The Government
of Northern Ireland
1922–72

'Students of state papers will have found that in their researches they may wade through years of . . . reports and find mere ordinary routine news, when, just as they are about to give up in despair, they suddenly stumble across a nugget of gold.'

F. B. F. Campbell, *Introduction to the Theory of a State-Paper Catalogue*, 1891.

The Government of Northern Ireland 1922–72

A Catalogue and Breviate of Parliamentary Papers

Arthur Maltby

IRISH UNIVERSITY PRESS

1974

Microfilm, microfiche and other forms of micro-publishing
© *Irish University Microforms Dublin Ireland*

Irish University Press Dublin Ireland

ISBN 0 7165 2151 2

FILMSET, PRINTED AND BOUND
IN THE REPUBLIC OF IRELAND

CONTENTS

* *The subjects in these classes are not dealt with by Stormont, but are covered by the Westminster Papers.*

INTRODUCTION

THIS volume is intended as a reference tool for historians and others who are interested in Irish social and economic history, education, transport, agriculture, industry and labour, health matters, town planning, and various other areas covered by 'blue books', 'white papers', and other Northern Ireland government reports. It should be viewed as a companion to and a continuation of the various select lists and breviates, produced by P. and G. Ford, which provide such an extensive survey of the range and content of British parliamentary papers. The aim of the present work is to catalogue and summarize the principal Northern Ireland papers for the fifty-year span from March 1922, the date of the first command paper, to the time of the prorogation of Stormont in March 1972. The catalogue entries and 'digests' of significant documents endeavour to present, in microcosm, the story of practical tasks and problems which the state has encountered and the views and recommendations of the various committees, commissions, working parties, or other specialists who have reported on these problems and tasks. The summaries should not be viewed as an adequate substitute for the examination of the original reports and papers if the latter are readily accessible; indeed it is hoped that they will rather promote the more frequent consultation of the originals. They may, however, prove a partial substitute where the source document is not available (all too few libraries, alas, have a set of Northern Ireland government papers which can be described as anything like comprehensive) and should also be of utility because their subject grouping with, in most cases, chronological sub-arrangement helps to reveal the evolving Northern Ireland social framework. An attempt has been made consciously to offset any weaknesses in the subject grouping chosen by means of cross-references and indexing. There is, nevertheless, some scattering of related material in the sense that statistical information on a topic, for instance, is widely distributed by the documents themselves. We thus find statistics on such diverse themes as forestry, rainfall and unemployment in the various area reports; shipbuilding statistics in an account of Northern Ireland's contribution to the 1939–45 war; and numerous statistics on many topics in the economic surveys. It is, however, maintained that the arrangement and indexing provided will satisfy most needs and is the best feasible plan.

The command papers, House of Commons and Senate papers, and departmental reports selected for inclusion do not, of course, represent the whole picture of the political evolution of Northern Ireland as told by its official documents. Acts of Parliament and statutory instruments can be examined to see just which proposals found their way into legislation and the way in which that legislation was implemented. There is a great deal of information too that is to be found in the reports of local government authorities and other appropriate institutions. Yet a substantial part of the story is told by the government documents that are summarized here. In reading these summaries it is interesting to reflect, on the one hand, upon the parallels that exist between the work of committees and other bodies appointed during the period by Stormont and those appointed by Westminster and, on the other hand, on links between the tasks undertaken by the Northern Ireland committees and their nineteenth-century equivalents. In the latter sphere, the Stormont reports on sugar beet, fictitious votes, forestry, cancer, the linen industry, civil disturbance and primary education—to quote a heterogeneous collection of examples—all have forerunners in the late nineteenth or very early twentieth centuries. Related Westminster and Stormont twentieth-century documents are also plentiful, although sometimes chronologically apart. In some instances, that of child adoption for example, we find proposed a legal pattern slightly different from that existing in England and Wales; in others, for instance the restructuring of local government, suggestions made in the official report are somewhat akin to Scottish thinking and legislation.

The volume endeavours to summarize reliably and objectively what the Northern Ireland government documents actually say. In no way does it try to assess any individual report or to either justify or criticize state policy. Descriptions of the machinery and evolution of government within the province can be found in two Stationery Office publications: *Northern Ireland 1921–1971*, Belfast: H.M.S.O. 1971 and *How Northern Ireland is Governed*, Belfast: H.M.S.O. 1963. Both of these were written by Hugh Shearman. There is, of course, an ample supply of other literature on Northern Ireland's government, and much of this offers some value judgements representing various political opinions. Whatever the merit of the latter type of material, I am convinced that there is a need for a reference book which is both a key to and an abbreviation of those source documents which have helped shape or influence government policy and action. These reports deserve more study and attention—both by experts and research workers in the various spheres and by the intelligent layman who, all too often, has been unreasonably and unnecessarily content to judge the reports by what the newspapers have said about them.

It is hoped that this book will not stand alone but will be one in a series of volumes which systematically display and summarize details of Irish official documents since the time of the Union, for, in association with Professor and Mrs. Ford, discussions are currently in hand for the production of similar keys to the range and content of the Dáil Éireann papers and Irish parliamentary papers of the nineteenth century.

A. Maltby.

Belfast, May 1972

A NOTE ON SCOPE AND ARRANGEMENT

The *Catalogue and Breviate* includes entries and summaries for those parliamentary papers which are considered to have lasting interest, especially those which made suggestions and recommendations that affected government policy. Non-parliamentary publications (issued by appropriate government departments) and a few other publications are included, where necessary, to ensure that the picture presented by the systematically arranged summaries is reasonably complete. Annual reports are listed in an appendix, but there are a few examples of reports which were intended to be issued regularly but which appeared once only. These are treated as individual reports and summarized in the main sequence.

The broad outline of the classification used by P. and G. Ford in their reference works relating to the Westminster papers has been perpetuated here, but subdivisions have been changed where necessary. The classification is supported by numerous cross-references and by a title index which includes entries under the first word of each report's title and other key words.

Librarians and others who may be interested in the methodology of the project or in problems of compilation will find a fuller account in the December 1971 issue of *An Leabharlann* (the journal of the Library Association of Ireland).

ACKNOWLEDGMENTS

My thanks are due to many people for help and advice given in the course of the project which culminated in the publication of this book. P.R. Lewis, who planned such a project before he left Queen's, provided much of the initial enthusiasm. Professor and Mrs. Ford have, both by example and in conversation and correspondence, helped to sustain and extend that enthusiasm and given me the benefit of their own extensive experience of such work. Successive part-time research assistants, Pamela Forsyth and Hazel Scott, have shared with me in the extensive sifting and intense scrutiny of many documents which must inevitably precede a volume of this kind and in the preparation of draft summaries. My wife has helped me with the checking of the manuscript and provided her usual unflagging support and encouragement.

Many local members of the library profession have been of assistance directly or indirectly. In various ways, I am particularly indebted to P. Havard-Williams, formerly Librarian at Queen's and the first director of its School of Library and Information Studies; to T. Hamilton and his colleagues in the Parliamentary Library at Stormont; to Miss F. Brown of Queen's University Library; and—for financial aid at the publishing stage—to the Institute of Irish Studies at Queen's.

Financial assistance for the project was provided by the British Academy and later by the Social Science Research Council. Her Majesty's Stationery Office in Belfast also assisted by the loan, for a long period, of a remarkably full set of Northern Ireland command and House of Commons papers.

I am grateful to these individuals and organizations for their support in the production of this volume. Any omissions or flaws are, however, my responsibility alone.

A. Maltby.

ABBREVIATIONS

The following abbreviations have been employed in various parts of the text:

Appendix	app.
Appointed	apptd.
Board	Bd.
Chairman	Ch.
Command	Cmd.
Commission	Com.
Committee	Cttee.
Departmental Committee	Dept. Cttee.
Diagrams	diagrs.
House of Commons Paper	H.C.
Illustrations	illus.
Joint Committee	Jt. Cttee.
Minutes of evidence	mins. of ev.
Ordered to be printed	o.p.
Pages	pp.
Photographs	photos.
Proceedings	proc.
Report	rep.
Senate Paper	S.
Select Committee	Sel. Cttee.
Signed	sgd.
Working Party	Wkg. Pty.

SUBJECT CLASSIFICATION AND LIST OF PAPERS

I MACHINERY OF GOVERNMENT

II NATIONAL FINANCE
Papers on this subject are published by the Imperial Government at Westminster.

III MONETARY AND ECONOMIC POLICY, FINANCIAL INSTITUTIONS

IV AGRICULTURE AND FOOD SUPPLY

1 General—Production, Supply, Output

2 Marketing

VIII POST OFFICE, TELECOMMUNICATIONS

Papers on these subjects are published by the Imperial Government at Westminster.

XII HEALTH

XIII A   HOUSING

XIII B   TOWN AND COUNTRY PLANNING

CATALOGUE AND BREVIATE

I MACHINERY OF GOVERNMENT

1 Parliament
2 Ministers
3 Civil Service
4 Local Government

5 Local Taxation and Financial
  Administration
6 Miscellaneous Papers

1 PARLIAMENT

The Law relating to Personation at Elections

Rep. of Dept. Cttee. of Inquiry, 1929. Cmd. 100, 18 pp.
Cttee. apptd. March 1929; rep. sgd. June 1929.

P. J. O'Donoghue (Ch.) and four members—R. H. Carson, Sir F. Henry Millar, S. C. Porter, J. Quail.

'To inquire into the existing laws relating to Personation at Parliamentary and Local Government Elections, and to make recommendations how these Laws might suitably be amended so as to secure the prevention of this evil.'

The present law is found to be generally adequate and certainly not materially at fault. There is some discussion of the evidence needed to prove personation and of the onus of prosecution, as well as of possible methods of prevention. These methods include systems for identifying voters and ways of keeping the electoral register updated. The committee recommend that the duty of prosecuting in cases of personation should be placed entirely upon the crown from the moment of arrest; that the law should be clarified and welded into a single statute; and that the power of committing for trial should be confined to one resident magistrate. There is also a suggested repeal of that part of the law which states that the evidence of two witnesses is needed before justices can return offenders for trial, and it is urged that if a returning officer is absent from the polling booth, poll clerks should be able to order the arrest of an individual suspected of personation.

A list of witnesses examined is given in a short appendix, and R. H. Carson, in a signed reservation to the report, quotes the majority of these witnesses as supporting his proposal that the guilty would have less chance of evading punishment if the trial were held before a single resident magistrate.

(Parliamentary) Privileges

Ten reps. as follows:
H.C. 805: 1948, 15 pp.
H.C. 914: 1950, 12 pp.
H.C. 1125: 1954, 3 pp.
H.C. 1341: 1959, 31 pp.
H.C. 1627: 1964, 8 pp.
H.C. 1726: 1966, 36 pp.
H.C. 1731: 1966, 71 pp.
H.C. 1944: 1969, 12 pp.
H.C. 2047: 1970, 39 pp.
S. 3: 1960, 18 pp.

These reports concern varied matters involving possible breach of privilege. Topics covered include the need for a B.B.C. press representative at Stormont as a check against communication error by government press officers (H.C. 805); the contents of letters to members of the House—Mrs. Dinah McNabb and Mr.

N. Minford (H.C. 914 and 1726); certain television remarks about the Royal Maternity Hospital (H.C. 1627); the revision of standing orders (H.C. 1731); newspaper comment on a bill involving possible change in licensing laws (H.C. 2047); and an allegation that vested interests have used the Senate to discredit the American publishing industry (S. 3).

Proceedings, minutes of evidence and appendices appear with the reports, where relevant.

Elections (House of Commons)

Rep. of Sel. Cttee., together with proc., mins. of ev. and apps., 1956.
H.C. 1185, 42 pp.
Cttee. apptd. January 1956; rep. o.p. February 1956.

R.W.B. McConnell (Ch.) and six members—A.B.D. Faulkner, I.G. Hawthorne, Capt. O.W.J. Henderson, S.T. Irwin, J.W. Morgan, W.J. Morgan.

'To consider whether the election of any of the following Members, that is to say:
1. Capt. the Rt. Hon. Sir Norman Stronge,
2. The Rt. Hon. Sir William McCleery,
3. Dr. Eileen Hickey,
is invalid on the ground that at the time of his or her election he or she held an office or place of profit under the Crown
. . . and to report whether any such Member appears on that account to have been incapable of election to this House, and, if so, what representations should be made to Her Majesty's Government.'

In its deliberations, the committee was guided by the reports of the select committees of the House of Commons at Westminster which considered the cases of Mr. Charles Alfred Howell and Mr. Charles Beattie.

The committee found that in acting, from September 1945, as a member of the Advisory Committee for the Belfast Area, set up under the Unemployment Assistance Act (N.I.), 1930, Dr. Eileen M. Hickey was entitled to claim travelling and other allowances, and that although she did not at any time apply for or receive remuneration or expenses of any kind, nevertheless the office constituted an office of profit under the crown, and in consequence, her election in February 1949 and her re-election in October 1953 were invalid.

In November 1944 Sir William McCleery was appointed an assessor under the Reinstatement in Civil Employment Act, 1944. Had he acted as assessor (which he did not) he would have been entitled to a fee. Hence he is deemed to have held an office of profit under the crown, and his election in 1945 and his re-election in 1949 and 1953 were consequently invalid. Sir Norman Stronge acted as chairman of the Central Advisory Council for the Employment of the Disabled, from June 1947. He did not apply for or receive any remuneration or expenses, which he would have been entitled to do, but nevertheless is deemed to have held an office of profit under the crown and his election was invalid.

All the members are considered to have acted in good faith, and the committee recommends that representation should be made immediately to Her Majesty's Government to introduce the necessary legislation to indemnify them.

Relevant correspondence and memoranda appear as appendices.

Elections (House of Commons)

Rep. of Sel. Cttee., together with proc., mins of ev., and apps., 1956.
H.C. 1192, 23 pp.
Cttee. apptd. February 1956; rep. o.p. February 1956.

R.W.B. McConnell (Ch.) and six members—A.B.D. Faulkner, I.G. Hawthorne, Capt. O.W.J. Henderson, S.T. Irwin, J.W. Morgan, W.J. Morgan.

'To consider whether the election of the following Member, that is to say:
Robert Samuel Nixon, Esq., M.B.
is invalid on. the ground that at the time of his election he held an office or place of profit under the Crown . . . and to report

whether such Member appears on that account to have been incapable of election to this House, and, if so, what representations should be made to Her Majesty's Government.'

Dr. Nixon held the position of appointed factory doctor under the Factories Acts (N.I.), 1938 and 1949, from May 1952. On 23 October he was elected a member of parliament and on 29 October resigned his appointment as factory doctor. Although he received no fees or emoluments from the Ministry of Labour and National Insurance, the office constitutes an office of profit under the crown within the meaning of the relevant statute, and his election was therefore invalid. Representations should be made immediately to Her Majesty's Government to introduce the necessary legislation to indemnify Dr. Nixon and to validate his election.

Relevant correspondence and memoranda are given in appendices.

Elections (Senate)

Reps. from the Sel. Cttee., together with proc., mins. of ev. and apps., 1956.
S.1, 42pp.
Cttee. apptd. January 1956; rep. o.p. February 1956.
S.2, 20 pp.
Cttee. apptd. January 1956; rep. o.p. February 1956. Sir Wilson Hungerford (Ch) and four members—Sir G.A. Clark, Mrs. M.J. Greeves, J.H.H. Pollock, H. Quin.

The election of Senators H. Fleming and Lt.-Col. H.S.C. Richardson is queried on the grounds that, at the time of their election, they held an office or place of profit under the crown. Deliberation and reference to precedents at Westminster indicate that both elections were invalid, but it is clear that the individuals concerned acted in good faith and without knowledge of the legal complexities involved. It is, therefore, proposed that representation be made to Westminster to introduce legislation which will indemnify them and make the elections valid.

Public Business

Standing Orders . . . 1964.
H.C. 1604, 40 pp.
O.p. February 1964.

It had been resolved in 1921 that the Stormont House of Commons should adopt the standing orders of the Westminster House. Various amendments have since been made, and revised orders are here set out, as several changes are currently being effected in the regulations relating to public business. These cover over twenty matters including sittings of the House, arrangement of public business, order in the House, closure of debate, divisions, petitions, public bills, public money, committees and the rules relating to strangers to the House. There is a full contents list and a detailed subject index.

Equivalent standing orders relating to public business for the Senate are set out in S.9: 1967, 10 pp. and S. 19: 1970, 11 pp.

The Future Development of the Parliament and Government of Northern Ireland

A consultative document, 1971.
Cmd. 560, 12 pp.

The reorganization of local services and the need for greater stability and unity in Northern Ireland society are two factors which suggest that some revision of the arrangements for Parliament and central government is justified.

The plan for three new functional committees to be added to the Public Accounts Committee (Opposition members are to chair at least two of the four committees) is mentioned, and alternatives to the present method of election to the House of Commons—the party list system and the single transferable vote—are discussed. An increase in the size of the House of Commons in the order of some twenty or thirty extra members seems wise in view of the fact that, from 1973, much business formerly in the hands of local authorities will be centralized at Stormont. This in itself implies a change in the method of election.

The Senate too could be enlarged and have about forty members to maintain the present situation whereby its present membership is half that of the House of Commons.

The continuity of one party in office (paralleled in the Irish Republic) has simply mirrored the wishes of the majority of the electorate. There is need for frank and open discussion on minority participation, but the cabinet—whatever the emphasis or attitudes of individual members—must be united in its fundamental outlook. The government could not join in a plan of 'collective responsibility' with those who do not:— recognize the maintenance of Northern Ireland as part of the United Kingdom, unequivocally resist organizations employing violence and coercion, and accept the process of a democratically elected Parliament. Because of deep divisions of opinion, a cabinet based on the idea of proportional representation is believed unworkable. The basis of government can, however, be broadened by the invitation of minority representatives of both religious groups to serve in the cabinet, provided they accept the three principles stated above. Ideally the province needs political parties each of which has roots in both communities, but this cannot be achieved quickly or by artificial means. The government argues that a start should be made on constructive decisions and that the evolution of the political structure should not await the decline of terrorism. The policy of a boycott on Stormont, now favoured by certain Opposition members, is seen as negative: 'before the Government can make decisions on participation, there must be participation in decisions.'

Political Settlement

Statements issued on Friday 24 March 1972 by the Prime Minister and the Government.
Cmd. 568, 8 pp.

The text of two statements is given. The first is Mr. Faulkner's account of the London meeting between himself, Senator Andrews, and the United Kingdom

prime minister and his colleagues. It is indicated that the meeting resulted in three definite ideas from the United Kingdom government for political change in Northern Ireland—a periodic referendum on the constitution, some 'movement' on the internment policy adopted in August 1971, and a proposal to appoint a secretary of state and to transfer security powers from Stormont to Westminster. Two of these were largely acceptable to Mr. Faulkner and Senator Andrews, but the final proposal was not. Reasons for considering it as unacceptable and indeed a concession to violence are given. This measure (and the implication that further radical changes might follow) resulted in the resignation of the Northern Ireland government. Mr. Heath thus indicated that the Stormont Parliament would be prorogued and that a bill would be introduced to place the powers of the government of Northern Ireland under a secretary of state. An advisory commission would also be appointed. At the conclusion of his statement on these matters, Mr. Faulkner appeals for people to work with calmness and determination, under the law, to make their opinions heard.

The second part of the document is a press statement by the Northern Ireland government. Mr. Heath and Mr. Faulkner had agreed that an initiative should be taken when they had met early in February. Since then, the government of Northern Ireland had reviewed options and proposals for a 'package of change'. Ideas considered included an easing of internment, a referendum, an active and guaranteed role for the minority, and the transfer of certain suitable border areas to the Republic of Ireland. The government had rejected some of these ideas but accepted others: it argues that it looked for responsible and realistic initiatives by reform of parliamentary structure (see above, Cmd. 560, *Future development of the Parliament and Government*), by a revision of the Government of Ireland Act to assist in combating any discrimination, by making internment policy a joint responsibility of the two governments, by considering legislation which would (after the cessation of violence) replace the Special Powers Act, and by certain proposals which, if accepted, would affect the law in the whole of Ireland and involve the setting up of an intergovernmental council to consider economic and social matters of mutual importance.

2 MINISTERS

Remuneration of Ministers . . .

Rep. of Sel. Cttee., 1921.
H.C. 3, 8 pp.
O.p. November 1921.

[Names of Cttee. Members are not given.]

'To consider what the Remuneration of Ministers, Parliamentary Secretaries, Assistant Parliamentary Secretaries and H.M.'s Attorney General should be.'

Evidence was not called, but a subcommittee was sent to England for advice, and an interview held with the lord chief justice of Northern Ireland. Statistics of salaries paid to ministers in the Dominions, and of the remuneration of managing directors and of higher officials in large municipalities were consulted. Recommendations are made for each post. It is considered that it would be a mistake to award pensions. Official residences are viewed as a negligible factor in determining remuneration. Travelling expenses should be reimbursed on a fixed scale.

Ministerial Salaries

Rep. of Sel. Cttee. on Ministerial Salaries and Payments and Allowances of Members of the House of Commons, 1943.
H.C. 605, 52 pp.
Cttee. apptd. October 1943; rep. published 1944.

Sir Milne Barbour (Ch.) and seven members—P. Agnew, T. Bailie, Dr. G. Dougan, W. Dowling, R. Elliot, Lt.-Col. S.H. Hall-Thompson, J. Johnston.

'To consider whether any alterations ought to be made in the remuneration of the Prime Minister, other Ministers, Parliamentary Secretaries and Assistant Parliamentary Secretaries; whether any alterations ought to be made in the payments and allowances made to Members of the House of Commons in respect of their expenses as Members of Parliament and to make recommendations.'

All aspects of ministerial salaries, i.e., the prime minister, cabinet ministers, parliamentary secretaries, members of parliament, attendance of members at committees, travelling expenses of members other than ministers and parliamentary secretaries, are taken into consideration. Comparisons are made, from documentary evidence, with the Imperial Parliament and the parliaments of the British Commonwealth, the Isle of Man and the Irish Free State. Details of remuneration of the prime minister, private members of the House of Commons and cabinet ministers, are listed in appendix A. Appendix B is devoted to information about ministerial salaries in Great Britain, the Commonwealth and the Irish Free State. These are followed by the minutes of evidence.

Ministerial Salaries

Rep. of Sel. Cttee., 1945.
H.C. 670, 7 pp.
Cttee. apptd. November 1945; rep. o.p. December 1945.

H.C. Midgley (Ch.) and six members— R. Getgood, T. Lyons, J. McSparran, H. Quin, F. Thompson, R.N. Wilson.

'To consider whether any alterations ought to be made in the remuneration of Ministers (other than the Prime Minister), Parliamentary Secretaries and Assistant Parliamentary Secretaries; and whether any alterations ought to be made in the payments and allowances made to Members of the House of Commons in respect of their expenses as Members of Parliament, and to make recommendations.'

This short report deals with members' allowances for expenses, compensation for loss of earnings, salaries and expenses for cabinet ministers, parliamentary secretaries and assistant parliamentary secretaries, payment for attendance of members at committees, and travelling expenses of members other than ministers and parliamentary secretaries.

Ministerial Salaries and Payments and Allowances of Members of the Senate and the House of Commons

Rep. of Sel. Cttee., together with proc., mins. of ev. and apps., 1954.
H.C. 1105, 84 pp.
Cttee. apptd. June 1954; rep. o.p. October 1954.

W.F. McCoy (Ch.) and eight members —H. Diamond, P.J. Gormley, Prof. F.T. Lloyd-Dodd, W.M. May, R.M.B. McConnell, Dr. R.S. Nixon, N. Porter, J.F. Stewart.

'To consider whether any alterations ought to be made in:
(1) the remuneration of the Prime Minister, other Ministers, Parliamentary Secretaries and Assistant Parliamentary Secretaries;
(2) the statutory salaries of the Speaker of the Senate, the Speaker of the House of Commons and the Attorney-General;
(3) the salary of the Chairman of Ways and Means;
(4) the payment and allowances made to Members of the Senate and of the House of Commons in respect of their salaries and expenses . . . ; and to make recommendations.'

Proposals are made based on documentary evidence relating to the situation in the Commonwealth parliaments and in the Irish Republic, and on changes in the purchasing power of sterling. Salaries recommended include £3,200 for the prime minister, £2,500 for cabinet ministers, £2,800 for the attorney-general and £2,000 and £1,000 respectively for the Speaker of the House of Commons and Speaker of the Senate. Many of the suggested salaries are, of course, to be supported considerably by appropriate expenses allowances.

Appendices give details of parliamentary and ministerial remuneration in the province since 1921, the details of salaries paid to equivalent ministers and secretaries in Britain and the Commonwealth and a memorandum from the members of the Senate criticizing the method adopted for calculating their expenses allowance. The bulk of the paper is devoted to the minutes of evidence received by the committee.

Ministerial Salaries and Payments and Allowances of Members

Rep. of Sel. Cttee., together with proc., mins. of ev. and apps., 1963.
H.C. 1557, 160 pp.
Cttee. apptd. July 1963; rep. o.p. October 1963.

I.G. Hawthorne (Ch.) and eight members —J. Burns, Capt. W.J. Long, H.I. McClure, N.O. Minford, R.H. O'Connor, J. O'Reilly, F.V. Simpson, C. Stewart.

'To consider:
1. (a) the remuneration of Ministers, Parliamentary Secretaries and Assistant Parliamentary Secretaries;
(b) the statutory salaries of the Speaker of the Senate, the Speaker of the House of Commons and the Attorney-General;
(c) the salary of the Chairman of Ways and Means;
(d) the making of a payment by way of salary to the Leader of the Opposition; and
(e) the payment and allowances to be made to the Members of the Senate and of the House of Commons in respect of their salaries and expenses . . . ;
2. The establishment of a contributory pension scheme for Members of the Senate and of the House of Commons;
3. The amendment or extension of the Ministerial Offices Act (N.I.). 1952, in relation to pensions payable thereunder; and to make recommendations.'

Documentary evidence with regard to comparable salaries in the United Kingdom, the Commonwealth and the Republic of Ireland is again examined. It is held desirable that there should be a range of salaries which will give a reasonable living for a member having no other income. Details are also given of a contributory pension scheme and of secretarial services that are to be provided. Salaries proposed include £4,500 for the prime minister, £3,250 for cabinet ministers, £4,500 for the attorney-general and £3,250 and £2,250 respectively for the Speaker of the House of Commons and the Speaker of the Senate. No recommendation is made for the payment of salary to the leader of the Opposition. Contributory pensions, for those who have completed eight years service in the House, involve a 5 percent deduction of salary and the 1952 Act will no longer apply; there will be no means test. The prime minister is to be excluded from the contributory scheme and remains eligible for eventual pension under the terms of the Act.

There is a list of six witnesses who provided evidence, and appendices give a memorandum from the Ministry of Finance plus statistics of comparative salaries and allowances. The latter draw particular attention to comparisons between Northern Ireland and New South Wales. Once again, the major part of the report provides the minutes of evidence received in the examination of witnesses.

3 CIVIL SERVICE

The Civil Service

Rep. of Sir R.R. Scott, 1926.
Cmd. 66, 5 pp.

'To report
(a) whether the general organization is on sound lines;
(b) whether there is a redundancy of staff;
(c) whether the standards of remuneration and conditions of service are reasonable;
and to make recommendations.'

The organization of most departments —finance, home affairs, commerce, labour, agriculture and education—is conceived on sound lines with little overlap, and thus no fundamental changes are proposed. Some rates of remuneration are equal to those of London and should be reduced so as to be equivalent to the pay of Imperial civil servants working outside the London area. Gradings on the whole are reasonable, but certain detailed changes might save about £15,000 per annum. Some higher clerical officers are performing duties more appropriate to junior executive grades. An improvement in the handling of routine work could result in the reduction of staff. Unsuitable and scattered accommodation has meant the maintenance of extra registry and typing staff.

Civil Service Regrading

Rep. of Dept. Cttee., 1930.
Cmd. 116, iii, 72 pp.
Cttee. apptd. October 1928; rep. sgd. July 1929.

G.C. Duggan (Ch.) and seven members —J.V. Coyle, G.T. Fidler, G.H.E. Parr, R.P. Pim, W. Robson, R.E. Thornley, A.N.B. Wyse.

'*(a) to take into consideration the grading of the posts comprised in the present Junior Executive, Higher Clerical and Clerical Grades of the Civil Service; and (b) to examine on similar lines the present position of the remaining Grades below the rank of Principal; and to make recommendations.'*

The committee were able to present an agreed report upon most of the matters covered by their terms of reference, but they found it necessary to produce majority and minority reports (see below) on the future organization of certain civil service grades. A review of the present organization and historical development of the service is followed by positive recommendations concerning salaries and future gradings. The present writing assistant, junior clerical, higher clerical and junior executive grades should be replaced by three grades which are (in ascending order) clerical officer, executive officer and junior staff officer. The higher posts are to be filled by promotion from below. Clerical officer, the only route to the higher posts, is to be filled by appointment on the results of examinations, although a proportion of the vacancies may be reserved for ex-service men. Existing officers will normally retain their present salary when the service is reorganized, and salary scales for women are, for the most part, unaffected. University-trained entrants are to be recruited by means of an appropriate examination. A change is recommended in the method of achieving the additional remuneration for the post of a private secretary to the minister.

A reservation signed by W. Robson presses for a better starting salary for older recruits to the service. R. P. Pim disputes the need for the committee to consider the tenure and appointment of a private secretary to the minister. He also queries the remuneration suggested for such secretaries. There are four appendices which concern proposals put forward for discussion and circulated to the Civil Service Representative Council, and memoranda received from that council and from the Committee of Assistant Principals. A note gives details of the subjects and syllabus for the examinations mentioned in the report.

The future organization of the civil service in grades not covered by Part III of the joint report.

Majority Report (signed by five members)

New grades and salaries are suggested to be substituted for the present gradings of superintending officer, assistant principal and higher executive officer. No attempt should be made in future to maintain a close discrimination between administrative and executive functions. University-trained entrants should receive training under staff officers (a new grade) in selected posts, and promotion to staff officer should be made from their ranks. Promotion to another new grade, that of deputy principal, would be made from the rank of staff officer. The post of private secretary to a minister should be included in the staff officer grade with

a special salary increase denoting the responsibility of the position.

Minority Report (signed by G.C. Duggan [Ch.], G.H.E. Parr and R.P. Pim)

The cardinal proposal of the minority is that a separate and distinct administrative grade should be perpetuated. Subsidiary recommendations deal with certain defects in that grading as it is at present and with minor disagreements about other matters in the majority report. It is felt that the plan proposed by the majority would gradually lower the standards of the service and place the graduate in an anomalous position.

4 LOCAL GOVERNMENT

Local Government Administration

Rep. of Dept. Com., 1927.
Cmd. 73, viii, 242 pp.
Com. apptd. April 1924; rep. sgd. September 1927.

Rt. Hon T. Moles (Ch.) (replaced by R.J. Johnstone, February 1925) and thirty-eight members—R. Andrews, H. A.M. Barbour, W.A. Bell, S. Bradley, Mrs. Dehra Chichester, R. Crawford, Lt.-Col. W.R. Dawson, F.W. Emery, N.D. Ferguson, G.T. Fidler, J. Freeland, J.S. Godden, D. Gray, Maj. G.A. Harris, M. Hopkins, O. Jamison, J.E. Johnston, Miss Harriet Johnston, Prof. R.J. Johnstone, Prof. J.A. Lindsay, J.A. Long, Prof. H.O. Meredith, W.T. Miller, W. Macartney, J.M. McCloy, H.J. McConville, Miss Mary M. McCrea, S. McGuffin, W. McLorinan, W.J. McMillan, L. McQuibban, M. Moore, H.S. Morrison, R.J. Newell, A. Robinson, S. Sloan, S. Watt, J.D. Williamson. (Prof. Meredith and S. Watt resigned before the report was completed.)

'(a) To enquire into the allocation amongst local authorities and local committees of their different powers and duties in connection with Local Government, Public Health, Poor Law, and Allied Services;

(b) to enquire as to the suitability and efficiency of the local administrative machinery . . . ;

(c) to enquire into the cost of such services generally, and . . . in the respective districts of local authorities and local committees;
(d) to recommend what alteration in the allocation of such powers and duties and in the local administrative machinery can be made with a view to increasing efficiency of the administration of such services, without . . . creating unnecessary additional burdens on the local rates or on public funds; and to report what consequential provisions will be necessary to give effect to such recommendations.'

Part I of the report gives a brief historical sketch of local government administration. There are at present in Northern Ireland six types of local authority: town commissioners, rural district councils, urban district councils, boards of guardians, county councils and county borough councils. Their more important functions (obligatory and permissive) are described in Part II, and overlapping and anomalies are discussed. Parts III to VII discuss poor relief, medical treatment, public health, roads administration and other miscellaneous functions, and make recommendations. Part VIII deals with county administration and suggests certain reorganization. Part IX covers local government administration in county borough areas. Part X, on the financial aspects, concludes with a summary of the extensive recommendations.

It is recommended that there should be separation of medical relief from relief of destitution; abolition of unions and boards of guardians; abolition of workhouses; establishment of county homes for certain classes of the destitute poor, of cottage homes for children (although boarding out is to be preferred); and provision for the insane and mentally defective. Amendments are suggested to the Children Act, 1908. Local health services, internal and external medical treatment, public health and housing should all be co-ordinated on a county basis. The recommended organization of the county health committee and of

hospitals is described. All patients should pay in accordance with their means.

The system of affording external medical relief under the Medical Charities Act should be continued but requires more local supervision, which should be achieved through setting up local dispensary committees in each district. There should be a district nurse and midwife in each dispensary district. Medical benefits under the National Insurance Acts should not be introduced. Domiciliary treatment of tuberculosis should be discouraged and institutions provided, as far as possible.

Urban and rural district councils should be retained as local administrative authorities for public health purposes. The smaller rural districts should be abolished, and powers given to the minister of home affairs to dissolve or otherwise alter any rural district. Recommendations deal with appointment of officers, sewerage schemes, markets and fairs, slaughterhouses and inspection of meat, milk production, notification of diseases, housing and town planning. All adoptive Public Health Acts should be made mandatory. Public Health Acts should be codified.

Miscellaneous recommendations are concerned with improvement of Class III roads, registration of births, marriages and deaths, preparation of electoral registers, salaries and appointment of officials, and surcharge in respect of illegal payments.

Recommendations concerning Londonderry and Belfast are made separately. Those for Londonderry are very similar to the county position. Rather than transfer the functions of the Board of Guardians to Belfast Corporation, it should be replaced by a Belfast County Borough Public Assistance Board. The Belfast Union Infirmary should become the Belfast County Borough Hospital, and the Belfast Workhouse should be retained as the Belfast County Borough Home. Administrative alterations are recommended: the number of committees should be reduced and a greater measure of authority vested in the chief officers of the corporation. The town clerk should be empowered to exercise an effective supervision over all the principal officials of the corporation.

Of the thirty-six signatures, thirteen are subject to reservation.

The first reservation, signed by nine members, concerns medical services and medical benefits. After an examination of the problem it concludes that a medical service is required for the working classes; that the dispensary system falls far short of the needs and that the majority's proposals for extending it are not convincing; that under existing arrangements the health of the people is suffering seriously; that medical benefit has been a success elsewhere; that the medical profession and the workers desire it; and that on economic grounds Northern Ireland's relations with the remainder of the United Kingdom require its introduction without delay.

The second reservation, signed by the same nine members, concerns county organization. They see no satisfactory alternative to an abolition of rural district councils, and they make suggestions for a unified county organization.

The third reservation, with eight signatories, advocates bringing the functions of both the Board of Guardians and the Water Commissioners into the hands of Belfast Corporation. Recommendations made for the reform of county services should be applied to the city. The reorganization would be most easily effected if the work of the city were placed, for a limited time, in the hands of commissioners.

The fourth reservation, signed by ten members, suggests the establishment of an appointments board, which would abolish the patronage at present existing in local authority appointments.

A reservation by J.D. Williamson comments on a variety of the recommendations of the main report, in particular as they affect the City of Belfast.

W.J. McMillan's reservation concerns conditions of opting out by urban districts from the county scheme for public health, and the interests of urban districts in the maintenance of interconnecting roads.

M.S. Moore feels that many of the most important recommendations will entail further considerable burden on the rates, and that it is not expedient nor feasible to carry them out in the form presented.

S. Sloan advocates new legislation for milk and milk products, and he would restrict any scheme of medical benefits to industrial workers.

Architect's Department of the Down County Regional Education Committee

[*Ministry of Education.*] *Rep. of Inquiry, 1935.*
35 pp.
Commissioner apptd. October 1934; rep. sgd. February 1935.

J. McGonigal (Commissioner), S. Baird (Assessor).

'To hold a Public Sworn Inquiry into . . . the administration and working of the department of the Architect to the Committee and of the other departments of the Committee in so far as they come into contact with the Architect's department; and also into such other matters relating to the administration and working of the said departments, or any of them as the Ministry may consider to be necessary or proper subjects of inquiry.'

The report investigates the practice of the secretary of the committee of sending direct to the architect paying orders in respect of the amounts due to builders on foot of their building contracts and in respect of amounts due to firms who were supplying equipment for schools. This practice of sending paying orders to the architect to be ultimately sent to the payees is entirely wrong and one which can be abused by the architect concerned, as has happened in this case.

Belfast Corporation Inquiry

Rep. of Public Inquiry, 1962.
Cmd. 440, 147 pp. map.

R.L.W. Lowry (Inspector) apptd. May 1961; rep. sgd. May 1962.

'To inquire into the observance of the existing law, including Belfast Local Acts, with regard to members of Belfast Corporation voting or taking part in discussion on matters in which they have a direct or indirect pecuniary interest or in which they have acted professionally, or in using knowledge which they have acquired through their membership of the Corporation for their personal advantage, and to consider whether the existing law on the subject is adequate or requires amendment.'

The principal case considered is one of several which concern Sir Cecil McKee and is an investigation of his acquisition of interest in land adjacent to Bridge Street prior to its redevelopment, and of whether or not his firm were agents for other property owners in the area. 'The Petrol Station Cases' concern Sir John Harcourt, J.S.R. Harcourt, and Mrs. M.E. Barter. The contract cases concern W.J. McCracken, Sir James Norritt, G. Kelso, Mrs. M.E. Barter, Mrs. Florence E. Breakie, J.S.R. Harcourt and Sir Robin Kinehan. Other cases concern S.H. Walsh, G. Fitt and Sir Percival Brown. Three principal points emerge:

1 Allegations of morally culpable acts by members of the corporation were comparatively few.

2 Ignorance of the statutory provisions governing the conduct of councillors was widespread, and even the principles upon which they were founded were but imperfectly understood.

3 The existing law is inadequate.

It is recommended that there should be a uniform code for every local authority. All the provisions governing the conduct of councillors should be brought together in one act, modelled, with certain modifications, on the Local Government Act, 1933. There should no longer be disqualification of members who are concerned in contracts with the local authority. Members should have to disclose pecuniary interest in matters

under consideration and withdraw from the meeting; the general prohibition against voting or taking part in discussion should continue, but the system of dispensation in force in England ought to be introduced and given a fair trial. Legislation should be introduced which would prevent a member from obtaining documents or information which would not be available to any member of the public and which relate to matters in which he has a pecuniary interest. The form of words used in the present Section 21, Belfast Corporation Act (N.I.), 1930, dealing with the conflict between duty as a councillor and professional duty to a client should be restated and clarified. Information gained through council membership should not be used to the member's advantage in dealing with persons without it: such dealings should be forbidden.

Penalties are suggested. For offences relating to conduct at meetings, conduct outside meetings, and use of knowledge, the penalties are more lenient for inadvertent misconduct than for breaches committed 'knowingly and recklessly'.

Statutory restrictions should be included in standing orders, and council members and officers should be conversant with them.

In the appendices are lists of witnesses, details of the cases investigated, extracts from laws relevant to the inquiry, and a map of the Bridge Street area.

Reshaping of Local Government

Statement of Aims, 1967 (reprinted 1968). Cmd. 517, 33 pp.

Preliminary conferences have been held with representatives of local government bodies, and the government now sets out tentative aims for reshaping local government with a view to providing information to Parliament, press and public, stimulating discussion and providing a basis for detailed consultations with all interested parties. A series of working parties would later translate proposals into administrative terms.

The functions of local government are

discussed; rationalization is possible in a number of areas of responsibility, e.g., there is a case for reducing road responsibility to two levels only. Alternative structures for local government are discussed, and the best solution is considered to mean a reduction in the number of local government areas to twelve to eighteen, based on the historic towns and their surrounding districts. The county council's responsibilities would in future lie in the field of social services: education, libraries, personal health and school health as well as welfare including child care.

Little can be said as yet of the financial impact of the proposals. The rates are likely to remain the basic source of local revenue. Miscellaneous revenues derived from rents, tolls, fees, etc., should be reviewed from time to time. Council house rents should be realistic, but experiment with a rent rebate scheme is suggested, as is a new approach to the subsidy structure. The government grant system could with advantage be simplified. Demands on the Government Loan Fund seem likely to exceed its resources, and some advice is given to local authorities on loans.

Greater delegation of work to the council's officers would relieve councillors of a heavy burden of detailed work. Management procedures are discussed. A regional advisory unit could be set up to assist change-over to the proposed area councils. Certain developments should be suspended while consultations are taking place—new administrative buildings, making of permanent senior appointments, and extension of boundaries.

Financial statistics of local authorities are given in the appendices, and also a short bibliography of background sources and recent academic works relevant to the subject.

Reshaping of Local Government

Further proposals following discussions and consultations, 1969.
Cmd. 530, 36 pp., map.

Many discussions have taken place with local authorities and professional and specialized bodies; interest shown by individual members of the public has been slight. There is evident desire for change, and the prospect of a better and simpler plan of local government has been welcomed.

Sixteen areas, shown on the map, are proposed, together with the City of Belfast as it stands. The prospect of integration of the three arms of the health service under specialized boards suggests that similar action might be taken with education and public library services, and there would no longer be any need for county councils.

Legislation is to be introduced to abolish plural voting, to provide for universal adult franchise in local government elections, and to appoint an independent statutory commission to review electoral areas. Final determination of wards and electoral divisions will have to be made by December 1970 so that elections may be held in autumn 1971.

Essentially, it is proposed to allocate to area councils responsibility for as many functions as can efficiently be discharged on a local basis, e.g. housing, slum clearance, action planning; to provide flexible intermediate arrangements for functions which go beyond local boundaries, e.g. water resources; and to reserve to government those responsibilities which are regional in character and essential to the economy of Northern Ireland as a whole—town and country planning policy, trunk motorways and trunk roads, etc.

Working parties will be set up to advise on finance, staff structure, standing orders, accounts and other matters. Less urgently, a review of the rating and valuation system as a whole is also to be undertaken.

Appendices list the existing local authorities; the populations, areas and rateable values of the proposed new areas; the main functions of area councils. They also give financial details of costs of services, payments and receipts of local authorities, rate burden according to types of hereditaments, etc. Finally, there are administrative notes on the proposed areas and on the points at which further local advice is desired.

Local Government

Rep. of Review Body, 1970.
Cmd. 546, 68 pp.
Body apptd. December 1969; rep. sgd. May 1970.

P.A. Macrory (Ch.) and five members—J.C. Baird, W.J. Blease, M.G. Bready, T.D. Lorimer, E.M.R. O'Driscoll.

'1. To review existing published government proposals for reshaping local government. . . .
2. To examine any further proposals which may be made to the Review Body.
3. To examine the consequences of the decision on housing [decision to set up a central housing authority announced in Cmnd. 4178, a Westminster report—see p. 222].
4. To consider any implications of that decision for the health, welfare, child care, education and public library services at present discharged by local government.
5. To advise on the most efficient distribution under the Parliament and Government . . . —whether under local government or otherwise—of the functions dealt with in proposals under 1 or 2 above.
6. To bear in mind the implications for elected local government of any courses of action which the Review Body may deem advisable.
7. To recommend how local opinion can best be brought to bear on administration.
8. To advise on the number of local government areas; and to submit interim reports if they think fit.'

The review body, which was assisted by a consultant from England (D.N. Chester) and three assessors nominated by local authority associations (A. Jack, A. McNeilly and A.R. Martin), reports that it elected to pursue a short and intensive investigation rather than a long-drawn-out inquiry. A basic aim is to reform the system developed in the nineteenth

century with its seventy-three, now uneconomical, small local authorities and create a structure which will last for at least a quarter of a century, based closely on the size, character and needs of the province. The Redcliffe-Maud Report on English local government reform was of considerable assistance, but a greater influence, on account of the size and population of the province, is Lord Wheatley's report on Scotland's local government.

It is thought that a system involving three or five major authorities and numerous small authorities with Stormont in a supervisory capacity would be inefficient and would perpetuate over-administration. The existence of Stormont as a regional government provides a unique factor, and the review body thus recommends a two-tier system involving a distinction between regional and district services to eliminate waste and duplication. Housing has been recommended as a centralized or regional service in an earlier government report. Other *regional services*, to be administered by Stormont, are defined as education, public libraries, health, planning, roads, water, sewerage, food standards, tourism, electoral arrangements, gas and electricity, harbours, fire services, motor taxation, and criminal injury compensation. Many of these lend themselves to some decentralization and delegation. Viable district councils, based on areas of population, are suggested for the administration of those matters defined as *district services*, best controlled locally. Twenty-six councils are proposed—Antrim, Armagh, Ballycastle, Ballymena, Ballymoney, Banbridge, Bangor, Belfast, Carrickfergus, Castlereagh, Coleraine, Cookstown, Craigavon (including Lurgan and Portadown), Downpatrick, Dungannon, Enniskillen, Larne, Limavady, Lisburn, Londonderry, Magherafelt, Newry, Newtownabbey, Newtownards, Omagh and Strabane. It is argued that these councils could be stronger than the ones they replace. Any future changes in boundaries would be likely to diminish, rather than increase, the number of councils. District services include parks and gardens, cleansing, markets, cemetery administration, civic improvement schemes, promotion of local entertainment and culture, bye-laws, and various regulatory services. Major local government functions would thus be transferred to Stormont, not only from small towns but from Belfast and Londonderry. However, the ancient civic dignities of these two cities would continue unimpaired, and it is significant that the Wheatley Report recommends a similar kind of exchange for Edinburgh and Glasgow. It is envisaged that there will be few district councils with a population of under thirty thousand. No place will remain for county councils in the envisaged structure.

It is proposed that there should be a single gas service for the whole province and that there could be a unified fire service, with the Belfast fire brigade as a valuable adjunct. The rate struck each year would be in two parts, a regional portion, uniformly applied, and a district portion which would be determined independently by each district council. Other proposals concern links between the government and the district councils, methods to ensure that local opinion is heard on local matters, and the need for the direct assignment of the regional services to individual ministries. Non-statutory community groups can be formed, where desired, to make known to a district council the views of residents in small localities. The implementation of the review body's views might profitably be followed by changes in the machinery for valuation and rating.

The report discusses the implications for local government staff, the effect of its proposals on councillors, and its reasons for not considering the question of proportional representation at this stage of local government reform. Appendices provide a statement by the review body as to its work, object, and attitude towards representations from local bodies, plus a statement made to the body at its opening meeting by Mr. Brian Faulkner, minister of development.

Report of Progress: Reorganization of Local Government and Other Services

[*Rep. of*] Ministries of Finance, Home Affairs, Health and Social Services, Education, Agriculture, Commerce, Development and Community Relations, 1971. 24 pp.
Not published by H.M.S.O.

This is a statement on progress in local government reconstruction up to November 1971. There is discussion of the functions of the twenty-six district councils, of the transfer of housing functions from the Housing Trust and local authorities to the housing executive, and of the implications for health and social services, education and libraries, roads, water and sewerage and various other services. The implications for finance, staffing problems and the transfer of property are considered, and details are given of the phasing out of the development commissions.

Further work and planning is necessary to effect the transition envisaged, but the new systems are expected to be in operation by April 1973.

5 LOCAL TAXATION AND FINANCIAL ADMINISTRATION

Valuation

Reps. of Dept. Cttee.   Cttee. apptd. June 1923; reps. published 1924.

Sir Ernest Clark (Ch.) and ten members —W. Abbott, G.A.S. Atack, J. Brown, Capt. W.C. Carlielle, C.W. Grant, H.E. Magee, J.A. McAuley, W.D. Scott, Maj. P.E. Shepherd, W.J. Ward.

'To inquire generally into the method of the valuation of property in Northern Ireland for the purposes of taxation and rating; and to consider what amendment, if any, of the present law or practice is necessary in order to obtain a uniform and equitable basis of valuation, . . . to remove anomalies at present existing, and to provide for a revision of the valuation from time to time.'

Interim Report.   Sgd. October 1923. Cmd. 23, 12 pp.

It is urged that all valuations made or revised since 1 March 1915 be reduced to 1914 standard of value plus 15 percent. All ratepayers affected should apply for revision of valuations in the usual way. For valuations or revisions made after 1 March 1924, the valuation authority should give individual notice of the valuation to the owner or occupier. A reservation, signed by W.J. Ward, disagrees with the method proposed for reducing anomalies.

Final Report. *Sgd. June 1924.*
Cmd. 26, 36 pp.

Main conclusions are that all hereditaments should be valued on the basis of what is deemed to be a reasonable net rent; that the existing central valuation system should be retained; that the Ministry of Finance should appoint a valuation advisory committee to determine when general revaluation is needed; that at least fifteen years should elapse between such revaluations in the case of agricultural land, and seven years in the case of other hereditaments; and that on general revaluation, the figure to be inserted in the valuation list should normally be the net annual value. Among several subsidiary recommendations, it is urged that returns of rent should be obtainable when needed and that a statement of the desired amendment should be given in any notice of appeal against a valuation. It is recognized that a general revaluation may not be required for a number of years, but it is strongly recommended that the other reforms outlined be introduced without delay. Three separate reservations, signed by J.A. McAuley, H.E. Magee and W.J. Ward, respectively, query the suggested time periods for revaluations. The report concludes with a specimen annual return form on which an owner or occupier is to give valuation particulars for rating and taxation purposes.

Rating Relief

Rep. of the Inter-Dept. Cttee. 1928.
Cmd. 89, 35 pp.

Cttee. apptd. May, 1928; rep. sgd. August, 1928.

G.C. Duggan (Ch.) and six members— D.L. Clarke, J.I. Cook, W. Crone, J.S. Gordon, W. Robson and W.J. Ward.

'To consider the application to Northern Ireland of a Scheme for the relief of rates similar to that proposed for Great Britain . . . or of any alternative method of granting . . . relief from State or local burdens.'

The committee recommend that agricultural land and farm offices be exempted from all rates except malicious injury, drainage and certain water rates. There should be partial derating of industrial hereditaments, except for malicious injury and certain water rates. The amount of rate relief from a similar partial derating of freight-transport hereditaments would be used largely for reducing freight charges on certain classes of traffic over railways and canals and through docks. There should be an annual government grant to each local authority to make good the consequent deficiency in rates. Transfer of road administration to county councils from urban areas with a valuation below £14,000 might mean an increase in county rates, and this should be made good by a government grant in the first year of working of the new system. The smallest area of charge should be the urban or rural district, but existing charges on special smaller districts should continue to be so assessed.

A prefatory note by the minister of finance explains minor deviations of the government proposals from the committee's recommendations. Statistical appendices deal with the cost of the whole derating scheme, and with the estimated total amount of rating relief for the three principal railways and their total gross annual freight receipts in respect of the commodities suggested for relief.

Rating Relief

Rep. of Local Authorities' Grants (Derating) Cttee., 1929.
Cmd. 95, 21 pp.

Rep. sgd. February 1929.

G.C. Duggan (Ch.) and five members—
T.E. Brown, G. Bryan, D.L. Clarke, J.I.
Cook and A.N.B. Wyse.

'To consider and report further on the
method of putting into operation that
portion of the recommendations made . . .
by the Inter-Departmental Committee on
Rating Relief, which related to the pro-
cedure for recouping to local authorities
. . . the loss of revenue which they will
suffer as a consequence of the derating of
agricultural land, industrial hereditaments,
and freight-transport hereditaments.'

The committee recommends that deficiencies in educational rates should be
met by a standard deficiency payment
based on expenditure in the year ending
31 March 1929, together with an un-
limited supplemental grant to meet increases in expenditure. County boroughs,
boroughs, urban district councils, town
commissioners and the Belfast City and
District Water Commissioners should
receive a single deficiency grant. County
councils should receive a standard deficiency grant based on expenditure in
the three years prior to 31 March 1929,
and, where necessary, a supplemental
grant limited to the equivalent of a rate
of sixpence in the pound. Existing charges
on special areas for water supply and
sewerage should be made district charges,
and there should be no special areas in
future. Relief of water rates should operate only where the rate is a general
public charge and not a payment for
water used. The Ministry of Home
Affairs or the Ministry of Education
should have power to reduce grants if
efficient services are not maintained.
Transfer of the administration of roads
in the smaller urban districts is not
appropriate to a bill concerned with
rate relief. Recommendations also cover
the transitional period, adjustments to
rate collectors' remuneration, and other
minor matters.

A reservation by J.I. Cook concerns
the payment and allocation of grants
and suggests an alternative to the proposal of the report which Cook regards
as inflexible.

The Financial Relations between the State and Local Authorities

Rep. of Cttee., 1931.
Cmd. 131, x, 116 pp.
Cttee. apptd. July, 1930; rep. sgd. August
1931.

J.G. Leslie (Ch.) and seven members—
Capt. J.L. Chichester-Clark, D.L. Clarke,
J.I. Cook, G.C. Duggan, M. Gordon, A.
Robinson and A.N.B. Wyse.

'Having regard to the resources of
Northern Ireland and its taxable and
rateable capacity, to consider the present
system of Government Grants in aid of
Local Authorities' expenditure and the
distribution of public expenditure between
the Exchequer and the Rates, and to
recommend what changes, if any, are
desirable.'

After an appropriate historical introduction, the report proceeds to summarize grants made and to compare
these with the situation in Great Britain;
to discuss present methods of distributing
grants in aid; to consider the rateable
and taxable capacity of the province; to
compare Northern Ireland's expenditure
on the police and education services with
that of Great Britain; and to debate the
benefits and effects of the present systems
of valuation and derating. Details are
given of suggestions made by local
authorities for the transfer of certain
services to the state. The committee are,
in the words of their chairman, 'compelled to indicate that it is only by
rigorous—even ruthless—reductions in
expenditure that the permanent financial
solvency of Northern Ireland is attain-
able'.

It is found that there is no case for a
redistribution of expenditure between
the Exchequer and the rates on any
considerable scale; that the distress
caused by abolishing all existing grants
in aid would be out of proportion to the
small relief this would give to the
Exchequer; and that derating has had a

serious effect upon local government finances. Any drastic change in the method of making grants is viewed as unnecessary. Substantial cuts in state and local expenditure are called for, as it is thought that the limit of taxable capacity has been exceeded and very little more could be expected from rates. Comparisons between Great Britain and Northern Ireland in the sphere of public finance are misleading, unless the different conditions prevailing in the two areas are considered. Recommendations include the suggestion that a revaluation of all buildings should be undertaken; that certain grants should be amalgamated and others abolished; and that there should be review and readjustment of certain state and local authority responsibilities and financial obligations. It is believed that the proposals should result in a net annual saving of over £38,000 to the Exchequer. Revaluation should yield a further £50,000 each year, but the revision of the standard derating grants is viewed as costing some £13,000. Total net saving per annum is, therefore, estimated as approximately £75,000.

There are two signed reservations to the report. One, by A.N.B. Wyse, argues that the proposed cut in the technical education grant is too drastic. The other, signed by D.L. Clarke and A. Robinson, presents a lengthy case opposing the abolition of certain grants relating to services associated with the poor law system. In a covering letter, printed at the front of the report, the chairman comments on this latter reservation and on his own view on another matter—that, strictly speaking, derating is outside the committee's terms of reference. The report is also prefaced by extracts from that of the Departmental Commission on Local Government Administration (Cmd. 73 of 1927) arguing that too much money is absorbed by the salaries of poor law officials and the upkeep of buildings.

Statistical appendices concern: expenditure of local authorities compared with corresponding government grants (a series of tables including one showing the effects of derating); central and local taxation in Britain and Northern Ireland, 1925–1931; state, rate and grant expenditure per head of population in the two countries, 1927–1931; comparison of rates in the countries' county boroughs and urban districts; rates in each Northern Ireland local authority for the years 1928–1931; the poor rate in rural districts over the same period. Further appendices give details of local government finance on the Isle of Man, some British dominions and certain European countries. There are also details of proposed grant increases and of grants which, it is suggested, should be abolished.

The Finances of Local Authorities

Rep. of Cttee., 1957 (reprinted 1963). Cmd. 369, 86 pp. Cttee. apptd. January 1955; rep. sgd. March 1957.

Maj. the Rt. Hon. Sir Ronald Nugent (Ch.) and seventeen members—Maj. D.M. Anderson, H. Boyd, G.A. Cathcart, Lt.-Col. D.J. Christie, G.N. Cox, W.S. Henderson, Maj. D.C.B. Holden, W.H. Jones, Prof. F.T. Lloyd-Dodd, W. McCaughey, Maj. G.R.B. McConnell, Maj. W.C. McKee, J.A. Oliver, H. Quin, H.W.F. Reid, R.B. Stevens, E.W. Thompson. (H. Boyd resigned October 1955, Maj. G.R.B. McConnell in June 1956, and G.N. Cox died January 1957. D.C. White and G.H.E. Parr were appointed members in April and October 1955, respectively, and J.M. Benn in June 1956.)

'To consider the finances of local authorities . . . with particular reference to:
(a) the rating system;
(b) the income derived from rates;
(c) the present system of Government grants; and
(d) the distribution of these grants; and to make recommendations.'

The existing rating system is sound, but revaluation of all property, including agricultural land and buildings, should be carried out and a system of continuous revision introduced. Industrial derating should cease as soon as similar action is taken in Great Britain, and other exemptions from rating should be strictly limited. The state's share of financial responsibility for certain items should be examined—certain education costs, arrangements for the care of old people, expenditure on roads, maintenance of young persons in training schools. The method of calculation of the General Exchequer Grant should be revised, and the state should be responsible for appointment and remuneration of coroners, and expenditure in connection with juror's lists, sheriffs' expenses, and advertisement of assizes. Rents for local authority houses should be fixed according to the value of the accommodation, but the circumstances of the tenant should be taken into account. All local authorities should contribute on the same basis under the Drainage Act (N.I.), 1947. Belfast should cease to pay an annual contribution to the cost of police and should be given the option of coming into an integrated fire services scheme. Levies under the Diseases of Animals Acts, and general agriculture and destruction of vermin levies should cease.

Appendices list bodies and persons who gave evidence; tables show the general exchequer contribution to different local authorities; a proposed new basis for the general exchequer contribution is described; a glossary gives some of the more technical terms used, and there is a table of the statutes cited in the report.

6 MISCELLANEOUS PAPERS

The Parliamentary Library

For details of this report see Class XIV p. 175.

Regularity of Some Scholarship Awards

Special rep. of Sel. Cttee. on Public Accounts, 1955/6, together with procs., mins. of ev. and apps.
H.C. 1247, 47 pp.
Rep. o.p. March 1957.

Prof. F.T. Lloyd-Dodd (Ch.) and six members—P.J. Gormley, S.T. Irwin, H.V. Kirk, J.W.N. Martin, N.O. Minford, W.J. Morgan.

The accounting officer of the Ministry of Education notified the Ministry of Finance and the comptroller and auditor-general that seven scholarships were awarded in 1955 and 1956 on the directions of the minister of education, who in giving these directions overruled objections by the accounting officer to the effect that in his opinion the statutory requirements were not fulfilled. This action relieved the accounting officer of personal responsibility for the possible irregularity of the payments. Six of the scholarships were awarded by the ministry at training colleges for teachers. In one of these, the candidate had been found unsuitable for training by two separate interviewing boards, and the committee considered the payments made in this case to be unlawful. The other five candidates had been rejected on medical grounds. In four cases, the committee find that the candidates failed to pass the test and any payments made are unlawful. In the fifth case, the degree of disability, one leg being shorter than the other, might not be such as to preclude the candidate taking part in the full training, and this case is referred back to the ministry. Following discussion by the cabinet, the Ministry of Finance approved extra-statutory payments being made in these cases to cover one year's expenditure. The committee are of the opinion that such approval does not regularize the position, and the payments remain unlawful.

In the one other case, a candidate was awarded a local education authority further education scholarship, grant-aided by the ministry, to pursue studies abroad. Such awards require the candidate to show evidence of superior ability, and the committee overrule the accounting officer's objections and find that the minister did not go beyond the exercise of his proper functions as head of the department.

Memoranda from the comptroller and auditor-general form appendices.

Tender Procedure for School Building Works

Ministry of Education. Rep. of Public Inquiry conducted by W.F. Patton, 1959. Cmd. 395, 11 pp.
W.F. Patton apptd. August 1958; rep. sgd. November 1958.

'To hold a public inquiry into the procedure which should be adopted in connection with tenders relating to school building works undertaken by local education authorities; and to consider the procedure followed by the Education Committee for the County of Londonderry, their members and officers, in relation to the consideration of tenders received by the said Committee for the supply and erection of structural steel for the new county intermediate school at Limavady.'

It is necessary to provide by direction or by standing orders for the precise procedure to be followed in regard to tenders, so that there may be no irregularities such as are found to have occurred with the Limavady school tenders. When a tender box is opened other than in committee, a list should be made of the contents.

Advertising should not be left entirely in the architect's hands. The powers of a member of committee, no matter how exalted, can only be exercised at a meeting of committee at which a quorum is present, and he has no right to issue instructions on his own responsibility. It should be impossible for a committee to adopt a recommendation made by a subcommittee unless it be in writing, or the minutes of the latter are before the committee.

The (Parliamentary) Kitchen and Refreshment Rooms

Special rep. of Jt. Sel. Cttee., together with proc., mins. of ev. and app., 1963. H.C. 1542, 48 pp.
Rep. o.p. January 1963.

I.G. Hawthorne (Ch.) and seven members—J. Cunningham, H. Diamond, Mrs. M.J. Greeves, J.S. Johnson, Capt.

W.J. Long, P.J. O'Hare and F.V. Simpson.

This committee was appointed to control refreshment arrangements at Stormont. Its first meeting in the present Parliament was in July 1962, and attention was drawn to the fact that the last meeting had been held more than three years previously and audited accounts since that date were not available. The committee had an auditor's report made, and this, together with a memorandum prepared by the clerk of the parliaments and dealing with the present catering arrangements, is given in appendices. The auditor's report includes statistics of income and expenditure. It is stressed that the committee is now engaged in a detailed study of catering arrangements and that members should make full use of the facilities in the parliamentary refreshment rooms.

The clerk of the parliaments and the accountant were the only witnesses called, and their names are given at the end of the concise report and immediately before the minutes of evidence. A further appendix gives the text of a letter dated September 1962, from a local catering firm, on the subject of charges for special functions.

[Further reports on this subject appear in H.C. papers:

1644 (1965);   1684 (1966);
1749 (1966);   1813 (1967);
1886 (1968);   1975 (1970);
2052 (1971);   2188 (1972).]

The 'Seenozip Case'

Special and first rep. from the Sel. Cttee. of Public Accounts, 1962–63, with the proc., mins. of ev. and apps. H.C. 1615, 398 pp.
Special rep. o.p. January 1964; first rep. o.p. July 1964.

D.W. Bleakley (Ch.) and six members—J. Burns, C. Healy, W.S. Hinds, H.I. McClure, P. O'Neill, W. Scott. (C. Healy resigned from the Cttee. at an early stage in the deliberations.)

The case concerns a company engaged in the manufacture of invisible zip-fasteners which transferred, to a site in Newry, plant and machinery to set up a Northern Ireland division and received substantial grants under the government's scheme for attracting new industry to the province. Five applications for financial aid were approved. The company experienced grave difficulties; a receiver was appointed and its two principal promoters were prosecuted for fraud.

The special report merely concerns correspondence between the committee and the prime minister. The first report deals with the financial aspects of the affair and the way in which the credentials of the company had been investigated by the ministry. Two members of Parliament had been prepared to join the company's board of directors, and there seemed good reasons for supporting

this enterprise. The nature of the product might have been more thoroughly investigated, and other precautions could have been taken. Nevertheless, apart from the possibility of discovering the fraud, the committee do not think that the most thorough investigation would have dissuaded the government from aiding this industrial development in an area of high unemployment. The case was most unfortunate but exceptional; it must be recalled that since 1945 nearly 3,000 projects have been investigated and over one-tenth of these have received governments grants.

Various appendices to the short reports give the legal and financial background, the employment and wage situation within the company, a note of the appointment of directors, an extract from the *Belfast Telegraph*, and some relevant correspondence. A list of witnesses called by the committee is also supplied.

II NATIONAL FINANCE

Papers on this subject are published by the Imperial Government at Westminster.

III MONETARY AND ECONOMIC POLICY, FINANCIAL INSTITUTIONS

Trustee Securities

Rep. of Cttee. of Inquiry, 1939. Cmd. 203, 27 pp. Cttee. apptd. February 1937; rep. sgd. October 1937.

Justice R.D. Megaw (Ch.) and seven members—W.T. Barry, A. Black, C.A. Brett, C.E. Duffin, G.C. Duggan, Sir Dudley E.B. McCorkell, W.F. Scott.

'(1) to consider the present state of the law . . . relating to the investment of trust funds by trustees, and to recommend what changes, if any, should be made therein. (2) to consider whether a Public Trustee ought to be constituted in Northern Ireland.'

It is concluded that stock and securities issued by the Northern Ireland government should be given full trustee status for both English and Scottish trusts and

that this status should also be granted to stock guaranteed by the government with regard to capital and interest. Trustee status for Scottish trusts should also be conferred upon stock issued by the municipal corporations, and stocks issued by large municipal corporations or by water companies should be given a definite statutory basis as authorized trustee investments for English trusts. The appointment within the United Kingdom of a standing statutory committee, to revise the list of trustee securities when required, is urged. It is also recommended that the authorized range of trustee investments should depend directly upon statute; that in future trustee status should be granted only by public statute; and that there should be no addition to the province's list of trustee securities.

The committee firmly denies the need

for a public trustee in Northern Ireland on the grounds that the volume of business would be small and receipts from fees insufficient. This conclusion is based largely on memoranda and statistics supplied by the deputy public trustee in Manchester. Appendices summarize details of appropriate legislation concerning trusts.

A prefatory note to the report, by the minister of finance, concerns the effect which the committee's proposals would have on British legislation and indicates that it was necessary to have the view of H.M. Treasury. The Treasury are unable to accept the notion of a standing statutory committee for the whole of the United Kingdom and reject the recommendations that stocks guaranteed by the Northern Ireland government be made trustee securities in Britain and that stocks issued by local government in the province should be accorded trustee status. They also comment on the recommendation that Northern Ireland government stock be given trustee status for English and Scottish trusts. They feel that the proposal has more value in relation to English trusts than to the Scottish.

An Economic Survey of Northern Ireland

Ministry of Commerce Survey rep. by K.S. Isles and N. Cuthbert, 1957. xxvi, 646 pp., charts, index, tables.

The report sets out to provide 'an independent study of the economy of Northern Ireland . . . made on the basis of academic research'. It is believed that such a survey 'might add to public understanding of Northern Ireland's economic conditions and problems; and . . . contain data and analyses which, though not by themselves capable of supporting a decision to adopt any specific measures of policy in preference to others, would throw additional light on the economic aspects of some of the considerations on which policy decisions depend'. The fundamental object of the whole report is essentially one of minute analysis and description rather than actual recom-

mendation. An attempt is made 'to gauge the general level of prosperity relatively to that in the United Kingdom as a whole—judging it by the separate tests of income and employment—and then to analyse the causes of, and the economic effects of various possible measures for dealing with, the resulting economic problems. More specifically, the aim is to examine the main facts regarding Northern Ireland's relatively depressed state, the principal conditions and difficulties hindering its economic development relative to that of Great Britain, the nature of the resulting economic problems facing the people and the government, and the economic effects of measures designed to overcome them.' The report divides into three parts plus detailed appendices. Part I is a factual study of the level and distribution of income and of employment patterns and trends. The long Part II studies the range and size of industries and the factors governing income, employment levels and the factors governing income, employment levels and the structure of industry, with special reference to divergences from the U.K. norm. Part III discusses economic policy problems.

Part I. *The General Level of Prosperity: income; the level of employment.*

During the war years, the total money income in Northern Ireland increased faster than it did within the U.K. as a whole, but after 1945 the relative growth fell somewhat behind. Income per head has grown faster in Northern Ireland in recent years, but it is still lower than the U.K. average. This is due to comparatively low earnings, high unemployment, a smaller proportion of the population falling within the working age group, the character of specialization in certain manufacturing industries and the high proportion of workers employed in agriculture. In 1949/50 Northern Ireland had 43.8 percent of its workers earning under £250, as opposed to 35.7 percent for the U.K. A comparatively large proportion of private income in the province is derived from investment abroad.

Lower incomes seem to result from lack of opportunity rather than inefficiency. Unemployment—in part, the result of fewer opportunities—may mean that plant and machinery are not worked near enough to full capacity. Although employment levels in all areas of the U.K. have improved, there is still persistently high unemployment in Ulster. It had apparently been thought that high regional unemployment was the result of the general depression, and the possibility of other, more lingering, causes was overlooked. Unemployment follows the pattern of British unemployment levels over a period of time, but the size of the industrial labour force has fluctuated much more in Northern Ireland. Greater industrial specialization, in relation to a fluctuating labour supply, has probably contributed to unemployment, which has been greatest in relation to male workers.

Part II. *Factors Controlling Economic Development: the industrial structure; the export trade; location of industry; the size of firms; the degree of industrial specialization; transport; investment and the supply of capital; the natural increase in the labour force; wages; potential labour supplies through inter-regional migration; short-term variations in labour supplies; production; economic interdependence with Great Britain.*

Agriculture is the dominant industry, providing jobs for more than a quarter of the employed males and about one-tenth of the working females in the province. (The proportion for the U.K. as a whole is 6 percent approximately.) The small family farm is the typical unit, and, on average, farms are smaller and less well equipped than their British equivalents. The ease of interchange of the labour force between industry and agriculture is a feature of the Ulster economy. A large proportion of those employed in production are concentrated in a few industries—shipbuilding, engineering, textiles, clothing, and, to a lesser extent, building, food and drink, and vehicle manufacture and maintenance.

In 1952, 42 percent of males employed in manufacturing were in the group comprising shipbuilding, engineering and textiles. The concentration of women workers in a few manufacturing industries is even greater; in 1952, 79 percent of women employed in manufacturing were working in textiles or clothing. Building attracts a great deal of male casual labour. Many workers are thus seen to be in capital-goods industries which are prone to economic disturbances and industrial fluctuations; a study of cyclical variations over a period of time in the major manufacturing industries is thus provided. The emphasis on light industries helps to explain why unemployment has been heaviest among males. The lack of heavy manufacturing industry helps to explain the relatively high proportion of men engaged in service industries. There has been definite growth, in the last twenty years, in male-employing industries, but this is insufficient to cure the problem of male unemployment.

The only manufactures which are usually able to compete successfully in overseas markets are those on which the direct and indirect transport costs are relatively low. About 60 percent or more of the value of total production is exported either abroad or to Great Britain. There is a remarkable statistical correlation between total civilian income from year to year and the total value of exports. The main changes in the level of income are promoted from without and come mainly from or via Great Britain. They stem from changes in production costs or in the external demand for goods. A study of employment trends in an industry closely connected with external trade, namely shipbuilding, shows the way in which vicissitudes parallel those of Britain.

Industry in Northern Ireland tends to be carried on in smaller units than is the case in the U.K. as a whole. There is a higher proportion of private companies in Ulster, and some of these are larger than their British equivalents, but the public companies are smaller. The average amount of capital per insured industrial worker is lower in Northern Ireland. Excluding agriculture, industry tends to be concentrated in and around Belfast. In 1947, 60 percent of insured workers came from the Belfast employment exchange area, the next highest percentage being 5.9 percent from the Londonderry exchange area. The heavier industries—engineering and shipbuilding—are especially concentrated in the Belfast region. It is argued that unemployment in the province is not due to industrial specialization but rather to costs of transport, dependence on imports, and the emphasis on production for exporting.

Northern Ireland's small share, in proportion to population, of the U.K. newly invested industrial capital is also a crucial factor in the high level of unemployment. Much investment that does take place is in companies in Britain, but the low level of domestic investment is certainly not due to a lack of propensity to save. It is due rather to a low expectation of profit on the part of investors and, among other reasons, to the preponderence of small private companies. Some limitations on investment in the province are due to the nature of the capital market—these could be eased by finding ways for sound companies to issue shares to the public at less expense than is involved in employing the London capital market and ways to enable firms, too small for a public issue, to find alternative and reasonable means of obtaining risk capital. A government-sponsored industrial investment and finance company would help improve the situation.

The growth rate in the population of working age has been significantly higher in Northern Ireland than in Great Britain. Despite this and notwithstanding higher unemployment rates in Ulster, the growth in wage rates in various industries up to the early war years matched that of the U.K. and exceeded it immediately after the war. This picture is distorted by certain factors, including variations in the length of the working week and in the different composition of the industrial structure in Northern Ireland in comparison with Great Britain. Northern Ireland has a high proportion of unskilled workers. The reasons for and solution to this situation are considered, as is the question of the effect of migration on the labour supply.

It is argued that geographical handicaps (difficulty of access to markets and natural resources) would not lead to persistent unemployment if wages were completely free to adapt themselves to the monetary demand for labour and the other agents of production. Given this flexibility and mobility of labour, industrial expansion could match that of Great Britain. Actual differentials must thus 'be due to the conditions determining the relation which the monetary demand for labour and capital, the physical supplies of these productive agents and their contractual rates of pay, bear to the corresponding quantities in Great Britain.' If, as a result of fiscal and economic policy, the total demand for labour in the U.K. as a whole is enough to match the total labour force, it will not yield full employment in Northern Ireland, as special measures are needed to offset the problems connected with labour migration, under-investment in the province, the imbalance in the industrial structure and similar matters. The Stormont government, as a subordinate Parliament, cannot employ all those measures enjoyed by a country with economic independence, but at times, when in Great Britain there is a need to relieve inflationary pressure on wages and prices, the measures required in the general interest conflict with those needed in Northern Ireland. Other regions within the U.K. are affected to some extent by this phenomenon too. Even if new investment could be distributed between the different regions in proportion to their unemployment problem, those with low income multipliers (like Northern Ireland) would tend to lag in any expansion of employment.

Part III. *Economic Considerations Relating to Policy: problems of economic policy; government assistance to industry; the economic powers of government.*

There is a discussion of the practical disadvantages facing the Stormont government in trying to promote the growth of industry and employment, and of whether the provincial economy would benefit if the delegated powers were extended. Efforts to overcome the economic problems of the province could be made by workers, by entrepreneurs and by Stormont. Workers could contribute more effort or accept lower pay than their counterparts in other regions of the U.K.; entrepreneurs could investigate the value of investment in further equipment, improve factory layout and review organization techniques; the provincial government could promote industrial training, provide appropriate subsidies to industry and offer other stimuli. A local capital institution, acting as an issuing house, underwriter and investment trust, is needed. More extensive delegation to Stormont, however, would separate the economy from that of the rest of the U.K.; so close co-ordination between the two governments and a clear acceptance by Westminster of direct responsibility for the Northern Ireland economy is necessary.

The Stormont government has taken measures to increase the number of new industrial undertakings, to promote the expansion of industry through the provision of capital and to encourage productivity on the farm. An even greater drive to attract new industry is required. The question of greater economic independence for the province concerns variations in taxation that might be desirable or possible and the use of a tariff to foster the growth of industries which do not, at present, exist in Northern Ireland. Such self-sufficiency would tend to involve the establishment of industries in which Ulster's comparative disadvantages are substantial. Fiscal and monetary autonomy would only serve to discourage the investment of British capital in Northern Ireland industry. Full self-government would be contrary to world trends and utterly against Northern Ireland's economic interest. A more effective answer lies in discerning support from the central government to keep growth and industrial employment compatible with that in Great Britain.

Appendices.

The report has eight appendices, one of these being entirely devoted to statistical tables. Appendix A concerns a discussion of private income and reviews the structure of salaries and wages, business profits, investment income and income from government securities. Appendix B deals with inter-regional investment, that is, external investment by citizens and corporate bodies in Northern Ireland and investment in Ulster by outsiders. Then, in appendix C, there is an attempt to measure personal and corporate saving. This is followed by a discussion, in a further appendix, of the change in the number of insured workers, within any given year, due to the increase in the population. The methods of calculation used in Part II of the report, with reference to the natural increase in the labour force, are discussed. Appendix E considers the potential for recruitment of female factory workers in rural districts, while appendix F concerns male workers and the fluctuating nature of the insured labour force in the twelve-year period 1926–1937. In appendix G, there is an examination of cyclical movements in the linen industry and their possible origins, with special reference to the U.S. market. Fluctuations in demand from the latter are most important, for it is considered that cyclical variations stem from the conditions governing the demand rather than from those determining the supply.

The statistical appendix provides fifty-two tables. Some show levels of employment and unemployment in various industries over a period of time (usually 1926–1953). The industries concerned include agriculture, engineering, shipbuilding, building and contracting, linen, food and drink, and clothing. Comparisons of employment levels for different regions of Great Britain are given. Other tables show wage rates, the volume of exports, the proportion of males among workers in manufacturing industry, incomes and saving. Some specialized tables relate to the textile industries and to the production and consumption of textile goods in the United States.

A hundred and thirty further tables within the main text of the report also give data relating to some of these subjects. They include, in addition, details of private income in Great Britain and Northern Ireland, the proportion of the total population of working age, the number and size of agricultural holdings, the value of exports, the average numbers of workers per establishment in various industries, the cost of importing and transporting coal, company trading profits, trade union membership, private (personal and company) saving, wage rates in certain industries and details of time lost in trade disputes. Other tables among those distributed throughout the report concern migration and emigration of workers, fuel costs in Northern Ireland and Great Britain, the cost of materials, the value of net output per employee, the duration of unemployment, the number of taxpayers, the total extent of savings, investments in government securities, the distribution of share capital and the paid-up value of shares in Northern Ireland companies. Some of the statistical tables are in index-number form, and some represent projections estimating future trends, but they are especially full with regard to information on incomes and employment. Serious gaps in the provision of official statistics for the province made the compilation of some of these tables difficult and reliant on estimates.

The Economy of Northern Ireland

Rep. of the Jt. Wkg. Pty., 1962.
Cmd. 446, vi, 89 pp.
Wkg. Pty. apptd. May 1961; rep. submitted June 1962.

Chairman of Wkg. Pty.: Sir Robert Hall

(original chairman, Sir Herbert Brittain, died September 1961).

'To examine and report on the economic situation of Northern Ireland, the factors causing the persistent problem of high unemployment, and what measures can be taken to bring about a lasting improvement.'

The working party was established following a meeting between United Kingdom and Northern Ireland ministers and was composed of officials from relevant departments in both administrations with a chairman from outside the civil service. When the completed report was considered, it was agreed that it should be published with the omission of a small amount of confidential material, and a few amendments were thus necessary in the published version.

The report begins by considering the economic position of Ulster—its political and economic characteristics, its staple industries, employment trends and economic problems. Some of the latter stem from the fact that Northern Ireland, although enjoying many benefits from being a part of the United Kingdom, is not free to pursue independent policies such as the use of extra tariffs. The promotion of exports and the diversification of industrial structure are seen as the key needs. The report considers measures to create employment and their efficiency; measures of financial aid; labour mobility; major individual industries (linen, shipbuilding, aircraft construction, agriculture and tourism); and the control of planning and development. There is also a short estimate of the effects of joining the European Economic Community and the effects if Éire were to join also. In dealing with considerations relevant to future policy, the working party argues that it would be wrong to give permanent subsidies to industries, but aid is needed and should be directed towards the growth of new industry rather than towards the support of staple industries, such as shipbuilding, now in decline.

As the working party could not agree

on the main proposal put by the Ulster government—that there should be an employment subsidy—it eventually rejected this proposed wage subsidy. However, many new ideas for bringing additional industry to the province were accepted. Derating for industry (despite its decline in Britain) is recommended to continue in the province. Other recommendations are that grants should be given to encourage the use by industry of management consultant services; further aid should be given to the linen industry and to promote tourism; the training of skilled labour should be accelerated; the subsidy on coal should be extended to other industrial fuels; and improvements are needed in the aircraft industry and in air traffic facilities. In agriculture, concentration should be on increasing efficiency rather than on increasing employment. The working party finds no case for the setting up of an economic planning council or any similar body devoted to economic development, as the work of such a body might overlap with that of the Northern Ireland Development Council.

The numerous appendices give statistical tables, with comment and explanatory remarks concerning the figures shown. There are useful appendices on financial arrangements between the governments, an employment estimate for Ulster in 1965 and efforts to assist employment, housing, agricultural aid, and the distribution of industry. The main statistical series in these and the other appendices concern the following themes:

Average weekly and hourly earnings in 1961: arranged by industry. Earnings of male manual workers are contrasted with British rates.

Insured employees: arranged by industry. Figures given for both Northern Ireland and Britain.

Employment changes in industry since 1950: for Britain and Northern Ireland. Figures given for agriculture, shipbuilding and textiles.

The linen industry: yardage of cloth woven, employment and output in recent years.

Population and employment 1950–1960: comparison of June figures each year for Northern Ireland and Britain.

Occupational analysis of the unemployed: arranged by industry with a special table for Belfast.

Comparison of public investment in Britain and Northern Ireland: figures for 1956–1962 with 1962/1963 estimates.

Housing building progress by public authorities: figures for 1954 to 1961 with future estimates.

Agricultural subsidies: for 1958–1961. Shown as a ratio of total output in Britain and Northern Ireland.

Economic Survey

Economic Advisory Office, 1963.
Cmd. 453, 75 pp.
Rep. dated April 1963.

This survey commences with a review of the general economic background, comprising a short account of the world economic situation, the United Kingdom economy, and conditions in Northern Ireland during 1962. Despite the slower growth of world trade over the last year and the recession in production and employment within the United Kingdom, the main sectors of the Northern Ireland economy were resilient and high levels of production and investment were maintained. At $7\frac{1}{2}$ percent, however, the rate of unemployment in the province was higher than in any other region within the United Kingdom. Government grants and the increased numbers benefiting from sponsored schemes of vocational training might help to some degree in meeting an increasing demand for skilled workers, as many of the jobless are unskilled men.

The remainder of the survey analyses the individual sectors of the Northern Ireland economy—employment, production, distribution, transport and finance. In the section devoted to employment there are details of wages, vocational training, and employment in new industries. Investment expenditure is also dealt with in this part of the survey. The section on production covers both agriculture and the major manufacturing industries, and there is a short review of tourism which reveals that the tourist trade brought some £12 million to the province in 1962. The section on distribution involves an analysis of retail sales, hire-purchase, and external and internal trading, while the short section on transport reviews the recent operating and financial results of the Ulster Transport Authority. Finally, in the area of the survey concerned with finance, there is an account of company registrations, banking, interest rates, savings, the work of building societies, bankruptcies and government financial operations.

There are, throughout the survey, many concise statistical tables showing recent trends in matters affecting the sector of the economy being reviewed. A more detailed analysis is given in the statistical appendix which provides over thirty tables, as follows:

Population: 1951, 1961 and 1962 (arranged by county and county borough).

Personal incomes: 1950/51 – 1961/62 (sub-arranged by source of income).

Employment and unemployment: 1950–1962 (sub-arranged by industry).

Average weekly earnings of male manual workers: 1960–1962 (arranged by industry and utilizing index numbers).

Vocational training: 1960–1962 (number of trainees, sub-arranged by types of establishment).

Gross fixed capital formation: given for certain years in the period 1950–1962 (arranged firstly by industrial group, then by sector and by type of asset).

New housing: statistics of dwellings completed in certain years during the period 1950–1962.

Public roads: details of new construction and maintenance in certain recent years.

New vehicle registrations: arranged by type, in certain recent years.

Farming output and expenditure: for certain recent years, with a 1962/1963 forecast.

Agricultural subsidies and grants: for certain recent years, with a 1962/1963 forecast.

Crop acreages and yields: 1946, and 1957 to 1962 (arranged by crop).

Livestock numbers on farms: for certain recent years.

Fish landings: arranged by type of fish, for certain recent years.

Capital grants to industry: in recent years (sub-arranged by industry).

Industrial production: in certain recent years (sub-arranged by industry and utilizing some index numbers).

Retail sales: index numbers 1960–1962 (arranged by type of shop).

Air transport: statistics of passengers and freight carried 1958–1962.

Financial results of the Ulster Transport Authority: 1950, 1958–1961.

Exchequer finance: 1960/1961 and 1961/1962.

Bank rate and interest rates: statistics for 1950–1961.

Other statistical tables provide information on capital investment in farming, agricultural output, hire-purchase transactions, internal transport, container traffic, company registrations, bankruptcy cases, bank advances and deposits, building society advances and receipts, other forms of saving. In each case figures are given for 1962 with some comparative statistics from earlier years.

Economic Development

Government statement and rep. of the economic consultant, Prof. T. Wilson, [1965].
Cmd. 479, 153 pp., diagrs., maps.
Consultants rep. sgd. December 1964.

Most of this document is occupied by Professor Wilson's detailed report, on which the Ulster government proposes to base its plans for economic development up to 1970. The framework of this report and the chief proposals of its various chapters are as follows:

Chapter 1, *Basis of the Plan*, argues

that the province needs an environment suited to promoting expansion and a fuller measure of employment. Growth centres need to be developed and efficient transport is essential. The need for the training of the semi-skilled is stressed. While the government must take positive action, a great deal depends upon the efficiency of management and labour.

Chapter 2, *Objectives for Manpower*, states that over the period 1964–1970, about 160,000 young people will reach the age of sixteen, so manpower is Ulster's chief economic asset. Certain industries, such as agriculture, will need a reduced labour force, while others—the service industries, for example—will attract more labour. A target of 30,000 new jobs in manufacturing during the years 1964–1970 is suggested for the government. Employment in the construction industry can be boosted by supporting a programme of investment which is outlined.

Chapter 3, *Location of Industry*, examines centres of growth, labour mobility and the development of industry in Belfast, Londonderry, Carnmoney, Carrickfergus, Bangor, Newtownards, Lurgan, Portadown, Larne, Antrim, Ballymena and some other towns. Belfast is viewed as likely to remain the most important base for industry, and the establishment of a development plan for Londonderry is urged. The Ministry of Development should establish a working party for each main town to consider its industrial needs and growth.

Chapter 4, *Amenity and Tourists*, suggests various ideas to promote the tourist industry. These include ways of making Belfast more attractive and improving its hotel accommodation. An air terminal is needed.

Chapter 5, *Transport Services*, points out the pressing need for the proposed urban motorway to relieve traffic congestion in Belfast. Larger airport buildings are needed, bus fares are unduly high and should be reduced, while extra services—such as car ferries—are needed in connection with sea transport. The abandonment of the public monopoly of freight transport is welcomed by this report. A general transport subsidy is not recommended.

Chapter 6, *New Plans for Training*, includes several recommendations on technical training in schools and on conditions of apprenticeship. Speedy training for the construction industry is imperative to provide a labour force to match the proposed investment programme. Employment exchanges need to be reformed and strengthened, and special rehabilitation courses for the unemployed require improvement. In view of the complexity of the responsibilities for the minister of health, there is the case for the setting up of a new ministry of employment and training, and it is appropriate that the government should bear a larger proportion of the cost of vocational training than would be customary in Britain.

Chapter 7, *Management Science and Industry*, points out the need to encourage the growth of science-based industries and suggests the setting up of a science and industry committee. More emphasis on research and development is needed, and a research centre for the biological sciences is proposed. A government inquiry into the question of the further diversification of Short Bros. and Harland's output is recommended.

Chapter 8, *Government Assistance with Industrial Expansion*, is concerned with government factories, inducements to industry, and taxation matters. A special expert inquiry into banking is recommended. Measures adopted to promote expansion should not merely act as a prop for inefficient industries and should, as far as possible, be consistent with policies adopted elsewhere in the United Kingdom.

Chapter 9, *Agriculture*, presents the prospect of rising incomes for a declining number of farmers, as it considers employment and productivity, marketing of farm products, the development of new products, fishing, and forestry. Further amalgamation of farms and greater co-operation is proposed, and there are some recommendations on education for farming. If Northern Ireland is to hold its share of the British market, it must improve the quality of produce and reduce costs further. Arguments against increasing the programme of afforestation are put forward. It is noted that the Ministry of Agriculture proposes to establish an agricultural trust to foster the growth of new processes and of new agricultural products.

Chapter 10, *The Programme for Investment,* outlines the financial resources required to achieve the planned programme and discusses investment in housing, fuels, transport, water and sewerage, education, industry, and health. Total investment expenditure, at 1963 prices, could amount to £900 million over the six financial years 1964/65–1969/70. A calculation is given of the amount of investment required to reach the set target of 30,000 new jobs in manufacturing industry. Specific recommendations include comments on the roads programme and on slum clearance, and it is stressed that a decrease in 'social' investment may not give impetus to industrial investment. The provision of more basic statistical information by the government is urged.

Professor Wilson's report has three appendices. The first gives estimates, sub-arranged by industry, of the province's gross domestic product at factory cost, at intervals between the years 1950 and 1962. The other appendices give details of training courses provided by the Ministry of Health and Social Services and details of the value of the inducements to new industry or firms planning to expand their Northern Ireland interests. There are also two diagrams which show the index of gross domestic product and national production, 1950–1963, and of civil employment (sub-arranged by industry) over the same period. Two of the individual chapters have their own special appendices. An appendix to chapter 1 gives a brief analysis of em-ployment structure in manufacturing, by reference to national employment changes, 1950–1958 and 1959–1962. The appendix to the chapter on agriculture gives statistics on the output of chief agricultural products for the year 1924/1925, at ten year intervals from 1940/1941 onwards, and finally for the recent years 1961–1963.

The report is prefaced by a government statement on economic development, with particular regard to its recommendations. This statement comments on each of Professor Wilson's chapters. The target of 30,000 new jobs for manufacturing over the six years is accepted and, indeed, any recommendations which are rejected essentially concern matters of detail only. Full attention is, therefore, to be given to the needs for training skilled workers for appropriate industries; to necessary readjustment in agriculture, 'the most important single industry' in the province; to certain transport reforms; and to the question of attracting more research and development work to Northern Ireland. A major investment effort is thus needed, and by 1969/70 it is hoped to achieve a level of investment in the public sector which will be almost 60 percent higher than that of 1963/64. The government is eager to accelerate the work of slum clearance and notes the recommendation for the building of 64,000 houses over the six years of the plan, based on the achievement of an annual completion rate of 12,000 houses by 1969/70. It is considered that Professor Wilson's work 'underlines the substantial progress which has been made in recent years and points in particular to the impressive record of rising output. It stresses, nevertheless, the considerable scope for further advance in line with the main objectives of national policy:- . . . full employment, the expansion of output and the strengthening of the balance of payments position.' This will require 'a proper emphasis upon the efficiency and adaptability of management and labour and the creation of the right kind of physical environment'.

Bank Interest Rates 1965–1966

Ministry of Finance. Rep. of Cttee. of Inquiry, 1966.
Cmd. 499, 62 pp.
Cttee. apptd. July 1965; rep. o.p. June 1966.

Prof. T. Wilson (Ch.) and two members —Prof. M. Gaskin, C.L. Woolveridge.

'*To study current overdraft and other credit facilities and services provided by the Banks in Northern Ireland and to comment on any differences . . . between Northern Ireland and other parts of the United Kingdom. The committee to take account of*
(i) economic conditions;
(ii) the operations of other financial institutions;
(iii) bank charges; and
(iv) various levels of Bank Rates.'

The first chapter of the report provides a brief review of the financial institutions in Northern Ireland, together with some reference to the economic environment in which they operate. Chapter 2 contains a factual account of the leading features of banking in the province, including an analysis of the structure of assets and liabilities, which differs in some respects from that of the clearing banks. In chapter 3, interest rates and bank charges in Northern Ireland are analysed and compared with corresponding rates and charges in England and Wales and in Scotland. The significance of these comparisons, which are by no means straightforward, is further discussed in chapter 4. Finally, in chapter 5, the committee's conclusions and recommendations are set out.

In some respects the practices of the Northern Ireland banks are defective, and there are always various respects in which the banks could improve their efficiency and methods of working. A more flexible system of interest rates and charges should be adopted. The practice of agreeing on a comprehensive set of uniform rates of interest and charges should be abandoned, and any future agreements restricted to the deposit rate of interest. The higher deposit rate for large sums should be extended to all deposits, and the banks should experiment with higher rates on term deposits. The undertaking of the banks that they would attempt to keep the cost of borrowing from exceeding that in England and Wales is welcome, and minimum levels for rates on advances, corresponding to those applied individually by the London clearing banks, should be permissible. The range of overdraft rates should reflect more fully the surrounding circumstances of each advance. Charges on some current accounts are too low, and there should be no maxima for such charges. Each bank should describe the changes to be made in its rates of interest and charges to the Bank of England or to an independent committee appointed by the government of Northern Ireland. New institutions, such as an agricultural mortgage bank and a special financial institution as suggested in Cmd. 479 (p. 105), would assist the provision of long-term finance for fixed capital to small and medium-sized business and to farmers. The banks should explore the ways in which their operating costs might be reduced, particularly by rationalization of their branch systems.

Persons, organizations and companies from whom evidence or memoranda was received are listed in the appendix. Evidence was sought but not received from Belfast Chamber of Trade, the Federation of Building Trade Employers, James Mackie and Sons Ltd. and F.B. McKee and Co. Ltd. Sixteen statistical tables in an appendix and fourteen in the text illustrate the many aspects of Northern Ireland banking.

Manpower: An Appraisal of the Position 1964–1970

For details of this report see Class X p. 97.

Area Development

For details of this report see Class XIII B p. 133.

Northern Ireland Development Programme, 1970–1975.

Rep. of the three consultants: Prof. Sir Robert Matthew, Prof. Thomas Wilson, Prof. Jack Parkinson, 1970.
227 pp., graphs, maps.

Part I   *Introductory Survey by the Consultants*

The object of this introduction is to explain the background to the programme and set the scene for its proposals in various spheres of activity.

Northern Ireland has long been held to be the least prosperous region of the United Kingdom, and political agitation has, during the past few years, drawn attention to demands for more houses and jobs. In mid-1969, unemployment was 6.8. percent compared with 2.2 percent for the United Kingdom as a whole, and output per head is relatively low, but the gross domestic product has been rising faster in Northern Ireland than in the remainder of the United Kingdom. The general environment must be made still more favourable for expansion. Training of workers and the creation of more jobs for unemployed males are clearly among priorities. While the promotion of 40,000 new jobs over the quinquennium had been deemed the minimum advisable, civil disturbances have made the figure appear as a formidable one to achieve. The Antrim/Belfast/Craigavon triangle is the hub of industry in the province and holds about 55 percent of the population, but Londonderry and Ballymena are two other centres designated for growth. In recent years at least, the area west of Lough Neagh has had its full share of public investment. Before 1969 Londonderry was the best placed area for industrial expansion and may still be when unrest ceases there.

The objectives of policy include better employment opportunity, a reduction in the flow of outward migration, an improvement in living conditions and the improvement and preservation of amenities in town and countryside. Transport efficiency needs to be raised, and agricultural activity needs reviewing, preferably by a special committee which could

be appointed for this task. The whole plan clearly needs integration of effort and the support of the Westminster Government and the Ulster people.

Part II   *Description of Programmes*

The fifteen chapters examine manpower; industrial development and training; industrial relations; housing; a physical development strategy; Londonderry, Ballymena and the key centres; the Greater Belfast area; mobility; transport; amenities and tourism; education; health and welfare; agriculture. The final chapter considers the implementation of the programme and administration and legislation relating to it.

From the analysis of unemployment by industry (appendix 3), it can be seen that Northern Ireland, in increasing employment, has exceeded the Great Britain average in almost all industrial orders and that, if this can be maintained, faster employment growth rates will be possible. By the use of graphs, the report examines unemployment trends, locations and percentages, and possible manpower patterns for 1975. The existing industrial base is seen as stronger than ever before, but new industries must be attracted and allocated to areas where workers are available, investment grants continued, and advertising and publicity provided. Two chapters on industrial training outline plans for the quinquennium and discuss the state of industrial relations.

On housing, the report summarizes the housing record and progress on slum clearance. Location of house building, 1970–75, rents and housing subsidies, home ownership, standards, and the idea of a central housing authority are all matters reported in detail. If the target of 75,000 new dwellings for the period is attained—as it can be—it should make a dramatic difference to the housing position in the province.

Physical development strategy can be divided into two aspects, each presenting its own problems:
1. Under-developed areas, where the difficulty is mainly due to the decline of

agriculture and lack of alternative employment.

2. The problem of the Greater Belfast area which is relatively prosperous but has an inadequate centre and a sprawl of largely unplanned suburbia. The growth centres designated as a result of the Matthew Report on Belfast (Cmd. 451, 1963; see Class XIIIB) and the Wilson Report (Cmd. 479, 1965; see above) are discussed, and the progress of such centres in the Belfast region is reported upon.

Mobility of population is required to bring unemployed labour resources into the larger urban areas and to aid the development of the city of Belfast. Growth centres in the Greater Belfast area will need to accommodate not only an influx of new industry but varying degrees of accelerated population growth too. It is proposed that a central mobility office be set up in Belfast to co-ordinate and advise on population movements.

Since one of Northern Ireland's main problems in encouraging industrial growth is its remoteness from the major centres of population in Great Britain, the transport links with Great Britain are of crucial importance in the creation of the necessary conditions for the attraction of new industry. Transport by sea, ports and harbours, air services, airport development, post and telecommunications, internal transport, road freight services, railways, and the roads programme are all discussed with this problem in mind.

The creation of an environment which will enable the people of Northern Ireland to lead full and interesting lives is a major objective, and the Amenity Lands Act, 1965, has under its provision seven areas of outstanding natural beauty, Lagan Valley, North Derry, Antrim Coast and the Glens, South Armagh, the Mournes, the Lecale Coast and the Sperrins. More action is required in the countryside to clean up eyesores such as derelict buildings, old airfields, rubbish dumps, exhausted quarries and overgrown churchyards. There is a need for an urban and rural development campaign to improve the appearance of both towns and country, both for the Northern Ireland people and the visitors to the province, thereby improving the tourism potential.

The programme for education for 1970–75 includes the provision of more new schools and extension of existing schools. There have been no major changes in school education since 1964. The raising of the school leaving age in 1972/73 will require careful planning of syllabuses and add a further dimension to the requirement for school building up to 1975. Further education and higher education (see the Lockwood Report, Cmd. 475 in Class XIV) are discussed in the chapter on education, together with plans for social and recreational facilities and the development of the library service in Northern Ireland (see the Hawnt Report, Cmd. 494 in Class XIV).

There are also planned developments in the health services. Six hospitals have been selected for development as key area hospitals: Craigavon, Belfast City, Royal Victoria Hospital, Altnagelvin, Ballymena, Ulster. The desirability of redeveloping and strengthening the major teaching hospitals in Belfast is also recognized. The existing programme appears to be adequate to provide a good average standard of community health and welfare services by 1975 in the designated growth areas.

In the last five years the Northern Ireland agricultural industry has raised its total production, and the farming population has continued to fall, helping to boost labour productivity by $6\frac{1}{2}$ percent per year. The central aim of Northern Ireland agricultural policy should be to increase efficiency as rapidly as possible and to achieve, during the period, maximum growth in the incomes of the smaller number of farmers who will be working the land. The more successful the industry, however, the fewer numbers of workers will be needed. The programme discusses the costs of feeding stuffs; pig and poultry production; livestock and grassland management; farm amalgamations; land and capital; labour;

animal health; marketing and food processing; pig, egg and milk marketing; the Agricultural Trust; education; advice and research; forestry and fisheries—giving statistical information and plans for development.

The last chapter of the programme deals with implementation of the development programme, administration and legislation. Appendices show estimates of gross domestic product (with tables and diagrams); the level of civil employment; a comparison of the growth of uninsured employment in Northern Ireland and Great Britain, analysed by industrial orders; the value of industrial inducements; a summary of the main recommendations of the Belfast Urban Area Plan prepared by Building Design Partnership; a summary of the main recommendations of the Belfast Transportation Plan prepared by R. Travers Morgan Ltd.; extensions of the Stopline (maps 1 and 2); written and oral evidence received; and statistics of transport costs. Appropriate statistics are also provided in various parts of the text of the report.

Development Programme, 1970–1975

Government statement, 1970.
Cmd. 547, 30 pp.

A programme for economic and social development over the next five years has been under consideration since May 1968. The consultants have now reported to the government, and their advice provides the basis for the extension of the Matthew Plan of 1963 (Cmd. 451 in Class XIIIB) and the Wilson Economic Plan of 1965 (Cmd. 479 above). The vigorous adoption of the current plan, which involves expenditure of some £75 million, should help to diminish the root causes of unrest in the province, but the consultants have indicated that, although great progress can be made with housing, the employment problem will continue to be a difficult one. It must be attacked by a continuing drive for new industries, by modernization of existing ones, and by the creation of new employment through local initiative. The target of

40,000 new jobs is partly dependent on the cessation of civil disturbance. The housing programme should aim at the completion of some 75,000 houses over the quinquennium. Slum clearance and redevelopment is receiving active attention and may be helped considerably by the new Central Housing Organization.

Other subjects considered in the statement, with regard to their quality and the new investment expenditure needed, include education, health services, agriculture, transport, tourism facilities and industrial relations. A physical development strategy based on the conception of growth areas is proposed, and areas designated for faster growth include Londonderry, Ballymena, Newry, the Coleraine triangle, Larne, Dungannon, Omagh, Enniskillen, Strabane and Downpatrick. In Londonderry and Ballymena, the area plans are already being put into operation by development commissions.

Details are given of the measures by which the government proposes to supervise and co-ordinate the programme. Statistical tables show the average annual public expenditure on various industries and services and the expenditure increases necessitated by the new five-year programme.

Northern Ireland and the European Communities

[Rep.], 1971.
Cmd. 563, 16 pp.

Information given concerns the likely impact of entry into the European Community on five main areas of activity: employment, social security, industry and trade, transport and agriculture.

The Safeguarding of Employment Act of 1947, which governs employment permits in Northern Ireland, will, in the event of entry, be observed for at least a further five years. The residence condition which affects the receipt of unemployment benefit in Northern Ireland must be modified to treat nationals of other member countries as residents of the U.K. Reciprocal rights will naturally exist for people from Northern Ireland who go to E.E.C. countries. In industry, there are implications for tariffs, aids to manufacturers, and company law. Some 19 percent of Northern Ireland's 1969 exports went to the E.E.C., and this does not suggest that the trading challenge would be different from that faced by other areas of the U.K. Great benefits can accrue from economics of scale, greater specialization and increased competition, provided local manufacturers can show the necessary initiative and flexibility. The regional policies adopted in the community might aid Northern Ireland, and membership could aid the bringing in of further industrial investment from overseas countries. If Éire and the U.K. enter the Community simultaneously, co-operation between Northern Ireland and the Republic for a common transport plan will be necessary.

In farming there should be benefits for those making extensive use of grassland. There should also be a growth in cereal production but problems for intensive livestock enterprises. Beef, sheep, milk (and possibly potatoes) are commodities which should benefit. The fruit and vegetable industry should not be significantly affected. Restructuring of the agricultural industry into larger farm units is already taking place but will probably be quickened by E.E.C. entry. If agricultural adjustment problems arise, there is a strong case for special help in view of the high proportion of workers who are employed in farming and the general high level of unemployment. Fisheries negotiations are still taking place with a view to necessary changes to meet the demands of a larger community. Modernization of the Northern Ireland fishing fleet and improved marketing methods are urged.

It is emphasized that the E.E.C. entry will mean change and adjustment, but also new privileges and opportunity for faster expansion. Frequent references are made to the relevant Westminster Papers *The Common Agricultural Policy of the E.E.C.* (Cmnd. 3274: 1967) and

The United Kingdom and the European Communities (Cmnd. 4715: 1971).

[The relevant government publication for Éire is *Membership of the European Communities: Implications for Ireland,* April 1970, 138 pp.]

Review of Economic and Social Development

Rep. of the Jt. Review Body, 1971. Cmd. 564, 16 pp.

Members of Review Body: Sir A. Cairncross, C.H. Villiers, D.H. Templeton.

'*To review the prospects for economic and social development in Northern Ireland as envisaged in the Development Programme (in view of the changed political and economic circumstances) with particular reference to the present and expected levels of investment . . . and to recommend to the United Kingdom and Northern Ireland Governments any further measures which might be adopted.*'

The Northern Ireland economy expended and diversified well in the mid-1960s, and even up to mid-1971 economic indicators revealed little sign of the civil unrest. The index of industrial production was very high, although unemployment levels were also high. The very satisfactory rate of production, however, is seen as the result of existing orders, and inquiries about new industrial development have been declining. Extra security measures and higher insurance costs are among factors affecting profitability.

In the private sector, machinery is needed to assist enterprises with sound prospects in the medium to long term, but now possibly threatened with closure or contraction because of civil strife. A new institution, to be named the Northern Ireland Finance Corporation, is suggested for this purpose. It would have £50 million financial support and a minimum life of three years, although its work could be reviewed after two years. Present levels of current assistance to manufacturing industry should be maintained, but the idea that the government might itself initiate and manage new industrial enterprise is rejected. It is proposed that the system of retraining workers by attaching them to firms should be extended and also that the Ministry of Health and Social Services should have sole responsibility for management training.

Public investment could be accelerated to atone for the decline in new private investment. The Development Programme is viewed as well balanced, and the excellent achievement and aims in house building could hardly be bettered or speeded up; it is possible, however, that new projects that could be started soon might be introduced. Extra employment could also be generated by speeding up the Urban and Rural Improvement Campaign.

Details of the individuals and organizations consulted by the review body are given.

The Feasibility of State Industry in Northern Ireland

Northern Ireland Economic Council. Rep. of a Subcommittee, 1971.
24 pp.

J.T. O'Brien (Ch.) and six members— A. Barr, J.H. Binks, P.F. Foreman, J. Grew, B.G. Harkin and T. McAteer.

'To inquire into the feasibility of the state initiating viable activities for the purpose of providing direct worthwhile employment.'

State participation in industry might possibly alleviate the unemployment situation. An examination is thus made of circumstances where such enterprise might be justified, the identification of suitable and viable projects, and the operational problems of state enterprise.

The latter include organization, finance, public accountability and the need to establish right relationships with the private sector. An industrial development board, with various appropriate divisions, is proposed. This board, to be created by the Northern Ireland Government, could evaluate the marketing and financial aspects of possible new projects, act as a holding company for state participation and a body for taking corporate risks, set up appropriate new enterprises (possibly, on occasion, in partnership with the private sector), and provide services and facilities for industry as a whole. The guaranteed investment programmes of the state participations could be a most useful steadying factor in times of recession. It is thus urged that this is a measure which would greatly assist in solving the employment problem.

The committee decided in the course of their inquiry that the study of individual projects was an unsuitable method for determining the value of state industry, but some projects considered at an early stage in deliberations—fish farming, apple growing and canning, a steel mill, carbon fibres, microwave heating, and the blast freezing of precooked foods—are indicated in an appendix. A further appendix sets out, with description and a diagram, the envisaged organizational structure and work of the suggested industrial development board.

A list of the several organizations and individuals consulted by the subcommittee is provided.

[A further report on this subject—sold but not published by H.M.S.O.—is *Local Enterprise Development Unit. Some Scope for Enterprise in Northern Ireland*, 1972, 30 pp.]

IV AGRICULTURE AND FOOD SUPPLY

1 General—Production, Supply, Output
2 Marketing
3 Production and Marketing of Particular Products
4 Forestry
5 Drainage, River Pollution, Coast Protection
6 Fishing

Note: Much useful information on Northern Ireland agriculture is also provided in the economic surveys which are summarized in Class III.

1 GENERAL—PRODUCTION, SUPPLY, OUTPUT

Agricultural Aid

Rep. of Cttee., 1923.
Cmd. 17, 7 pp.
Cttee. apptd. June 1923; rep. sgd. July 1923.

Rt. Hon. Viscount Pirrie (Ch.) and seven members—H. Adams, Sir Basil S. Brooke, J. Cunningham, J. Hill Dickson, R. McKinlay, A.J. Pilkington, H.E. Thompson. (J. Cunningham was ill and did not hear evidence nor sign the report.)

'To enquire into and report on the present depression of the farming industry . . . and to recommend what measures should be taken.'

The depression is due to the general decrease in purchasing power after the war, but more particularly to the recent high quantities of potatoes available in the United Kingdom which left Northern Ireland farmers with surplus stocks. It is recommended that the proposed grant of £128,000 should be used chiefly for the relief of rates on agricultural land. Other recommendations include the encouragement of more specialization in contrast to the mixed farming at present prevalent, the marketing of agricultural produce in accordance with suitably approved standards, improvement of transport facilities, and adequate preservation of goods during the period of transportation. Statistical tables show the average amount of rates paid on each holding by farmers and by the state in 1923/1924 and the number of holdings of various sizes in each of the six counties. Latest returns reveal that out of a total of 129,000 farms, no less than 115,000 are under fifty acres.

The Agricultural Output of Northern Ireland, 1925

Ministry of Agriculture. Rep. on certain statistical inquiries made in connection with the Census of Production, relating to the output of agricultural produce, with a survey of the agricultural statistics of Northern Ireland from 1847 to 1927, 1928. Cmd. 87, 84 pp.

Rep. sgd. November 1928 by D.A.E. Harkness.

The report considers crops, livestock, agricultural holdings, population and organization, and it is accompanied by many graphs and statistical tables.

During the five years 1923–1927, out of a total area of 3,351,444 acres no less than 2,977,225 were used for agricultural purposes, that is nearly 89 percent of the total area of the province. The average area of crops and pasture was 2,455,366 acres during 1923–1927, of which, however, only 584,021 acres were under tillage. The extent of ploughed land in Northern Ireland has shown an almost continuous decline—apart from the war years 1914–1918—since 1861, when the extent under the plough attained its maximum of 1,117,298 acres. The increase in the average yield per acre has, however, counteracted to some extent the decline in the area devoted to several of the principal crops.

Changes in the livestock population have been relatively slight in comparison with those in the case of crops. Whereas during the past sixty-five years there has been a decline of 49 percent in the tilled area, the numbers of livestock have been relatively well maintained. Today the livestock industry is by far the most important branch of the agricultural economy. The estimated value of the output of the agricultural industry in the six counties in 1925 was £15,073,000, of which £11,824,000, or 78 percent, represented the output of livestock and livestock products. The value of the materials not produced on farms in Northern Ireland purchased by farmers in 1925 amounted to approximately £3,888,000, of which £3,100,000 was in respect of animal feeding stuffs. The net output of the agricultural industry was thus £11,185,000.

Simultaneously with the agricultural census conducted by the Ministry of Agriculture, an industrial census was taken by the Board of Trade. The value of the net output of the industries and trades covered by the industrial census for Northern Ireland was £24,237,000. It thus appears that the agricultural industry is responsible for approximately 32 percent of the total production of the country, exclusive of the merchanting and distributive trades. The only single trade which approaches agriculture in importance is the linen industry, with a net output of £9,201,000 in 1924.

The net output of £11,185,000 from the soil of Northern Ireland is the result of the individual efforts of the occupiers of 104,410 separate farms exceeding one acre in size. The average area of crops and grass on farms in Northern Ireland is only 23.5 acres in comparison with 33.2 acres in the Irish Free State, 63.5 in England and Wales, and 61.8 in Scotland. The great bulk of the agricultural labour of Northern Ireland is performed by farmers and members of their families. In 1925 there were 146,809 male persons engaged in agriculture in Northern Ireland, of whom only 37,951 were hired labourers. Large numbers of the women members of farmers' families also share in the work of the farm.

Appendix I gives certain statistics relating to the output of timber from woods in Northern Ireland during 1924/1925. Appendix II concerns the flax scutching trade. In the first census of production in 1907, this trade was included in the industrial census. In 1925 the ministry was asked to include the scutching industry within the census of agriculture. Finally, nine statistical tables show, for various years, output; acreages; and numbers of livestock, of holdings, of persons and of different kinds of agricultural implements.

Conditions of Employment and Wages of Agricultural Workers

For details of this report see Class X p. 100.

The Agricultural Inquiry

Rep. of Cttee. Cttee. apptd. April 1943; reps. published 1943, 1947.

Rt. Hon. Lord Justice A.B. Babington (Ch.) and fourteen members—J.E. Bailey, G. Ervine, A. Grant, D.A.E. Harkness, J.P. Herdman, J. Keating, A.A. McGuckian, W.B. Maginess, Rev. R. Moore, A. Morrison, D. Munn, Major F.A. Pope, J.G. Rhynehart, Miss Dorothy Robertson. (Rev. R. Moore resigned May 1943, and Maj. F.A. Pope, July 1943. Maj. W.G. Nixon and T. Lyons apptd. October 1943, and A.E. Swain, November 1944. W.B. Maginess resigned August 1945.)

'To inquire into ... the future of agriculture in Northern Ireland, and to advise upon the steps necessary to effect its maximum development and improvement, and all matters bearing directly or indirectly thereon, including the marketing and transport of agricultural produce and the development of industries ... for the processing of agricultural produce.'

Interim Report. *Transport.* Sgd. October 1943.
Cmd. 222, 16 pp.

Amalgamation and co-ordination of road and rail transport would be more economic and no less efficient. The one mile limit within which a farmer may carry his neighbour's goods should be increased to two. Two members of the Transport Board should be appointed by the minister of agriculture. Consideration of cross-channel transport is deferred to the final report.

A reservation by A. Morrison disagrees with extension of the permitted radius for farmers' vehicles. A minority report by J.P. Herdman suggests that proper application of the Transport Act of 1935 might render unnecessary any amalgamation of transport services.

Second Interim Report. *Rural Housing.* Sgd. November 1945. (Published with final report as Cmd. 249.) 46 pp.

The rural housing situation is much

worse than that found in either Scotland or England and Wales. Housing is a problem of the greatest urgency and should be dealt with in future as a national problem and a responsibility to be borne by the whole community. The lack of adequate housing, and social amenities generally, has been one of the contributory causes to the drift from the land. A central housing authority, free from local interests, should be responsible for provision of all publicly owned housing. It should not share responsibility with local authorities as does the Housing Trust. Allocation and management of the housing should be supervised, but should be in the care of the local authorities, and any surplus from the rents and a uniform charge on the rates should be paid to the housing authority. Private enterprise should be encouraged by subsidies, loans, and guarantees to building societies, and assistance should be given for reconditioning old houses on the smaller farms. There should be special reservation of houses in each district for agricultural workers. Minimum standards should be adopted. Up-to-date by-laws of universal application should be devised.

An appendix gives an extract from the evidence of Mr. John Fisher (Gibson Trust) concerning the procedure when a grant is requested.

Final Report. *Sgd. December 1946.* *Cmd. 249, 240 pp.*

Agricultural Policy and Production

The government's policy is to establish a system of assured markets and guaranteed prices for the principal agricultural products. The recommendations of the United Nations Conference on Food and Agriculture, Hot Springs, 1943, may be taken as a guide.

The tendency to an increase in livestock production should be encouraged, as being suitable to the climate and the size of holdings. The decrease in tillage area is offset by increased yield. Livestock production requires an adequate market-ing and processing system, a steady improvement in grassland management, and free importation of feeding stuffs.

Cattle A dual purpose breed will best suit the small farmer, and English Dairy Shorthorn is recommended. Ultimately all subsidised bulls should be of the dairy shorthorn type. Setting up artificial insemination centres will speed improvement of milking qualities and help eradicate disease.

Sheep Encouragement to improve stocks of Blackface, Border Leicester and Suffolk breeds is necessary and should be given by financial assistance towards purchase of good quality rams. Early castration of commercial ram lambs is desirable, and price discrimination against uncastrated lambs should continue.

Pigs Pig production was greatly stimulated after the stabilization of prices in 1933. Large White pigs have thicker skins than Large White Ulster pigs, bruise less easily, are less sluggish, and therefore more suitable for transport alive. Ulster pig breeders should concentrate on this breed and endeavour to improve the quality by widespread pig recording for an official register, combined with a premium boar scheme. Research is needed into pig houses suitable for small farms.

Poultry The chief methods through which poultry improvement has been carried out have been the county poultry stations, the accredited farms, the official laying tests at Stormont, an official breeding station now discontinued, and the blood testing of birds to eliminate carriers of bacillary white diarrhoea. The use of pure-bred breeding stock is very desirable, and production of cross-bred chicks on accredited farms should be controlled. The number of such farms should be increased and an official breeding station established, to run in conjunction with the laying test. Hatcheries should be licensed and sexes registered. Breeding of table ducklings should be encouraged.

Horses Licensing of stallions, and the premium scheme for stallions of good standard are valuable. The new system of leasing Clydesdale sires to a group of farmers is welcomed. Highland Garron or Irish Draught stallions may be found more suitable for the type of mare from mountainous areas. The quality of stock bred from premium stallions should be recorded.

Grassland Much grassland is of unsatisfactory quality. Grassland management should be studied at an experimental farm in County Fermanagh. Silage making needs investigation. Grass should be part of the normal rotation cycle.

Tillage Inspection and certification of oats, similar to the scheme for rye-grass, would ensure the full benefit being gained from improved varieties. The main development in potato growing will probably be in the export of seed potatoes. Heavy yielding varieties for stock feeding require further investigation. Attempts should be made to improve flax production by research and by education, but the acreage will certainly fall unless there is either a subsidy or a guaranteed price.

Horticulture There is potential for a big expansion in horticultural crops. Bramley's Seedling apples are usually of better quality than those grown in the south of England. The Marketing of Fruit Act (N.I.), 1931, enforced proper standards of quality, grading and packing, but further advance is possible. The provision of gas storage is essential to deal with gluts, and inferior fruits could be processed, perhaps into apple juice. Compulsory spraying of all orchards would remove the hazards presented by derelict orchards. The growing of many other fruits is possible. The Ministry of Agriculture should foster co-operation between processors and producers, and between wholesalers, retailers and producers of tomatoes.

Forestry The percentage of land afforested in Ulster is the smallest of any country in Europe except Iceland. The present rate of planting is too slow. Land values are now higher than pre-war and the ministry must be enabled to pay up to eight pounds per acre. Replanting of private woodlands should be encouraged by generous replanting grants, and acquisition of such land, or state management of existing private forests, should be possible.

Agricultural Marketing and Processing

It is strongly recommended that the government should continue the policy of guaranteed prices, related to production costs, for all major farm produce. Licensing of dealers is an essential preliminary to quality control, and where grading is carried out, it is desirable that it should be by officials of the ministry. Pooling of transport costs prevents farmers in outlying areas being at a disadvantage.

In the absence of guaranteed prices, marketing boards should determine prices. Where war-time schemes are to be discontinued, they should be replaced by establishment of a fatstock marketing board and fatstock commission, a milk marketing board and milk commission, a pigs marketing board and pig industry council, an egg marketing committee which would include poultry marketing, a fruit and vegetable marketing committee, a potato marketing association and a joint committee to grade and fix prices for flax. Slaughter of fatstock should be prohibited, except by the fatstock commission, and the government should consider the provision of a modern slaughterhouse to deal with all fat cattle and sheep at present shipped alive, thus preventing weight loss and retaining by-products which could be the basis of new industries. The Ministry of Agriculture should constantly study developments in processing methods for all agricultural produce.

Education

Education of value to a rural community should include courses in elementary science in the primary schools and in general science in the junior secondary schools. The technical schools should provide junior agricultural courses similar to the junior technical courses. Agricultural subjects should be available in senior secondary schools, especially in rural areas, and should be included in part-time continuing education when it becomes compulsory. Further agricultural education should be the responsibility of the Ministry of Agriculture. The limited demand for places at the Greenmount Agricultural College makes it unnecessary to extend its facilities, but as the farm at Greenmount is most suited to grazing and stock rearing, whereas that at Loughry, Cookstown, is suited to mixed farming, it is recommended that the Agricultural College and the Ulster Dairy and Poultry School at Loughry should change places. There is another centre for training girls, the North-West School, Strabane. The Vaughan Institute, Kesh, County Fermanagh, could be developed as a centre for short courses. There should be a diploma in horticulture similar to that awarded in Great Britain.

Ancillary Services

A central advisory service is recommended, similar to the National Agricultural Advisory Service of Great Britain. Research sponsored by the Ministry of Agriculture is briefly surveyed and commented on. The Veterinary Research and Plant Breeding Divisions should move to a farm near Belfast, and Stormont can be developed as a poultry breeding station.

For agricultural land which has ceased to be subject to an annuity, the provisions of the Land Act of 1881 prohibiting subdivision or subletting should be re-enacted, and the system of letting in conacre should be continued. The Land Improvement Scheme, by which grants are given for improvement of drainage and roads, and removal of whins, bracken and scrub, and the Land Fertility Scheme and Marginal Land Scheme, which encourage land improvement through the use of fertilizers, should be continued. The extension of water and sewerage services to agricultural areas is highly desirable, but the committee disagrees with the Planning Advisory Board's recommendations on organization.

The Ministry of Agriculture should be the central drainage authority recommended by the Drainage Commission and should be responsible for the maintenance and improvement of the main rivers.

A survey should be undertaken to access the costs of a comprehensive rural electricity supply scheme. Problems arise mainly from the cost of the supply lines, which might be reduced by local co-operation in erecting poles and by an examination of existing standards for line equipment, which may be unnecessarily high. Tenants who have wired their premises should be able to recover the value of the system from their landlords upon quitting. It is in the interests of the whole province that there should be one public non-profit-making authority to generate and distribute electricity.

For short-term loans farmers normally obtain bills or overdrafts from the banks. There is no agricultural credit corporation in Ulster similar to those in Great Britain and in Éire. Statistics are given of loans made by the Ministry of Finance and Ministry of Agriculture, and it is recommended that existing schemes continue and that certain conditions regarding securities and advertisement be relaxed to make the schemes more attractive to the farmer.

It is very important that Ulster's interests be represented in the control of cross-channel shipping. The government should negotiate to obtain this.

Control of sheep scab and sheep dipping, at present undertaken by county councils, should be transferred to the Ministry of Agriculture which is responsible for all other animal disease regulations. Contagious abortion and trichomoniasis should be notifiable diseases. Livestock diseases will not be eliminated unless similar legislation and regulations are in force in both Ulster and Éire, and an attempt should be made to have all such regulations made reciprocal.

It is suggested that a central agricultural council be established, representative of all agricultural and rural life, which would bring the needs of the rural community before the government. It would be the governing body of a proposed agricultural institute, which would foster agricultural interests and encourage social and cultural activity.

A reservation by D.A.E. Harkness stresses the need for an improvement in general education for rural children, rather than the provision of special courses.

A minority addendum, with four signatories, makes suggestions for reform of agricultural courses given at the university.

Appendices list the witnesses and publications consulted by the committee and give statistical tables concerning numbers and sizes of holdings, quantities and value of produce, acreage under crops, production of principal crops over a number of years, yield per acre, and numbers of livestock over a number of years.

Agricultural Co-operation

Rep. by Prof. J.R. Parkinson in collaboration with the Economics and Statistics Division of the Ministry of Agriculture, 1965.
Cmd. 484, 92 pp., map.

'An investigation into the place of co-operation in the future development of Northern Ireland farming.'

Co-operation must be seen as one of a number of alternative ways of organizing agricultural development and not as something to be encouraged for its own sake. The Ministry of Agriculture should ensure, by its educational work, that farmers are aware of the principles of co-operation, and should give advice to new and old co-operatives if required. The Ulster Agricultural Organization Society should continue to receive financial support from the government for a further three years, by which time the agricultural trust mentioned in the Wilson Report on Economic Development

(Cmd. 479) would be operational and could take responsibility for forms of development which are inappropriate for the ministry. The report includes an historical account of co-operation until 1939 and an account of co-operatives which are in operation today, and both text and appendices contain statistics concerning the numbers, interests and finances of agricultural co-operatives. Appendix 4 gives the results of a farm survey held in 1964, and appendix 5 tabulates the output and expenditure of farming in Northern Ireland from 1954–1964. There is a list of the organizations consulted and of useful reference sources on co-operation in agriculture.

An accompanying statement by the ministry comments on the number of the more pertinent points in the report and agrees with its findings on the lack of interest in and education about co-operation, and on the part which co-operation can still play, in spite of the various marketing boards, provided a suitable line of activity is chosen and there is top quality business management. Comment also covers the ministry's loan schemes for machinery syndicates, and grants under the Market Development Scheme, and it is agreed that the Ulster Agricultural Organization Society should receive an increased grant, which would be discontinued after three years.

Northern Ireland and the European Communities

For details of this report see Class III p. 33.

2 MARKETING

The Transit, Prices and Marketing of Agricultural Produce

Ministry of Agriculture. Rep. of Dept. Cttee., 1927.
Cmd. 75, 20 pp.
Cttee. apptd. April 1927; rep. sgd. November 1927.

J.M. Mark (Ch.) and eleven members A. Adams, G. Barry, H. Crawford, W. Grant, W. Jackson, J. Johnston, G.

Leeke, W.J. McGuffin, J. Price, J.E. Wellwood, D. Wright.

'To inquire into
(a) the cost of transit of farm produce;
(b) the causes of the difference in prices obtained by producers and the prices charged to consumers; and
(c) the methods of marketing . . .
and to submit recommendations.'

In dealing with the themes indicated, the report refers to such products as apples, potatoes, dairy produce, flax, livestock and pork. With regard to transit, it is recommended that carrying companies should consider reducing rates for agricultural traffic. Price differences could be attacked by lowering the postal rates for farm produce. Marketing would be improved by grading and by the imposition of a system of compulsory inspection. Such inspection is already urgently needed in the case of potato exports.

It is also stated that primary education in rural districts could be given an agricultural trend; that the production of inferior butter should be discouraged; and that farming finance might be aided by reviewing the system of motor taxation and, more especially, by the setting up of credit banks for the agricultural community. Every effort should be made to promote greater co-operation between farmers. The past record in this latter respect is not encouraging, but educative propaganda might help.

The Marketing of Northern Ireland Agricultural Produce

[*Ministry of Agriculture.*] *Rep., 1932. 159 pp., maps, photos.*

The inquiries upon which this report is based were carried out with the aid of a grant from the Empire Marketing Fund, approved in April 1928. A. McGibbon acted as marketing investigator from June 1928 to October 1929. C.P. Mac-Auley, who was appointed produce inspector from September 1928, succeeded Mr. McGibbon, and T.C. Small was appointed produce inspector from January 1930. The report is signed by

D.A.E. Harkness, March 1932.

Legislation aimed at improving the quality of Northern Ireland produce already exists in the form of licensing of wholesale dealers and prescription of recognized standards and grades for eggs, potatoes, dairy produce, meat and fruit. While the quality and handling of certain agricultural produce is thus subject to government administration and control, the problem of bringing about an improvement in the marketing methods of farmers and other producers has in the main still to be confronted. This report surveys the existing marketing structure with a view to a future improvement in the machinery of marketing.

Part I, the General Report, discusses the numbers of dealers and the historical development of markets and fairs and gives details of the markets of Northern Ireland and their tolls for various commodities. The declining popularity of markets is discussed and suggestions are made for reform. Grading of produce facilitates marketing as well as guaranteeing quality, and the introduction of voluntary grades, used as a basis for price quotation, might be worth considering, especially for flax. A licensing system for dealers in commodities not at present requiring licence might be introduced, and limitation of the number of licence holders is desirable. Re-examination of co-operative marketing is urgently called for.

Subsequent sections examine the marketing of specific types of produce and make suggestions for improvement.

The marketing of cattle is probably the field in which there is the greatest need for improvement. An excessive number of fairs is held, and some form of control seems desirable so that fairs which are redundant or which have no adequate accommodation should be closed down. Cattle grading and sale by weight rather than by head would increase efficiency, and the provisions of the Markets and Fairs (Weighing of Cattle) Act, 1891, should be put into operation in all markets. As a prelude to legislation, the ministry should issue model rules for the conduct of a cattle fair and attempt to secure the constitution of responsible authorities at certain of the more important fair centres. The ministry should appoint one officer to report on transactions at all fairs and thus secure reliable, uniform reports.

Prices paid for pork fluctuate according to the supply at any particular market, and the farmer cannot predict prices at the time he kills his pigs. There should be collective bargaining between the farmers' representatives and the bacon curers to fix an agreed weekly price. Markets should have suitable accommodation for pork carcases, and those which exact tolls should employ a 'pork trier' to arbitrate on the soundness of carcases. Farmers do not like buying young pigs directly from other farmers, but existing dealers are unsatisfactory; introduction of sale by auction would be of benefit.

The report on marketing of fat and store lambs is an introductory survey confined to counties Antrim and Down; no recommendations are made.

The practice of buying poultry by weight should be extended, perhaps by legislation, as it is of more benefit to the producer. Introduction of definite grades and standards for poultry should be considered. A system of licensing poultry dealers would probably eliminate the worst types of dealer. Turkey marketing is also surveyed.

A large number of statistical tables in the text and appendix deal principally with total numbers, volume of trade, and prices of different commodities—cattle, sheep, pigs, poultry—and with tolls and weighing charges, and numbers of buyers. Fluctuations in numbers of livestock and acreage of ploughed land since 1847 are shown.

Markets and Market Tolls

Ministry of Home Affairs. Rep. of Com., 1934.
Cmd 162, v, 52 pp., charts.
Com. apptd. February 1934; rep. sgd. October 1934.

D.L. Clarke (Ch.) and ten members—J. Archer, D.H. Christie, W.M. Cronin, T.H. Hardy, D.A.E. Harkness, W. Jackson, J.M. Mark, J. Ritchie, A. Robinson, R.C. Young.

'To inquire into the position of Markets and Fairs . . . and into the tolls or other charges made by Market Authorities in respect of marketing commodities and marketable animals, and to make recommendations.'

The report is divided into eight chapters and includes an historical survey, a discussion of the existing situation and recommendations for future organization of markets and fairs. It concludes that markets fulfil a useful function, and the government should take no action which would render them uneconomic. There should be the fullest co-operation between marketing authorities and marketing boards. The law relating to markets and fairs should be uniform as far as possible. Urban district councils should acquire all market rights, but rural district councils should only do so where facilities are required and cannot be provided otherwise. Powers vested in central government should be centralized. Markets provided by local authorities should be self-supporting, but if this can only be through the charging of excessive tolls, subsidy from the rates is permissable if a substantial number of ratepayers benefit from the market. Any increases in charges should be with the approval of the ministry. Weighing charges and tolls should be separated, and no toll should be charged unless a service is provided. Tolls should be payable when an agreement is made within the market limits and the goods sold are within these limits, or when goods are subsequently delivered there and their price relates to the market price. Where modern weighing facilities are lacking in a district, they should be provided by the local authority. Auction marts should be encouraged, and local authorities should have power to appoint or employ auctioneers.

Three appendices give a summary of the conclusions and recommendations of the Royal Commission on Market Rights and Tolls, 1891; a table showing the markets in Northern Ireland and the nature of ownership in each case; and details of tolls and weighing charges imposed at market centres.

3 PRODUCTION AND MARKETING OF PARTICULAR PRODUCTS

LIVESTOCK

Diseases of Animals

Rep. of proceedings under the Acts, 1926. 33 pp.

This report of the chief veterinary officer for the year 1926 begins by listing the new orders for the year and summarizing the outbreaks of animal disease under the list of scheduled diseases—cattle plague, foot-and-mouth disease, pleuro-pneumonia, rabies, glanders and farcy, anthrax, epizootic lymphangitis and sheep pox.

The returns for livestock exported from Northern Ireland for the year show a decrease in the total number of animals shipped as compared with the previous year, and because of sporadic outbreaks of foot-and-mouth disease in Great Britain, a small number of animals were imported.

A section of the report deals with 'transit' reports on investigations carried out by an inspector:
1. Inspections of the condition in which livestock from Northern Ireland arrive at the various landing places in Great Britain.
2. Inspections of the conditions under which animals are detained at landing wharves and of the methods adopted for forwarding them to licensed paddocks, lairs, markets and farms.
3. The inspection of the cattle-carrying arrangements on Canadian vessels, including an inspection of the condition generally of cargoes of animals and the arrangements for their unloading.

Conditions on the whole are found to be good, but there is still room for im-provement in the cleansing and disinfecting of paddocks, lairs, etc., used before sales of cattle. With the rapidly increasing number of animals carried by road in motor vehicles, it is evident that steps will have to be taken to ensure the proper cleansing and disinfection of such vehicles. Numerous and regular inspections were carried out at the various railway stations on all systems in Northern Ireland in connection with the loading of stock taking place at fairs and markets. No case of abuse of animals was found. Periodic inspections were carried out during the year by an officer of the ministry at each of the ports in Northern Ireland from which stock are exported, and the conditions were found to be satisfactory.

Appendices to the report show the List of Orders in force on 31 December 1926 and also give statistical tables including information on diseases of animals and import and export of animals.

[No further reports were published as separate items.]

Spahlinger Experiments, 1931–1934

*Ministry of Agriculture. Rep. sgd. September 1935.
47 pp., graphs.*

This report covers the experiments carried out with Mr. Henry Spahlinger's bovine anti-tuberculosis vaccine during the period 1931–1934.

Section I sets out, in non-technical language, the objects of the experiment, the methods adopted in testing the vaccine and the general results of the test. It was found that the Spahlinger dead vaccine had conferred on the animals a very high degree of immunity to a lethal dose of tubercle bacilli injected into the blood stream six months after vaccination and at least an equally high degree of immunity to intense natural infection during a continuing period of approximately two years.

Section II is a technical report and an appendix which contains the results of the detailed post-mortem examination of all the animals included in the experiment. Graphs show, in accordance with the control groups, the number of days after inoculation that the calves died.

Although the results were highly satisfactory, it is recommended that, before adopting the compulsory use of the vaccine, a further experiment should be carried out in which the vaccinated animals are submitted to continuous and intense forms of natural infection through the lungs and the alimentary canal, the experiment to be designed with a view to determining, amongst other factors, the period for which the immunity conferred by the vaccine lasts.

The Slaughter of Young Calves

Rep. of Sel. Cttee., together with proc. . . . mins. of ev. and apps.
H.C. 771, 111 pp.
Cttee. apptd. June 1947; rep. o.p. December 1947.

W.F. McCoy (Ch.) and four members—H. Downey, T. Lyons, M. McGurk, H. Minford.

'To inquire into the causes of the slaughter . . . and the relation of such slaughter to the present shortage of store cattle, and to make recommendations.'

Since 1942, when milk received priority, the killing of calves has caused concern. This is the direct result of the relatively low price for beef in comparison with the financial returns obtainable from milk production. Unauthorized slaughter means that the actual death toll of calves is higher than figures supplied to the Ministry of Agriculture would indicate. Thus measures are needed to preserve the balance of production between milk and beef.

It is recommended that a subsidy of four pounds should be paid for all calves of a type suitable for beef, and for dairy or dual-purpose animals when the calf is six months old. A similar subsidy should be paid for every in-calf heifer. The price for bulls up to the age of two-and-a-half years should be raised to the level of steer beef. The ministry needs to assist farmers to obtain and keep first

class dual-purpose bulls, such as the Shorthorn and British Friesian, for breeding purposes, to ensure the maintenance of the store and fat cattle trade. Suitable feeding stuffs are to be made available as a priority, to help farmers to rear the increased stocks.

The bulk of the document contains minutes of evidence, and the report, excluding appendices, occupies only two pages. A list of witnesses is provided, and there is also a list of individuals and organizations who supplied documentary evidence. Tables in the appendices give statistics showing exports of cattle of Éire origin, 1939–1946; total cattle exports for this period; monthly numbers of calves killed, 1940– May 1947; classification of fat cattle (home bred and imported) and numbers purchased, 1940–1947; details of milk utilization during approximately the same period, including dried and skim milk.

Survey of Livestock Management in Northern Ireland

Ministry of Agriculture, 1959.
97 pp., photos.

The survey was directed by a senior officer of the Ministry of Agriculture's Livestock Inspectorate; field work was carried out by three graduates in agriculture; and finance was provided, under a 1952 agreement, from counterpart funds arising from the Economic Co-operation Agreement between the governments of the United Kingdom and the United States (signed 6 July 1948). The survey, carried out during 1954 and 1955, aimed to provide precise information as to which factors of management limit production and efficiency.

Sampling methods are discussed, and the national herd and cattle breeding practices are surveyed. Following the survey of dairy cow feeding and management, it is concluded that not enough care is given to the provision of water and suitable diet, to giving regular feeding and attention, and to obtaining the maximum output from grassland. There is considerable scope for improvement in calf rearing by the provision of adequate diet, improvement of housing and hygiene, and dishorning of male calves intended for fattening. The response of cattle to any fattening system depends on their breeding and early feeding. In the survey period there was abnormal variation in the price of store cattle, as well as a change in the marketing arrangements. Progress could not be assessed on a valuation basis, and there are therefore no conclusions.

The survey found a lack of knowledge of any more than the general principles of pig rearing. Deficient diet and bad housing are common faults. A general improvement of all aspects of pig husbandry is needed, especially with regard to finding the most suitable diet for each age group.

A hundred and forty-seven tables throughout the report give detailed relevant statistical data.

Survey of Livestock Diseases in Northern Ireland

Ministry of Agriculture, 1960.
192 pp., bibliography.

This survey, like the Survey of Livestock Management, was carried out in 1954 and 1955, with the aid of funds arising from the Economic Co-operation Agreement between the governments of the United Kingdom and the United States. The survey was directed and carried out by officers of the ministry's Veterinary Research Division, with assistance from the veterinary field staff, and the report of the survey is by J.F. Gracey. The main part of the investigations was carried out on a random sample of some 600 farms. Based on the findings, estimates of total losses of cattle, sheep and pigs for the whole of the province are made. Subsidiary information on disease incidence and meat condemnation losses, obtained by the setting up of a system of meat inspection recording in seventeen abattoirs, is also presented, as well as data on notifiable diseases.

Of the 6.2 percent calf losses which were found to occur, over half (3.4 percent) were due to abortions and still births. The remaining 2.8 percent of deaths were due, in order of importance, to bacterium coli infections causing septicaemia or white scour; to weak, premature or abnormal calves and those injured at birth; and to non-infective conditions of the digestive tract, pneumonia, joint-ill, and lead poisoning. The high mortality rate of many calf diseases is shown by the relatively little difference between the death rate and the total sickness rate.

Losses in cows are most often associated with metabolic disorders such as milk fever, hypomagnesaemic tetany and acetonaemia, followed by infections of the genital system and mammary glands, specific diseases, and the complications of pregnancy and parturition. As a single condition, acute metritis was the most common cause of death. Over half the disposals from herds are due to disease, mainly in the form of infertility and mastitis, the commonest disease of cows.

In heifers and steers, the commonest cause of death was found to be parasitic bronchitis, with the most prevalent diseases being hoose, liver fluke disease, parasitic gastroenteritis, and ringworm and other skin diseases.

Pre-natal losses of lambs amounted to 3.8 percent of all those born, and post-natal losses were nearly three times as great (11.2 percent). The majority of the latter were due to exposure and starvation, with pulpy kidney disease being the next most frequent cause of death. The chief single cause of ewe mortality was twin-lamb disease, which can be prevented by more attention to feeding and management. Protective inoculations are available against pulpy kidney disease, black disease, louping ill and contagious pustular dermatitis, and more widespread use of these, with planned anthelmintic measures against fascioliasis and parasitic gastroenteritis, would alter the pattern of sheep mortality and ill-health very considerably. A large number of sheep, especially lambs, succumb to bad weather conditions in winter and early spring; these losses would be reduced by provision of suitable shelter belts.

Pre-weaning mortality of piglets is high, 19·1 percent, but this is somewhat less than is found in other countries. It is due principally to overlaying, still births and death within a few hours of birth, with scouring and piglet anaemia also important. Later losses occur mainly in the immediate post-weaning period, during which more careful management is required; bowel oedema was the commonest cause of death, followed by pneumonia and gastroenteritis. Gastroenteritis and virus pneumonia cause most of the clinically obvious pig ill-health, but tuberculosis is a common cause of rejection of carcase meat. Pig productivity would improve with better management and further disease research.

Statistics are given for notifiable diseases. Bovine tuberculosis and sheep scab show a satisfactory reduction. Anthrax has a low incidence and arises from infected imported feeding stuffs. Jöhne's disease (paratuberculosis), which is increasing in Great Britain, is infrequent here, although it has been found in all counties except Tyrone.

Throughout the report it is stressed that study of livestock diseases would be greatly benefited if abattoirs were in a position to make precise diagnosis of conditions found.

The 192 tables given in the report show statistics relating to disease and death, and the numbers of animals affected. A glossary of terms is also provided.

Fatstock Marketing

Rep., 1966.
Cmd. 500, 23 pp.

A meat and livestock commission with an advisory function has been set up in Great Britain. The ministry suggested several alternative types of body which might be appropriate to Northern Ireland conditions and held consultations with various interested organizations. The producers were anxious for a major reorganization, and the trade organiz-

ations were relatively content with the present system but not unwilling to accept some type of new body provided its powers and duties were not too sweeping and it was representative of all interests. The ministry's view is that there should be a board which could buy fatstock and sell it and which could create financial incentives for any form of marketing which it favoured but particularly for deadweight sales. The board would consist of members appointed by the minister and independent of any trade interests, and it would be advised by a committee representative of all the various parties involved in the fatstock and meat industry. It would provide a system of selling fatstock offered to it by producers; buy fatstock either in accordance with a limited scheme of 'support buying' or in order to honour contracts with factory abattoirs and others; create a system of carcase classification; finance its operations by a levy on producers; advise the government on marketing and breeding policy; and provide a meat intelligence service. Other powers might be exercised from time to time, but the board would have no compulsory powers of purchase or sale and no power to control marketing. It would help producers or buyers on a voluntary basis.

Statistical tables in the appendices illustrate the production and disposal of fat cattle, fat sheep, and fat cows and bulls, over a number of years, and the organizations consulted by the ministry are listed.

The Production and Marketing of Northern Ireland Meat

Ministry of Agriculture, 1967.
62 pp.

This publication is intended as an overall review of the meat industry, excluding the marketing of bacon pigs.

The cattle and sheep population increased following the Second World War, and although cattle numbers are still rising, the peak sheep population occurred in 1962. Government measures to encourage livestock production include both production schemes and subsidies, and improvement schemes. The ministry is satisfied that it is technically possible for farmers to increase beef production by ten thousand animals per year. If a healthy and stable beef industry is to develop, it will be important to plan marketings of fat cattle on a more even basis throughout the year. This will mean more winter feeding and more finishing in the first six months of the year, which will require suitable incentives and satisfactory market prices. The situation is similar for fat lambs and fat sheep.

Northern Ireland is free from most of the livestock diseases prevalent in other countries and is in a favourable position to export disease-free meat. Great Britain is by far the most important market, but Northern Ireland meat commands a lower price than English meat, and if this price differential is to be overcome, an overall marketing programme must be developed. This should include the institution of a classification system for carcase meat, the development of a distribution service which would enable sales direct to retail outlets, and an advertising and promotion campaign.

It is government policy to encourage the slaughter of fatstock in Northern Ireland and the export and shipment of meat and meat products. The two main reasons for this policy are the desire to create additional employment and the hope of reducing the adverse price differential. In addition, it is more humane, and it is difficult to secure adequate shipping space for animals in the autumn. However, the shipment of dead meat to Great Britain will develop only if it can provide the producer with an equal or better return for his fatstock than live shipment, which is frequently not so. Legislation and policy concerning slaughterhouses is discussed and fuller details given in appendix I.

Northern Ireland and Irish Republic meat plants sell in the same markets, and the Northern Ireland plants were put at a disadvantage when the government of the Irish Republic decided, in February 1965, to pay a subsidy to their meat

plants. In September 1966 the minister of agriculture appointed a firm of industrial consultants, Harmood-Danner, Cash, Stone & Mounsey, to make a report on the problems of meat plants. The preliminary report (September 1966) and final report (November 1966) are published in full here as appendices III and IV. They list nine reasons for the economic difficulties of meat plants, the principal ones being the price differential and the Irish Republic subsidy, and they recommend concentration on quality, grading, market research and publicity. The consultants reported that the plants were operating at less than one-third of their capacity, and the minister decided to give the industry a limited amount of financial assistance for a period of at least three years.

A livestock marketing commission is being set up to advise the ministry, encourage better marketing arrangements, conduct and foster research, and disseminate information.

It is suggested that prices might be maximized by the introduction of a carcase classification system; the use of publicity and sales promotion; an evening out of seasonal fluctuations in marketing; the development of market research and market intelligence services; and the introduction of schemes to improve the quality of carcases, hides and offal.

Costs may be minimized by the appropriate use of production and improvement schemes for livestock: also by the evening out of seasonal fluctuations in the supply of fatstock; and by the coordination of research and the dissemination of information on new techniques.

Statistical tables show numbers of cattle and sheep, 1960–66; payments of subsidies for cattle and sheep, over a number of years; channels of sale chosen by farmers; figures for cattle and sheep marketing, disposal and exports; and sources of U.K. meat supplies. Average auction prices in England and Northern Ireland for fat cattle and sheep are compared, and financial data from the United States meat packing industry are given.

Shipping costs are shown for the carriage from Northern Ireland to Manchester of a live bullock and a dressed carcase.

Appendices to the consultants' report give further figures for prices of fat cattle, through-put of cattle and sheep at Northern Ireland meat plants, production and disposal of fat cattle and sheep, analysis of slaughtering at meat plants and other abattoirs, and analysis of sales.

PIGS

The Pigs Marketing Scheme (N.I.), 1933

Memorandum containing the scheme as approved by Parliament, 1935.
Cmd. 167, 15 pp.

The constitution of the Pigs Marketing Board is stated, as are conditions of holding office, and procedure. A register of producers shall be kept by the board. Provision is made for election to the board, the administration of funds, the keeping of accounts, marketing provisions and the principal powers of the board, and arrangements for arbitration between the board and any aggrieved producer. A schedule lists products which may be produced by the board from pigs.

The Pigs Marketing Board

Ministry of Agriculture. Rep. of investigators appointed . . . to inquire into the administrative and financial arrangements of the Pigs Marketing Board . . . , 1939.
Cmd. 205, 66 pp.
Investigators apptd. September 1938; rep. sgd. February 1939.

Investigators were two members of the ministry staff, A. Cope and J.F. Mc-Mullan.

'To enquire into the report on—
  (1) the arrangements of the Pigs Marketing Board . . . in regard to the purchase and sale of pigs and the administrative and financial control of those arrangements;
  (2) the general administrative and financial arrangements of the board.'

The Marketing Board consists of eleven members elected by registered producers of pigs and three nominated by the min-

istry. Administration has, since October 1937, been in the charge of the secretary/manager, and there are four departments —secretarial, marketing, accounts and intelligence. In the first part of the report, the investigators scrutinize the working of these departments and refer to documents from the board's files, in order to explain the board's administrative and financial workings. The second part of the report concerns the purchase and sale of pigs. The board has a virtual monopoly of trade in live pigs of bacon weight, and, in addition to reviewing the circumstances and method of this trading, the investigators report on the sale of pigs injured in transit, sale of porkers, offal sales, pig insurance, the remuneration of agents, travelling allowances and other expenses of the board. From the facts revealed in relation to these matters, it is concluded that the board's present administration and finance are highly unsatisfactory and that there are several irregularities in its practice.

Appendices show expenses claimed for overseas travel by officers of the board, correspondence between the investigators and the board's marketing officer, and an auditor's statement. The report includes some outline statistics of the purchase price of pigs in the years 1935–1938.

The Pigs Marketing Board

Rep. on the general administration, organization and financial arrangements of the pigs marketing scheme to the Ministry of Agriculture by the members of the Pigs Marketing Board appointed on 28 February 1939, 1939.
Cmd. 208, 33 pp.

Members reporting—D.E.B. McCorkell, J. Graham, S.J. Crowe, J. Patrick, and M. Speir.
Following the earlier report of investigators (see Cmd. 205 above), an amending order changed the constitution of the board. This report, made by the new board, sets out to re-examine the 'numerous charges of inefficiency and maladministration against various executive officers of the [old] Board . . . giving those

concerned an opportunity to refute the allegations laid against them'.

The duties and record of the previous secretary/manager and accountant are examined in some detail, and it is considered that inefficiency occurred in the marketing and accounts areas rather than in the secretarial and intelligence departments. Most of the strictures of the investigators submitting the earlier report are found to be justified, but the former board did achieve much good work and succeeded in increasing the pig population to three times its size in approximately three years. The new board has been active in achieving certain economies, in initiating some staff re-organization, in seeking to eliminate some administrative faults and irregularities, and in drawing up regulations to control the future payment of travelling and subsistence allowances to staff.

The signatories requested that, having taken these steps and duly reported, they should be relieved of their positions on the board to permit its formation on a different basis.

Marketing of Pigs

Rep. of Cttee. of Inquiry, 1970.
Cmd. 545, 78 pp.
Cttee. apptd. August 1968; rep. sgd. May 1970.

Prof. J. Ashton (Ch.) and four members —A.W. Buller, H.O.H. Coulson, J.H.A. Swinson and N.A. Whitaker.

'To examine the Pigs Marketing Board's purchasing and selling arrangements for pigs and future trends in the demand for, and in the marketing of, pigs and pig products, and to recommend consequential changes which might be desirable in:
(a) the pattern of marketing; and
(b) the power necessary to the Pigs Marketing Board to ensure continuing growth of the pig industry and maximum returns to pig producers.'

An introductory historical outline of the industry considers developments before 1939, war-time and post-war control, and developments in both Great Britain and Northern Ireland since decontrol in 1954. This is followed by a detailed review of the current organization pattern in the industry and the structure of marketing and consumption. The steady tendency towards diversification in the U.K. industry in recent years and the production of several distinctive types of pig for different purposes is commented upon.

The remainder of the report is devoted to a consideration of the principal issues involved in making an appraisal of the industry and in drawing appropriate conclusions. It is proposed that the production of Wiltshire bacon as a specialized objective in Northern Ireland should cease and that the industry should, in addition to its sales of this product, endeavour to gain a substantial share of the growing market for other pig products. It is urged that the system of marketing through the monopoly of the Pigs Marketing Board should radically change and that future marketing should be based upon contracts negotiated between producers and processors, although producers wishing to do so should be able to market their pigs through the board. Contracts should be registered with the board for records purposes. In addition, the board should withdraw from the Ulster Bacon Agency Limited and liquidate its factory partnership interests in the processing industry. The board's monopoly would thus cease, as would the quota scheme. The latter has, in the opinion of the committee, diminished the producer's ability to be selective and hindered the effect upon him of the merits or faults of the type of production he has followed. In future the powers of the Pigs Marketing Board should be slanted away from processing and selling and towards production and marketing. The board could profitably employ suitable technical officers to promote research and development. It should be a small body, and changes for the system of election to it are proposed. The ending of the board's monopoly powers would represent a drastic change, but it is believed that it could encourage producers to diversify and select the type of production in which they wish to engage. They can thus become more flexible in response to a changing market situation. The trend towards larger and fewer production units, with more specialization, is expected to continue.

Appendices provide details of the 1933 Pigs Marketing Scheme; the quota scheme and the curer's margin; and of deductions from producers marketing through the Pigs Marketing Board; and the board's revenue from government sources. There is a list of visits made, including some to Denmark and Holland, and of individuals and organizations supplying evidence. Twenty-seven statistical tables, most of which appear in a special appendix, include data on pig numbers, production and marketing, curers' margins, the sharing of the bacon market, revenue and costs per pig, the structure of the bacon curing industry, sow breeding and sow disposal.

OTHER AGRICULTURAL PRODUCTS

The Egg Industry

Rep. of Com. on the Natural and Industrial Resources of Northern Ireland, [1924].
Cmd. 27, 15 pp.
Com. apptd. June 1923; rep. sgd. February 1924.

The Rt. Hon. the Viscount Charlemont (Ch.) and twenty-three members—W. Addis, R. Armstrong, T.H. Burn, J.F. Cleaver, H. Conacher, G.M. Donaldson, F. Gilliland, E.D. Hill, Capt. S.J. Hutchinson, O. Jamison, Sir Samuel Kelly, W. Logue, R. McClung, W.J. McGuffin, Prof. H.O. Meredith, J.A. Pringle, W.D. Scott, Prof. R. Stanley, D.P. Thompson, D. Wright. (In addition, J. Hill Dickson and J.S. Gordon were appointed, October 1923, and Prof. J.K. Charlesworth, January 1924.)

'*To consider and report as to how the Natural and Industrial Resources of Northern Ireland can be best developed with a view to increasing the general prosperity and reducing the extent of unemployment.*'

The report sets out to investigate the importance of the industry as one which affords a means of livelihood to a large part of the state and the necessity for prompt government action against the practice of exporting stale or badly packed eggs to Britain. It is thought that the practice may be checked by demanding in future that each wholesaler or exporter holds a Ministry of Agriculture licence, by stressing that covered accommodation should be obligatory in market places where eggs are packed and by investigating the value of the system of date stamping eggs and grading them by size or weight.

The development of the industry in the province is then considered, and it is believed that the poultry population of the six counties could be increased and also a higher annual output of eggs per bird achieved. The plans of the ministry to subsidize demonstration poultry farms, to organize marketing exhibits at agricultural shows and to publicize poultry farming's benefits are approved. The report proposes that this work might be aided by giving agricultural education to pupils in rural schools and by more press publicity.

Appendices indicate statistics of the quantity and value of eggs exported from Ireland, 1904–1923, and the import of eggs into the United Kingdom, 1919–1923. There is a list of the witnesses called by the commissioners.

The Practicability of Establishing the Sugar Beet Industry

Rep. of Com. on the Natural and Industrial Resources of Northern Ireland, 1926.
Cmd. 60, 17 pp.
Com. apptd. June 1923; rep. sgd. April 1926.

The Rt. Hon. the Viscount Charlemont (Ch.) and twenty-three members—F. Anderson, R. Armstrong, H. Barbour, T.H. Burn, J.F. Cleaver, H. Conacher, F. Gilliland, J.A. Grey, E.D. Hill, Capt. S.J. Hutchinson, O. Jamison, W.J. McGuffin, J. Mackie, Prof. H.O. Meredith, J.A. Pringle, W.D. Scott, Prof. R. Stanley, D.P. Thompson, D. Wright. (In addition, J. Hill Dickson, J.S. Gordon, and Maj. G.A. Harris were appointed in October 1923, and Prof. J.K. Charlesworth in January 1924. In October 1925, R.R. Bowman was appointed in place of H. Conacher who had resigned.)

'To consider and report as to how the Natural and Industrial Resources of Northern Ireland can be best developed with a view to increasing the general prosperity and reducing the extent of unemployment.'

The average yield of beet per acre in England during 1924 was eight tons, and the advantages and problems of growing this root crop, particularly through reducing the amount of land devoted to potatoes, are considered. There is no guarantee that sugar beet would provide the Ulster farmer with a reliable return, but the existence of a sugar beet factory and the task of its construction would help unemployment. The suitability of climate and soil for this crop is discussed. Many of the commission members were doubtful about this, but the introduction of the De Vecchis process, whereby roots are preserved against decay and sugar loss, and the extractive period thus extended over many months, would help a great deal. It is concluded that it would be best to postpone for two years the question of a state subsidy for this crop, but that the Ministry of Agriculture should test the suitability of conditions for growing it on a commercial scale. This would involve a limited amount of land (some thirty acres) being used for beet by selected farmers in various districts. The ministry would purchase the crop at the current price paid by British factories and sell it to a factory in England or Scotland.

An appendix gives the names of the witnesses called by the commission.

4 FORESTRY

Afforestation

Rep. of Com. on the Natural and Industrial Resources of Northern Ireland, [1925]. *Cmd. 35, 16 pp.*

Com. apptd. June 1923; rep. sgd. December 1924.

The Rt. Hon. the Viscount Charlemont (Ch.) and twenty-six members — W. Addis, F. Anderson, R. Armstrong, T.H. Burn, J.F. Cleaver, H. Conacher, G.M. Donaldson, F. Gilliland, J.A. Grey, E.D. Hill, Capt. S.J. Hutchinson, Sir Samuel Kelly, W. Logue, R. McClung, W.J. McGuffin, J. Mackie, Prof. H.O. Meredith, J.A. Pringle, W.D. Scott, Prof. R. Stanley, D.P. Thompson, D. Wright. (Later appointments were J. Hill Dickson, J.S. Gordon, Maj. G.A. Harris, October 1923, and Prof. J.K. Charlesworth, January 1924.)

'To consider and report as to how the Natural and Industrial Resources of Northern Ireland can be best developed with a view to increasing the general prosperity and reducing the extent of unemployment.'

This subject attracted the attention of the commission both from the point of view of a useful, but somewhat neglected natural resource and as a measure for decreasing the extent of rural unemployment. Northern Ireland relies heavily upon imported timber, and only 1.2 percent of its acreage is afforested. This is considered the smallest figure for any European country save Iceland. The need to encourage home-grown supplies, especially considering the likely future world shortage of softwood, is stressed. The climate is quite suitable and some coniferous trees grow to perfection in Ulster's relatively humid atmosphere. Money invested in afforestation should show a sound return, and the handling and working of timber utilizes some ten times as much labour as would the devotion of the same amount of land to the grazing of pasture. State action in this context in Great Britain and in Scandinavian countries is briefly discussed. It is proposed that the Northern Ireland Ministry of Agriculture should press on with its programme on forest land and give help to farmers who have small but suitable areas which they are prepared to use for tree growing. A suitable scheme of grants is outlined; alternatively, small holders may elect to receive plants at a reduced price.

Appendices provide a list of witnesses called and statistics showing the character, extent and location of Ministry of Agriculture forest land, with details of the rate of planting during 1920 and 1924. A further table gives the quantity and value of softwood imports in some recent years and indicates country of origin.

Forestry in Northern Ireland

(Rep.), 1970.
Cmd. 550, 47 pp.

A review is made of the history of forestry in Northern Ireland and its changing aims; production and marketing; the area and type of land that should be devoted to forests; and past, present and future employment in state forestry. Reference is also made to investment and profitability, forest accounts, private forestry, and other uses of state forests—the latter including education, recreation and wildlife conservation. It has been decided that the target of a hundred and fifty thousand acres by the end of the century should be increased to three hundred thousand, with much planting taking place in the next fifteen years because of the short-term unemployment position. Management must concentrate upon economy, good planning and marketing, and the maximum value of wood production compatible with conservation, and scenic and similar considerations. Private tree planting and afforestation is to be encouraged.

The above objectives need to be continually reviewed in the light of current circumstances, and surveys of progress are planned to take place at five-year intervals.

Appendices give statistics on forest land and employment, many of which are broken down geographically within counties. Rate of attendance in recent years at those forest parks where a charge is made is shown. Balance sheets for Ministry of Agriculture forestry operations are also given.

5 DRAINAGE, RIVER POLLUTION, COAST PROTECTION

Flax Water

[Ministry of Agriculture.] Rep. of Cttee., 1924.
22 pp.
Cttee. apptd. July 1923; rep. sgd. October 1923.

T.H. Maxwell (Ch.) and four members— W.J.M. Menzies, Capt. J.A. Miller, R.D. Pinkerton, J.W. Stewart.

'To inquire and report what steps should be taken, having regard to the interests alike of fishery protection and of the flax industry, to provide for the innocuous disposal of water in which flax has been steeped; and to submit recommendations as to the modifications, if any, which should be made in the existing Law on the subject.'

Flax water should be retained in a catch dam until the month of January, except in conditions of flood, or should be discharged over land. If neither method is practicable, the advice of the local board of conservators should be sought. The Privy Council should be empowered to exempt certain waters. It should be permissible to ret flax in registered mill races. The consent of the local board of conservators should be obtained prior to the institution of any prosecution, and private prosecutors or informers should no longer be awarded one-third of the penalty. Water bailiffs should be sworn in similarly to police constables. Minimum penalties are suggested.

The appendix gives details of chemical analyses of flax water, and of experiments designed to show the relative danger to trout of the various constituents of flax water. Data are given for a series of records of temperature, oxygen requirement, acidity and sulphuretted hydrogen content.

Bann and Lough Neagh Drainage

Ministry of Finance, Works and Public Buildings. Dept. rep., 1926.
Cmd. 63, 48 pp., map.

To investigate and report on *'measures to alleviate the flooding caused by Lough Neagh and the River Bann'*.

i) *Report of Director of Works, Major P.E. Shepherd. Proposals for measures to alleviate the flooding caused by Lough Neagh and the River Bann. Sgd. March 1926.*

The history of the River Bann, from the time of Mr. McMahon's scheme for drainage and navigation—about 1859—until the present day, is one continuous record of engineering reports and royal commissions, resulting in no actual remedial works. Due to deterioration and silting up since 1859, a complete new survey had to be organized before preparing a scheme. Proposals include the provision of sluices; rock excavation; dredging and reconstruction at the various weirs on the Lower Bann; dredging of the bar in Lough Neagh south of Toome; and dredging of the Upper Bann, Blackwater and Moyola rivers. The reliability of formulae and tables used when calculating flood levels was confirmed by an independent expert, C.H.J. Clayton. A table is given showing maximum flood levels for most years between 1859 and 1926 and a calculated maximum level under the present scheme. The cost of the scheme is estimated. If a hydroelectric scheme is adopted, work should be co-ordinated with the drainage scheme. The failure of Mr. McMahon's scheme was not entirely due to silting, but also to underestimation of and increase in run-off, and to non-completion of the scheme. Eel weirs do not obstruct the flow of water so much as was previously reported. Salmon fishing and through navigation should not be adversely affected by the proposals except during construction work.

ii) *Departmental Report on Financial Aspects of the Scheme. Sgd. September 1926 by W.B. Spender, G.C. Duggan, R.E. Thornley, P.E. Shepherd, W.J. Ward.*

Benefit is received by flooded areas, saturated areas and the remainder of the catchment area in a 4:2:1 ratio, and the charges should be fixed accordingly. The proportion of the capital and maintenance costs chargeable to each zone of benefit should be raised by means of a rate upon the poor law valuation of the assessable property. Tables show the effect of any government contribution at 25 percent, $33\frac{1}{3}$ percent and 50 percent of the total costs. There would be a substantial saving if navigation facilities were sacrificed. Drainage and navigation maintenance should be under a single control. A hundred and fifty-five square miles of the catchment area lies in the Irish Free State.

Drainage of Lough Neagh and the River Bann

Drainage Advisory Committee. Cttee. constituted under the Drainage Act (N.I.), 1925. Reps. published 1927, 1928.

Maj. J.C. Boyle (Ch.) and thirteen members—W. Abbott, Commander J.L. Chichester-Clark, J. Hill Dickson, G.C. Duggan, C.W. Grant, T. Hegan, H. Kirkpatrick, J. Lusk, H.P. Nicholson, Lt.-Col. J. Patrick, J. Pimlott, Maj. P.E. Shepherd, J.E. Wellwood. (By 1928, C.W. Grant had been replaced by A. Robinson, J. Pimlott by J. Getty, H.P. Nicholson by Capt. G.E. Barcroft, H. Kirkpatrick by T.A. Graham.)

[*To advise the Minister of Finance regarding the proposed Bann Drainage Scheme and its financial aspects.*]

Interim Report. *Sgd. March 1927. Cmd. 72, 25 pp.*

The hydroelectric scheme cannot proceed as an economical proposition without the drainage scheme. The latter will not be acceptable to county councils unless its cost can be reduced, and the only tangible method of reducing the cost materially without impairing the efficiency of the scheme is by combining it with a hydroelectric scheme. Subsidiary drainage works carried out by county councils will be seriously hampered or become much more expensive unless the

Bann Drainage Scheme is carried out in its entirety.

(Major P.E. Shepherd considered it would be improper for him to sign the report as it embodies committee opinions on the scheme which he had drafted.)

Appendix A gives the report of the Antrim Electricity Supply Bill Sub-committee. The bill provides for the erection of a dam and weir above the existing Carnroe weir, which will create a reservoir extending up river to Portna and flooding seven hundred acres. A full development of the water power of the river cannot be attained without a much larger storage of water in Lough Neagh than the interests of arterial drainage permit above fifty-two feet ordnance datum, or the interests of navigation and fisheries permit below that level. Navigation will be severed by the new power dam, and there will have to be a means of conveyance of launches and small boats from one reach of the river to the other, and a public right of way. Royalties could be charged for the use of water power. In the event of the drainage and hydroelectric schemes being treated as interdependent, the drainage works should not be begun until the government has adequate guarantees or security for the carrying out of the hydroelectric works by the company.

Other appendices deal with conditions relating to regulation of discharge of water from Lough Neagh, and they also list persons examined.

Final Report. *Sgd. November 1928. Cmd. 90, 16 pp.*

The committee approves the government's decisions that the county council's contribution to the cost of the scheme be limited to £200,000, that the government assumes responsibility for future maintenance of the drainage works in the Bann channel and that agricultural land and farm buildings be relieved of navigation rates. Test borings by Major P.E. Shepherd showed more soft strata than had been anticipated, and an amended scheme could be carried out, independent of a hydroelectric scheme, for about £650,000. This is recommended. Previous recommendations as to rating are abandoned, and it is now suggested that each county council levy a rate evenly throughout the catchment area, including urban districts.

T. Hegan, representing County Tyrone, wished the county council to have the option to raise their charge over the county at large.

A. Robinson, newly appointed to the committee, did not sign.

A schedule compares the original estimate of costs with the revised estimate.

Objections Lodged Against the Draft Scheme (for Bann and Lough Neagh Drainage)

[*Ministry of Finance.*] *Rep. of Inquiry, 1930.   28 pp.*
F.W. Crofts apptd. as Inspector, June 1930; rep. sgd. July 1930.

The report divides the objections into three classes. Class I covers all formal or 'standard' objections such as access to the river, farm interference, nuisance, damage to trees, wells and rights of way, etc., with suggestions as to how objections may be met.

Class II is devoted to commercial objections from the Toome Eel Fishery Limited and the Diatomite Company Limited. Objections by the former are carefully considered, and many useful suggestions are made as to the most economic and successful means of eel fishing under different methods. Should the experiments prove impracticable and unsatisfactory, then the report recommends paying compensation on the basis of the actual results obtained. The objections raised by the Diatomite Company were found to be mainly invalid, and the matter, therefore, calls only for compensation to cover their purchase of the mining rights and loss by disturbance.

Amenity objections, such as damage to land, trees, a boat slip, obstruction of views and destruction of beauty spots along the river, are all noted under individual objections in Class III. Where possible, alternative boundaries for the dump are put forward to maintain property value and appearance and to preserve the beauty of certain places on the river.

In conclusion, F.W. Crofts states that he can find nothing in the objections against the draft scheme, in principle, and nothing that cannot be met by compensation or a slight modification of detail.

The report is followed by two schedules listing respectively the objections in Class I and Class III.

Lough Erne Drainage

Rep. upon remedial measures to alleviate flooding, 1929.
Cmd. 119, 36 pp., maps.

Lough Erne Drainage Board is elected by drainage ratepayers in Northern Ireland and the Irish Free State, and it was agreed in 1927 that a joint commission of inquiry into the drainage problem of the lough should be initiated. This report by Major Shepherd, director of works, Ministry of Finance, Belfast, outlines four alternative schemes. The first would cost over £800,000 and would give total relief from all flooding. The alternatives are cheaper but less satisfactory; the last suggested scheme, which would lower all the worst winter floods, would cost nearly £500,000. The estimates are accompanied by reasoning and the necessary technical details, and a map is provided. It is calculated that the two more costly schemes, by reducing the saturation level, would indirectly benefit a large acreage of land beyond the area directly assisted.

The Drainage of Lough Erne

Rep. of the Drainage Advisory Cttee., 1932.
Cmd. 143, 17 pp.
Rep. sgd. March 1932.

Maj. J.C. Boyle (Ch.) and eleven members—W. Abbott, Capt. G.E. Barcroft, Commander J.L. Chichester-Clark, J.H. Dickson, G.C. Duggan, J. Getty, T.

Greer, J. Johnston, Lt.-Col. J. Patrick, A. Robinson, Maj. P.E. Shepherd.

Four schemes, differing in cost and efficiency, which were outlined in an earlier report by Major Shepherd (see Cmd. 119 above) are considered, but none are recommended, as even the least costly is thought uneconomic. Evidence was heard from witnesses representing farming, fishery and urban interests, and there is no evidence that interested parties would be willing to contribute to a new drainage scheme. It is recommended that government engineers should take control of the Belleek sluices for a period to collect data on the effect of varying the level of the lakes, and that the idea of the control of these sluices passing into the hands of a government department should be contemplated. Negotiations should be opened with the pottery company to decide upon cash compensation for their surrendering the right to be provided at all times with a full head of water. A short reservation, signed by J. Johnston, opposes the plan to remove sluice control from the Lough Erne Drainage Board.

An appendix lists persons examined by the committee.

Erne Drainage and Development

Ministry of Finance. Agreement between the Ministry . . . and the Electricity Supply Board, Dublin, executed on 4 September 1950, 1951. *14 pp.*

The board is developing water power from the River Erne for the purpose of generating electricity, and certain work in County Fermanagh, as well as in Donegal, is needed to facilitate this. The agreement indicates the extent of the work to be done and the proposed division of labour. Arrangements are made for payment by the board for work carried out by the ministry, for the indemnity of the ministry by the board, and for arbitration should this be required. Records of water levels, as measured by apparatus in both Donegal and Fermanagh, are to be interchanged.

Drainage

Reps. of Com. apptd. April 1941. Reps.
published 1941, 1942.

Major J.M. Sinclair (Ch.) and seven
members—J. Blane, R. Crawford, R.D.
Duncan, G.A. Locke, S.H.W. Middleton,
I. Pimlott, Maj. P.E. Shepherd.

(i) To carry out an arterial drainage
survey [and] . . .
ii) to consider . . .
  (a) the arterial drainage schemes which
  should be undertaken and the order of
  priority in which they should be executed;
  (b) whether any of these schemes would
  contribute to an increase in the acreage
  under cultivation during the period of the
  war;
  (c) the modifications, if any, required
  in the existing administrative machinery
  for the execution of these schemes;
  (d) the method by which these schemes
  should be financed;
  and
iii) to make such recommendations as
may be pertinent.'

First Interim Report. Sgd. June 1941.
Published with second interim report.)
Cmd. 216, 16 pp.

An extensive survey was planned, but the
lack of suitable engineers limited activ-
ties. Investigations suggest that drainage
could not increase the amount of land
available for food production until 1942–
1944 and that the full benefits would not
be seen until the latter part of this period.
Nevertheless the problem is so acute that
drainage operations ought to start
promptly, and the government should
bear the bulk of the cost—a preliminary
programme might involve some £500,000.
This estimate excludes the work of drain-
ing the Erne, the Upper Bann and other
larger rivers. The problem of the removal
of weirs and other artificial obstructions
needs attention also. It is thought that
any arterial drainage undertaken will do
little to ease the war-time unemployment.
R. Crawford did not sign the report, and
his objection, concerning the commis-

sion's suggestion that local ratepayers
should support government expenditure
by contributing one quarter of the financial outlay on a drainage programme
plus maintenance costs, is recorded. His
name does not appear in the list of
signatories of the subsequent reports.

Second Interim Report. Sgd. October
1941. (Published with first interim report.)
Cmd. 216, 16 pp.

The further deterioration in the position
with regard to the availability of skilled
engineers means that even the limited
survey envisaged cannot be carried out.
Thus the commission has restricted its
activities to the examination of ten
schemes already prepared and to the
consideration of rivers where a weir or
dam is the chief cause of flooding. A
war-time drainage programme with government grants up to a maximum of 75
percent and with the object of increasing
food production is visualized, along with
an examination of the long-term drainage
problem. The cost originally estimated
has been reduced because of the restricted
programme now planned as a short-term
measure for the war period. The Ministry
of Home Affairs should supervise drainage schemes initiated in the war years,
but county councils should remain the
drainage authorities for their areas.
Schemes should be designed for execution
by the use of mechanical plant where
possible, and where loans are involved
the period of repayment should be
relatively short.

An appendix gives details, in tabular
form, of the ten complete schemes already
proposed.

Final Report. Sgd. March 1942.
Cmd. 217, 8 pp.

Drainage, prior to the war, was carried
out in a sporadic and localized fashion,
and the commission has sought in all its
deliberations to enable 'some drainage
to be carried out immediately and to
clear the ground for the continuance of
drainage measures on a comprehensive
scale in the future'. For the long term,
it is recommended that there should be

established a central drainage board with executive powers to undertake all arterial drainage plans. The board should carry out an appropriate survey and be responsible for the maintenance of all arterial rivers. Its work should be supervised by the Ministry of Agriculture, but local authorities should have representation on the board and provide 25 percent of its finance. Special consideration is needed with regard to the drainage problems of the rivers Erne, Blackwater, Lagan and Upper Bann.

6 FISHING

Sea Fisheries and Fishery Harbours

Rep. of Com. on the Natural and Industrial Resources of Northern Ireland, [1925].
Cmd. 39, 18 pp.
Com. apptd. June 1923; rep. sgd. March 1925.

Rt. Hon. the Viscount Charlemont (Ch.) and twenty-seven members—W. Addis, F. Anderson, R. Armstrong, H. Barbour, T.H. Burn, J.F. Cleaver, H. Conagher, G.M. Donaldson, F. Gilliland, J.A. Grey, E.D. Hill, Capt. S.J. Hutchinson, O. Jamison, Sir Samuel Kelly, W. Logue, R. McClung, W.J. McGuffin, J. Mackie, Prof. H.O. Meredith, J.A. Pringle, W.D. Scott, Prof. R. Stanley, D.P. Thompson, D. Wright. (Later additions were J. Hill Dickson, Maj. G.A. Harris, and Prof. J. K. Charlesworth.)

'To consider and report as to how the Natural and Industrial Resources of Northern Ireland can be best developed with a view to increasing the general prosperity and reducing the extent of unemployment.'

A general survey of the fishing industries and fishing harbours is followed by accounts of herring fishing and the need for an adequate central harbour; inshore fishing and the present condition of the smaller harbours; and the possible development of a deep-sea fishing industry. Recommendations are made concerning harbours, dredging, loans to fishermen, the restocking of shellfish beds and the

need for the furtherance of technica instruction for fishermen. Among pro posals made are the suggestions that a large central harbour be constructed or the County Down coast; that Ardglass and Killough harbours be surveyed to see which is best for the construction o a large central fishery harbour; that a site just inside Magilligan Point in Lough Foyle be surveyed for the construction of a wharf with possible expansion into a deep-sea harbour; that berthing and landing accommodation needs improve ment; and that the government should acquire a dredger for clearing out the coastal fishery harbours. The herring fishery offers extremely good develop ment prospects.

One appendix lists witnesses examined by the commission. Two others give figures relating to landings of herrings 1910–1914 and 1918–1924, and export of pickled herrings during the same periods.

The Development of Fishery Harbours

Rep. of Dept. Advisory Cttee., 1927.
Cmd. 81, 47 pp.
Cttee. apptd. February 1927; rep. sgd February 1928.

W.D. Scott (Ch.) and four members— W. Abbott, R.R. Bowman, W. Crone an G.H.E. Parr.

'To consider and report whether, having regard to the physical, geographical, in dustrial, and other relevant considerations improved or additional fishery harbou accommodation might justifiably be pro vided at the expense of public funds . . having regard to the cost involved . . . an the resultant advantages.'

Reference is made at the outset to th conclusions of the report on sea fisherie made by the Commission on the Natura and Industrial Resources (see Cmd. 3 above). This present report support most of these. There is then some dis cussion on the extent of the fishin industry in the province, and it i calculated that there are nearly fourtee hundred fishermen of whom just ove half are fully engaged in that occupation. The disposal of the fish caught is next considered, and it is asserted that difficulties lie in the development of the white fishing industry on account of the selective character of local demand. Expenditure on harbour accommodation solely for this type of fishing is hard to justify, as facilities at Belfast, Larne and Londonderry could be developed. It is believed that the summer herring fishing gives very little direct benefit to Northern Ireland, and heavy expenditure on a large central harbour for this purpose on the east coast cannot be supported by present benefits. Certain remedial works need to be effected promptly at Ardglass, but there is no immediate likelihood of a commercial harbour or mail packet station being established at Killough. Present harbour facilities are inadequate for the purposes of the inshore fishing communities. Repairs needing immediate attention in certain of the minor harbours are specified. The existence of a government-owned dredger would greatly benefit these minor harbours. It is believed that the most pressing need for remedial work is in the harbours owned by local authorities, and the cost of this work should be shared by the government and the authorities concerned.

The report provides details in tabular form of many individual harbours in 1926, stating the number of fishermen, the number of boats, the approximate value of fish landed and the type of fishing mainly practised in each harbour concerned. There is also a statistical table showing quantities of fish (other than herring and shellfish) imported in the years 1922–1926, with estimated monetary values. Reports by the consultant engineer, R.G. Nicol, on the Ardglass, Killough and Ballycastle harbours are submitted as appendices.

Fishing and Shooting Rights on Lough Erne

Rep. of Cttee. of Inquiry, 1930.
Cmd. 111, 25 pp., map.
Cttee. apptd. April 1929; rep. sgd. December 1929.

A.P. Magill (Ch.) and five members—J.I. Cook, W. Crone, Lieut.-Col. J.R. Darley, R.D.W. Harrison and J.H. Scaife.

'To consider:- (a) to what extent and under what conditions fishing in Lough Erne should be permitted to persons other than patentees; (b) the relations between the Ministry of Finance...and the Ministry of Commerce; (c) the position of patentees and the leasing of fishing rights; and (d) the conditions under which the shooting of wild fowl, etc., ... on Lough Erne should be permitted; and to make recommendations.'

The committee concludes that the interest of trout anglers should have priority in regulation of the fishing where such angling conflicts with other methods; that the netting of coarse fish under supervision should be undertaken in trout areas if funds become available; that cross lining should be entirely prohibited; that permits for coarse fish angling should be abolished; that there should be a maximum length of net and a minimum size of trout taken; and that protection should be given to spawning beds in the inflowing rivers. It is also suggested that an extension of the close season for shooting wild-duck would be advisable and that the taking of wild-duck eggs should be prohibited. Steps should be taken to destroy vermin and to reduce the number of gulls. As for shooting, it is argued that leases should continue to be given to responsible persons and that a limited number of permits for shooting over unleased portions of the loughs could be granted for a small annual fee.

A reservation to the report by J.H. Scaife concerns the ownership of crown rights in fishing. An appendix discusses parts of the loughs at present excluded from netting, and these, together with additional areas recommended for such exclusion, are given in a map.

The Use of Bag Nets for the Capture of Salmon

Ministry of Commerce. Rep. of Cttee., 1930.

Cmd. 124, 20 pp.
Cttee. apptd. June 1930; rep. sgd. October 1930.

J.H. Monroe (Ch.) and four members— W.L. Calderwood, W. Crone, Col. J. Patrick, and Prof. G. Wilson.

'To consider and report to what extent, if any, it is desirable to amend the law . . . in relation to the use of bag nets for the capture of salmon.'

The report outlines the present position with a view to ascertaining if the law needs amendment. It is thought that no step should be taken to secure the general substitution of an equal number of bag nets for the fixed draft nets at present in use, but that the fishery authority could consider suppressing groups of fixed draft nets and employing bag nets in the ratio of one bag net for every three fixed draft nets. The authority should also investigate drift netting and should obtain a patrol launch to regulate salmon drift netting and to assist in combatting offences by steam trawlers. The Royal Ulster Constabulary might be used more to suppress fishery offences, particularly those concerning river pollution. Appendices include a list of witnesses, diagrams of a draft salmon net and of a bag net with leader, plus a lengthy extract from the report of the 1902 Commission on Salmon Fisheries in Great Britain.

Local Fishery Administration, 1932–33

Rep. of Cttee., 1933.
Cmd. 152, 35 pp.
Cttee. apptd. September 1932; rep. sgd. May 1933.

A.P. Magill (Ch.) and six members—J.A. Barlowe, W. Crone, Maj. T.W. Dickie, Capt. J.L. Kinnaird, J.C. McDermott, H. O'H. O'Neill.

'To examine
(a) the functions of Boards of Conservators in relation to the administration of the Fishery Acts in Northern Ireland,
(b) the existing law relating to the constitution of such Boards and the election

of members thereof,
(c) the areas of the existing Fishery Districts and Electoral Division, and to report what changes, if any, are desirable in the interests of the general administration of the Fishery Acts.'

The general superintendence of fisheries and the determination of broad questions of policy should rest with the Ministry of Commerce, matters of local administration being left in the hands of the boards of conservators. The ministry should fix licence duties, should prescribe the form of accounts which the boards submit (these should be audited by a government auditor), and should have power to impose a licence duty for taking trout by rod and line in certain areas where they think fit. The other powers and duties of the boards should remain. The Royal Ulster Constabulary should keep in touch with officers of the boards as regards protection of the fisheries, and water bailiffs employed by a board should be responsible only to that board. The fourteen-day salmon licence should be replaced by a ten-shilling seven-day licence. Licence duties should be increased for draft nets used in tidal waters, drift nets over 750 yards in length, bag nets, and for box, cruive or drum nets used for taking salmon or trout in weirs.

The present constitution of the boards of conservators is discussed and compared with similar boards in England and Wales and in Scotland. The electors of a board of conservators should be divided into two groups—the holders of salmon rod licences on the one hand, and the holders of all other forms of licence on the other. Each group should elect its own representatives, the ratio of the representatives of different interests being fixed according to the district. The number of votes to which an elector is entitled should be proportionate to the licence duty paid. The committee make recommendations as to the qualifications for ex-officio members of a board. Existing legislation should be revised and embodied in one consolidating act.

Sale of salmon and trout should be prohibited between 15 September and 1 February, and of immature salmon and trout at all times. It is recommended that an offender against the fishery laws may be disqualified from holding a licence for up to a year, and trial should either be in the district where the offence is alleged to have occurred or where the defendent resides, or in any petty sessions district adjoining either. Any person aiding and abetting an offence should be punishable as if he were a principal offender.

Appendices list witnesses, summarize the income and expenditure of boards of conservators during 1926–1931, and describe the fishery districts, the present elected membership of each board, and the waters to be protected in each district.

[This was the only report published.]

Inland Fisheries

Ministry of Agriculture. Rep. of Fishery Advisory Cttee., 1963.
Cmd. 455, 38 pp.
Cttee. apptd. February 1961; rep. sgd. February 1963.

G.H.E. Parr (Ch.) and fifteen members —Maj. J.L. Baxter, J.P. Camac, A.C. Coyles, J.C. Davison, J. Edwards, J.G. Lennon, W. Marshall, G. Moore, G. McCartney, P.F. McGovern, A.H. Noble, J.S. Patterson, H.J. Perkes, G.B. Slipper, K.U. Vickers. (Sir Antony Macnaghten replaced Maj. Baxter in November 1961.)

'To review the present position of inland fisheries . . . with special reference to the improvement of rod angling facilities, and to make recommendations.'

The original terms of reference were rather narrower but were revised at the committee's request. Central administration of all fishery services, for which the Ministry of Commerce was responsible from 1 April 1923, passed to the Ministry of Agriculture on 1 April 1963. Local administration is the responsibility of boards of conservators for the conservancy districts of Coleraine, Enniskillen and Ballycastle, and the Foyle Fisheries Commission for the conservancy district of Londonderry. The boards, first established in 1848, do not have sufficient power or income and are unsatisfactory in many ways. They should be replaced by a central fishery authority responsible, among other things, for improvement and development of fishing facilities; the making of by-laws dealing with close seasons, methods of fishing, licence duty and conditions; and the collection and administration of fishery rates, licence duties, etc. Owners of fishing rights should be compelled to register their titles, and the central fishery authority could maintain a register of all rights. Unclaimed rights should be vested in the central fishery authority.

Setting of eel nets in the Queen's Gap should be permitted. The minimum weight restriction on 'silver' eels should be abolished, but a minimum weight should be prescribed for 'yellow' (immature) eels. The question of substitution of bag nets for draft nets in salmon fishing should be re-examined, and commercial netting in fresh water should be prohibited. The committee strongly recommend the establishment of a freshwater fisheries research organization. Tourism would be aided by improved access to coarse fishing waters and suitable accommodation.

Pollution is not found on the same scale as in Great Britain and is due mainly to the older industries, inefficient sewage disposal, the effluent of piggeries, and sand-washing installations. Protection should be extended to estuaries and tidal waters, and the maximum penalties increased for pollution and for poaching. Recommendations are made for protection of fisheries in the design and execution of drainage schemes.

Legislation affecting fisheries should be consolidated.

The committee's recommendations also cover the use of explosives, poisons, nets, lights, spears, etc.; licences, salmon registers; collection of statistics; and provisions concerning the farming and sale of rainbow trout.

The text contains statistics comparing the catches of freshwater fish in Northern Ireland, England and Wales, and Scotland. Appendices list persons and bodies submitting evidence, receipts and expenditure of boards of conservators for the five years ended 31 October 1961, and suggestions for the organization and programme of research.

The Sea Fishing Industry of Northern Ireland

Ministry of Agriculture. An economic study by P.H. Hughes, 1970.
155 pp., bibliography, diagrs., map.

This study provides a comprehensive body of information about the sea fishing industry and an analysis in the light of that information. In section I, 'Catching', the characteristics of the industry are discussed: the fleet, the fishing grounds, productivity, finance, employment, and the various ports and marketing methods. Section II, 'Marketing', analyses the market, efficiency in retailing, the different uses of fish, the wholesale trade, the newer developments in presentation of fish, consumption of fish, and the issues involved in increasing sales and improving marketing. Section III, 'Develop-

ment', discusses potential development of the fleet and the fishing grounds, marketing, subsidies, and the cost and benefit of various proposals for expansion. Many suggestions are made to improve efficiency at all levels; fishermen and wholesalers should be kept aware of the consumers' preferences, and greater care should be taken in the handling and display of fish, to maintain the quality. Openings in the North American and the continental markets should be investigated. Harbour accommodation is inhibiting the industry from reaching its optimum potential, and after discussion of alternative developments in County Down harbours, it is concluded that a new harbour at Kilkeel and additional accommodation at Warrenpoint associated with investment in the fleet and in processing provide the best solution. (Since the study was made the decision has been announced to carry out the full-scale development of Kilkeel Harbour.)

In addition to thirty-eight statistical tables and three diagrams in the text of the study, an appendix contains thirty-nine tables concerned with all aspects of the fishing trade: numbers of boats, landings of fish, earnings, retail outlets, prices, etc. There is a two-page bibliography.

V TRADE AND INDUSTRY

1 **General**
2 **Location of Industry**

3 **Particular Industries and Trades**
4 **Company and Commercial Law**

1 GENERAL

Trade Boards

For details of this report see Class X p. 94.

Industrial Art

Rep. of Cttee., 1935.
Cmd. 169, 54 pp.
Cttee. apptd. July 1933; rep. sgd. October 1935.

Sir Roland T. Nugent (Ch.) and eleven members—Lady Mabel Annesley, V.F.

Clarendon, J.H. Craig, G.F.M. Harding, J.F. Hunter, G.H.E. Parr, Maj. R. Stanley, H. Strain, N.F. Webb, R.J. Woods, and A.N.B. Wyse.

'To examine and report upon the present position of Industrial Art . . . especially in connection with the textile and printing trades, and, having regard to the increasing importance of artistic design as a factor in industry, to recommend steps . . . to correlate more closely the work of art schools with industrial requirements.'

The growth of design in industrial life and the rapidity of fashion changes have created a need for greater artistic research and closer co-operation between art and industry. In Northern Ireland, linen is the outstanding commodity offering scope for design, but furniture, printing and shipbuilding are among other industries presenting great opportunities. The report surveys existing facilities for art education in elementary, secondary and technical schools, and detailed recommendations are made for the future of art education in these schools, and also with regard to Belfast College of Art, and the training of apprentice craftsmen. It is considered that a central art council should be set up and also that an Ulster art institute should be established. The institute would promote research, and it would have in its charge a central art school which would relieve the pressure on the Belfast College of art resulting from students from all parts of the province, who seek advanced art courses, applying there. It is also suggested that the Belfast Museum should be raised to the status of an Ulster museum and given more accommodation to serve the province appropriately.

A reservation by Major Stanley opposes the creation of a new art school or college within Belfast. In an appendix there is a Ministry of Education memorandum on existing facilities for art studies and their use; art examinations, exhibitions and scholarships; and the co-ordination of art studies with known local industrial needs.

The Feasibility of State Industry in Northern Ireland

For details of this report see Class III p. 35.

2 LOCATION OF INDUSTRY

Location of Industry

Interim rep. of the Planning Advisory Board Cttee., 1945.
Cmd. 225, 32 pp., chart.

Maj. D.M. Anderson (Ch.) and six members—T. Coote, W. Crone, G.H. Mc-Alister, W.F. Scott, H. Turtle, R.C. Wilson.

'To consider
(1) The present geographical distribution of industry in Northern Ireland.
(2) Measures of physical planning calculated to foster the further development of industry—
and to report whether the location of industry should in future be brought under State control, and, if so, to what extent and by what means.'

The equivalent report for Great Britain is that of the Royal Commission on the Distribution of the Industrial Population (Cmd. 6153 of 1940), but the character of population distribution and industrial siting in Northern Ireland has certain unique features. The staple industries of linen and shipbuilding have declined, and there is a lack of industrial diversification with a distinct migration of population towards Belfast.

The present report divides into three sections which deal respectively with the three parts of the terms of reference. An examination of the present distribution of the urban population shows that most towns need to grow considerably to reach a size (estimated at approximately 15,000 population) suitable for the economic provision of amenities. No town within the Counties Tyrone and Fermanagh has a population of more than 6,000. There is no one major industry apart from agriculture, outside of Belfast, but in view of the better health of country workers, evidence of their higher morale and other factors, it is concluded that new industries should be attracted, if possible, to towns other than Belfast.

It is decided that location planning, despite some disadvantages, is essential to the prosperity of the province and that a zoning system for industry and housing might prove advantageous. With regard to the setting up of industrial zones, study must be made of industrial estates in Britain, and there is a description of some of these trading estates and the way in which they have promoted the diversification of industry in England and Scotland. It is argued that the province may need one or more of such trading estates and that this matter should be studied by the government. Other areas of possible state action include promotion of liaison between local authorities and industrialists; the provision of advice on industrial location; and the provision of current information on the location and equipment of areas zoned for industry.

Statistics are given, in appendices and in the body of the report, on: the population, and birth and death rates of certain urban areas in 1901, 1911, 1926, and 1937; registrations of births and deaths, 1934–1938; and the industrial and geographical distribution of employees. Details are given of the numbers employed in 1935 in major industries (excluding agriculture) within six principal towns other than Belfast. Some two-fifths of the whole population live in or near to Belfast at present, and in the period 1926–1937 this city accounted for 98 percent of the province's total population increase.

The 'Seenozip' Case

For details of this report see Class I p. 19.

Londonderry as a Location for New Industry

Ministry of Commerce. Rep. of Northern Ireland Economic Council, 1966.
20 pp.
Rep. sgd. February 1966.

B. Faulkner (Ch.) and seventeen members —D. Andrews, A. Barr, W.J. Blease, G.E. Cameron, H.E. Campbell, Senator N. Kennedy, D.C. Lamont, W. McCormick, S. McGonagle, E.D. Maguire, J. Morrow, J.T. O'Brien, Prof. J.R. Parkinson, Dr. D. Rebbeck, R.L. Schierbeek, W.L. Stephens, R. Thompson.

Londonderry has many advantages for industry, and since 1945 new industry now employing over 2,600 people has been established. There is still, however, an unacceptable level of male unemployment—15.4 percent in 1965. The report examines facilities for industrial growth

in the city and environs, urban development and housing, transport, labour training, social amenities, and Londonderry's links with other centres. It is thought that organizations representing the industrial and commercial life of the city should appoint a standing committee to ensure that appropriate measures to win industry to the area are implemented. Road and rail links with Belfast and Ballymena/Larne need improvement. Tourism should be developed and housing targets set. The development of the Maydown area for industry ought to continue.

A fully co-operative effort from all authorities and other organizations concerned is urged for the implementation of suggestions such as those mentioned in this report's twenty-five recommendations.

3 PARTICULAR INDUSTRIES AND TRADES

The Retail Bespoke Tailoring Trade

For details of this report see Class X p. 100.

The Linen Industry

(Ministry of Commerce and Production.) Rep. of Linen Industry Post-War Planning Cttee., 1944.
22 pp.

Cttee. apptd. January 1943; rep. sgd. February 1944.

H.L. McCready (Ch.) and ten members —H. Boyd, D. Campbell, R.W. Charlesson, E.S. Clarke, J.E. Finney, A.C. Herdman, J.P. Herdman, G. Larmor, H.B. McCance, H.G.H. Mulholland.

'To consider the problems with which the Northern Ireland Linen Industry is likely to be faced in the post-war period, and advise as to the measures which could best be taken to ensure the maintenance and development of the industry in future years.'

The pattern of world trade in the post-war years is still unknown, but the committee review the major domestic problems which must in any event be considered.

A flax buying corporation, representative of the whole industry, should be set up, to be the sole purchaser and distributor of home-grown and imported fibre and imported yarns required by the whole United Kingdom linen industry. Thus farmers could be induced to grow flax by having a guaranteed market and an attractive price. The additional price, if any, which would be needed to pay the home producer in order to secure the home acreage and to maintain the export trade should be a joint liability of the industry and the state. It is desirable that about one-third of the flax required should be home produced.

Government contracts should give preference to materials prepared from home-grown flax. Until there is enough flax to meet requirements, sufficient supplies of alternative fibres and yarns should be made available in order to utilize spinning and weaving facilities fully.

The present high taxation prevents the modernization and improvement of plant and machinery and the accumulation of profits to form working capital. The committee recommend a refund of 20 percent of excess profits tax paid and the provision of low-interest government loans for modernization, improvement or development of plant and machinery.

Flax and linen research should be under unified control, with a headquarters located in Northern Ireland, and the industry should have the determining voice as to the precise purposes to which the money available should be devoted. The existing Linen Industry Research Association at Lambeg seems an appropriate headquarters and is already suitably organized for co-ordination and centralization of research. A more liberal contribution to research finance is called for from the linen industry; the remainder of the cost might be borne by the Department of Scientific and Industrial Research and the government of Northern Ireland. A statutory levy, administered by the Flax Corporation, is desirable to raise contributions from the industry for both research and publicity. Publicity funds, augmented by government grants, should be in the hands of the Irish Linen Guild.

The internal structure of the industry is discussed, and reference is made to the recommendations, in 1928, of a committee consisting of four representatives of the principal branches of the industry. The ultimate objective then suggested was the amalgamation of the entire industry into one unit. While the present committee see points of merit in the idea, it is considered impracticable. Their view is that a policy of vertical grouping of many of the firms now operating independently is much to be preferred to any plan of price regulation. The effect of raw material control, supported in other directions by a policy of co-operative action between groups, should first be tried.

A comprehensive statistical service would be of value, providing data on which to base authoritative conclusions which would assist in the formulation of policy.

More use should be made of the training facilities available at the Belfast College of Technology; introduction of a trade scholarship course is suggested. The establishment of a school of textile design should be considered.

If good labour relations are to continue, the industry must recognize the need to pay wages at the highest level practicable and to continue to improve working conditions.

The Production of Bricks

Ministry of Commerce. Rep. of Cttee., 1945.
55 pp.
Cttee. apptd. July 1944; rep. sgd. March 1945.

J.P. Graham (Ch.) and seven members —H.W. Gooding, J.J. Hartley, J. McGladery, F. McKee, A. Ryan, J.H. Stevenson, H. Turtle.

'To enquire into the present position of the brickmaking industry . . . , to report

thereon and to make recommendations for the increased production of bricks or slabs of any material of satisfactory quality at an economic price, bearing particularly in mind the urgent requirements of the post-war period and the necessity to provide for an increased demand.'

The report describes, with much technical detail, the combinations of raw materials which can be used in brickmaking, the six stages of the process of clay-brick manufacture, other raw materials used in brickmaking, and the defects of bricks and how these can be minimized. A standard specification for common clay bricks is given with details of tests for the determination of efflorescence, compressive strength and soluble salt content. Post-war demands and methods for increasing production are discussed, together with the cost of production and selling price. The government should set up an advisory council to promote control and co-ordination within the industry.

The committee concludes that good quality bricks can be made in Northern Ireland provided that brickmakers give attention to all manufacturing processes. The present output of walling units does not meet potential requirements, and new works should be provided, or existing ones expanded, to improve production. Control of the industry must be continued for a limited period, and arrangements should be made speedily for the necessary accumulation of brick stocks. It is believed that the selection of suitable mortars is an important factor in the efficient use of bricks. The committee also urges the government to carry out a survey with the object of discovering, within the province, the most suitable clay and shale deposits.

Lists of persons and organizations providing evidence form an appendix to the report. Some statistics within the text of the report give details of clay-brick production during several pre-war years.

Northern Ireland's Furniture Industry

Ministry of Commerce. Rep. of Advisory

Cttee. on Furniture Production, 1945. 16 pp.
Cttee. first met February 1945; rep. sgd. September 1945.

R.W. Charlesson (Ch.) and fourteen members—Jean M. Armour, J. Drennan, J. Duff, Mrs. Maud I. Girvan, J. Glover, G.F. Hamilton, L. Hyman, W. Jamison, A.L. Keeble, J.E. McKelvey, W. Neasham, J.H. Stevenson, W.E. Stewart, A. M. Wallace. (Mrs. Girvan died in May 1945.)

'To consider and advise the Minister upon such matters as affect the Furniture Industry and Trade in Northern Ireland, with special reference to its organization, expansion and improvement in the post-war period.'

The pre-war output of locally made furniture was about 25 percent of total requirements. Possible reasons for this low figure are listed.

In the transitional period following relaxation of the utility furniture scheme, minimum standards of materials, construction and finish should apply; price should be controlled; but specification and design should not.

Long-term problems are also considered. Existing machinery in factories is largely obsolete. Manufacturers should be enabled to obtain government loans to re-equip their factories. All furniture manufacturers should be registered; minimum standards of production, maintenance of adequate factory premises, and observation of the wages and working conditions laid down by the Joint Council Agreement should be conditions of registration, which should not be granted to new firms until such time as firms already in business in 1939 have had an opportunity to attain normal production. A grade label, the manufacturer's registration number, and possibly an 'Ulster mark' should be applied to all furniture.

Good design should be encouraged, perhaps by a pool of designers under the auspices of the Ulster Furniture Federation, by scholarships to promising young craftsmen, and by the establishment of a design centre financed jointly by the industry and the government.

The Ministry of Commerce should establish an inspectorate to enforce standards, grades, and registration, but should be guided by a body representative of employers, trade unions, distributors, appropriate government departments, and consumers.

Facilities for kiln drying timber should be improved. Recommendations are made for a drastic reorganization of the softbedding industry, in which registration should be granted only to satisfactory firms. Surplus government stores should pass through the channels of trade normally used for such goods when manufactured for civil trade.

Specifications for minimum standards of materials, construction and finish, in three grades, are given in the appendix.

The Tourist Industry

Interim rep. of the Planning Advisory Bd. Cttee., 1964.
Cmd. 234, 22 pp.
Rep. sgd. August 1945.

W.I. Cunningham (Ch.) and eight members—R. Bell, Miss F.J. Davidson, Miss R. Duffin, J. Edwards, R. Ferguson, R.F. Green, W. Malcolm and F. Storey. (W. Malcolm died before the work of the committee was completed.)

'To consider in what respect and to what extent the accommodation, amenities and facilities likely to be available to tourists . . . after the war will be adequate for the purpose of catering for increased demands, and to make recommendations as to what steps should be taken towards improving or extending such accommodation, amenities and facilities with a view to making Northern Ireland more attractive to tourists.'

The annual value of the province's tourist industry has been calculated at £1¾ million, and the trade is thus a leading export. There is, however, a need to improve upon the quantity and quality of accommodation, to lengthen the season by the spreading of holidays, and for government assistance similar to that provided in other countries. The Ulster Tourist Development Association suggests, in evidence to the board, that cross-channel shipping might be improved and extended during the high season. Other witnesses make various suggestions about improvements in travel, and in amenity provision. The Development Association has done much to publicize the province as a holiday centre, but it would have been unsuitable for (and indeed is reluctant to undertake) the implementation of some of the proposals of the present report.

The Ministry of Commerce is thus urged to set up a board for the tourist industry which will inspect, register and grade hotels and boarding houses; make appropriate grants and loans to local authorities; consult and co-operate with government departments; and carry out planning and direction over the whole area of tourist development and amenities.

Appendices show lists of witnesses who gave evidence to the earlier committee on tourism (the MacDermott Committee appointed in 1938, but dissolved during the war years without issuing a report), and of those providing evidence for the present committee. They also give details of the average rainfall, temperature and hours of sunshine, during the summer months, in Northern Ireland.

Computer Inquiry

Ministry of Commerce. Rep. of N.I. Computer Inquiry Cttee., 1966.
12 pp.
Cttee. apptd. November 1965; rep. sgd. June 1966.

W.T. Underwood (Ch.) and two members —J.C. Browne and W.E. Tetlow.

'To review the existing and potential usage of computers . . . and to compare it with the facilities available and likely to be provided.'

The committee made an interim report

in February 1966 (apparently not published) dealing with the urgent need for appreciation courses and the importance of encouraging interest among young people in careers in programming and systems analysis. This conclusion has been reinforced by the answers to questionnaires and by evidence given to the committee. The potential impact of computers on the commercial life of Northern Ireland is only now beginning to be appreciated. Nevertheless, the need is not for a centralized computer service, but for the organization of educational facilities to demonstrate to the business community the practical application of computers to their organizations, and to train competent staff. Co-ordination of computer activities in Northern Ireland could be undertaken by an existing organization such as the British Institute of Management. There may be value in establishing a clearing house for available computer time, and there could also be some contribution made locally to the National Computing Centre's work on the development of standard programmes.

Tables showing the coverage of the questionnaire, and an analysis of its results, showing the use of computers by various types of organization, form appendices to the report.

4 COMPANY AND COMMERCIAL LAW

Bankruptcy Law

Rep. of Dept. Cttee. apptd. by the Minister of Commerce, 1926 (!).
27 pp.
Cttee. apptd. September 1926; rep. sgd. January 1927 (!).

J.H. Robb (Ch.) and seven members— W.M. Knox, J. McGonigal, W. McMullan, G.H.E. Parr, S. Ross, R. Wallace, A.J. Weir.

'To consider and report what amendments in Bankruptcy Law, as it applies in Northern Ireland, experience has shown to be desirable.'

The bankruptcy laws in the province need to be codified and consolidated. No drastic changes in the administration of the Acts are necessary, but to facilitate the speedy conclusion of proceedings, the second sitting before the court should be abolished in the case of arrangements and compositions after bankruptcy. Numerous changes in points of law should be effected by an amending statute, pending a consolidation act. These changes include stricter regulations as to the keeping of accounts by traders, and the extension of the bankruptcy laws to married women or minors who carry on a business. Fraudulent preference and a return of 'no goods' by the sheriff should be declared acts of bankruptcy, and provision should be made to remove the minimum limit of twenty pounds for the act of bankruptcy when a debtor's goods are seized. Departing from or remaining out of Northern Ireland to avoid creditors must become an act of bankruptcy. The provisions of the English law on such matters as creditors' rights, rash speculation by bankrupts, and fees for accountants administering a debtor's affairs need to be extended to Northern Ireland.

Company Law Amendment

Rep. of Dept. Cttee., 1960.
Cmd. 393, 42 pp.
Cttee. first met July 1956; rep. sgd. July 1958.

W.F. Patton (Ch.) and six members—R. Bell, G.E. Cameron, J. Edwards, G.C. Holt, J.C. Taylor, P.T. Watson.

To consider 'how far the Companies Act (N.I.), 1932 calls for amendment after the lapse of twenty-five years and in the light of the amendments which have been made in Great Britain by the Companies Act, 1947.'

Any departure from British law in regard to public companies might have a deterrent effect upon the British investor, but greater independence of attitude is called for in regard to private companies, to encourage local capitalists to invest in them rather than in public companies in Great Britain. The sections of the 1947 Act which the committee approves are listed in a schedule. The remaining sections are considered individually. Recommendations aim to ensure proper conduct of private companies and fair treatment of minority shareholders. They cover conduct of meetings, statement of accounts, regulations regarding directors, and winding up of companies.

The appendix sets out the amending provisions of the Companies Act, 1947; the comparable sections and schedules of the Companies Act, 1948; and the sections or schedules of the Companies Act (N.I.), 1932, which would be affected.

VI COAL, FUEL, POWER, WATER

1 General
2 Coal
3 Electricity

4 Water
5 Peat Utilization

1 GENERAL

Mineral Resources

Rep. of Com. on the Natural and Industrial Resources of Northern Ireland, 1925.
Cmd. 43, 91 pp., map.
Com. apptd. June 1923; rep. sgd. March 1925.

Rt. Hon. the Viscount Charlemont (Ch.) and twenty-six members—W. Addis, F. Anderson, R. Armstrong, H. Barbour, T.H. Burn, J.F. Cleaver, H. Conacher, G.M. Donaldson, F. Gilliland, J.A. Grey, E.D. Hill, Capt. S.J. Hutchinson, O. Jamison, Sir Samuel Kelly, W. Logue, R. McClung, W.J. McGuffin, J. Mackie, Prof. H.O. Meredith, J.A. Pringle, Prof. R. Stanley, D.P. Thompson, D. Wright. (Further appointments were J. Hill Dickson, and Maj. G.A. Harris, in October 1923, and Prof. J.K. Charlesworth, January 1924.)

'To consider and report as to how the Natural and Industrial Resources of Northern Ireland can be best developed with a view to increasing the general prosperity and reducing the extent of unemployment.'

The report reviews first of all the province's coal resources, and proved and probable coal-bearing areas. The resources of other minerals are then considered, these being iron ore, rock salt, potash, bauxite, felspar, diatomite, clays and sands, lignite, building stones, lead, copper, bog iron ore, manganese and glauconite.

It is considered by the commission that the state should assist the mining industry by means of housing subsidies, by helping local authorities with essential public services, and by securing the necessary co-operation of the railways. A thorough geological revision of Northern Ireland is also needed. There are numerous suggestions with regard to coal and coal boring, and it is recommended that surveys should be carried out by the government to ascertain the extent, quality and characteristics of several other minerals. Exploratory boring for the remaining resources of lead ore is not justified. A reservation signed by G.M. Donaldson, W. Logue and R. McClung urges that, in view of other countries' recent experience, the mines should be nationalized. This fundamental idea is ignored in the report, despite the agreement on the need for state aid.

Appendices give the names of witnesses providing evidence, analyses of seams in various coalfields and of other mineral deposits, and the quantity together with the value of minerals produced in the province during the years 1922 and 1923. They also include a list of bauxite mines, a list of the Antrim iron ore mines, and a memorandum on the geological features of the country. There are also many statistics within the report itself relating to the output and value of various minerals. A map contrasts coal bearing areas in the province with those of the Scottish Lowlands.

Power Resources

Rep. of Com. on the Natural and Industrial Resources, 1926.
Cmd. 59, 32 pp., map.
Com. apptd. June 1923; rep. sgd. April 1926.

The Rt. Hon. the Viscount Charlemont (Ch.) and twenty-two members—F. Anderson, R. Armstrong, H. Barbour, T.H. Burn, J.F. Cleaver, H. Conacher, F. Gilliland, J.A. Grey, E.D. Hill, Capt. S.J. Hutchinson, O. Jamison, R. McClung, W.J. McGuffin, J. Mackie, Prof. H.O. Meredith, J.A. Pringle, Prof. R. Stanley, D.P. Thompson, D. Wright. (Additional members were J. Hill Dickson, and Maj. G.A. Harris, appointed October 1923, Prof. J.K. Charlesworth, January 1924, and R.R. Bowman, appointed October 1925 to replace H. Conacher, who resigned.)

'To consider and report as to how the Natural and Industrial resources of Northern Ireland can be best developed with a view to increasing the general prosperity and reducing the extent of unemployment.'

Little advantage, outside of Belfast and Londonderry, has been taken of benefits resulting from the greater use of electricity. There is need for the development of a comprehensive public supply capable of satisfying power, traction, lighting, heating and general domestic needs. The situation is surveyed with consideration of future demand and sources of supply, and reference is made to the 1918 report of the Coal Conservation Subcommittee embodied in the Electricity Act, 1919.

It is suggested that the Electricity Commission should be able to prohibit schemes which might render proposed undertakings unable to participate in any future comprehensive system of supply. No economic advantage would come from linking the Belfast and London-derry electricity stations. Estimated total demand for bulk power in load centres could, at present, be supplied by Belfast Corporation without demanding added capital expenditure. A generating station, using Coalisland coal, should be made available in the future at Lough Neagh. This would augment the supply of bulk power obtainable from other sources. Electricity demands in agricultural and rural areas are not yet sufficient to be economically met, but short-distance railway electrification would be profitable.

Other proposals include the idea of establishing, under the Electricity Commissioners, a public board to deal with erection, maintenance and operation of transmission networks, high-tension mains, switchgear, and transformers. The expert advice of a consulting engineer is needed to effect the co-ordination and growth of future supplies. The Electricity Commissioners could be profitably given additional powers, and the public board referred to should receive government help in raising capital. Alternative ways of achieving the last recommendation are outlined.

A map displays Northern Ireland's existing and proposed power stations, transmission lines, and other relevant details. Appendices contain a list of witnesses giving evidence; particulars of existing electricity undertakings; and a table showing actual electricity demands in Belfast and Londonderry and estimated demands in various load centres.

Geophysical and Drilling Exploration in Northern Ireland

Ministry of Commerce. Progress rep. by W. Bullerwell, 1964.
12 pp.

A programme of regional geophysical exploration began in 1959, and this report reviews the results of drilling and makes recommendations for the future programme. It was concluded in 1961 that an exploratory borehole should be drilled to examine the Lough Foyle gravity trough, that similar exploration in the Larne gravity basin was justified, and that the same procedure should be followed in the Dungiven–Ballycastle trough at a location and time determined by a seismic trial employing the Vibroseis system. At the Larne borehole, it has now been found that there are considerable salt reserves, that coal resources in the neighbourhood are too deep for present-day exploration, and that this is a potential area for oil and gas storage. The earth structure here contains many deposits of economic interest and improves hopes that Northern Ireland may become a worthy commercial proposition for oil and gas. These findings and those at the Magilligan borehole in the Lough Foyle basin offer a more optimistic outlook than seemed possible in 1958. There are grounds for confidence that suitable sites for further exploration can, on the basis of the present geophysical evidence, be selected now.

Recent drilling results also suggest that suitable localities can be established for the examination of geological structure in the Dungiven–Ballycastle and Portglenone-Maghera basins. It is therefore concluded that further exploration is justified and that three further boreholes, within these areas, should be authorized. Appendices indicate and review the cost of operations to date, give some technical details relating to the Larne borehole, and indicate considerations (such as site choice, complexity of structure, area and costs) relating to the exploration of six basins at Lough Neagh, Larne, Strangford Lough, Lough Foyle, Portglenone–Maghera and Ballycastle–Dungiven.

2 COAL

Lough Neagh Coal Basin

Interim rep. of Com. on the Natural and Industrial Resources, [1923].
Cmd. 24, 8 pp.
Com. apptd. June 1923; rep. sgd. October 1923.

The Rt. Hon. the Viscount Charlemont (Ch.) and twenty-five members — W. Addis, F. Anderson, R. Armstrong, W. Boyd, T.H. Burn, J.F. Cleaver, H. Conacher, G.M. Donaldson, F. Gilliland, J.A. Grey, E.D. Hill, Capt. S.J. Hutchinson, O. Jamison, C. Litchfield, W. Logue, R. McClung, W.J. McGuffin, J. Mackie, Prof. H.O. Meredith, J.A. Pringle, W.D. Scott, Prof. R. Stanley, D.P. Thompson, D. Wright. (An additional member was J. Hill Dickson, appointed October 1923.)

'*To consider and report as to how the Natural and Industrial Resources of Northern Ireland can be best developed with a view to increasing the general prosperity and reducing the extent of unemployment.*'

The coal-bearing possibilities of the Lough Neagh area and the resources of the Coalisland coalfield were investigated by the commission in the earliest stages of its work. It is considered that, although these resources will automatically be developed, their utilization should be aided and accelerated by means of state aid.

Coal Rationing

[Plan for] temporary scheme, 1942.
Cmd. 218, 4 pp.

No coal is produced in Northern Ireland, and the question of the rationing of imported supplies for domestic use is inevitably linked to that of rationing gas and electricity. This measure is not recommended, but a simple coal rationing scheme, whereby each domestic coal user is limited from August 1942 to three-quarters of his annual supply and in which one quarter of the new supply may be slack or briquettes, is proposed. No occupier will be compulsorily restricted to less than two tons per annum during the rationing period. Provisions under this scheme apply to clubs and hotels, but not to coal bought solely for industrial or agricultural purposes. A more rigorous system, to be employed if the temporary scheme is ineffective, is outlined.

Coal Distribution Costs

Rep. of Cttee. of Inquiry, 1958 (reprinted 1960).
Cmd. 386, 79 pp.
Cttee. apptd. March 1956; rep. sgd. April 1958.

Sir Thomas Robson (Ch.) and five members—C.T. Brunner, Prof. A.D. Campbell, Mrs. F.H. Cantwell, Sir Graham Larmor, W.J.P. Webber.

'To ascertain what are the various items which make up the difference between the prices received by producers of coal, coke and manufactured fuels in the United kingdom and those paid by consumers in Northern Ireland; to investigate the merchant's distribution costs and profit margins in respect of these supplies and to make recommendations.'

The size of the coal market in the province is reviewed and details given of consumption by public utilities, industry and domestic users. Costs incurred in Britain and in the sea transport of coal are examined, as is the pricing of coal and allied fuels within the province.

Substantial supplies of coal from Scotland are not likely to be available for some years, and Northern Ireland must continue to depend on coal which incurs heavy transport charges from pithead to port of shipment. No firm conclusion is possible, but information obtained suggests that there is not excessive profit made on sea freight nor on distribution. But these should be checked periodically by the Ministry of Commerce, which fixes maximum prices. The ministry should keep in close touch with price movements if it decides to decontrol retail prices. A representative of the ministry should attend the meetings of the shipping company which allocates supplies to importers. There is too little competition among distributors in the Northern Ireland coal trade, and this affects costs adversely.

Many figures for tonnage, prices, and costs are given throughout the report and in the appendices. These figures include costs of various grades of domestic coal in different Northern Ireland towns as effective in August 1957. Those individuals and organizations who gave evidence to the committee are also listed in an appendix.

Domestic Coal

(Ministry of Commerce). Reps. of Domestic Coal Consumers' Council, 1958. Council apptd. September 1957.

W. Mawhinney (Ch.) and thirteen members—H. Bell, W.J. Burton, S.J. Campbell, G.R. Hyde, J.S. Kennedy, W.R. Knox, R.T. Luney, R. Malcomson, A. McClure, Mrs. O.H. Proctor, Sir William Scott, Mrs. Hilda F. Wilson, D. Wylie. (Mrs. R.N.A. Bailey and Mrs. J. McCormack were added in May 1958.)

'To consider and keep under review all matters concerning domestic coal.'

First (Interim) Report. *Sgd. March 1958. 7 pp.*

There are seen to be arguments both for and against a summer price scheme, such as operates in Great Britain. The introduction of such a scheme would not necessarily result in more coal being imported in summer and retained for use in times of shortage, and the advantage to those who could build up stocks would be offset by the problems for those who could not. It is thus thought that the use of the scheme in Northern Ireland would be unwise.

Annual winter and summer imports of domestic coal, 1949–1958, are shown in a table.

Second (Interim) Report. *Sgd. June 1958. 6 pp.*

A review is made of prices, shipping and sea freight charges, and grades of household coal in use. The advantages and drawbacks of competitive marketing free from Government control are considered. It is believed that the best way to reduce retail coal prices is to import a high proportion of coal from coalfields near to the ports on Great Britain's west coast.

Domestic Coal

[*Ministry of Commerce.*] *Rep. of Domestic Coal Liaison Cttee., 1960.*
7 pp.
Cttee. apptd. September 1959; rep. sgd. November 1960.

W. Mawhinney (Ch.) and thirteen members—H. Bell, W.J. Burton, S.J. Campbell, G.R. Hyde, J.S. Kennedy, W.R. Knox, R.T. Luney, Mrs. E.F. McCormack, R. Malcomson, A. McClure, Mrs. D. Proctor, Sir William Scott, D. Wylie. (Mrs. E.F. McCormack resigned, and Mrs. Hilda F. Wilson and Mrs. J.E. Rodgers were appointed.)

'To maintain contact between the Northern Ireland domestic consumer, the National Coal Board and the coal trade generally and to advise the appropriate authorities on any problems arising from the supply and distribution of domestic coal in Northern Ireland.'

The introduction of a summer price scheme was discussed more than once, and many of the committee were in favour of trying such a scheme, but in a subsequent scheme the majority thought it would not be in the best interests of Northern Ireland consumers.

Information on the prices charged for domestic coal has not been available since the end of government price control in July 1958, but the committee fear that regular publication of such information might cause all prices to rise to the level of the highest. In accordance with the committee's advice, therefore, the Ministry of Commerce has established a voluntary panel of importers and merchants prepared to provide regular information on their prices so that the ministry may periodically publish a review of general trends revealed.

The committee examine the prospects of obtaining coal from pits in Great Britain with lower transport costs to Northern Ireland than from the present main sources of supply in the East Midlands, but they conclude that there is no immediate prospect of this being possible. They recommend that the situation should be kept under continuous review in view of its fundamental importance to the province. A table shows the present pattern of supply.

The National Coal Board price for coal sold to the Irish Republic is said to be thirty-five shillings less per ton than the corresponding Northern Ireland price, but this is because the former is treated as an export market in which prices must compete with prevailing world prices. The committee find that this has not so far been disadvantageous to Northern Ireland.

Some distributors are making an additional charge per bag for delivery of coal to flats. The committee find this not unreasonable but have drawn the attention of the relevant authorities to the need for coal storage and delivery problems to be considered by those responsible for the design of flats.

Coal Inquiry

Ministry of Commerce. Rep. of Cttee. Cttee. apptd. January 1961; reps. published 1962, 1963.

B.J. Fox (Ch.) and three members—G.E. Cameron, J. Morrow, Sir William Robinson. (Sir William Robinson died and was replaced by M.F. Gordon, apptd. February 1962.)

'To inquire into the level of coal prices in Northern Ireland and to ascertain whether they give excessive profits to the trader; to inquire into the general efficiency of the coal trade in Northern Ireland; and to make such inquiries into the supply and cost of transport of coal as would enable the Committee to assess whether costs could be reduced.'

Interim Report. *Sgd. February 1962.*
Cmd. 447, 35 pp.

The National Coal Board gives priority
to the requirements of consumers nearest
to particular coalfields, and in consequence, most of Northern Ireland's
domestic coal comes from the more
distant coalfields and carries a high
transport charge. Most supplies come
from the most profitable coalfields, at a
pit price higher than the cost of production, so that the Northern Ireland
consumer has been helping to subsidize
the price of coal mined from the unec-
omic pits. There is little prospect of
obtaining cheaper coal from more convenient areas. No evidence was received
that the quality was below that of coal
supplied to mainland consumers.

Competition from fuel oil is a safeguard against excessive charges for non-
domestic coal.

The monopoly position of the National Coal Board and the prohibition on
importation of foreign coal place an
obligation on the board to ensure that
its system of pricing and distribution is
fair to Northern Ireland consumers.

Appendices give the National Coal
Board's methods of determining prices
and statistics relating to prices, tonnage,
and inland transport charges. Two maps
show the locations of coalfields, and
delivery-zone prices.

Written observations of the National
Coal Board discuss the price changes
made in May 1962 and justify the principles governing prices and zones.

Final Report. *Sgd. June 1963.*
Cmd. 460, 32 pp.

There is little scope for a reduction in
existing coal prices as far as the charges
for sea freight are concerned, or the
charges for distribution—with the reservation that prices charged for domestic
coal could be reduced where the trader
is obtaining substantial quantities of
cheaper coal through Blyth. There is a
reasonable case for a reduction in the
National Coal Board's charges for domestic coal supplied to Northern Ireland;

the committee find it difficult to follow
the board's concern that each consumer
should be charged the economic cost of
transport when the pit prices are unrel-
ated to the cost of production, and they
consider that the board's system of
zoning involves an element of 'postaliz-
ation' (uniform transport charge within
an area), which it rejects when applied to
Northern Ireland.

Reports by a firm of chartered accountants on a shipping company with
major coal interests, and on five coal
importing businesses show profits to be
not excessive, although there is no effective price competition between traders.
There should be a periodic investigation
into coal prices. Traders should be
required by law to declare to the buyer
the N.C.B. group number of the coal.
The introduction of a differential price
scheme would be disadvantageous to
those without finance or storage accommodation for summer stocking, and it
is not recommended.

Appendices include a list of those
submitting evidence, statistics on profits
and losses of collieries and on coal imports, and an extract from the report of
the Committee on Shipping Services to
Northern Ireland.

3 ELECTRICITY

Electricity Development: Scheme for
South-Eastern Area

Interim rep. by J.M. Kennedy, 1930.
Cmd. 122, 24 pp.

'. . . *to furnish a comprehensive report
on the following matters:-*
*(a) The present state of electricity deve-
lopment . . . and the further measures
necessary to ensure the provision of
supplies of electricity adequate to the
requirements of the industries and population of the Province generally, and more
particularly the steps to be taken forthwith
for the development of electricity supply
in the area to the west of Belfast comprising
the western portion of the County of Down
and northern portion of the County of
Armagh, and to the eastward of Belfast,*

*the northern portion of the County of
Down.
(b) The technical aspects of the policy
to be followed in the development of
existing areas of supply by the alternative
methods of extension of the local generating stations, or by the inter-linking of
existing load centres by a system of main
transmission lines.
(c) The districts which should be included
in any scheme or schemes of comprehensive
development, together with estimates of
the capital cost and the financial prospects
of such schemes.
(d) The line of development best calculated to secure a co-ordinated system of
electricity supply throughout the various
districts and the Province generally.'*

The consultant selected to prepare this
report had been closely connected with
the recently developed British electric
grid systems. For this area of Northern
Ireland, Mr. Kennedy outlines a scheme
of supply by means of transmission lines
based upon bulk supplies from Belfast,
which he is convinced will be a sound one,
both technically and economically, for
what he sees as the most promising area
for comprehensive electrical development. His estimates show that, if the
scheme is effected by a single non-profit-
making authority, electricity can be made
available at a lower cost than would be
possible under the individual development of separate generating stations.
Attention is drawn to the new sections of
transmission line that are most urgently
required. A special reference is made to
the situation at Lurgan, where the undertaking urgently needs extra generating
plant, and some comments are made
regarding areas not dealt with specifically
in the report—Antrim, the north-west
of the province and the Enniskillen district.

Schedules set out at the conclusion of
the report show a list of towns and
villages to be connected with the suggested transmission system, together with
estimates of their probable electricity
demand over the next decade. The likely

capital costs and annual recurrent expenditure for this period is set out in
some detail, while a map shows the
existing transmission lines within the
area and those now proposed by the
consultant.

In a foreword to the report, the
minister of commerce indicates that it is
the government's intention to adopt
these proposals for the future electrical
development of the defined area, with
their basic aim of a transmission system
of 33,000-volt lines based on Belfast, and
capital expenditure (including transfor-
mer stations) of an estimated £245,000.

Electricity Development: Scheme for Western Area

*Supplementary rep. by J.M. Kennedy,
1930.
Cmd. 123, 16 pp., map.
(Terms of reference are as for the previous
report.)*

The defined area, of approximately 1,400
square miles, is divided into eight districts. Each of these is to be supplied
from a 33,000-volt transmission line
drawing supplies from Londonderry and
from the system of County Down and/or
Antrim. Capital expenditure for a decade
is estimated at £1,013,000. The Strabane
region is the district most suitable for
initial development, for it is the largest
town in the whole western area without
any supply and could supply electricity
to nearby areas in the Irish Republic. The
other districts identified in the report are
based on Omagh, Enniskillen, Londonderry, Limavady, Draperstown, Cookstown and Clogher.

Appendices show estimated capital
and annual expenditure in some detail.
The large map shows the geographical
districts with their population density
and indicates proposed 33,000-volt and
11,000-volt transmission lines. The report
also makes some supplementary proposals and costings relating to the electricity scheme for the south-eastern area.

Electricity Development

(Ministry of Commerce), 1947.
Cmd. 250, 11 pp.

There are three generating authorities, the Ministry of Commerce, Belfast Corporation and Londonderry Corporation. Electricity is distributed by the Electricity Board, except in Belfast and Londonderry, and although the stations are interconnected by the Electricity Board transmission network, there is no formal co-operation and no central organization. It is proposed to transfer government generating stations to the Electricity Board. Co-ordination of generation will be entrusted to a joint electricity committee consisting of a chairman appointed by the Ministry of Commerce, the city electrical engineer of Belfast Corporation and the chief engineer of the Electricity Board. Whether or not Londonderry joins the scheme is a matter of only local concern, as it represents a very small proportion of the total load. The joint committee would direct the operation of the generating stations; form development schemes; pool all current generated and sell energy to the distributing authorities; arrange for purchase, sale or exchange of energy supplies with the Éire Electricity Supply Board (which due to the method of generation, has periods of under- and overloading the reverse of those in Northern Ireland); and determine what proportion of the annual cost of main transmission lines should be included in the joint cost of production. Ultimate responsibility would rest with a minister advised by three eminent electrical engineers. The guarantee system whereby rural consumers cover much of the cost of installation within five years is to be abandoned. Shortage of equipment will restrict rural expansion for some years, but it is hoped that later development will not be curtailed by the need to balance accounts, as it will increasingly involve long distances between consumers and high-tension lines, and hence increased costs.

Tables give details of undertakings acquired by the Electricity Board, and of new undertakings, and statistics showing progress during 1932–1944.

Electricity Supply

(Ministry of Commerce), 1956.
Cmd. 355, 26 pp.

The report attempts to provide details of the need for the further development of electricity supplies in view of increasing demands, and of the matters which affect development. Some indication of plans to meet immediate needs is given, together with a forecast of the scope for future developments. The paper is divided into three parts which deal respectively with past and present development (that is, development before and after the 1948 Act) and the progress of rural electrification; present problems, including sources of power, the use of atomic power and hydro-electric schemes; and programmes for action. Two programmes are outlined. One is a limited one designed to meet the real needs of the years 1960–1962; the other involves later and fuller development and assumes the establishment of a new major atomic station with large generators which could be expanded. A further large power station would be needed by the early 1970s. Some estimate of the financial implications is made.

Statistical tables in appendices show the maximum system demands and generating capacity under past and present developments and immediate future plans. Further estimated demands in relation to the availability of plant plus additions in hand are also shown. A further appendix gives explanations of technical terms used in connection with electricity supply.

Administration of the Electricity Supply Service

Ministry of Commerce. Rep. by Sir Josiah Eccles, 1963. Rep. sgd. June 1963.
8 pp.

The Electricity Board for Northern Ireland and the corporations of Belfast and Londonderry own and operate the electricity supply service, but statistics show that the board is becoming the dominant supplier. A common practice and operational policy is an economic necessity, and it is proposed that the board acquire the assets and rights of the two municipal authorities and become the sole generating authority. Staff can be transferred to the board from the city undertakings. The role of the Joint Electricity Committee, set up in 1948 to co-ordinate the industry, is considered, and it is recommended that this committee now be dissolved.

A Ten Year Programme for Electricity Supply

Ministry of Commerce, 1965.
Cmd. 478, 16 pp.

The paper reviews a decade of future electricity needs in terms of new plant, generating capacity and co-ordination of supply and transmission arrangements. The principal sections cover the growth of the industry, the proposed generation programme, choice of plant to meet this programme, details of the new fossil-fuelled power station which is to be sited at Ballylumford, and facts concerning transmission and system control. Frequent references are made to the advice given by Sir Josiah Eccles in his 1963 report on 'The Administration of the Electricity Supply Service' (see above). It is proposed to improve co-ordination by forming a new body to replace the Joint Electricity Committee. However, legal ownership of and responsibility for power stations is to remain with the three electricity undertakings existing at present.

Numerous statistical tables are scattered throughout this report, and these deal chiefly with plant capacity and anticipated demand.

Electricity in Ireland

Ministry of Commerce. Rep. of Jt. Cttee.
on Co-operation in Electricity Supply,

March 1966. Cttee. apptd. March 1965;
rep. sgd. March 1966.
28 pp.

Sir Josiah Eccles (Ch.) and four members —A. Harkin and R. McDowell, (representing the Republic of Ireland), C.M. Stoupe and R.P. Watson, (representing Northern Ireland). (R.P. Watson retired in December 1965 and was replaced by E.N. Cunliffe.)

'To investigate the scope for agreement in cross-border co-operation between the electricity supply systems, to advise on the economic and technical problems involved and to estimate broadly the savings in cost which might be achieved.'

There is an interconnected electricity supply system in the Republic of Ireland, provided and operated by one undertaking, the Electricity Supply Board. There is an interconnected supply system in Northern Ireland, where distribution is effected by three undertakings. The establishment of a substantial connection between the two supply systems is technically practicable and economically desirable since there may be a difference in peak demand in the two systems, reserve generating capacities can be pooled, and the most economical generators can be run at maximum output regardless of ownership. A connection between Tandragee and Maynooth would be most suitable, with the necessary transformers, isolating switches, etc., located at Dundalk. Subsidiary connections between the two systems could also be made, perhaps at Strabane-Letterkenny and Ballyshannon-Enniskillen. (The systems should not be connected at voltages below 110kv.)

If the systems are to be connected, there should be established a permanent liaison panel of the top managements to handle all matters of planning, administration and the principles of co-ordination; and a joint operating panel of senior technical staff to provide cost data and operating instructions to the control engineers of both systems, and to co-ordinate maintenance programmes. And there should be a control and communications system to enable co-ordinated operation to be effectively carried out.

Graphs show the annual indicated maximum demand in both systems, and typical load curves for a day in winter. The appendix gives typical principles of planning and operation of interconnected electricity supply systems.

Electricity Supply

Ministry of Commerce. Rep. on an inquiry into the characteristics of the system in Northern Ireland, 1971.
iv, 20 pp., map.
Rep. sgd. March 1971.

'To enquire into the characteristics of the electricity supply system to determine if a more flexible system would give greater security of supply'.

This investigation was carried out by three experts from England, N.F. Marsh and D.V. Ford of the Electricity Council plus G.T. Shepherd of the London Electricity Board. It arose because of serious cuts in supplies during the previous December, resulting from a 'work to rule' and overtime ban, but the inquiry is concerned not only with these cuts, for it explores various situations where generating plant might be idle.

It is decided that there is adequate generating plant for the needs of the province and that additional plant would probably not have eased matters at the end of 1970. The disconnection of load was handled competently then, although it is possible that a more supple and useful Electricity (Industrial Purposes-Restriction) Order could be devised. Extra transformers planned at Ballylumford and Coolkeeragh are needed, as is the new control room that is already under construction. The planning of generating equipment to meet the anticipated load position throughout the decade is discussed. The transmission link with the Republic is viewed as having great utility, and a link with Scotland, although expensive, would add to the security of the Northern Ireland system. A single unified electricity authority would facil-

itate control and communication and would be a boon in other ways.

The map shows power stations and the main transmission system. An appendix gives the names of C.B.I. and trade union representatives met by the investigators.

4 WATER

Water Supplies for North Down

Ministry of Home Affairs. Rep. of Cttee., [1938].
Cmd. 194, 16 pp.
Cttee. apptd. October 1937; rep. sgd. June 1938.

W. Malcolm (Ch.) and eleven members —S.W. Allworthy, J.A. Cleland, H. Diamond, J. Hill Dickson, R. Edgar, S.C.B. Erskine, T.S. Graham, C.F. Milligan, Sir Roland T. Nugent, J.M. Small, F. Storey.

'To consider methods of providing an improved supply of water for the Borough of Bangor, the Urban Districts of Holywood and Newtownards, and places in the Castlereagh and Newtownards Rural Districts, with special reference to the possibility of obtaining a supply from the Belfast and District Water Commissioners; to inquire into the cost of providing such improved supply and the proportions of the expenditure to be borne by the respective local authorities concerned, and to make recommendations.'

Three schemes formulated by the engineers of the north Down councils were considered, and the report favours that termed the Bow Lough scheme which involves an estimated capital outlay of a little over £150,000. The suggested apportionment of the cost is set out, and it is recommended that representatives of the authorities concerned set up a joint board to establish and administer the scheme.

A reservation signed by C.F. Milligan believes that the proportion of the costs allocated to Bangor is too high. The three alternative systems are outlined in appendices.

Problems of Water Supply and Sewerage

Planning Advisory Bd. Rep. of Water and Sewerage Cttee., 1944 (reprinted 1945). Cmd. 223, 11 pp.
Rep. sgd. August 1943.

W.F. Neill (Ch.) and nine members—J. Blane, W.M. Cronin, R.D. Duncan, R. Ferguson, J.A. Higgins, S.H.W. Middleton, J. Shuttleworth, S.B. Thompson, Prof. W.J. Wilson.

'To consider and report on the problems of water supply and sewerage and the adequate provision of these facilities in urban and rural areas throughout the Province.'

Government grants are necessary to bring about the needed improvements in water and sewerage facilities. As it is impossible to achieve this economically with a multiplicity of small authorities, the achievement of co-ordinated development through regional water and sewerage authorities with a central co-ordinating committee is urgently recommended. The proposed duties of the co-ordinating committee and of the regional authorities are set out, with particular reference to the position of the Belfast Water Commissioners in the recommended system. A map of the province, showing the suggested regional boundaries, is provided.

5 PEAT UTILIZATION

Peat Bog Survey

Council of Scientific Research and Development. Fuel and Power Cttee. Final rep. of the preliminary survey of peat bogs, 1956.
171 pp., maps.

Prof. A.H. Naylor (Ch.) and seven members—D.H. Alexander, H.R. Ayton, T.G. Christie, G.T.P. Hill, Prof. K.S. Isles, J.H. Jones, Rt. Hon. Sir R. Nugent.

'To examine the principal bogs of Northern Ireland and to locate those, which so far as preliminary examination would show, were suitable for development as sources of fuel and raw material.'

This preliminary survey shows that, although there is a considerable area of peat in Northern Ireland, there are no large areas of relatively level bog such as may be seen further south, and hill bog is predominant. The survey covers thirty areas of not less than 200 acres each, and the field reports show details of depth and quality of the peat. Peat deposits can be divided into two types: blanket and basin. The former is a relatively thin layer usually found on high moorland in areas of high rainfall or high relative humidity. Peat deposits lie mainly in the counties of Antrim, Londonderry, Tyrone and Fermanagh. Those deposits found in Down and Armagh are usually very small, occupying local depressions and especially inter-drumlin basins.

The major peat resources are the Altahullion, Garry, Black, Rasharkin, Gortfinbar and Fivemiletown bogs, which would in total yield around 7 million tons. The Garry Bog probably contains the greatest amount of peat. The remaining five bogs are mainly blanket bogs suitable for development using the conventional machine methods of peat production, but they can be divided into two groups. Firstly, the Black Bog, in the eastern part of Tyrone, and the Rasharkin Bog, in the western part of Antrim, differ from the surrounding peats in structure, moisture content, degree of composition, and plant types, and apart from the difficulties encountered in bog preparation, and winning and harvesting the peat, there would be changes in the quality and usefulness of the product. The second group, Altahullion in northern Londonderry, Gortfinbar in Tyrone and Fivemiletown on the borders of Tyrone and Fermanagh, are typically blanket bogs, and these present problems peculiar to their respective topographic situations, i.e., problems such as severe gradients, unfavourable climatic conditions prevailing at high altitudes, and drainage. Indiscriminate cutting of some of the bogs presents difficulties for the subsequent mechanical harvesting of peat in these areas. Basin type bogs in general do not offer many possibilities of development for the mechanical winning of peat except for the basin bogs of Armoy, the clusters of the Grove and Fairywater, Moneygal and Sluggan Moss.

Hill bogs, although readily drained, are in many cases shallow and heavily contained and therefore present difficult problems when conventional methods of mechanical winning are considered.

The appendices at the end of the report cover the thirty field reports of the preliminary survey, with a map for each area; the botanists report on the surface vegetation, calorific and ash content of composite peat samples; wax content of peat samples, 1952 and 1953; and the survey and sampling procedures.

VII TRANSPORT

1 General
2 Railways

3 Road Transport
4 Shipping and Harbours

1 GENERAL

Transport Conditions

Rep. by Sir Felix J.C. Pole, 1934.
Cmd. 160, 54 pp.
Rep. sgd. June 1934.

'The problem of transport . . . has been giving . . . considerable concern, and the co-ordination of road and rail transport here is now a matter of urgency . . . it is of great importance that we should be able to formulate a policy which will be fair to the interests concerned and at the same time will ensure an efficient system.'

A detailed survey was made of road and rail transport, and evidence and proposals collected from various transport organizations and from chambers of commerce. There is 'an unanswerable case for co-ordination of road and rail services'. The idea of proposing the establishment of a Northern Ireland transport board to achieve such co-ordination is considered. It is rejected because six of the railways concerned operate partly on the Irish Free State and some have their headquarters there. Alternatives are leaving transport in the hands of existing operators with a new supervisory body to achieve regulation and control, or the constitution of a Northern Ireland road transport board which would take over passenger and goods road motor services and work in liaison with the railway companies. This latter alternative is preferred; the board should be a small body, whose chairman should be experienced in transport work, and members should include nominees of the railway companies, the Belfast Omnibus Company, H.M.S. Catherwood Ltd., and Belfast Corporation. A proposal by the railway companies that road transport should be more heavily taxed and that railway companies should become the sole providers of public transport in their respective areas is emphatically rejected. It is thought that the road transport board and the railway companies should, as an incentive to the avoidance of wasteful competition, pool their receipts in Northern Ireland.

Other recommendations include the suggestion that transport be administered in future, not by the Ministry of Commerce and the Ministry of Home Affairs, but by a single government department; that a transport appeal tribunal should be established to hear complaints about fares, services and transport conditions; that certain extra powers and privileges should be granted to the railway companies; and that a system of regulation and licensing should be enforced for road transport. Finally, there is a simple diagrammatical representation of the new organizational structure envisaged. An appendix gives a draft outline of the proposed traffic-receipts pool, and in other appendices and in the text of the report there are statistics concerning the number of motor vehicles in Northern Ireland, 1921–1933; the volume of railway traffic over an approximately equivalent period; railway receipts; the cost of road maintenance and improvement; income from motor taxation; road and railway mileage; and the number of licensed buses in use. There are also some detailed statistics relating to the individual railway companies.

Public Transport

Reps. of Commissioner holding the Public Inquiry and of the Cttee. of Inquiry, 1938. Cmd. 198, 127 pp. (in toto).

The Public Inquiry. Report by Commissioner H.M. Thompson.
Apptd. April 1938; rep. sgd. June 1938. 33 pp.

'To consider representations from the public or other interests desirous of being heard in regard to existing transport facilities and charges.'

The background leading to the 1935 Act, designed to place the operation of all public services under the control of one body, the Northern Ireland Road Transport Board, is discussed. With a view to encouraging co-operation between road and rail transport, the Act provided for the pooling of the net receipts of the board and the railway companies. The board experienced difficulties with both passenger and freight services but most particularly in regard to the latter. The criticisms levied against each other by the railways and the board are considered. It is alleged, for example, that the railway companies have failed to close many uneconomic branch lines, while the charge is made against the board that it acquired the freight undertakings in a manner which led to disorder and dislocation. The railway companies also asserted that they had been kept in ignorance of the financial losses incurred by the board.

Judge Thompson sees the unhappy partnership which arose from the Act as stemming from a basic divergence of both views and methods. Although there have been some instances of co-operation and co-ordination, there is little mutual confidence; and each side seems jealous of the other's contributions to or drawings from the receipts pool. The system of management under a joint committee with an appeals tribunal in the background for the settlement of matters in dispute has not, alas, succeeded, and the task ahead is to devise a better plan. The railway companies pointed out that, despite the recommendation of Sir Felix Pole (see Cmd. 160 above), no member of the board had previous experience of transport work; the government, however, believed that the transport industry needed the direction of men whose experience did not restrict them to a departmental view of the problems involved.

An appendix lists organizations and individuals giving oral or written evidence to the commissioner. His report expresses regret that the railway companies did not give evidence.

The Committee of Inquiry. *Cttee. apptd. February 1938; rep. sgd. November 1938. 94 pp.*

Sir William McLintock (Ch.) and two members—Sir Herbert A. Walker and J.S. Nicholl.

'To investigate and report on the working of the Road and Railway Transport Act (N.I.), 1935, and to advise what improvements . . . are necessary in order to secure on a sound economic basis an adequate and efficient transport system.'

The Act has lamentably failed to secure an effective and co-ordinated pattern of transport, and bold action is urgently needed. To enable public road transport to compete adequately with privately owned vehicles, the requirements of the Act concerning wages and employees' conditions should be extended to embrace private road undertakings also, and a comprehensive scheme of licensing for goods vehicles other than those operated by the board must be introduced. Concessions given to farmers are being abused and need to be exercised with more discrimination. Legislation should provide heavy minimum penalties for the illegal operation of vehicles.

Co-ordination of road and rail services is best achieved by bringing the commercial side of road and rail transport under unified management. However, as the Great Northern Railway operates partly in Éire, such a plan must necessarily be modified. A new body should be formed uniting the road services with those railways operating solely in Northern Ireland, and the new organization should enter into a pooling arrangement with the Great Northern Railway. Details are given concerning the valuation of the enterprises and the composition of the stock and capital of the proposed new body. The Northern Ireland Road Transport Board and the Belfast and County Down Railway Company would cease to exist, the stocks of the new concern being held by the Northern Ireland Government; the London, Midland and Scottish Railway Company; persons holding stock in the two concerns passing out of existence; and the Great Northern Railway Company. The new body should have a small board of six or eight appropriately elected members and, when it achieves a sound revenue earning position, Belfast Corporation should transfer their transport undertaking to it. Londonderry Corporation should no longer share in the profits from public transport, and the pooling scheme devised in the 1935 Act should be regarded as inoperative from its inception, for it has never been successful.

Numerous statistical appendices give the number and kinds of motor vehicles in Northern Ireland, 1921–1937; the volume of traffic and traffic receipts on the individual railways over approximately the same period of time; details of road expenditure and maintenance in 1913 and over the period 1927–1937; and details of traffic on the roads in 1936 and 1937. Some of the statistics of railway traffic utilize index numbers with 1924 as the base year.

Public Transport

(Ministry of Commerce), 1946.
Cmd. 232, 8 pp.

The development of road transport has broken the monopoly of the railways, and rail services which are beneficial to community development may no longer be economic to operate. The problem has been obscured by increased demands on all forms of transport during the war years, but with the return to normal conditions a solution must be found. This paper considers a number of alternative courses and concludes that the only efficient and solvent system requires the merger of the Road Transport Board, the Belfast and County Down Railway, the system of the Northern Counties Committee of the London, Midland and Scottish Railway, and the system of the Great Northern Railway (Ireland) in Northern Ireland. Existing rights of Belfast Corporation, of farmers, of Belfast and Londonderry carriers, of special trades (furniture removal, burials and others), and of private owners carrying their own goods shall not be affected. A tribunal shall be set up to hear appeals concerning rates, charges and services.

Transport Tribunal

Rep., 1952.
Cmd. 310, 76 pp., maps.
Tribunal commenced Public Inquiry March 1952; rep. sgd. November 1952.

The Rt. Hon. Sir Anthony B. Babington (Ch.) and two members—R.G. Manson and M.P. Sinclair. (M.P. Sinclair died, July 1952.)

'To inquire into the operation of the Transport Act (N.I.), 1948, and the manner in which the Ulster Transport Authority have carried out their duties under the Act and such other matters relating to transport in Northern Ireland (including transport services to and from

Northern Ireland) as might appear . . . to be relevant.'

A brief history of Northern Ireland's transport services is given, together with summaries of previous reports—Sir Felix Pole's report (Cmd. 160, above), reports of Judge Thompson and Sir William McLintock's committee (Cmd. 198, above), the joint select committee's report (H.C. 472, below), the white paper of 1946 (Cmd. 232, above).

The tribunal concludes that the Ulster Transport Authority has performed its duties satisfactorily, that financial difficulties arise from increases in wages, taxation and general costs, and that it is not yet possible to tell whether the economies made by the authority will enable it to be self-supporting. It should be assisted over this difficult period by the government liquidating the losses up to date and assuming liability for deficits for a stated period. Main railway lines should be retained until it is quite clear that they cannot be profitable; if diesel trains are found satisfactory after trial, they should replace steam. The development of the Belfast Central Line should be taken up. Wider public service vehicles are advocated, and the introduction of one-day licences for buses. The authority should set up a public relations department and a consultative committee which would represent public opinion to the authority. The tribunal should sit annually to hear reports from the authority and representations from the public. The hotels should be retained, at least initially, and the authority should be empowered to build up a reserve fund if and when possible. Cross-channel sailing tickets should be dispensed with as soon as possible.

Appendices give statistics over a number of years for receipts, expenditure and traffic on the railways, road freight and road passenger services; details of the organization of the U.T.A.; and lists of witnesses examined. The maps show organizational areas and routes over the whole province, and details of the Belfast Central Railway.

2 RAILWAYS

Railways

Ministry of Labour. Rep. of the Railway Com. in Northern Ireland, 1922.
Cmd. 10, 84 pp., map
Com. apptd. May 1922; rep. sgd. November 1922.

Rt. Hon. Mr. Justice T.W. Brown (Ch.) and six members—G.M. Donaldson, H. L. Garrett, W. Grant, W. Jackson, S. Kyle and Major D.G. Shillington.

'To advise . . . as to what changes, if any, are desirable in the administration of the railway undertakings . . . and in particular to report on:-
(a) The financial position and earning powers of the several railway undertakings, including those in receipt of baronial guarantees.
(b) The best means of consolidating or otherwise working the different railways in the future and of providing the rolling stock and other equipment used. . . .
(c) The remuneration and conditions of employment of the salaried and wages staff and arrangements for the future settlement of questions relating to such matters.
(d) Any other matters affecting the working and administration of the railways upon which . . . it is expedient to report in the interests of the proprietors of the railway companies, the employees and the public.'

Majority Report (signed by T.W. Brown and four members).

The history of the railway system is outlined, and the four points identified in the terms of reference are then considered in turn. With regard to the consolidation and future working of the railways, nationalization, unification and amalgamation are all considered, but, after reviewing the position in many overseas countries and the existence of competition from other forms of transport, it is asserted that the best solution lies in the continuance of the present system of private management. The Clogher Valley Railway should be absorbed by the Great Northern, and the

Midland Railway should take over the Ballycastle Railway, in the interests of efficiency. Railway companies should consider how far the common use of plant and rolling stock could be profitably extended. Conciliation machinery should be established to deal with questions relating to salaries, wages and conditions of service, and this machinery should immediately investigate the possibility of paying the same wage rates as are applied in Great Britain. It is proposed that a railway rates tribunal be established also.

Appendices include a list of witnesses and those providing written evidence, and there is a folding map illustrating the railway system as it existed in 1922. Statistical tables in the report give a detailed analysis of railway receipts and traffic volume; a comparison of railway wage rates in Great Britain and Ireland; and particulars of hours and service conditions on Northern Ireland railways. A further appendix provides figures on the financial position of each of the privately owned railways for 1913 and 1921 with estimates for 1922.

Minority Report (signed by G.M. Donaldson and S. Kyle).

It is claimed that, as there are eight separate railway undertakings in the province and five other railways part of whose line runs through Northern Ireland, the acceptance of the principle of public ownership can best achieve cohesion. It is regretted that there has not been a joint commission for Northern and Southern Ireland and that the recommendations of the commission in the South are not yet known. If it favours nationalization, a joint commission of nine persons should be established and an arbitration tribunal of four members appointed. The tribunal should decide upon the terms of state purchase of the Irish railways, while the joint commission will have ultimate responsibility for wages and service conditions and should receive advice from a national railway council that is representative of all grades of workers. Wages ought to be stabilized at existing levels pending nationalization, and if the Irish Free State does not agree to nationalization and the joint working of all Irish railways, a minister of transport should be appointed to co-ordinate the achievement of public ownership in the North.

Clogher Valley Railway

Ministry of Commerce. Rep. of Cttee. of Investigation, 1927.
38 pp., chart.
Rep. sgd. November 1927.

W. Abbott (Ch.) and two members—A. H. Coote and H. Kirkpatrick.

'To enquire into the affairs of the Clogher Valley Railway Company Limited, and the administration and working of the undertaking; to report whether, and under what terms and conditions, the railway should continue working, or, in the alternative, what arrangements should be made to close down the railway and to liquidate the Baronial Guarantee; and also to ascertain if and what alternative transport facilities would then be required in the districts concerned.'

The railway company dates back to 1883 but has never earned a dividend, and in most years working expenses have exceeded revenue. Deficiencies have been met by ratepayers and government funds, but, in view of the poor management record and the competition of road services for both passengers and freight, the future of the service is in doubt. Public meetings were held at Aughnacloy, Fivemiletown and Brookeborough to enable ratepayers to express their annoyance in respect of their liability for the railway and to enable the company directors' case to be heard. A report by a specialist from Scotland, R. Killin, is provided, but the committee of investigation believes that it would be unwise to undertake the capital expenditure which he states is necessary for the continuation of the passenger service. The committee therefore propose that the company should be taken over by county councils and the railway operated purely as a goods service, that staff be reduced and capital equipment reviewed, and that the bus service operated by the Belfast Omnibus Company should be subjected to competition if it abuses the result of the closing down of the railway passenger service. A renewals fund is to be set up to spread the cost of heavy repairs and renewals over a period of years.

The report by R. Killin is provided as an appendix, and other appendices give statistics of traffic returns on the railway and the amounts of money contributed by ratepayers and the government. Mr. Killin's report has appendices of its own, and these give details of staff, stations, track, rolling stock and the proposed new freight service.

Road and Rail Transport

Rep. of Jt. Sel. Cttee. together with proc. and apps.
H.C. 472, 155 pp.
(The report is also published with mins. of ev. as a 'blue book' of 1,062 pp.) Cttee. apptd. December 1938; rep. o.p. June 1939.

J.C. MacDermott (Ch.) and twenty-three members—J. Beattie, Maj. J.C. Boyle, R. Byrne, T.J. Campbell, G.A. Clark, Rev. Prof. R. Corkey, J. Cunningham, Sir J. Davison, Maj. A.F. Dobbs, R. Elliott, Sir E. Herdman, J. Johnston, J. G. Leslie, J. Maguire, T. McLaughlin, H. Minford, Rev. R. Moore, J. Nixon, Sir R. Nugent, Capt. J.R. Perceval-Maxwell, Major H.C. Robinson, H. Taylor and the Mayor of Londonderry (Sir James Wilton).

'To consider the Reports of His Honour Herbert M. Thompson . . . and of the Committee presided over by Sir William McLintock . . . in regard to public transport . . . and to report whether any, and if so what, modifications in the recommendations thereof are deemed to be necessary or to suggest an alternative scheme which will place transport . . . on a sound and economic basis.'

This report is particularly concerned with an appraisal of the findings of Sir William McLintock's committee (Cmd. 198 above), with a view to establishing whether these or variant conclusions ought to be implemented. Geographic and economic features are seen as profoundly affecting the issue of transport co-ordination in Northern Ireland, and a primary problem is that of competition between public and private transport. There is a brief review of the present situation in regard to the individual railways, with appropriate statistics, and a discussion of the poor degree of road/rail co-ordination achieved to date.

The McLintock committee had maintained that both the public rail service and the public road service should be continued and that the former should be assisted at the expense of the latter. These proposals are reviewed in the light of grave current transport problems. Part of the railway service could, it seems, be abolished, but not all; the public road freight service certainly merits retention. The interpretation of the way in which road transport should support the railways calls for review. The proposals of the McLintock Committee are then viewed in two distinct categories—basic recommendations, which concern the promotion of co-ordination and the protection of public transport, and what the present committee describes as subsidiary recommendations. The achievement of co-ordination is approved, but proposals different from those favoured by the McLintock Committee are put forward to achieve it, as it is considered that the earlier suggestions would mean attempting too much too soon. The counter-proposals involve the appointment of a transport adviser to work with the responsible minister in the government and the suggestion that a consultative committee should be set up. Other recommendations in this area include the proposal that the pooling scheme and standing joint committee established under the Act have failed and should thus be abolished; the suggestion that surplus and redundant road and railway stock and other assets should be sold—even if a loss is involved; and the recommendation that a remission of road freight services be made to local hauliers in certain rural areas.

The matter of the protection of public transport involves a discussion of wages and conditions of service, illegal and unfair competition, the proposed licensing system, and the rights of individual trades. There is agreement with the McLintock Report in many matters relating to this area and certainly with its general principles. However, some additional recommendations are made relating to wage rates for certain classes of private goods transport, a less cumbersome licensing system than that advocated by the McLintock Report, limitations to be imposed on the drawing of trailers and the dimensions of goods vehicles, and penalties for unlawful competition. The remaining recommendations of the McLintock Committee are also commented on and slightly enlarged by the present report. These are viewed as relatively minor, since they do not so directly affect the future of public transport. They concern the stockholders of the Road Transport Board, the position of the corporations of Belfast and Londonderry, the Clogher Valley Railway, the local carriers of Belfast and Londonderry, and a future firm endorsement of the McLintock Report's condemnation of the pooling scheme drawn up under the 1935 Act. A plea is made for a more positive and decisive government policy on transport. Not all the new recommendations could be speedily implemented, but it is urged that the measures suggested for the protection of public transport are urgent, as is the appointment of a transport adviser.

Most of the appendices give further statistical information. They include figures on the volume of railway traffic and traffic receipts, 1913 and 1922–1938; financial results of railway companies, 1937 and 1938; some recent comparative figures of Road Transport Board receipts and costs; statistics of local carriers in Londonderry and Belfast; and statistics

of local hackney cars believed to be competing with the omnibus services of the Road Transport Board. There is also a memorandum on the Clogher Valley Railway, particulars of recent issues of Northern Ireland transport stock and a relevant transport regulation quoted from the *South Australian Government Gazette*.

Great Northern Railway Board: Termination of Certain Services

Ministry of Commerce. Rep. of Inquiry dated 11 September 1956, 1956. 71 pp.

Inquiry held jointly by Rt. Hon. Sir Anthony B. Babington, chairman of the Transport Tribunal for Northern Ireland, and Dr. J.P. Beddy, chairman of the Transport Tribunal, Dublin.

'*To consider a proposal for the termination of the common services . . . over certain of the common service railway lines . . . , to hold a Public Inquiry thereon and to report . . .*'

The sections of railway line to which the proposal refers are: Omagh-Enniskillen-Newtownbutler; Portadown-Armagh-Tynan; Bundoran Junction-Belleek; and the sections of line between the last mentioned stations in each case, and the border.

The two chairmen failed to agree, and their reports are given separately. Both reports discuss the statutory position and the responsibilities of the Great Northern Railway Board (established 1953), and in addition to considering the evidence given to the inquiry, both reports refer at some length to two earlier reports.

A joint investigation committee, composed of one representative of the Great Northern Railway and three of the Ulster Transport Authority, opened its inquiry in April 1953 and submitted its report in June 1954. The report was not published. The committee recommended various economies, the closure of certain rail services (including those listed above), and the adoption of diesel traction on the remaining rail systems, and it considered that this would reduce the level of losses or even eliminate it.

However, before the joint investigation committee had submitted its report, the Great Northern Railway Board set up a committee, in September 1953, to investigate the working of the railways as a separate organization, and in March 1954 this committee was told to confine its investigations to branch lines and the elimination of small stations, because 'it has now been decided *as a matter of policy* that there will be no abandonment of main and secondary lines'. The findings of the joint committee were therefore overruled by the board before they were presented, and the two reports are in direct conflict with regard to secondary lines. The board's committee reported in September 1954, recommending complete conversion to diesel power, the closure of certain branch lines (not including the three above), and closure of some small stations and halts.

Evidence to the inquiry from the general manager of The Great Northern Railway Board gave the board's considered opinion that no main or secondary line should be closed without a fair trial being made of its proposals for the complete modernization of the undertaking and its operation by diesel traction. Rather than examining small sections of railway line in isolation, it would be fairer and more reasonable to consider the matter on the basis of closing the system as a whole. An officer of the Ulster Transport Authority gave evidence about the capability of his authority to deal with increased road traffic following any closure. Other bodies and individuals, listed in the appendix, also submitted evidence about the legal position, and the effect of closures on trade, tourism, pilgrimage and unemployment.

Sir Anthony Babington concludes that it is impossible to see where any substantial accretion of traffic is to come from in any areas other than those in the environs of Londonderry, Belfast or Dublin, or from an increase in traffic between these centres of population. The termination of the three services is therefore a necessary step, and he recommends their discontinuation unless the Northern Ireland Government is prepared to assume responsibility for the deficits which the board may show even after modernization.

Dr. Beddy advises against termination of the services. He doubts the legality of the proposal and considers that the information available is not sufficient to judge the ultimate effects, and that the proposal should not be considered in isolation but by reference to the settled policies of the governments of Northern Ireland and the Republic of Ireland in regard to the provision of public transport as a whole.

Railways

Ministry of Home Affairs. Rep. by H. Benson, 1963 (reprinted 1964).
Cmd. 458, 99 pp., maps.
Investigator apptd. February 1962; rep. published July 1963.

'To investigate the position of the railways . . . , to make recommendations about their future, and to report on the effect which the recommendations would have on the transport system of the Ulster Transport Authority as a whole.'

The initial chapters consider the past, present and future of the railway services. Reference is made to the existing transport legislation, to the financial position of the railways, to administrative economies and methods of modernization, and to the problems of attracting more passengers and more freight to rail transport. It is thought that the 1958 Transport Act, which recognized that unprofitable railway lines should be closed, was a step forward, but that the notion that the authority should be self-supporting by September 1966 is unrealistic. Present services are mediocre and costly. Both freight and passenger traffic have shown a downward trend for some time, and increases in charges or fares would be unlikely to yield extra revenue.

Railways are then considered in relation to roads, with the aim of establishing the respective roles of rail and road transport and assessing the effect of railway closures on the roads. Although there is heavy traffic congestion in Belfast and certain other towns, the road system is good, and it should be able to carry extra traffic arising from any rail closures recommended. The questions of passenger traffic and freight are dealt with next as distinct issues. With regard to the former, it is considered that in view of a survey of population development, journey times, and other factors, commuter rail lines should remain open. Other passenger lines, however, are pronounced uneconomic, and their closure is recommended. A review of freight charges and road transport alternatives leads to the conclusion that the rail freight service can be discontinued entirely.

Proposals for a new service include details of the closure programme; the question of border service; redundancy payments—estimated at some £550,000 for the 1,100 workers displaced; effects of the new service on the railway revenue; and the capital costs of changing to the new service. Net capital expenditure for the reorganization is estimated at £1,075,000, but the changes proposed would greatly reduce the railways' annual deficit, and the services cannot be continued indefinitely at a loss. If these proposals are ignored, the alternatives are to close the railways altogether or to continue with existing uneconomic policy. It is emphasized that the aim is to reshape the service so as to offer only fast and comfortable passenger commuter services, and this could be achieved in approximately four years. Although no freight would be carried, there would be provision for mail and for passengers' parcels, and the Portadown to Dundalk line, although not strictly a commuter service, should be retained. Services would be provided for Belfast–Larneharbour, Belfast–Portadown–the Border, Belfast–Bangor; all other lines would close. It is also proposed that special attention be given to the co-ordination of road and rail services; that the link-line between Belfast's Great Victoria Street and Queen's Quay stations be retained and improved; that stations should have good car-parking facilities; and that, as the sites of the Belfast stations are too large, part of them could be developed for commercial purposes. The changes mean a distinct reduction in the manpower employed, but when appropriate decisions have been made, every effort should be taken to re-establish morale and promote recruitment of suitable personnel. It is recommended too that the constitution of the Ulster Transport Authority be changed to allow for the appointment of more full-time members to its board.

There are some thirty appendices, most of which provide statistics. The first gives a list of organizations and individuals supplying written or oral evidence. Maps indicate the extent of the Northern Ireland rail services in 1914 and 1962; road improvements schemes planned for the next decade; and the recommended new service with Belfast's terminals and link-line. Other information provided in appendices includes a schedule of railway closures since 1914 and tables of statistics on engine miles per annum in recent years; volume of freight (merchandise and livestock) carried by rail in the last decade; and number of passenger journeys and miles of rail open in the ten years ended September 1962. There are also various tables showing recent financial returns, the cost of change, and the financial effects of the new railway system. Other tables give details of rolling stock and vindicate the report's assertion that much of the railway's capital is antiquated and nearly obsolete. There is a special list of the stations and halts that would remain open when the new service was fully implemented.

Ulster Transport Authority versus Tyrone County Council and Others

For details of this report see Class XVI p. 197.

3 ROAD TRANSPORT

Roads

Rep. of Com. on the Natural and Industrial Resources of Northern Ireland, [1924].
Cmd. 31, 15 pp.
Com. apptd. June 1923; rep. sgd. July 1924.

The Rt. Hon. the Viscount Charlemont (Ch.) and twenty-four members—W. Addis, F. Anderson, R. Armstrong, H. Barbour, T.H. Burn, J.F. Cleaver, G.M. Donaldson, F. Gilliland, J.A. Grey, E.D. Hill, Capt. S.J. Hutchinson, O. Jamison, Sir Samuel Kelly, W. Logue, R. McClung, W.J. McGuffin, J. Mackie, Prof. H.O. Meredith, J.A. Pringle, Prof. R. Stanley, D.P. Thompson, D. Wright. (Additional appointments were J.Hill Dickson, in October 1923, and Prof. J.K. Charlesworth, January 1924.)

'To consider and report as to how the Natural and Industrial Resources of Northern Ireland can be best developed with a view to increasing the general prosperity and reducing the extent of unemployment.'

Witnesses to the commission suggested that dual authority exercised over main roads by county and rural district councils does not lead to wise road maintenance and reconstruction; that foundations are defective on large stretches of road and many of the resurfacing methods used have been inadequate; that expenditure involved in necessary repairs is too great to be met by local authorities alone; and that, pending improvements, regulations regarding the weight and speed of heavy vehicles should be strictly enforced. The road fund, derived from taxes on vehicles and from fines plus licence fees, might help with the necessary finance, especially if the government provides aid on the understanding that it is repaid from the future income of the fund. The volume of criticism voiced against the condition of the roads is stressed, and it is alleged that, because of their inferiority, repair and maintenance costs in the six counties are some 33 percent higher than in Great Britain.

Thus essential road improvement schemes demand speedy implementation.

A reservation signed by F. Gilliland suggests that the report pays too much heed to recent administrative changes and to criticism from rural district councils. He urges state-guaranteed loans rather than the use of the road fund. Statistical appendices give an analysis of traffic on important roads in County Down during two months of 1921, and details of expenditure on roads in the six counties and the boroughs of Belfast and Londonderry in the financial year ended March 1922, with the proportion contributed by government funds shown. A list of witnesses called is shown in a separate appendix.

Taxation of Motor Vehicles

Rep. of the Dept. Cttee. 1925.
Cmd. 55, 22 pp.
Cttee. apptd. 1923; rep. sgd. September 1925.

W.D. Scott (Ch.) and three members— J.I. Cook, Maj. G.A. Harris, and Capt. S.J. Hutchinson.

'To submit . . . recommendations with regard to the taxation of motor vehicles . . . and more particularly of the heavier class of both hackney and commercial vehicles.'

Majority Report

Two fundamental questions to be decided were those of finding a satisfactory alternative method of taxation and modifying the present system in the light of objections against it. It is argued that the 'quantum' of road user should be a principal factor in determining the taxation payable. Motor fuel best represents this, but no tax on it seems to be practical, and so the report examines other amendments to the present system. For commercial and hackney motor vehicles, two scales of payment are considered and set out as scales A and B. Scale A would tax the heavier vehicles much more heavily and would mean an annual increase in revenue for the road fund of some £45,000. Scale B would not yield so much extra revenue but might be regarded as more equitable, for it does not tax the heavier vehicles so severely that their value and efficiency in the community might be diminished.

The committee, with the exception of Mr. Cook, attended during 1923–1924 the meetings of the equivalent body appointed by the British government.

Minority Report (of S.J. Hutchinson)

Argues against a proposed motor spirit tax on the grounds that, although it is an equitable tax, it is not applied in Britain, and uniformity of practice in this matter is desirable. The intervalidity of licences and registration between Great Britain and Northern Ireland is viewed as being important. Hutchinson believes that the existing taxation favours commercial and hackney vehicles, but he cannot support either of the proposed new scales, for he believes that their imposition, in a time of trade depression, would affect industry adversely.

Belfast County Borough By-laws with respect to Omnibuses

Ministry of Home Affairs. Rep. on inquiry and correspondence regarding consequent agreement, 1928.
Cmd. 85, 75 pp.
Rep. sgd. October 1928.

The report was prepared for the ministry by two members of its staff, D.L. Clarke and G. Bryan, and concerns the co-ordination of services and rationalization of the duties of the Belfast trams and privately owned buses operating within and without the city. The conclusions of the inquiry are that transport in Belfast should, subject to safeguards, be a municipally owned monopoly, for the present competition threatens the future of the tramways and greatly increases the city traffic dangers. Omnibuses are needed to support the trams, but, despite overcrowding at certain times which might have been avoided, the tramways are an efficient part of the Belfast transport services, and their financial administration has been excellent. If the present competition continued and the tramways closed, there would be serious financial results. It is recommended, therefore, that city traffic should all be in the hands of Belfast Corporation; that appropriate new by-laws be submitted by the corporation, as the ministry should not confirm the existing ones; and that protection should be given to private operators providing a satisfactory service on a particular country route. A list of witnesses, a list of documents handed in, and details of existing Belfast traffic stands with their accommodation are given in appendices.

The details of the inquiry and the resulting recommendations are prefaced by correspondence between, on the one hand, the ministry and the Ulster Motor Coach Owners Association, and, on the other, between the ministry and the general manager of the city tramways in Belfast. The coach owners can see that benefits are likely to accrue from the new by-laws and are willing to accept the removal of their rights to the traffic solely within Belfast subject to conditions protecting existing private proprietors operating outside the city and providing road passenger service into it. The letter from the tramways manager sets out in detail the proposed basis of arrangement for the co-ordination of tramway and omnibus traffic in and around Belfast. The ministry replies confirm and clarify the new arrangement, indicating future steps which the tramways should take and stating that it accepts the bulk of the content of the coach owner's proposals, although it cannot guarantee compensation to private owners should the city boundary ever be extended. It welcomes the fact that the ideas outlined in the correspondence are so close to the recommendations of the so recently completed inquiry.

Road Fund Finance

Rep. of Inter-Dept. Cttee., 1930.
Cmd. 115, 32 pp.

Cttee. apptd. June 1929; rep. sgd. February 1930.

G.C. Duggan (Ch.) and four members—G.W. Brownell, D.L. Clarke, J.I. Cook and Capt. C.H. Petherick.

'To examine the position of the Road Fund and, having regard to the future commitments of the Fund, to make recommendations for such changes in the taxation of motor vehicles, as may appear desirable, on the understanding that the revenue of the Road Fund must be sufficient to meet its expenditure without any grants from the Exchequer.'

The accrued income of the fund has been considerably depleted in recent years, and the report carefully examines each item of income and expenditure. By dropping the charge made on the fund for police services in detecting unlicensed vehicles and reducing the cost to the fund of police engaged in point duty, about £8,000 per annum could be saved. Reduction of road fund grants would save some £10,000 annually. In Northern Ireland, motor taxation receipts are low and mileage of roads is high per head of the population, and therefore the state of the road fund would not admit of introduction of the lower rates of taxation found in Great Britain. The rate of tax for ordinary private vehicles is identical, but higher rates must continue for those vehicles which contribute most to the damage of the roads. Proposed increases in revenue from commercial goods vehicles, road locomotives and tractors, motor hackneys, motor cycles, and driving licences would realize nearly £43,000 per annum. These methods of saving on expenditure and obtaining additional income would, in combination, remove most of the existing £67,000 deficit. No specific recommendation is made for covering the 'small problematical deficit' that remains.

An appendix gives a comparison of present and proposed rates of duty on various vehicles and the proposed new scales for driving licences. The statistical tables distributed throughout the report give details of road expenditure and revenue, including rates of duty, and give some comparative figures for Great Britain and the Irish Free State.

Road Transport Fares Tribunal

Decision on general principles in the matter of the applications of the Belfast Omnibus Company Ltd., the London, Midland and Scottish Railway Company, and the Great Northern Railway Company, 1932.
42 pp.

Tribunal members—D.L. Clarke, L.L. Macassey, A. Robinson.

The applications concern the revision, with certain exceptions, of fares for the passenger road transport services operated by the applicants. It is particularly urged that a standard and economic rate of fare per mile be fixed. Suggestions for this are made along with proposed details of weekly and monthly tickets and reductions offered for young people and female passengers.

The tribunal considers these proposals along with objections from those who oppose the applicants in these matters. Objections claim inefficiency in the services and urge greater competition. After consultation with independent authorities, the tribunal urges that a comprehensive service, as outlined by the applicants, is very necessary and rejects the appeal of opponents that fares on a particular service should provide no more than the financial return needed to operate that one service. It examines the question of the basis on which fares should be fixed and considers goodwill, working costs and the problem of capital depreciation. The tribunal favours a uniform rate of fare, although there is seen to be a case for slightly reduced fares within a zone of a ten-mile radius from the centre of Belfast. The system of 'privilege' weekly or monthly tickets has been abused, and reform is required.

The tribunal recognizes that their decisions will reduce fares in some areas but increase them in others, and this in a time of economic depression. They defend the long-term objectives of their conclusions, affirming also as their duty the need to see that higher charges are justified.

Road and Rail Transport

For details of this report see this class p. 85 above.

Road Communications

Rep. of Planning Commission. Commission apptd. August 1942. Reps. published 1946.

(Composition at February 1946) W.R. Davidge (Ch.) and twenty members— J.M. Aitken, J.W. Charlton, H.W. Craig, J. Crossland, D.A. Davidson, R.B. Donald, R.D. Duncan, J. Getty, B.G.L. Glasgow, W. Grigor, A.S. Hamilton, S.H.W. Middleton, E. McConnell, T.N. McLay, R.H.S. Patterson, Maj. J.H.A. Patton, T.F.O. Rippingham, J.G. Wilkin, R.S. Wilshere, D. Winston.

'To prepare planning proposals for submission to the Ministry of Health and Local Government and to make recommendations as to any legislative or administrative action necessary in connection therewith.'

Interim Report. *Sgd. February 1946. Cmd. 241, 19 pp., map.*

Members of the commission are drawn from county and county borough councils, Belfast Harbour Commissioners, Belfast Water Commissioners, the government departments of finance, commerce, health and local government, agriculture, and one additional member.

A survey of the principal roads should be carried out immediately. With certain exceptions, county councils should be the road authorities for all public roads in their respective county areas. There should be two new classes of road, the arterial road developed from certain Class I roads, and the motorway, and

they should be provided and maintained by Central government. A motorway should be provided from Belfast to Portadown as soon as possible. By-passes are needed for certain towns. Arterial and important Class I roads should be of the standards specified in Ministry of War Transport Circular No. 575, or any desirable modification thereof, and the remaining Class I roads also improved to a more uniform standard. Legislation is urgently needed to control ribbon development.

A map illustrates the proposals, and centres of population where by-passes are considered necessary are listed in an appendix.

Public Road Freight Transport

[Rep. 1956]
Cmd. 361, 16 pp.

This is an examination of the carriage of goods by road and the problems which would arise if the present rights of the Ulster Transport Authority were abandoned or modified. Statistics are given for the numbers of vehicles engaged in road transport and the volume of goods carried by road, and there is a description of the present policy. Different aspects of the problem are discussed, and there is a summary of the licensing system in operation in Great Britain. It is concluded that a competitive system of public road transport has considerable merits and could include a road freight service of the U.T.A. Introduction of such a system would cause immediate deterioration in the finances of the railways and probably further closures; the U.T.A. might be involved in higher costs and would have to charge more. The U.T.A. would no longer have an obligation to carry unremunerative traffic, and neither would carriers, whether restricted by licence or not. A selective licensing system would be unlikely to have special advantages and would not necessarily prevent illegal operation. Public safety and the interests of employees are safeguarded by other legislation and agreements.

4 SHIPPING AND HARBOURS

Note: Shipping services to Northern Ireland are discussed in a British government publication of this title, published in 1963 by the Ministry of Transport.

Sea Fisheries and Fishery Harbours

For details of this report see Class IV p. 58.

Improvement of Entrance to Coleraine Harbour

Rep. of Com. on the Natural and Industrial Resources of Northern Ireland, 1925. Cmd. 47, 16 pp.
Com. apptd. June 1923; rep. sgd. June 1925.

The Rt. Hon. the Viscount Charlemont (Ch.) and twenty-four members—W. Addis, F. Anderson, R. Armstrong, T.H. Burn, J.F. Cleaver, G.M. Donaldson, F. Gilliland, J.A. Grey, Capt. S.J. Hutchinson, O. Jamison, Sir Samuel Kelly, W. Logue, R. McClung, W.J. McGuffin, J. Mackie, Prof. H.O. Meredith, J.A. Pringle, W.D. Scott, Prof. R. Stanley, D.P. Thomson, D. Wright. (To the above, J.Hill Dickson, Major G.A. Harris, and Professor J.K. Charlesworth were later added.)

'To consider and report as to how the Natural and Industrial Resources . . . can be best developed with a view to increasing the general prosperity and reducing the extent of unemployment.'

This report arose out of the request of the Coleraine Harbour Commissioners for state assistance towards the carrying out of certain improvements at the mouth of the Bann River. Two stone moles there had subsided so much that they could no more adequately protect the mouth of the river from heavy seas nor confine the river between necessary narrow limits at its entrance. T.S. Gilbert, the engineer consulted, confirmed that the deterioration of the moles could be checked. His proposed restoration would take two years and cost some £89,000. There is some discussion of the history and present significance of the harbour and of ways in which the Harbour Commissioners might raise finance—by increasing harbour dues, for instance.

It is recommended that the government make a relief grant to cover half the wage bill of the scheme (total estimated wage bill is £30,000), and that a further contribution of approximately £10,000 be made provided the Harbour Commissioners themselves raise £60,000 towards the cost of the proposed works. A reservation, signed by F. Gilliland, opposes the idea that the government contribution to the wage bill should be conditional on the workers being engaged via Ministry of Labour exchanges. Appendices provide a list of witnesses and the report, plans and estimate of the engineer.

The Development of Fishery Harbours

For details of this report see Class IV p. 58.

Port Facilities

Ministry of Commerce. Rep. of a Wkg. Pty. on port facilities, 1965.
42 pp., map.

'To examine the capacity and usage of the main ports in Northern Ireland, to estimate future requirements having regard to the trend of urban development, and to make a forecast of the future demand for the facilities of particular ports.'

The ports which are available for commercial usage and operate according to a regular schedule of sailings are Belfast, Londonderry, Larne, Newry, Warrenpoint, Coleraine and Portrush. Unfortunately, although the coastline of Northern Ireland is long, it is lacking in natural shelter combined with deep water, and this limits the potentialities for new harbour developments. The report, using tables, indicates the present freight traffic through the main ports and gives a forecast of future freight traffic. Again using tables, a pattern of freight traffic outlines the relative importance of each port for each commodity group imported and exported.

The cost of road haulage in Northern Ireland is an important element in the usage of particular ports; therefore, the report divides the main ports into areas of influence (i.e., an area surrounding each of the main ports from which it will be cheaper to consign goods rather than to haul them by road to another port). The four areas of influence are Londonderry, Coleraine/Portrush, Belfast/Larne, Newry/Warrenpoint. Using these four areas of influence, the report forecasts the maximum demand for facilities for other dry cargo in 1971 and 1981. (Other dry cargo is the term used to describe cargo that is and can be transported as a unit load to the port, is shipped as a unit across the channel and is driven to its destination.)

The report considers the main ports in the light of the foregoing traffic analysis and forecasts, outlining their suitability for development and expansion. For passenger traffic, the report finds no immediate problem in the three ports at present handling passengers. The possibility of developing other ports such as Kilkeel, Carrickfergus and Ardglass is investigated, and the report finds that location, natural facilities, and costs do not make such developments economical.

Appendices give tables indicating the port traffic, 1953 and 1963, to cross-channel and other ports. A map showing four areas over which the various ports have influence is also given as an appendix. Numerous tables in the body of the report give statistics of imports and exports during recent years for each of the various ports.

VIII POST OFFICE, TELECOMMUNICATIONS

IX PATENTS, COPYRIGHT, INVENTIONS

Papers on these subjects are published by the Imperial Government at Westminster.

X LABOUR

1 General
2 Labour Supply and Demand. Cost of Living
3 Industrial Relations. Wages Councils

4 Wages and Conditions in Particular Employments
5 Employment of Women and Young Persons
6 Retail Shops

1 GENERAL

Trade Boards

Ministry of Labour. Rep. of Advisory Cttee., 1922.
Cmd. 7.
Cttee. apptd. November 1921; rep. sgd. July 1922.

The Rt. Hon. The Marquis of Dufferin and Ava (Ch.) and fifteen members— W. Addis, F. Anderson, J.A. Dale, G.M. Donaldson, Miss Mary Galway, H.L. Garrett, D. Gordon, R.P. Hogg, S. Kyle, R. McBride, J.D. McClure, J. McGuffin, L.F. O'Brien, Brig. Gen. A.St.Q. Ricardo and J.A. Turkington.

'To advise the Minister of Labour as to the application of the Trade Boards Acts to Northern Ireland.'

The Trade Board Acts of 1909 and 1918 were the result of agitation over sweated labour, and this committee, in reporting on their application to Northern Ireland, considers oral evidence from witnesses representing most of the Irish trade boards. The report discusses alternative machinery to trade boards, demarcation between trades, the powers of the boards, and the enforcement of their decisions. It is argued that the trade board should be retained in Northern Ireland or established in any trade where the minister of labour believes that the rate of wages is unduly low, but that certain legislative amendments might be beneficial.

A memorandum, signed by Miss Galway, and Addis, Donaldson, Gordon, Kyle, McBride and Turkington, argues the case for a trade board in agriculture. Appendices include a draft of the model constitution and objects of an industrial council, and a list of trade boards in operation in Ireland at the end of 1931.

Sheltered Employment

Rep. by General Advisory Council on the Employment of the Disabled, 1960.
H.C. 1401, v, 25 pp.
Rep. sgd. April 1960.

R. McCreary (Ch.) and twenty members —Maj. D.M. Anderson, Flying-Officer H.W. Bailie, Capt. J.L. Bennet, Brig. J.Y. Calwell, A.E. Carswell, Dr. E.M. Condy, Prof. P.T. Crymble, J. Ferguson, Mrs. Ogilvie Graham, C.W. Grant, Lt. Col. R.G.G. Harvey, J.W. Hutton, Mrs. Jasper Johnstone, W.J. Leeburn, A.C. Menzies, T. McKee, Lt. Com. A. Niblock, Rev. S.J. Patterson, G. Porter, The Hon. Mr. Justice Shiel. (Rev. S.J. Patterson died 26 January 1960).

'To consider the adequacy of existing facilities (for disabled persons) and whether any additional and practicable measures could be taken to improve them.'

The existing arrangements of sheltered employment are reviewed, problems involved and preparation for open employment being considered.

All disabled people should be encouraged and assisted to return, ultimately, to ordinary employment, if necessary, after a course of rehabilitation at one of the ministry's industrial rehabilitation units. Although it is agreed that the latter could not easily extend courses of training, the council think that there should be greater liaison between hospitals and rehabilitation units. The most promising type of training was that given on an employer's premises, and every effort should be made to extend it through the assistance of local welfare authorities.

It is contended that the existing facilities, except those intended for blind persons, are inadequate. Severely disabled persons should be able to make a significant contribution to production in the sheltered workshop. The establishment of an organization similar to Remploy Ltd. would not be the best way of providing sheltered employment; instead it is recommended that increased financial assistance be given to voluntary organizations and that sheltered workshops should fully explore the question of sponsorship schemes. Because many blind persons are seeking and obtaining open employment, it is recommended that the possibility of placing severely disabled sighted persons in the workshops for the blind should be fully explored by the ministry. The council recommend that the cripples' institutes be encouraged to expand their activities.

There should be closer liaison between the employment officer of the special care committees and the local disablement officer to deal with the difficult employment problems of special care patients. From medical evidence presented to the council, it is shown that some mentally ill and special care patients could be placed in open employment. If the register of handicapped persons indicated a need for further sheltered employment, then it would be desirable for the Hospitals Authority to set up a workshop for the mentally ill and special care patients living in the community who might be capable of employment. The physically handicapped should be admitted to that workshop by arrangement with the Ministry of Labour and National Insurance.

The names of organizations from which evidence was received are noted in appendix I. Appendix II is a table on the number of registered disabled persons, 1958 and 1959. The number of registered disabled persons unemployed in 1958 and 1959 and the number of unemployed registered disabled persons requiring sheltered employment in 1958 and 1959 are arranged in tables in appendices III and IV respectively.

2 LABOUR SUPPLY AND DEMAND. COST OF LIVING

Cost of Living

Ministry of Labour. Reps. of Dept. Cttee. Cttee. apptd. September 1922; reps. published [1923].

J. H. Robb (Ch.) and sixteen members— S.D. Bell, L.A. Bullwinkle, J.A. Dale, T. Donald, J. Freeland, Miss Mary Galway, S. Geddes, F. Gilliland, D.L. Hall, Maj. R.J. McCormack, D. Mc-Randal, Prof. H.O. Meredith, H. Midgley, H. Richardson, W.W. Robertson, L.M. Thomas.

'To consider the Cost of Living in Northern Ireland as compared with that in Great Britain, and the causes of differences, and to make such recommendations as they think proper, and to report on the advisability of publishing a separate Cost of Living Index Number for Northern Ireland.'

Interim Report. *Sgd. December 1922. Cmd. 12, 16 pp.*

Comparison is difficult because official data on the cost of living in Ireland is scanty in comparison with that for Great Britain. The idea of visiting households to collect accounts of expenditure was rejected, as this would involve much time and money and because current depressed conditions would make the findings untypical. Instead the retail prices of articles, chiefly foodstuffs, in the United Kingdom and Ireland are compared. There is little difference in the cost of food between Northern Ireland and Great Britain, but the relative increase in the cost of food over the 1914 level is higher in Northern Ireland.

Final Report. *Sgd. September 1923. Cmd. 20, 46 pp.*

The additional inquiry of 1 March 1923 confirms that there is no large difference between food costs in Northern Ireland

and Great Britain, but modifies the conclusion that the cost of food had risen more quickly in Northern Ireland since 1914. Comparison of prices reveal that Northern Ireland seems to have retained its pre-war advantage in the sphere of rent and rates, but appears to be at a disadvantage with regard to fuel and light.

Possible causes for these differences are outlined. These include transportation difficulties, differences in building costs, and education as a cost of living factor. The committee is not in favour of a separate cost-of-living index number for the province but recommends measures for filling gaps in the existing statistical record.

Statistical appendices include: average retail prices in Northern Ireland and the United Kingdom in October 1922 and March 1923; comparison of food prices in the two countries in 1914, 1922 and 1923; monthly indices of price movements, January 1921 to April 1923, with 1914 as the base year; comparison of the cost of articles in the food budgets of the two countries in 1914, 1922 and 1923; increase in railway fares since 1914. Minor reservations to the conclusions of the report are made by F. Gilliland and L.M. Thomas.

Unemployment

Reps. of Sel. Cttee. Cttee. apptd. 1940.

Sir Wilson Hungerford and ten members —J.E. Bailey, J. Beattie, J. Brown, T.J. Campbell, W. Dowling, Rev. Prof. R. Corkey, J.F. Gamble, J. Johnston, H. Minford and F. Thompson. (Sir W. Hungerford and J. Johnston left the committee at the end of the 1940/41 parliamentary session and did not sign nor assist in the preparation of the final report. W. Dowling took over the chair for committee sittings in the 1941/42 session.)

'To inquire into the nature and extent of unemployment . . . and to make recommendations for its alleviation by measures which are capable of being put into force

by the Parliament and Government of Northern Ireland having regard to the war situation and also the probable conditions of the post-war period.'

Interim Report. *O.p. December 1940. H.C. 515, 6 pp.*

As unemployment is worse in the textile trade than in any other, the committee concentrated upon textiles in their preliminary investigations. A survey was made of the linen and allied trades, and it was found that the numbers of unemployed were nearly 30 percent higher than the average for the industry in Great Britain. Causes of this excessive unemployment are viewed as being shortage of raw materials, control of markets, insufficiency of war orders placed in Northern Ireland, and the effect on bleachers and dyers of the Limitation of Supplies (Woven Textiles) Order.

It is recommended that more flax factories should be established, that special attention should be given to the development of the export trade, that greater effort should be made to obtain government orders, and that the Limitation of Supplies Order and similar restrictions on the home market should be modified. Urgency of action to check the further growth of unemployment is stressed.

Second Interim Report and Special Report. *O.p. February 1941. H.C. 520, 6 pp.*

The possibilities of land drainage as an alleviative measure for unemployment are discussed. Suggestions include the proposal that all land, irrespective of ownership, should be brought within the improvement scheme; that a drainage commission should be appointed; that county surveyors should be empowered to organize certain labour schemes on behalf of farmers; and that the question of weirs and water rights requires investigation.

The special report merely indicates that the work of the committee is not yet complete and recommends its continuance in the next parliamentary session. (The interim reports and special report are also published with proceedings, minutes of evidence and appendices as H.C. 537, 1941. The appendices given here show statistics of unemployment in Northern Ireland and Great Britain; give details of numbers of occupiers of agricultural holdings of various sizes, and acreages of crops and grass in 1939 and 1940; and provide a statement on drainage schemes in England and Wales.)

Final Report (with proc. and mins. of ev.) *O.p. January 1942. H.C. 552, 99 pp.*

The report itself occupies only three pages and points out that the unemployment position has improved during the time of committee sittings, because of the war effort. The consideration of postwar conditions gives rise to recommendations on town planning, the problem arising from the redistribution of industries, and the alleviation of unemployment through the rebuilding of damaged areas and the initiation of new water and sewerage schemes. The immediate postwar problem can be best tackled by investigating methods and schemes for promoting employment and by beginning at once to develop a general plan for the future.

A list of witnesses examined by the committee is provided.

[Statistics on unemployment are found in many other reports, especially the economic, agricultural and regional surveys. See Classes III, IV and XIII B.]

Manpower: An Appraisal of the Position 1964–1970

Northern Ireland Economic Council rep., 1967. 44 pp., chart.

B. Faulkner (Ch.) and seventeen members—D. Andrews, A. Barr, W.J. Blease, G.E. Cameron, H.E. Campbell, N. Kennedy, D.C. Lamont, W. McCormick, S. McGonagle, E.D. Maguire, J. Morrow, J.T. O'Brien, Prof. J.R. Parkinson,

Dr. D. Rebbeck, R.L. Schierbeek, W.L. Stephens, R. Thompson.

The aim of the report is to indicate the findings of the Economic Council with regard to manpower, in the light of the targets set in the Economic Plan (Cmd. 479 in Class III) for 1964–1970—30,000 additional jobs in manufacturing industry, 30,000 in the services sector and 5,000 in the construction industry. The number of additional jobs available in service industries is at present behind target. This is partly the result of a reduction of employment in public transport. The service industries cover a wide and complex range of tasks, and accurate manpower forecasting is thus difficult. Notwithstanding this, the target of 2 percent growth rate on the present labour force in the services sector is seen as reasonable. The target for the construction industry is seen by the Economic Council as a minimum requirement.

Agricultural employment has declined at the rate of some 2,000 persons per annum, and the total net decrease in the six-year period under review is estimated as between 10,000 and 12,000 workers. Growth in the important manufacturing industries relies heavily on the recruitment of suitable labour, especially skilled workers. A questionnaire sent out to firms with twenty-five or more employees suggests that the target of 30,000 additional jobs should at least be achieved, perhaps surpassed; however, the questionnaire had a 50 percent non-response, and this is taken as a sign of lack of awareness in industry of the value of manpower planning.

Allowing for the predicted growth in the labour force in manufacturing, services and the construction industry, and subtracting the figures for workers leaving agriculture, the additional demand for labour in this six-year period is estimated at 49,000. Population growth, proportions prepared to seek employment, and migration and the factors governing labour supply—these suggest a 33,000 increase in the number of workers over the 1964–1970 period. By a

coincidence this is the average number of monthly unemployed—urging schemes of rehabilitation and training. A larger supply of trained workers would, it is contended, attract new industry to the province.

The final section of the report examines area development and labour mobility. Outside of Belfast, the community is still chiefly an agricultural one. The spread of industry away from the capital needs to be accelerated and urbanization encouraged in the areas suggested as centres of development in an earlier government report. Labour mobility, within the province is viewed as being of great importance. The report was completed at a time of economic recession (mid–1966), but it is contended that good progress is being made in manpower utilization and planning.

Appendices show statistics of employment, output and net output per person in the engineering, textile, clothing, food and drink and other manufacturing industries. These 1965 figures are accompanied by appropriate explanatory comment. Further appendices show the results of the questionnaire sent to manufacturing firms employing more than twenty-five persons. From these results, projected figures of probable employment in the various industries for 1966–1970 are provided. There is a note on civil employment, accompanied by a chart showing a graph for the period 1959–1970. Tables give statistics showing the 1964 unemployment level and national assistance rate. A final appendix attempts to discover characteristics of the unemployed—age, attitude to work, qualification, physical and mental condition being some of these. A table gives proportions of males and females in each category, attempting to show which of the unemployed have good employment prospects and which have not.

3   INDUSTRIAL RELATIONS. WAGES COUNCILS

The Establishment of a Wages Council for the Retail Food Trades

Ministry of Labour and National Insurance. Rep. of Cttee. of Inquiry, 1947.
18 pp.
Cttee. apptd. July 1946; rep. sgd. March 1947.

His Hon. Judge I. Copeland (Ch.) and four members—Miss A.N. Daunt, J. Duff, C.W. Grant, S.J. McCoubrey.

'To inquire into and to report on an application . . . for the establishment of a wages council for the retail food trades.'

The majority report is signed by four of the five-member commission, who find that the Joint Industrial Council formed in 1944 is unable to enforce its decisions. A reasonable standard of remuneration is not being and will not be maintained amongst all retail food workers. Improvement in the present machinery is possible only if both employers and workers are well organized so that the council is truly representative. The nature of the retail food trades makes this unlikely, and hence the commission recommend the establishment of a wages council, embracing workers in the retail grocery and provisions, cooked meats and other cooked foods, fruit, vegetables and flowers trades, with certain exceptions.

A minority report by Miss Daunt considers that establishing a wages council at this time would increase the difficulties of a trade already overburdened with restrictions and would make it impossible for the employer to differentiate between good and bad workers. The machinery of the Joint Industrial Council has not been sufficiently utilized; the council is not well enough known; and if it were to bring a few recalcitrant firms before the National Arbitration Tribunal, this would have a salutory effect.

Appendices list witnesses, details of press notices, and cases cited in evidence.

The Establishment of a Wages Council with respect to Road Haulage Workers and Their Employers

Ministry of Labour and National Insur-

ance. Rep. of Com. of Inquiry, 1948.
19 pp.
Com. apptd. November 1946; rep. sgd. March 1948.

Lord Justice S.C. Porter (Ch.) and four members—G.C. Lynn, W.A. Mullen, G. Porter and the Master S. Reid.

'To inquire into and report on the question whether a wages council should be established with respect to certain workers engaged on road haulage work.'

The commission reports that existing agreements relate only to a portion of the transport workers and that generally it is not the practice among employers who are not parties to agreements to remunerate their workers in accordance with the provisions of those agreements. It is unlikely that the degree of organization amongst transport workers will reach a level at which effective voluntary wage-fixing machinery could be established, and since a reasonable standard of remuneration is not being, and will not be maintained among all the workers, the commission recommends the establishment of a wages council. With certain exceptions, all transport workers, in whatever industry and in whatever grade they may be employed, should be brought within the scope of the same machinery. Those recommended for inclusion are defined in an appendix. Other appendices give press notices and list organizations and witnesses giving evidence, employer organizations party to wage agreements with the trade unions, and rates of wages cited by the Amalgamated Transport and General Workers Union for different areas.

The Establishment of a Wages Council for the Catering Industry

Ministry of Labour and National Insurance. Rep. of Com. of Inquiry, 1964.
18 pp.
Com. apptd. March 1964; rep. sgd. August 1964.

R.D.C. Black (Ch.) and four members—

J.H. Binks, J.B.E. Hutton, J. Little, H.V. Taggart.

'To consider the question whether a Wages Council should be established with respect to any of the workers and their employers engaged in the catering industry.'

The commission finds that existing wage agreements cover only a very small proportion of the workers engaged in the catering industry and that such machinery as exists for regulating remuneration and conditions of employment is not adequate for the purpose and no improvements are practicable. A reasonable standard of remuneration is not being, and will not be, maintained, and the commission recommends the establishment of a wages council with respect to all the workers and their employers engaged in the catering industry, with the exception of catering workers employed by a hospital management committee or a hospital board of management. Certain branches of the industry may wish to express their views to the council from time to time, and authority should be sought from Parliament for the appointment, on a request from a wages council, of a standing advisory committee with respect to any of the workers within the field of operation of the council.

Tables give examples of existing wage rates in Northern Ireland and in Great Britain, and appendices give the text of the press notice and of a letter issued to interested organizations, and list those organizations invited to give evidence and those who did so.

4 WAGES AND CONDITIONS IN PARTICULAR EMPLOYMENTS

For salaries of professional workers, e.g., teachers, nurses, members of Parliament, see appropriate class.

The Retail Bespoke Tailoring Trade

Ministry of Labour. Rep. of Cttee. of Inquiry, [1923].
Cmd. 21, 28 pp.

Cttee. apptd. January 1923; rep. sgd. October 1923.

A. Black (Ch.) and eight members— R. Adair, C.C. Doherty, J. Freeland, J.A. Grey, J. McKee, Mrs. Julia Mc-Mordie, R.N. McNeill and H. Tracey.

'To inquire into and advise . . . upon the following matters in connection with the Retail Bespoke Tailoring Trade . . . :—
(a) Dilution of labour.
(b) Employment of day's wage men, and
(c) Employment of apprentices.'

Majority Report

Some background discussion on the trade and the classification of its principal branches precedes the investigation of the three distinct matters that form the basis of the report. It is concluded that employers should be permitted to use more female labour, and demarcation with regard to women's work should therefore be reviewed. Acceptance by employers of the principle of additional dilution of labour must be coupled with an undertaking that no work is to be sent to outside firms. It is agreed that training by day's wage men is the best system for the instruction of apprentices; so such men are to be employed and used for this purpose on the understanding that they do not receive preferential treatment over piece-workers in slack seasons. A joint conciliation board should be set up to deal with matters concerning dilution schemes.

Minority Report (signed by C.C. Doherty, J. Freeland and H. Tracey)

The idea of dilution is firmly opposed, and the system of employing day's wage men pronounced obsolete. It is also urged that the public should be protected by law against the description 'tailor-made' being applied to ready-made garments.

Conditions of Employment and Wages of Agricultural Workers

Rep. of Cttee. appointed by the Ministry of Agriculture, 1938.

Cmd. 199, 34 pp.

Cttee. apptd. May 1938; rep. sgd. October 1938.

D.A.E. Harkness (Ch.) and fourteen members—A. Adams, P. Agnew, J. Beattie, J. Bradley, E.C. Ferguson, J.F. Gamble, J. Getty, R.J. Hale, H. Hezlett, H. Midgley, R. McClung, J. Pimlott, R.H. Todd, D. Wright. (J. Beattie resigned, June 1938.)

'To consider and report upon the conditions of employment of agricultural workers . . . and to make recommendations for the establishment of machinery for the fixing of agricultural wages and conditions of employment.'

The report deals firstly with the number of persons engaged in agriculture in Northern Ireland, discussing some discrepancies in past statistics and giving figures for the urban and rural populations in 1901, 1911, 1926 and 1937. It then discusses the engagement of farm workers, the agricultural labourer's wage, housing conditions, holidays, hours of work, and machinery for fixing agricultural wages. A typical wage at the time was fifteen shillings per week plus perquisites in the form of farmhouse meals. Appendices to the report give details of the number of male agricultural labourers employed from 1925 to 1938, the wages of rural surfacemen in 1935 and 1938, and the numbers of cottages erected under the provisions of the Labourers' Acts, 1883–1937.

Recommendations for future policy include the suggestion that a single agricultural wages board should be established for Northern Ireland and that it should have the power to fix minimum wage rates. It is suggested that farm workers should have six days holiday with pay per annum, and should have a half-day each week plus extra remuneration for Sunday work. Rural district councils should be encouraged to provide labourers' cottages in their areas, and the government should improve the economic lot of the farmer by giving as much assistance as possible to agriculture.

Catering Industry

Rep. of Cttee. of Inquiry, 1945.
Cmd. 228, 14 pp.
Cttee. apptd. February 1944; rep. sgd. December 1944.

Sir A.Wilson Hungerford (Ch.) and thirteen members—P. Agnew, Mrs. Ethel M. Dunbar, R. Eagleson, D. Gordon, D. Graham, W. McCarter, Mrs. Blanche M. McGowan, W.F. Minnis, R.M. Moore, A. Morrison, Lt.-Col. G.W. Panter, F. Storey, R.B. Thomas. (An additional member, W.I. Cunningham, was appointed in March 1944 and P. Agnew resigned, due to ill-health, in April.)

'To consider existing provisions for regulating the remuneration and conditions of employment of workpeople employed in the Catering industry . . . and to make recommendations . . . [also] to make such further recommendations . . . as they think fit as to the steps which should be taken towards the development and improvement of the Catering industry.'

The industry, as defined in this report, includes hotels, guest houses, industrial catering, school canteens, railway meals and all shops providing food or light refreshment of various kinds. The industry is an especially important one in the province in view of the tourist trade. There is some evidence of low wages, but what is more apparent is the lack of uniformity of wage rates, due largely to the absence of trade union regulation.

It is recommended that a catering wages board be established to work for the standardization of wages, hours, and employment conditions. Such a board could also consider suggestions for the welfare and development of the industry made by any government department. Other findings of the committee lead to the recommendation of the grading, licensing and inspection of establishments; the registration of catering establishments under defined categories; the regular medical examination of employees who handle and prepare food; the setting up of a training school for cooks and chefs; and the provision of financial assistance by the government in certain specified situations.

A list of witnesses is given as an appendix, and a second appendix notes the trade union agreements and National Arbitration Tribunal awards referred to in evidence.

Technical Education for the Textile Industry

For details of this report see Class XIV p. 170.

5 EMPLOYMENT OF WOMEN AND YOUNG PERSONS

The Instruction of Unemployed Juveniles

Rep. of Cttee., 1938.
Cmd. 193, 77 pp.
Cttee. apptd. December 1936; rep. sgd. May 1938.

F.W. Ogilvie (Ch.) and sixteen members —J. Beattie, R.R. Bowman, R. Byrne, Dr. H. Garrett, W. Grant, J. McGonigal, H. Midgley, Mrs. Elizabeth Montgomery, Mrs. Dehra Parker, J. Pyper, T.A. Shillington, J. Smyth, Maj. R. Stanley, J.M. Thompson, R.V. Williams and Capt. J.M. Wilton. (R.R. Bowman was replaced by J.A. McKeown for some committee sessions. H. Midgley resigned, and W.W. Robertson was appointed, February 1937.)

'To advise on the types of courses of instruction to be provided in accordance with . . . the Unemployment Insurance Act (N.I.), 1936, and the extent to which such courses should be provided, and to make recommendations.'

The introduction to the report gives an historical outline of the problem, estimates the present unemployment of juveniles, describes the Belfast juvenile instruction centre, and surveys the law relating to this subject. There is then a consideration of the different kinds and different needs of unemployed young people, the possible curriculum for special 'junior courses', the length and enforcement of attendance at such courses, their staffing and organization and sundry miscellaneous matters relating to them. The emphasis on these courses results from the fact that instruction, curriculum, staffing and other matters relating to the suitable training of young people who are out of work are stressed as urgent matters for investigation, in the committee's extended terms of reference.

It is believed that younger and older juveniles should be taught apart as far as is possible; that juveniles aged sixteen or over would benefit particularly from a junior course; and that rural areas pose special problems in arranging suitable facilities. The curriculum should be varied, with a strong emphasis on practical work (gardening, decoration, bookbinding and upholstery, for example, plus subjects suited to the student's sex, e.g., cookery, metalwork) and physical exercise. There should be instruction for some fifteen hours each week on such courses, and younger boys and girls may be taught together. The staff would be specially selected and, in some cases, should have experience of factory or workshop conditions. It is recommended that no class should normally have more than thirty pupils and that one to twenty is a good staff/student ratio.

Certificates may be issued to those doing well in the junior courses. The committee also comment on the prevalence of blind-alley occupations for the young and the long hours worked in many such jobs, although the employment problems of young people over the age of eighteen are, strictly speaking, beyond their terms of reference. An additional note, by J. Beattie, urges that full-time instruction should be made compulsory up to the age of fifteen, rather than applying junior course instruction to juveniles as young as fourteen simply as and when they are unemployed. This note also recommends adequate financial safeguards for the instructors at junior courses should a falling-off in attendance warrant reduction of staff numbers.

A list of witnesses, detailed notes on the proposed junior course curriculum and a summary of the existing relevant legislation are given in appendices. The report contains some statistical tables showing the numbers of children leaving school before the legal age, the occupations of boys in the fourteen-to-seventeen age groups, and a record of the unemployed juveniles in certain areas during 1937–1938.

[On this subject, see also Appendix: Select List of Annual Reports.]

Training of Apprentices

Rep. of Jt. Cttee., 1945
Cmd. 231, 20 pp.
Cttee. appd. July 1944; rep. sgd. April 1945.

Capt. S.W. Irwin (Ch.) and seventeen members—A. Black, W. Boyd, R.H.W. Bruce, H.E. Campbell, R.W. Charlesson, G.A. Hind, J. Little, G.H. McAlister, A. McAteer, J. McAteer, Maj. J.W. McConnell, G. Porter, J.B. Rowntree, Miss Betty Sinclair, W.H. Smyth, A.C. Williams and G.W.A. Woolmer. (After the second meeting two employers' representatives, G.A. Hind and G.W.A. Woolmer, were withdrawn. J.B. Rowntree retired on account of illness at this stage and was replaced as a trade union representative by J.W. Kerr. A. McAteer served on the committee throughout the period of its work but did not sign the report.)

'To advise upon the question of finding the most effective system of training for apprentices in trade and industry and to make recommendations on the facilities to be made available for the training of apprentices, the nature of the training to be given and the method of administration and finance for whatever schemes are suggested.'

The committee consisted of representatives of employers in six industries and representatives of trade unions, the Ministry of Education and the Ministry of Labour.

The definition of the term apprentice is considered, but a clear meaning acceptable to all trades could not be discerned. It is certain, however, that there are many young people who need continued education and many employments in which apprenticeship is defined and recognized. There is an obvious need for new and improved training methods, and the committee reviews the content of courses, provision for day attendance, finance, and the need for flexible proposals to be made.

It is urged that apprentices should, during their first year of employment, be released to attend classes for part of a day each week, with a minimum of four hours tuition. The aim would be to work towards the attainment of a widely recognized certificate. At the end of the second year, obligation to attend evening classes, in order to bring the minimum weekly total of tuition hours to six, should cease. Full-time day-class attendance is proposed for those who reach a third year of this training; after this, day release should end, except in certain cases where the apprentice shows outstanding ability. Pay during periods of release is to be made by employers in most cases. Trade unions are to pay tuition fees for member apprentices; non-members pay their own fees. Any remaining costs must be met from public funds. It is also recommended that suitable advisory committees be set up for the trades and professions concerned and that, to implement the scheme, certain improvements in the technical schools should be made.

Appendices provide a tabular presentation of schemes of apprentice training already in operation for motor engineering, vehicle building, cine operators, trade scholarships, and the baking and printing industries; schemes for future training in the building and linen industries, proposed before the joint committee made its recommendations; and a questionnaire and memorandum issued by the committee to selected and representative trade and industrial associations.

Vocational Guidance and Employment Services for Young Persons

Rep. of Cttee. of Enquiry, 1959.
Cmd. 394, 24 pp.
Cttee. apptd. May 1957; rep. sgd. October 1958.

The Rt. Hon. The Lord Coleraine (Ch.) and two members—Prof. T. Finnegan, Dr. D. Rebbeck.

'To examine vocational guidance and youth employment services for young persons under the age of 18 . . . ; and to recommend such changes as may be required to meet local needs and conditions.'

The Ministry of Labour and National Insurance, in consultation with the Ministry of Education, should establish a youth employment service responsible for vocational guidance and placing, and covering the whole of Northern Ireland with the exception of the areas where the local authority runs a service approved by the ministry. Schools and approved schools should be encouraged to provide confidential reports on pupils leaving at school-leaving age. Further advice should be available if required up to the age of eighteen. Vacancies unfilled in one area should be circulated to others. Training courses should be provided for careers masters. A central advisory committee and local advisory committees should be set up to advise the ministry.

Individuals and organizations who gave evidence are listed in the appendix.

Employment and Training of Women

Rep. of Cttee., 1970.
100 pp.
[Not published by H.M.S.O.]
Cttee. apptd. May 1966.

Mrs. M.A.F.E. Haughton (Ch.) and sixteen members—Miss E.O. Bartley, Miss B. Boyce, Mrs. K.M. Courtney, D. Ewart, F. Hughes, Mrs. A.M. Irwin, Miss M.W. Lillie, J. McGuckian, D.J. McNeill, Miss E.H. Maxwell, Miss S.M. Murnaghan, J.G. Peile, J.C. Quinn, Sister M.P. Rooney, Miss E. Sinclair, H.S. Wickens (Mrs. C.G. Neill replaced Miss E.H. Maxwell who resigned in September 1967).

'To investigate the problems associated with the employment and training of women workers.'

The committee was established by the Central Employment and Training Advisory Committee. Its report is divided into two parts covering new entrants into the labour market and the position of married women at work.

About one-third of the total labour force of Northern Ireland is made up of women. Table 3 in the appendices indicates that as economic prosperity increases, the proportion of women in the labour force tends to rise also. A large proportion of young women will return to work at a later stage in their married life and, accordingly, it would seem even more important that they receive a good basic education and adequate training in their first spell of employment, so that their re-entry into the labour market may be made as easy as possible. The committee stresses that in choosing a job or career, the individual should have freedom of choice. This is a practical aim, which, if achieved, would show very practical results in terms of higher productivity, reduced labour turnover and increased job satisfaction. The committee was also disturbed about the lack of representation of women on public boards, committees and other bodies, and it considers that women of appropriate knowledge should be appointed in the numbers required to make each body fully representative.

Tables and graphs in chapter 2 show the current and future pattern of female employment. Chapter 3 goes on to discuss the last years of school and vocational guidance. About three-quarters of all girls leave school before they are seventeen, the majority of these being fifteen years old. When the school-leaving age is raised to sixteen, the committee considers that the last two years should form a general preparation for adult life, and that the introduction of courses with a vocational bias is an important part of general education. In order to introduce these courses successfully, the schools and the Youth Employment Service would require considerable assistance from employers. Local education authorities should consider extending the provision of courses in industry and commerce for teachers, especially those involved in vocational guidance in schools. All girl school leavers should have the opportunity of at least one series of vocational visits.

In considering the role of the Youth Employment Service, the committee feels that they should approach the Confederation of British Industry and other relevant bodies, with a view to preparing a handbook covering the opportunities for girls leaving school. The committee further considers that all employers should, wherever possible, recruit young people under eighteen years of age through the Youth Employment Service.

The restrictions which operate on freedom of choice of occupation might be the unavailability of a particular job, or academic qualifications required by an employer, or they might arise because the job requires the girl to live away from home. The committee suggests that all employers should scrutinize their minimum entry requirements to make sure that these are all set at the required level, and it considers that further hostel facilities are necessary for girls living away from home.

The committee agrees as a general principle that all girls on starting work should receive a period of instruction and of planned systematic vocational training. It recommends that employers, training boards and other bodies responsible for the training function should continue to extend facilities for the training and retraining of women, especially married women, and that training boards should provide adequate grants for such training. The training

facilities for all types of employment are summarized in chapter 5.

On completion of training the school leaver can expect only a comparatively short working life before marriage. (The average age of marriage for girls in Northern Ireland in 1964 was 24–26 years.) High labour turnover might be reduced if girls were given adequate advice on initial occupation from schools, parents and the youth employment officer. High absenteeism in some instances is caused by routine and uninteresting jobs and conditions at work. Earnings and 'equal pay' are two matters considered by the committee. It recommends that equal pay with male workers should apply where women are doing identical work. The committee also feels strongly that women should have equality of opportunity in career prospects and that in selecting workers for promotion—at any level or in any occupation—men and women should be treated completely as equals.

The report continues by outlining the position of married women at work and the employment patterns of married women. Seventeen percent of all working women work part-time. Married women account for 44 percent of the total female labour force. The committee investigated to what extent their level of education and educational qualifications affected married women in securing employment and found that the higher the level of education, the greater likelihood of women obtaining higher-level employment.

The most frequently named incentive for women to return to work was the financial one, although part-time women workers placed more importance on the companionship and outside-interest incentive. The principal drawbacks to married women working were found to be (a) difficulty in caring for children (72 percent), (b) difficulty in looking after the house (38 percent), (c) difficulty in caring for husbands (11 percent), and (d) interference with social activities (7 percent).

It is clear from the figures produced

that in the period up to 1981, the demand for female labour will be much greater than the supply in most occupations and can be met by increasing the proportions of married women in employment. There is a need for industrial workers, social workers and academic and professional workers. For the latter, retraining and/or refresher courses are especially important. The difficulties in part-time employment will have to be overcome to meet these needs, and employers should consider the adoption of suitable variations in hours of service and leave arrangements to facilitate the discharge of women's responsibilities in the home.

There is evidence of a large demand for accommodation for children of pre-school age in nurseries and nursery schools, with which existing facilities could not cope. The committee recommends that the Ministry of Education should make every effort to extend the provision of nursery schools and of nursery classes in primary schools and that they should remain open longer during the day and during the normal school holidays. The Ministry of Development should give their attention to the urgent need for the inclusion of nursery schools in any future programme of developments in town or growth areas, and in any development of 100 houses or more, provision should be made for open space in play areas. All pre-school playgroups must register with welfare authorities and must be inspected regularly to ensure that the standards prescribed by the Northern Ireland Pre-School Play Groups Association and the welfare authority are observed. Besides the problem of children to care for, many women are unable to work because of elderly or infirm relatives. To overcome this difficulty, the committee recommends that a specialized well-trained corps of graded home helps should be established, capable of undertaking simple care of children and old people as well as helping with domestic chores, and that the Ministry of Health and Social Services should establish through the local authorities a standardized home-help service throughout the province.

There is a need for a research project to investigate the reasons for job preferences among girls. The committee, having accepted the principle of equal pay, feels that the merits of equalization of the retirement ages of men and women should be examined. Each section of industry and all spheres of employment should analyse their occupational needs and shortages in terms of woman power.

Appendices to the report contain statistical tables illustrating such information as age, earnings, activity rates, international comparisons, and an occupational analysis. Appendices 2 and 3 list those firms visited by the subcommittee and those who submitted evidence.

6　RETAIL SHOPS

The Shops Acts

Rep. of Cttee., 1939.
Cmd. 202, 64 pp.
Cttee. apptd. August 1936; rep. sgd. November 1938.

J.C. Davison (Ch.) and sixteen members —S.S. Bagder, T.J. Campbell, G.W. Clarke, R. Crawford, W. Crone, W. Grant, Lt. Com. R.M. Harcourt, W. Jackson, J.A. Kirkpatrick, W.R. Knox, H.C. Midgley, W.J. McCaghey, J. McVeigh, W. Sweeney, H. Todd, Capt. J.M. Wilton. (Additional member, J. Shaw, apptd. August 1936. T.J. Campbell resigned and J. Kirkpatrick died before completion of the report.)

'To inquire into the existing provisions of the laws relating to the Regulation of Shops . . . and to report as to the advisability of bringing such laws in Northern Ireland into conformity with those in Great Britain.'

Part I of the report, an historical survey, gives briefly the provisions of the Shops Acts of 1912 and 1913 and summarizes the amending legislation subsequently passed by the Imperial Parliament and not extended to Northern Ireland. The committee recommends that the laws should conform with those in Great Britain, and Part II discusses the laws and modifications which may be desirable.

The shops legislation should be universal in its application. Hours of employment in licensed and all other trades should be a maximum of fifty-two hours per week for adults and forty-eight or forty-four hours respectively for young persons above or below the age of sixteen. Other provisions are recommended for the health, comfort and holidays of employees. General closing hours should be fixed, and there should be a half-day closing every week, with certain exemptions, qualifications and suspension on occasions. Persons carrying on trade elsewhere than in shops should conform to the same conditions as shops. Exemptions to Sunday trading restrictions are permitted in certain trades and areas. Procedure for the making of regulations is indicated, and responsibility suggested for enforcement of the different provisions.

A reservation by H. Midgley concerns the maximum working hours and exemptions from general closing hours. A reservation by J. McVeigh concerns Sunday trading by Jewish shops and provisions for holidays with pay. G.W. Clarke makes a reservation about regulations for inspectors and shop assistants. R. Crawford and W. Grant wish further restriction on the sale of refreshments on Sunday.

the hours and conditions of work in shops . . . is practicable and expedient.'

The Shops Act of 1946 repealed the old imperial statutes so far as they related to Northern Ireland, re-enacted the most desirable of their provisions and added numerous new provisions, thus both consolidating and reforming. The Act proved awkward to administer in some respects and gave ground for great discontent. Complaints arose mainly from Part I, dealing with the closing of shops, and only minor points in Part II, conditions of employment, require change. In all, recommendations are made on such matters as retention of closing hours, mixed trading, Sunday trading, change of half-day, and the sale of specific products such as ice-cream, mineral waters and newspapers. Some proposals concern staff matters— hours of employment, overtime, and holidays with pay. There is some comment too on the application of the law to kiosks, theatres and cinemas. It is suggested that the committee's recommendations, if accepted, should be embodied in a general bill which would re-enact those portions of the present Act to be retained, so that one Act will contain all the law on the subject.

Appendices give a suggested form of combined notice concerning hours worked by employees, and a form of record of hours worked by young persons.

Shops Legislation

Ministry of Home Affairs. Rep. of Cttee., 1951.
Cmd. 298, 60 pp.
Cttee. apptd. May 1949; rep. sgd. September 1951.

J.V.S. Mills (Ch.) and four members— F.L. Hopkins, Mrs. Dinah McNabb, W.J. Morgan, and R. Thompson. (R. Thompson resigned and H. Downey was appointed, October 1949.)

'To inquire into . . . what amendment of the law governing the hours of trading and

The Shops Acts

Rep. of Jt. Sel. Cttee., together with proc. H.C. 1107, 28 pp.
(Also available with mins. of ev. as a 'blue book', 294 pp.) Cttee apptd. March 1953; rep. o.p. October 1954.

Original Cttee: T. Bailie (Ch.) and nine members — J. Cunningham, H. Diamond, Sir Wilson Hungerford, Prof. F.T. Lloyd-Dodd, J. McNally, H. Quin, J.F. Stewart, A.F. Wilson, and W.M. Wilton. (This cttee. was dissolved with the dissolution of Parliament in October 1953.)

New Cttee: A.F. Wilson (Ch.) and nine members—C. Bradley, J. Cunningham, H. Diamond, Sir Wilson Hungerford, Prof. F.T. Lloyd-Dodd, J.K. McCormick, J.W. Morgan, H. Quin, J.F. Stewart. (Mr. Wilson was absent due to illness on most occasions and the chair was taken by Sir Wilson Hungerford.)

'To consider the Shops Act (N.I.), 1946, the [Mills] Report [Cmd. 298] . . . in regard to Shops Legislation and the Shops (Amendment) Bill given a First Reading on February 28th, 1953, and to report whether any, and, if so, what, alternative modifications or amendments of the Shops Act . . . are . . . advisable in the public interest.'

The 1946 Act has proved ineffective and has created many anomalies. Indeed, because of the difficulties created, many of its provisions have still not been put into force. The present report considers the current position under the Act, including regulations for the sale of various goods, staff conditions, invidious or anomalous situations permitted by existing legislation, and the question of Sunday trading. Fines are suggested to cover certain offences in the latter sphere.

It is suggested that 10 P.M. be made the statutory closing hour for all shops (9 P.M. on Sundays); that there should be a maximum week of forty-eight hours for assistants, with a statutory half day leave and at least one week's holiday with pay per annum; that existing compulsory closing orders should be abolished to eliminate problems associated with 'mixed trading'; and that the Shops Acts should be administered by the Ministry of Home Affairs. The 1946 Act should be repealed to bring these reforms into effect and a shops council or shops tribunal should be established to guide the minister in revising and administering the law relating to shops. It is stressed that catering establishments and chemists and druggists should be outside these proposals. The former should be controlled by the Tourist Board and the latter by the health services.

The report also provides a list of witnesses and organizations whose representatives appeared before the committee, and a list of the acts, bills and reports considered in formulating proposals for reform.

XI SOCIAL SECURITY

Unemployment Insurance and Employment Exchanges

Reps. of Cttee. of Inquiry. Cttee. apptd. December 1921. Reps. published [1922].

Maj. D.G. Shillington (Ch.) and eighteen members—E. Bain, S. Bradley, J.R. Bristow, J.A. Dale, Miss M. Dougherty, J. Freeland, D. Gordon, W. Grant, J.A. Grey, H. Howard, D.S. Irvine, T. Mackie, J. Maxwell, S. McGuffin, S.J. Payne, A. Scott, H.C. Speirs, J.A. Woods.

'To consider the application of the National Unemployment Insurance and Employment Exchange system . . . and to make representations thereon.'

Interim Report. *Sgd. March 1922.* Cmd. 2, 7 pp.

Local employment committees, consisting of representatives of workers and employers, have operated well in Britain since 1917 and should be set up in Northern Ireland. These committees should be closely associated with the employment exchanges. In Britain, all claims for benefit under the 1921 Unemployment Insurance Act are referred to the local employment committees. Because of the work involved, it is proposed that claims should be so referred in Northern Ireland only when there is doubt as to the eligibility of the claim.

Final Report. *Sgd. December 1922.* Cmd. 11, 19 pp.

Unemployment insurance should continue on parallel lines with Great Britain, and the employment exchanges should keep in close touch with key industries such as shipbuilding. It is suggested that the Northern Ireland Government should press for an adjustment of the proportions of funds for unemployment insurance contributed by its own and by the Imperial Exchequer and for a recovery of the cost of repairing and improving those exchanges which are below British standards. The unemployment insurance scheme should cover the whole industrial population of the province. The co-operation of employers with the exchanges is urged, and the possibility of simplifying the administration of unemployment insurance, at some future date, is discussed also.

A list of witnesses and a list of organizations declining to provide oral evidence appear as appendices. There is also an appendix which shows statistics of the estimated insured population in June 1922.

Unemployment Insurance (Agreement)

Memorandum explaining financial resolution, 1926.
Cmd. 57, 6 pp.

The resolution is required to give financial authority (and to provide for a charge on the appropriate vote of Parliament) for an agreement which is set out in an appendix to the memorandum. The agreement is required because the burden of unemployment in proportion to the insured population is greater in Northern Ireland than in Great Britain, and a state of parity, which assumes equal insurance benefits and contributions within the two areas, is sought. The plan proposed is that within each financial year, a contribution shall be made, from one exchequer to the other, of three-quarters of the sum required to achieve equality of contribution, per head of the population of the two countries, to the unemployment funds. The Ministry of Finance is given power to advance to the fund, from April 1926 onwards,

any necessary sum up to £1 million. Some statistics show the percentages of insured persons unemployed in Great Britain and Northern Ireland for the years 1922–1925.

Financial and Other Circumstances of Retirement Pensioners

Rep. of Inquiry by the Ministry of Health and Social Services with the National Assistance Board, 1966.
ix, 107 pp.

The inquiry was conducted on similar lines to one currently taking place in Great Britain. Co-operation was sought from a carefully selected balanced sample of pensioners, and information was supplied both by these individuals and from the ministry's pensions records about them. Ninety-four percent of those contacted agreed to help.

The report examines the character of pensioners' incomes, noting total income, sources of income, and ability to save. Under the heading of 'Need', a chapter is concerned with the relationship between net available resources and needs, housing costs in relation to need, and need in relation to former occupation and to the amount of pension now provided. Some individuals regarded as entitled to supplementary pensions were asked why they had not applied for aid; reasons given stemmed from misunderstandings, ignorance, or pride and the wish for independence. A chapter on living accommodation deals with home ownership, housing costs, amenities and type of dwelling. Some other circumstances of pensioners are investigated also. These concern health, mobility, laundry arrangements, domestic help (paid and unpaid) and the use of the 'meals on wheels' service.

In the analysis of findings, a distinction is made between the situation of married couples and of single men and women. The results are compared with those of similar groups in Great Britain. Although incomes and savings tend to be lower in Northern Ireland, housing costs are also lower, but the standard of housing amenities, such as piped water, is found to be much lower in Northern Ireland. The proportion of pensioners in the different types of dwelling does not differ significantly from that in Great Britain. With regard to actual income, two-thirds of the married couples have incomes of less than ten pounds per week. Over two-thirds of the single men and over three-quarters of the single women receive less than six pounds a week. Incomes are higher among younger pensioners and, as far as married couples are concerned, are higher as a rule in the case of house-holders.

Appendices give notes and definitions, explain the structure and quality of the sample, and assess provisional entitle-ment to national assistance. The text of the minister's letter, inviting pensioners to participate in the inquiry, is also given.

The seventy statistical tables in the text and appendices give a detailed picture of various aspects of the income, savings and needs of pensioners; their housing and health; domestic help pro-vided; laundry costs and facilities; and the total number of retirement pension-ers within the population of the province.

XII HEALTH

1 General Health and Medical Services
2 Hospitals
3 The Nursing Profession

4 Particular Problems and Diseases
5 Food Purity

1 GENERAL HEALTH AND MEDICAL SERVICES

Medical Benefit

Rep. of Inter-Dept. Cttee., 1930.
Cmd. 113, 26 pp.
Cttee. apptd. September 1929; rep. sgd. February 1930.

W.R. Maconkey (Ch.) and six members —L.A. Bullwinkle, H. Diamond, W.A.B. Iliff, G.R. Lawrence, A. Robinson, W. Robson.

'To consider and report on
(a) the effect on the Exchequer, Health Insurance Funds and the finances of local authorities of introducing . . . a scheme of medical benefits;
(b) the effect of such a scheme on the dis-pensary medical service and its personnel, and to report what alterations, if any, in that service will be . . . necessary;
and to make such recommendations as may be pertinent.'

Part I of the report concerns the first of these two themes and discusses differ-ences between Great Britain and Nor-thern Ireland in the past with regard to medical benefit and contributions to health insurance funds. The report is, however, chiefly devoted to the second theme, and Part II suggests that the introduction of medical benefit will enable almost £10,000 to be saved in the salaries of dispensary medical officers or that the saving may be effected by a change in the capitation rate payable for insurance practice. (A prefatory note to the report by the Ministry of Finance indicates that the latter alternative is preferred.)

The report endorses also the recom-mendation of the Local Government Commission that the adoption of tuber-culosis schemes should be made man-datory. Its appendices give statistics of Exchequer grants to county authorities for the institutional treatment of this disease and a detailed analysis of the effect of the proposed salary reduction for dispensary medical officers.

Sickness Visitation by Approved Societies in Northern Ireland

Ministry of Labour. Rep. of the Dept. Cttee., 1932.
13 pp.

Cttee. apptd. March 1932; rep. sgd.
June 1932.

J.F. Gordon (Ch.) and nine members—
Sir J. Davison, P.J. Grant, D. Gray,
Maj. S.H. Hall-Thompson, W.A.B. Iliff,
S. Kyle, R.J. Meller, C. Neill, J.D.
Nugent.

*'To inquire into and report on, the existing
arrangements . . . and to make recommendations in regard to the extension and
development of the present service by
Approved Societies themselves and within
the amount at present available to (them)
. . . for the administration of benefits.'*

Forty-seven societies replied to a memorandum sent out by the committee
regarding details of sickness benefit
schemes and opinions on the value of
sickness visitation in connection with
such schemes. The arguments for and
against visits by agents and by 'whole-
time' sick visitors are summarized. Cost
appears at present to be a factor re-
stricting visitation arrangements outside
of Belfast. Sickness visitation is seen as
a necessity for administering the benefits
of the National Health Insurance
Scheme, and an experimental scheme
for the whole of the province except
Belfast is proposed as an extension of
existing arrangements. Visitors are to
be women, and during the experimental
period a fraction only of the scheme's
cost should fall on the societies. The
latter are believed to be capable of
making their own unaided arrangements
for such visitation within Belfast.

Sickness Visitation by Approved Societies in Northern Ireland

*Ministry of Labour. Rep. of the Dept.
Cttee., 1937.*
10 pp.
*Cttee. apptd. October 1936; rep. sgd.
May 1937.*

J.F. Gordon (Ch.) and nine members—
Sir J. Davison, E.C. Farmer, P.J. Grant,
D. Gray, J. Hackett, Major S.H. Hall-
Thompson, W.A.B. Iliff, C.G. Izard, H.
Midgley.

*'To inquire into and report on the working
of the co-operative scheme of sickness
visitation established by the Approved
Societies Sickness Visitation Committee
and to make recommendations . . . in
particular with regard to the extension of
its scope to include insured persons resident in the County Borough of Belfast.'*

The scheme proposed in the earlier report
had been effected and was a success in
its experimental period. Details of its
costs are provided. Extension to Belfast
is recommended, to introduce 'a scheme
of sickness visitation more comprehensive in its scope than anything of the
kind in the United Kingdom'. Difficulties seem to lie in the additional costs
and possible problems arising from the
fact that visitors and those visited may
be of different religious persuasion. The
extension of the scheme for a trial period
is urged, and details of the cost for
societies are calculated. If this results in
some full-time workers from societies
becoming redundant, compensation will
be paid to them. Denominational societies have the right to require that visitors
to their members in Belfast are of the
appropriate denomination.

Health Service

*Special, interim and final reps. of Sel.
Cttee. on Health Services, together with
proc., mins. of ev. and app.*
H.C. 601, 768 pp.
Cttee. apptd. December 1942.

H. Stevenson (Ch.) and nine members—
J.E. Bailey, T. Bailie, T.J. Campbell, Dr.
G. Dougan, Lt.-Col. S.H. Hall-Thomp-
son, J. Johnston, Dr. W. Lyle, H.C.
Midgley (replaced by Mr. J.W. Nixon
in May 1943) and H. Minford.

*'To investigate and consider the Health
Services of Northern Ireland.'*

Interim Report. *Presented to the House,
6 July 1943.*
2 pp.

Attention is drawn to inadequate salaries
paid to nurses, and it is proposed that the
scale recommended for Scottish nurses

be adopted in Northern Ireland, some form of state grant being introduced to cover the additional costs. Changes in salaries and conditions of service should, as far as possible, be put into effect from the same date as in Great Britain, although the implementation of certain recommendations must await improvements in nurses' accommodation. The development of a comprehensive superannuation scheme for the U.K., unaffected by staff mobility from hospital to hospital, is urged.

First and Second Special Reports. *Presented to the House 16 February and 19 October 1943 respectively.*
1 p.

The first of these indicates that the select committee was unable to complete its investigation in the parliamentary session 1942/43, while the second requests that the time allocated should be extended further, until the end of the new parliamentary session, because of the volume of evidence to be heard.

Final Report. *O.p. January 1944.*
36 pp.

It is made clear that the whole range of public health services, apart from housing questions, has been considered. The problems of special sections of the community and the present services available are discussed. These sections and services include the blind, mental defectives, children and their welfare, tuberculosis sufferers, midwifery services, hospital services, sanitary inspectors, veterinary services, fever hospitals and dispensary medical services.

It is proposed that a ministry of health be set up, to act as a controlling authority for the whole of the province. All services would be transferred to this ministry, and it would have all necessary powers to carry out suitable policies. It should receive advice from an honorary health council. It is further proposed that uniformity in the manner of notification of infectious diseases be established. The county council with a medical officer appointed by the minister is to be the

health authority for the county, although large local authorities can opt out of the county scheme. It is argued that in Belfast, maternity and child welfare clinics, particularly ante-natal and post-natal, should be excluded. The city of Londonderry's health services lag behind those in other parts of Northern Ireland, and remedial measures are needed as a matter of some urgency. Numerous specific suggestions are made with regard to each of the special sections of the report. These recommendations include the idea that blindness should be treated as a notifiable disease; that there should be a colony for mental defectives other than schoolchildren; that medical inspection of children under the age of sixteen should be a compulsory feature of the educational system; that two additional tuberculosis sanatoria be established; that a well-developed maternity service, entirely dissociated from the poor law, is needed; that hospital accommodation demands improvement; that posts such as dispensary doctors and sanitary inspectors need better salaries and conditions of service to boost recruitment; and that an up-to-date public health code should be published. There should be a single controlling authority dealing with milk production to ensure a pure supply, and milk, whether pasteurized or not, must be of good quality.

The final report is followed by the detailed minutes of evidence. There are provided an alphabetical list of witnesses called; lists of individuals and bodies submitting documentary evidence; and a list of acts, statistical data and other printed matter supplied to the committee for reference.

Health

First rep. of Advisory Council,
Cmd. 238, 16 pp.
Council apptd. November 1944; rep. covers period November 1944–December 1945.

H. Stevenson (Ch.) and nineteen members—W. Allen, L. Arndell, W.J. Bailie,

Miss M.A. Beaton, B.R. Clarke, T.L. Cole, Lt.-Col. J.M. Foreman, Lt.-Col. A.R.G. Gordon, J. Hamilton, Dr. J. Stuart Hawnt, J.M. Hunter, G.G. Lyttle, Miss Dorothy Melville, F.P. Montgomery, P. Murphy, Dr. J.H. McBurney, H.I. McClure, Prof. W.J. Wilson, C.J.A. Woodside. (J. Hamilton resigned in January 1945 and was replaced by S. Orr. H. McCullough and P. Brown were also appointed, in February and July 1945 respectively.)

'To advise the Minister of Health and Local Government upon matters which he may refer to them from time to time, to draw his attention to matters which it seems to them fit that he should consider and to advise him upon the general administration of the health and medical services.'

Recommendations are made by appropriate committees of the council on children's health services, hospitals, maternity and infant welfare, nursing services, and tuberculosis. These proposals include the need for the improvement of school medical services and the institution of compulsory medical inspection of school children; the need to improve the standard of ante-natal and child-welfare schemes and to continue war-time emergency arrangements for blood transfusions; an examination of the role of assistant nurses; the necessity to study the diagnosis and treatment of cancer and to devise a unified scheme in order to make a concentrated attack on tuberculosis; and the need to improve hospital services in the Londonderry Area. A general proposal urges that the functions of the registrar-general should transfer from the Ministry of Finance to the Ministry of Health.

A note on the implementation of the recommendations is provided by the minister of health and local government. [No further reports, as separate items, were published.]

The Health Services

Ministry of Health and Local Government. Rep. of Cttee., 1955.

Cmd. 334, 88 pp.
Cttee. apptd. June 1954; rep. sgd. April 1955.

H.G. Tanner (Ch.) and two members— Sir George H. Henderson and J.V.S. Mills.

'To advise on criticisms and suggestions made by members of both Houses of the Northern Ireland Parliament about the operation of the health services.'

The report is in three parts. Part 1 consists of a brief analysis of criticisms of the health services in Parliament and by parliamentary witnesses. Part 2 describes the organization of the services and gives some account of their development since 1948. In part 3 the committee discusses criticisms of the services and states conclusions. Recommendations deal with the membership and organization of the Health Authority. Suggestions are made to relieve pressure on the Royal Victoria Hospital and to improve outpatient services generally. The functions of the Tuberculosis Authority should be transferred soon to the Hospitals Authority and possibly, in part, to the health and welfare committees. The position of the Mater Infirmorum Hospital is discussed and also the desirability of removing the technical bar to contact and co-operation between the Mater and the state services. The membership and organization of the General Health Services Board is also discussed, and a survey advised of certain problems of general practice. More frequent consultation between the board and dentists would remedy the latter's lack of confidence in the board. Expansion of local authority health and welfare services should be encouraged. Better liaison is required between different services, and the ministry should be more active in co-ordination of services. The Northern Ireland Health Services Liaison Committee is a useful body and may need to expand its activities.

Appendices list those who gave evidence to the committee and give details of committees and subcommittees of the

Hospitals Authority, of hospital committees, and of committees of the General Health Services Board; and notes on hospital endorsements in Scotland and on provision of lodging accommodation for out-patients in the South-Western Region. Graphs show costs of drugs and numbers of prescriptions in different parts of the United Kingdom, 1952–1954.

Remuneration of General Medical Practitioners

Ministry of Health and Local Government. Rep. of Jt. Wkg. Pty. of Representatives of the British Medical Association and the Ministry of Health and Local Government. 1961.
27 pp.
Rep. dated January 1961.

Representatives of the profession—W.H. Belford, J. Bleakley, S.E. Browne, D.L.W. Chapman, N.S. Dickson, R.J.T. Gardiner, G.W. Houston, C.W. Musgrave, J.S. McKelvey, N.D. Wright. Prof. R.G.D. Allen and the Headquarters Staff of the B.M.A. acted as consultant advisers to the profession's side. The ministry representatives are not named in the report.

'Bearing in mind the recommendations of the Joint Working Party in Great Britain and in the light of the Social Services Agreement, to negotiate proposals for general practitioners' remuneration.'

Under the present system the same fees are paid to doctors as in Great Britain, but certain payments made in Great Britain have no counterpart in Northern Ireland, whereas, on the other hand, the Northern Ireland Mileage or Rural Practitioners' Fund is proportionately about three times as large as the corresponding fund in Great Britain. The working party compares the remuneration of general practitioners in Northern Ireland with other parts of Britain and discusses the introduction of a pool system similar to that in Great Britain, but concludes that, for the next few years at least, the present system should be retained with certain modification. An

appropriate purposes fund should be set up, corresponding to amounts normally distributed in Great Britain by way of inducement payments and trainee practitioner grants, and to the Group Practice Loans Fund. A further sum, the Transitional Fund, should be for distribution to doctors with relatively small lists. The Rural Practitioners' Fund should be reduced and its distribution reviewed. The reasons for the recommendations are then explained, and an account given of the uses to which the funds will be put.

The eight appendices give a summary of the working party's proposals, details of arrears for the year 1960, terms of reference of the Mileage Subcommittee and details of distribution of the Transitional Fund. Tables show types of practice and practice expenses, 1955–56; the effect of the working party's proposals on the 1960/61 and the 1961/62 estimates and their net effect on receipts; and (in the text) comparisons between Great Britain, England and Wales, Scotland, and Northern Ireland as regards average number of patients per doctor and average income.

Prescribing and Sickness Benefit Costs

Rep. of Health Advisory Cttee., 1969. Cmd. 528, 91 pp.
Cttee. apptd. December 1964; rep. sgd. December 1968.

Prof. J. Pemberton (Ch.) and nine members—Prof. E.A. Cheeseman, N. Dugdale, G.W. Houston, C.W. Kidd, H.A. Lowry, R.P. Maybin, A.T. Park, R.M. Shearer, Prof. O.L. Wade.

'To enquire into the factors contributing to the higher cost of prescribing and of payments for sickness benefit in Northern Ireland compared with Great Britain, and to make recommendations.'

The average cost of sickness benefit per insured person and the average cost of prescribing per person on doctors' prescribing lists are higher in Northern Ireland than the average in Great Britain, although there are wide variations in the average costs in different areas within each country. Employed men and single women make relatively fewer claims to sickness benefit than their counterparts in Great Britain, but they tend to remain on benefit considerably longer. Married women and self-employed men also tend to remain on benefit longer but make relatively more claims than corresponding categories in Great Britain. The chief factors giving rise to relatively higher sickness benefit costs in the year ended 31 May 1964 were the longer average duration of incapacity and the greater average number of dependants compared with Great Britain.

The average total cost per person of prescribing costs was much higher in Northern Ireland than in England or Scotland in 1963–1966, but it was similar to that in Wales. The average cost per prescription was highest in Northern Ireland, and the average prescription frequency was greater than in England and Scotland but not so great as in Wales. Many factors influence the average prescribing costs. The proportionately greater number of small pharmacy businesses means a greater use of relatively small packs and higher average percentage-on-cost allowances.

Social and economic factors may influence sickness benefit—a higher rate of unemployment; lower average earnings and standard of living; a greater proportion of partly skilled and unskilled persons in the working population; emigration of healthy young adults to Great Britain who return when ill. A study in 1960 had revealed no appreciable differences in sick leave experience among civil servants in Northern Ireland and Great Britain.

The committee recommends all measures designed to improve social, economic, and environmental conditions; a vigorous policy of direct measures in preventive medicine; and the development of health education and community medicine. A research and intelligence unit within the ministry should carry out or foster the many studies which are suggested. General practitioners and hospital consultants should be acquainted with the efficacy of drugs and the relative cost of proprietary drugs and non-proprietary equivalents. It is desirable that the number of pharmacies in the province be limited. The committee supports the measures being taken to promote high standards of certification and effective and economic prescribing. These are described in appendix I. Additional information on prescribing costs, dispensing doctors, and stock orders is given in appendix II. Fifteen statistical tables cover data discussed in the report.

The Administrative Structure of the Health and Personal Social Services in Northern Ireland

[*Ministry of Health and Social Services*], *1969.*
35 pp.

This paper reviews the present administrative structure of the health and personal social services in Northern Ireland and makes tentative proposals for change as a basis for public discussion and consultation with representative bodies. The need for reorganization is linked with the proposed alterations in local government structure (Cmd. 530), and due consideration has been given to the recent tentative proposals regarding the health and personal social services of Great Britain. A similar need for change in the education service is recognized but not dealt with in this paper.

It is suggested that the health services should form a fully integrated system: area boards would replace the Hospitals Authority, hospital management committees and the General Health Services Board, and would take over many of the functions of local health authorities. Local authorities should be represented on the boards, which would be responsible directly to the government. The responsibilities of area boards in relation to existing health services are examined.

Welfare departments are already more 'integrated' than in Great Britain, and this trend towards a comprehensive social welfare service is considered desirable. Alternative systems of administration are outlined, and some form of partnership with the health services is favoured. The paper then discusses the organization of services under a new structure, finance, and the membership and organization of the area boards.

Comments on the proposals are invited.

2 HOSPITALS

Administrative Structure of Hospital Management Committees and Hospital Committees

Ministry of Health and Social Services, Northern Ireland Hospitals Authority
Rep. of Jt. Wkg. Pty., 1966.
58 pp.
Wkg. Pty. apptd. January 1965; rep. sgd. June 1966.

J.S. Hawnt (Ch.) and eight members— J. Andress, R. Garnsey, W. Harvey, W. Hawthorne, C.W. Kidd, R. Moore, R.T. Spence, S.E. Taylor.

'Having regard to . . . the Report of the Committee of Inquiry into the Health Services, 1955 (the Tanner Committee) [Cmd. 334], to examine the administrative structure of the hospital service at the level of hospital management committees and hospital committees, and to make recommendations designed to promote the most effective distribution and discharge of management functions.'

The first chapter of the report describes the collection of evidence, and other reports relevant to the party's terms of reference. The second chapter deals with the relationships between the Authority and the management committees and recommends delegation to management committees of certain powers to determine numbers of staff, and of decisions with regard to carrying out minor capital works. Suggestions are made for improvement in the standard of liaison and consultation at various levels.

In chapter 3 the grouping of hospitals is examined. A regrouping is advocated,

as indicated in an appendix, with fifteen instead of twenty-nine groups. When regrouping causes redundancy in the higher administrative grades, adequate arrangement should be made to place these officers in suitable posts as soon as possible.

The fourth chapter is concerned with the internal administrative practice of management committees. Recommendations generally aim at simplification of the system by abolition of hospital and house committees and of medical superintendents, except in certain psychiatric hospitals, and by reduction of functional management committees to three, dealing with finance, works, and medical and allied services, respectively. Lesser matters should be delegated to these functional committees, and managerial functions to the management committee's chief executive. Recommendations also cover liaison and discussion between the various interests.

Recruitment and training of administrative and clerical staff is discussed in chapter 5. A representative Staffs Committee should be set up to survey the situation and make proposals for measures to improve it.

Appendices give relevant extracts from Cmd. 334 (Rep. of Cttee. of Inquiry into the Health Services, 1955); list those submitting evidence; give the present grouping and proposed regrouping of hospitals, with details of bed complement in each case; list those hospitals which have a hospital or house committee; and set out the proposed pattern of responsibility for staff appointments.

The Hospital Plan, 1966–75

Ministry of Health and Social Services, 1966.
Cmd. 497, 35 pp.

The building programme outlined in 1963 has shown slower progress and higher costs than estimated and must be reconsidered. The plan sets out the various factors which will shape the development of hospital and specialist services over the next decade and then shows how these factors in turn mould the hospital building programme and govern decisions on particular schemes. Estimates of the size, composition and distribution of the population in 1975 must be translated into probable needs of hospital beds and supporting facilities. Ratios are discussed for acute, maternity, geriatric, and mental illness, and special care beds, and the situation in Northern Ireland is compared with that in England and Scotland. The service is to be centred on six key units: the Royal Victoria and City Hospital complexes in Belfast, which between them would provide a comprehensive range of specialties, including regional specialties serving the entire province; and four area hospitals, located at Ballymena, Craigavon, Dundonald and London-derry, each of which would provide a comprehensive range of specialties, the regional specialties excepted. Linked with these would be a limited number of hospitals which would be required for the foreseeable future, such as Forster Green Hospital for diseases of the chest, some of the psychiatric hospitals, and those smaller general hospitals which would provide in-patient accommodation and services for at least the basic specialties and for some long-stay patients. Lastly, there would be a number of hospitals serving a variety of local needs, staffed mainly by general practitioners. Criteria are given for determining priorities in the building programme, on which basis schemes are listed for completion in the first quinquennium (1965–1970) and also schemes which should be started by 1970.

Appendix A lists major schemes planned to begin in 1966/67 and gives details of their postponement or rephasing. Particulars of the works, except minor works, included in the programme and of the broad phasing of expenditure on them are shown in appendix B.

Review of the Hospital Plan, 1968–78

Ministry of Health and Social Services, 1968.

Cmd. 524, 30 pp.

Most of the schemes due to be completed or started within the early years of the 1966 plan have been completed or are proceeding in accordance with their allotted time-schedule and within their cost limits. The scale of hospital services envisaged appears to have been adequate, with the exception of geriatric accommodation where an upward adjustment of the bed-ratio of 1.5 per 1,000 population seems desirable. In addition, further provision needs to be made for the community, and possibly also for the residential aspects of the special care service.

A Standing Medical Advisory Committee was set up in 1967 under the chairmanship of Professor Sir John H. Biggart. A report of this committee forms appendix A of the review. The report endorses the pattern of care outlined in the 1966 plan but criticizes the failure to make early provision for the development of regional specialties and argues for a more rigorous ordering of priorities; the present system of medical staffing and management structure will need to be revised to conform with the clinical area concept. The ministry and the authority accept the report, with certain reservations, which are discussed.

Three new schemes need to be included in the plan for the next few years: the provision of facilities at the Royal Victoria Hospital for neuro-surgery, cardiac surgery and a regional accident centre; the provision of additional geriatric beds; and the provision of further special care accommodation. The cost of these schemes will necessitate postponement of schemes for new maternity beds at Mid-Ulster Hospital, Lagan Valley Hospital, and Whiteabbey Hospital (which will also need to postpone the new out-patient facilities planned). The financial limit governing schemes for minor works is raised.

Appendix B tabulates major schemes to be completed or started during the ten years to 31 March 1978.

Second Review of the Hospital Plan, 1970–75

Ministry of Health and Social Services, 1971.
Cmd. 556, 24 pp.

Good progress has been made, and the government report on the development programme (Cmd. 547) indicates an increase in capital allocation for hospital services. A review is made of the scale of these services and the pattern of hospital care. The building programme up to 1975 is also outlined. From 1973, the administration of health and social services will come under the new area boards, and thus there will no longer be a hospital plan as such. Resources will, however, be undiminished, and the momentum of hospital expansion and improvement should be maintained.

Appendices give details of all hospital building schemes involving outlay of over £75,000 each which are to begin or be completed in the five years ending March 1975. They also give information on the distribution of specialists within Belfast hospitals.

3 THE NURSING PROFESSION

General Nurses

Rep. of Cttee. [on] Salaries and Conditions of Service of Nurses and Midwives in Hospitals (other than Mental Hospitals). Cttee. apptd. February 1946; reps. published 1947.

C.J.A. Woodside (Ch.) and fifteen members—Miss Flores, H. Airey, I.E. Bell, P. Brown, V.F. Clarendon, R.W. Craig, J. Dinsmore, R. Getgood, J.W. Haughton, A. McConnell, Miss Dorothy Melville, A.C. Menzies, S. Orr, Miss Marjorie Sheehan and Miss Marjorie W. Sparkes. (P. Brown resigned and was succeeded by C. Scott. A. McConnell also resigned before the completion of the first report. In the interim between the reports, Miss Sheehan's place on the committee was taken by Miss Margaret A. Beaton.)

'(a) To examine, and report on the scales or rates of remuneration, including emoluments, at present in operation . . . ;
(b) to draw up . . . and submit agreed scales of remuneration . . . if existing scales . . . are found to require revision;
(c) to examine and report on existing conditions of service . . . as to hours of work and length of holidays . . . and to draw up and submit recommendations embodying agreed conditions of service.'

First Report. *Sgd. September 1946.*
Cmd. 244, 44 pp.

Recommends salaries and emoluments based on English scales and current cost of living conditions. Recommendations for minimum working conditions include comments on hours of work, meal times, accommodation and discipline. There are also proposals concerning promotions, increments, special allowances and probationers' salaries. Definitions are given to clarify the question of the officer or rank referred to, and the date for the application of the various proposals is discussed. A series of schedules sets out suggested salaries and emoluments for general, children's and special hospitals; for male nurses and tutors; and for staffs of maternity homes. One major requirement foreseen is the need for a coordinated superannuation scheme for nurses in all hospitals.

Second Report. *Sgd. May 1947.*
Cmd. 252, 35 pp.

This report is divided into two parts. The first considers the salaries and conditions of service of district nurses, domiciliary midwives and public health nurses. The second offers further recommendations for the salaries and conditions of nurses and midwives. These latter proposals concern part-time nurses, sick pay and the service allowance for midwives. They are intended to add to, or amend, the proposals in the first report. The suggested salary scales for male and female post-registration student nurses are given in detail, and some indication of proposed salaries for part-time nurses and enrolled assistant nurses is also given.

The recommendations concerning domiciliary staff include definitions and proposed salary scales. They also give details of recommended allowances, of proposed service conditions, and of the suggested date of application of the proposals.

This report is furnished with a subject index, as is its predecessor.

Mental Nurses

Reps. of Cttee. on Salaries and Conditions of Service of Nurses in Mental Hospitals and Mental Deficiency Institutions. Cttee. apptd. February 1946; reps. published 1947, 1948.

T. Carnwath (Ch.) and twelve members —J. Holland, W.J. Hyndman, J.P. Jamison, J. Keating, J.N. Lamont, G. Leyburn, E.K. McGrady, W.J. Maynes, A.C. Menzies, H. Millar, Miss Sarah A. Robb, Miss Annie Torrens. (J.N. Lamont resigned and was replaced by J. Davidson who also resigned before the completion of the first report. When the committee reported a second time, this vacant place had been taken by Rev. E.V. MacGowan and Miss Mary A. Shields had replaced Miss Robb.)

'(a) To examine and report on the scales or rates of remuneration, including emoluments, at present, in operation . . . ;
(b) to draw up . . . and submit agreed scales of remuneration . . . if existing scales . . . are found to require revision; (c) to examine and report on existing conditions of service . . . as to hours of work and length of holidays . . . and to draw up and submit recommendations embodying agreed conditions of service.'

First Report. *Sgd. September 1946. Cmd. 245, 40 pp.*

The report gives definitions of staff posts and duties; recommends conditions of service with regard to matters such as hours of duty, training and discipline; and recommends revised salary scales based on those put forward earlier in the year in the reports of the appropriate Scottish committee. Various schedules set out the proposed new scales for male and female nurses and details of suggested payment of arrears for the years 1943–1946. Special allowances are recommended for those whose training has been interrupted by war service.

Second Report. *Sgd. November 1947. Cmd. 256, 16 pp.*

Further recommendations on the salaries and conditions of service of nurses in these hospitals are set out. These concern revised scales for matrons, deputy matrons, chief and deputy male nurses, and male tutors. The recommendations had been delayed pending the findings of the Scottish Nurses Salaries Committee, but recommended scales for these officers plus a scale for nurses taking post-registration training are now set out.

Both these reports have a subject index.

Hospital Domestic and General Staffs

*Rep. of Cttee. [on] Salaries and Conditions of Service of Domestic Staff in Hospitals, 1947.
Cmd. 247, 16 pp.
Rep. sgd. February 1947.*

Mrs. M. Gwladys Bailey (Ch.) and twelve members—Mrs. Rose Alexander, Mrs. Catherine Barrett, R.W. Craig, H.J. Curlis, S. Ferguson, R.W. Harland, J. Hopkins, Mrs. May S. McLeavy, M. McGurk, A.C. Menzies, Miss Saidie Patterson, Miss Marjorie W. Sparkes.

'(a) To examine and report on the scales or rates of remuneration, including emoluments, at present in operation . . . ;
(b) to draw up . . . and submit agreed scales of remuneration . . . if existing scales . . . are found to require revision; (c) to examine and report on existing conditions of service . . . as to hours of work and length of holidays . . . and to draw up and submit recommendations embodying agreed conditions of service.'

Recommendations are made concerning hours of duty, holidays, off-duty hours, supervision of staff health, accommodation, discipline, and recreation and social life. On the subject of remuneration the report recommends grades for female and some male staff based on a compromise between the rates suggested by employers and those requested by the employee panel. No agreement based on such compromise could be made, however, with regard to the majority of the male staff involved. Tables show recommended scales for appropriate categories of female staff and employers' and employees' recommendations for the categories of male staff where agreement was not reached. The report has a subject index.

4 PARTICULAR PROBLEMS AND DISEASES

Maternity Mortality and Morbidity

Ministry of Home Affairs. Rep. of Maternity Services Cttee., 1943.
Cmd. 219, 32 pp.
Cttee. apptd. December 1936; rep. sgd. June 1939.

Prof. R.J. Johnstone (Ch.) and nine members—J. Boyd, L.A. Bullwinkle, Miss E. Alletta Clark-Kennedy, Mrs. Lily Coleman, R. Crawford, A.J. Irwin, Prof. C.G. Lowry, Mrs. Dehra Parker, N.C. Patrick. (After Dr. Patrick's death, J.M. McCloy was appointed to the committee. Professor Lowry, a member of the committee from its inception, became chairman following the death of Professor Johnstone.)

'To examine the conditions under which the organisation of maternity services is carried on . . . and to recommend such alterations in the existing system as may be desirable for securing adequate nursing and medical services for domiciliary maternity cases, and improved efficiency in the services generally.'

The scope and nature of the problem is examined by discussing maternity statistics and the factors which make mother-hood safer; by outlining the essentials of an adequate service as laid down in earlier reports; and by first reviewing and then criticizing the existing Northern Ireland services. Proposals for an improved service include the recommendation that public maternity services be removed entirely from poor law. They should be organized on a county basis by county councils and county boroughs, supervised by the Ministry of Home Affairs. A central midwives board should be set up. It is further recommended that there should be a medical superintendent officer in each area to co-ordinate midwifery services along with other public health activities; that there should be better training and remuneration for midwives; and that ante- and post-natal clinics should be set up in each administrative area. Minor suggestions concern consultant services, mothers suffering from malnutrition, institutional accommodation, transport facilities, sterilized dressings, and provision for disinfection where needed. It is stressed that strong action should be taken against the practice of unqualified 'handy women' attempting the midwife's work. These proposals would certainly add to the cost of the public maternity service, and extra expense should be divided approximately equally, as in Great Britain, between the Exchequer and local authorities.

L.A. Bullwinkle records, in a signed reservation, his dissent from the idea of organization on a county basis, arguing that two regions plus Belfast would suffice.

Attached to the report as appendices are a list of witnesses and of persons and institutions supplying evidence, a list of papers submitted to the committee and a memorandum on grants for the training of nurses in midwifery. There is also an analysis of maternal and infant mortality in Northern Ireland during the decade 1927–1936 with some figures for 1937 and 1938.

[For reports on this subject see also Appendix: Select List of Annual Reports.]

Treatment of Cancer in Northern Ireland

A memorandum on the measures necessary for dealing with cancer in Northern Ireland. Ministry of Health and Local Government. Recommendations by the Health Advisory Council, 1946. 31 pp.

H. Stevenson (Ch.) and twenty-one members — Lt.-Col. A.R.G. Gordon, W. Allen, L. Arndell, W.J. Bailie, Miss M.A. Beaton, P. Brown, B.R. Clarke, T.L. Cole, Lt.-Col. J.M. Foreman, J.S. Hawnt, J.M. Hunter, G.G. Lyttle, Miss Dorothy Melville, F.P. Montgomery, P. Murphy, J.H. McBurney, H.I. McClure, H. McCullough, S. Orr, Prof. W.J. Wilson, C.J.A. Woodside.

The council examines measures taken to diagnose and treat cancer in Great Britain up to and after the passing of the Cancer Act, 1939. Greater detail is given of the North of England Scheme, the Manchester Scheme and the Liverpool Scheme. The council accepts the view that it is impossible to provide an adequate cancer service for a small population. Legislation similar to the Cancer Act, 1939, is required in Northern Ireland. There should be a statutory body responsible for the organization of a cancer scheme for the whole province, financed by county and county borough councils with the aid of grants from the Exchequer. The scheme should provide for the establishment of diagnostic centres at suitable hospitals, for the treatment of patients in a special treatment centre at or near the Royal Victoria Hospital, Belfast, for the education of the public in certain aspects of the cancer problem, for research, for the education of medical students and for the giving of post-graduate instruction to medical practitioners. Suggestions are made for temporary arrangements to be put into operation whilst the main scheme is being planned and developed. It would be an advantage if the Radium Commission could extend its operations to Northern Ireland.

Appendix I, and a table in the general text, give details of deaths from cancer in Northern Ireland, 1928–1944. Some figures are also given in the text for deaths in England and Wales and in Éire. Appendix II lists the provisions of the Cancer Act, 1939.

Mental Deficiency in Northern Ireland

[Ministry of Health and Local Government.] Rep. of Mental Health Services Cttee., 1946. 38 pp., chart.

Lt.-Col. A.R.G. Gordon (Ch.) and fourteen members—D.B.M. Lothian, P. Agnew, R.S. Allison, L. Arndell, Mrs. Irene Calvert, D.H. Christie, N.B. Graham, J. Harper, J. Holland, G. Leyburn, M. McGurk, Miss Sarah A. Robb, H.H. Stewart, Prof. W.W.D. Thomson.

'To report . . . on the steps which should be taken to deal with the problem of mental deficiency.'

In England and Scotland, Mental Deficiency Acts have been in force since 1913. In Northern Ireland, there is no Mental Deficiency Act, ascertainment is inefficient, provision for the care of mental defectives is inadequate, and the responsibility for dealing with mental defectives has not been placed by statute on any authority. The central authority responsible for mental defectives should be the Ministry of Health and Local Government. Local administration of the scheme should lie with a regional authority composed of representatives from the county and county borough councils and other interested bodies, such as the Association of Education Committees, the Child Guidance Council, etc. Local mental health committees should advise the regional authority. Applications and submissions for care and treatment should be decided by medical officers of the regional authority, from whose decisions appeal may be made to the ministry, and there should be no system of judicial certification or judicial order such as is used in Great Britain.

Mental deficiency is defined, and four different classes of defective are recognized. A colony should be provided by the regional authority for the young trainable mental defectives, and recommendations cover matters such as their 'boarding out' and the provision of sheltered employment. Defectives of dangerous or violent propensities should be sent to the state institutions in England. Penalties should be prescribed for certain offences against defectives, and an amendment to the Matrimonial Causes Act (N.I.), 1939, is desirable. Other recommendations aim to improve the level of ascertainment and to provide for finance, medical research, etc. The committee stresses the urgency of the problem.

An appendix gives statistical tables showing (for different districts) the numbers of ineducable mentally defective children, 1932–1944; the 1943 return of mentally defective and mentally backward children; the numbers of mental defectives in poor law institutions in January 1945, of mental defectives maintained in Éire mental deficiency institutions in January 1945, and of mental defectives in N.I. mental hospitals at 31 December 1944; a summary of the foregoing tables; and a chart illustrating a mental health service for children of school age. It is emphasized in the text of the report that the tables illustrate the varying levels of efficiency of ascertainment rather than the true numbers of defectives in each area.

Accident at the Gangway on the Whale Factory Ship *Juan Peron* **on 31 January 1951**

Ministry of Labour and National Insurance. Rep. of Tribunal of Public Inquiry, 1951.
23 pp.
Tribunal apptd. February 1951; rep. sgd. March 1951.

O. Faber (Investigator) and H.A. Mc-Veigh (Assessor).

'A formal investigation . . . into the accident, and of the causes and circumstances of the accident, which occurred on the

31st day of January, 1951, at the whale factory ship Juan Peron in the Musgrave Channel, Belfast.'

The accident occurred at 5.23 P.M., when a gangway leading from the ship, *Juan Peron,* was crowded with men waiting for the signal to stop work. There were sixty to seventy men on the gangway, stationary because it was still too early to leave the ship and they could see the assistant manager and two assistant foremen painters on the quay. Had the gangway no faults, its safe load would have been forty men stationary or twenty walking, but it was old and faulty, and the safe load must have been considerably less. It broke, and eighteen men were killed and forty-one seriously injured. No blame falls on those who recently inspected the gangway, but the faulty timber should have been seen at the time the gangway was made. The date of its construction is not known, but it was certainly before 1945. The tribunal is satisfied that although there were no notices to that effect, the men knew that they should queue on the deck of the ship and not on the gangway. A code of practice should be formulated to establish a standard of strength and security of gangways in the same way as is already done for buildings. Proposals for draft regulations appear in appendix II to the report. Appendix I is a list of the witnesses examined.

Byssinosis in Flax Workers in Northern Ireland

Ministry of Health and Social Services, 1965.
vii, 172 pp. bibliography, photos.

Prof. J. Pemberton asked to investigate by the Ministry of Labour and National Insurance, April 1960; rep. submitted November 1963. Research team and authors of rep.—G.C.R. Carey, P.C. Elwood, I.R. McAuley, J.D. Merrett, J. Pemberton.

Answers to the following questions were sought:

1. Can a counterpart to byssinosis amongst

cotton workers be identified in workers in the 'preparing' stages of the flax or hemp industries, attributable to the conditions in which they work?

2. If so, does the disease result in an advanced condition which is characterised by chronic respiratory embarrassment and in which demonstrable degenerative changes in the lungs have occurred?

3. If the disease can be identified, what characteristics distinguish it from conditions experienced by the general population causing respiratory symptoms?

4. If the disease occurs together with some other condition causing respiratory symptoms, can the degree of disability resulting from the occupational condition alone be determined?

5. What is the relative importance of clinical findings and occupational history in distinguishing the disease from non-occupational disability in individual cases?

The committee defines technical terms, refers to previous reports on the subject and reports on the various technical surveys carried out. These surveys involved testing in no less than twenty-three appropriate mills, but it proved impossible to investigate byssinosis in hemp workers also, as no mill spins hemp only and the term itself is imprecise.

The following conclusions are reached in relation to the ministry's five questions:

1. A condition similar to byssinosis among cotton workers is also found among flax workers, is commoner among workers engaged in the dustier processes and increases in relation to the dustiness of the room in which work takes place. The term 'hemp' applies to a number of different fibres, and it seems likely that dust from these also can cause byssinosis.

2. Byssinosis was found to be associated with breathlessness, and advanced cases were more likely to have chronic respiratory embarrassment than those with little or no byssinosis. Bronchitis incidence was significantly associated with type of occupation in the mill, being greater among 'preparers'.

3. The most typical feature of flax byssinosis is the Monday syndrome. This consists of tightness of the chest and sometimes coughing, occurring within a few hours of return to work on Monday mornings. Later, the symptoms occur on other days, and they are clinically indistinguishable from emphysema and bronchitis as they occur in the general population.

4. As bronchitis and dyspnoea are common in the general population, it is not possible to assess the proportion of disability in a flax worker due to occupational conditions.

5. An occupational history of exposure to a dust known to cause byssinosis is essential for diagnosis.

The many statistical tables in the text give details of numbers of workers interviewed, numbers and degree of byssinosis found, smoking habits, age and occupation, similar data for workers who had left the industry, results of ventilatory capacity tests, and levels of airborne dust. The appendices include a questionnaire used in the survey, illustrative case histories, results of experiments, statistical analyses, and an extensive list of references to the literature.

Geriatric and Psychiatric Services for the Elderly

Ministry of Health and Social Services. Rep. of Subcttee. of Medical Advisory Cttee., 1970.
21 pp., bibliography.

Prof. O.L. Wade (Ch.) and eight members—G.F. Adams, E. Casement, J.J. Cosgrove, J.H.P. Giff, W.O. McCormick, J.B. McKinney, W.H. Moffatt, W.A. Norris.

Increasing numbers of elderly people and shortages of accommodation are straining the resources of the health and welfare services and creating in some areas an emergency situation. Senile, confused and demented patients present the most serious problem.

It is recommended that geriatric medicine should remain an integral part of general medicine; that geriatric and psychiatric hospital units should be sited with, or at least linked closely with, general hospital services; and that more beds for elderly patients should be provided, either in hospital or hostel accommodation sited with a hospital. General physicians should continue to care for a proportion of elderly people, and they should be given adequate facilities, such as hospital wards designed to separate these patients from the busier section of the ward, and long-stay beds for elderly people in smaller local general hospitals. More money should be spent now on community services, particularly housing, residential homes and domiciliary services, to keep as many old people as possible out of hospital. Day services from geriatric and psychiatric hospitals should be increased and special transport provided where necessary. Joint assessment treatment and care of patients should be undertaken by teams closely linked with the community services, comprising a geriatric physician, a psychiatrist and one or more general physicians. The proposed integrated administrative structure for the health and personal social services will have enormous advantages for old people if the distinction between hospital and domiciliary services is removed.

Geriatric medicine and psychiatry should be part of the training curriculum of doctors and nurses. An operational research unit should be established to analyse data and recommend priorities. Research into the clinical and sociological aspects of ageing should be undertaken.

A list is appended of references and further reading. In appendices, statistical tables are given, comparing the elderly population of Northern Ireland with that of England and Wales and giving details of numbers of beds, welfare places and dwellings for old people in the different areas of the province.

[Other reports, not summarized in this volume, relating to the elderly include G.F. Adams and E.A. Cheese-man: *Old people in Northern Ireland, (Northern Ireland Hospitals Authority) 1951,* and a pamphlet published by the Ministry of Health in 1966, entitled *Memorandum on Development of Services for the Elderly.* This latter document contains many useful statistics.]

[*On the financial situation of pensioners see p. 109.*]

5 FOOD PURITY

Adulterated Wine

Rep. of Sel Cttee., together with proc.,...
mins. of ev. and apps.
H.C. 450, 107 pp.
Cttee. apptd. April 1938; rep. and mins. of ev. o.p. November 1938.

J.E. Warnock (Ch.) and nine members— P. Agnew, J. Brown, R. Byrne, Prof. R. Corkey, W. Grant, Lt.-Col. A.B. Mitchell, Capt. J. Patrick, Capt. J.M. Sinclair and F. Thompson.

'To enquire into the composition of "Red Biddy" or "Tony Wine"; the methods of its manufacture, preparation and admixture with deleterious ingredients (if any), the extent of its consumption, its effect upon the habits and health of those consuming it, and to report what restrictions upon its sale or consumption may be desirable.'

Most of this document is devoted to an account of the minutes of evidence provided by the twenty-five witnesses examined over a period of eight days. The report itself is extremely concise. It describes how the committee purchased sample bottles of cheap wines and submitted them to the public analyst. Most examples had no added deleterious substance, but two had been adulterated with methyl alcohol. Wine consumption in the province has, however, increased from 191,000 gallons of British wine during 1929 to 415,000 gallons in 1937. The growth in the purchase of such wine is unfortunate, especially when consumed by young people, since the results when the wine is taken to excess are worse than is the case with beer or spirits, and the cheap wines seem to promote violence in those who are drunken. A large increase in price as a deterrent is recommended; this could be achieved by government regulations or, preferably, by a large increase in the duty payable.

The report concludes with two paragraphs on which there was some disagreement among committee members, and the views of individuals are indicated. There is a list of witnesses examined and a list of persons submitting documentary evidence. Appendices give the analyst's report on the twelve wine samples tested; correspondence from the Customs and Excise and from the Belfast medical officer of health; and the present duty paid on British wines.

Food and Drugs

Proposed consolidation and amendment of legislation, 1958.
Cmd. 382, 7 pp.

Present legislation is scattered over some thirty statutes, dating from 1733 onwards, and requires up-dating. New legislation must seek to remedy any defects at present existing in the law with regard to food composition, adulteration, nutritive values, and false or misleading description of food products. Various proposals are therefore made for law amendments concerning hygiene, labelling, sampling powers, and poisoning (caused otherwise than by bacteria). Possible extensions of the system of registration and, where need be, disqualification of traders are discussed.

XIII A HOUSING

1 General   2 Belfast

1 GENERAL

Increase of Rent and Mortgage Interest (Restrictions) Act, 1920

Ministry of Home Affairs. Final reps. of Dept. Cttee., [1923].
Cmd. 22, 47 pp.
Cttee. apptd. April 1923; reps. sgd. September 1923.

T.M. Greer (Ch.) and ten members—Maj. H. Conacher, J. Cooper, T. Donald, W. Dowling, H.H. Graham, W. Grant, Maj. G.A. Harris, R. McBride, H. Midgley, G.H.E. Parr.

'To advise . . . as to what alterations, if any, should be made in applying to Northern Ireland the recommendations . . . regarding the continuance or amendment of the Increase of Rent and Mortgage Interest (Restrictions) Act, 1920.'

Majority Report. (Signed by the chairman and eight members.)

Rent Restriction Acts were introduced to cope with an acute housing shortage. The removal of rent controls is now urged, although it is realized that it cannot be achieved immediately. The first of May, 1926, is recommended as the date for the decontrol of rents on all houses. Increases of rent, as permitted by the principal Act, are only to be permitted if a tenant sublets. Provisions enabling a tenant to apply to a court for a suspension of an increase on sanitary grounds are to be continued. Houses, except those with a valuation of eight pounds or less, becoming vacant after the passing of the Act should be removed from its scope. The landlord's responsibility for repairs should be clearly defined in any new legislation, and it is proposed that landlord and tenant be empowered to enter into agreement on schemes to increase the latter's security of tenure. Modifications should be made in the chief Act in respect of the grounds on which a landlord may reclaim possession of a property. It is also argued that in the case of low rents, proceedings against tenants should be taken before a court of summary jurisdiction; that licensed premises may be repossessed if there is a breach of licensing laws;

that the consent of the landlord is needed for sublettings; and that restrictions on mortgage interest should be continued. Existing legislation should continue to cater for such miscellaneous matters as furnished lettings, key money and assessment of new houses.

The committee's brief interim report of May 1923 is not published separately but is provided as an appendix to this final report. There are four separate reservations to the final majority report, signed by J. Cooper, T. Donald, Major Conacher, and W. Grant and R. McBride, respectively. They register dissent from the report's recommendations on various matters chiefly in connection with permitted rent increases, vacant houses and the landlord's right to recover possession.

Minority Reports (of W. Dowling and H. Midgley.)

Dowling's report is the longer and argues against the choice of May 1926 as a date for the removal of controls, on the grounds that it is too soon. He also opposes the idea that vacant houses should only be decontrolled in certain cases. He offers proposals, which he claims will give incentives for the building of houses, while protecting tenants on the vital issues of rent and eviction.

Midgley's report also queries the selected date for the removal of controls and takes up issues concerned with rent increases, vacant houses, subletting, and the landlord's right to recover possession. Machinery should be established to deal impartially with any disputes which arise.

Rents

Rep. from Sel. Cttee. together with proc., . . . mins. of ev. and app.
H.C. 249, 338 pp.
Cttee. apptd. October 1931; rep. and mins. of ev. o.p. December 1931.

R. Crawford (Ch.) and twelve members —J. Beattie, Maj. C. Blakiston-Houston, R. Byrne, Rev. Prof. R. Corkey, J.H. Collins, J.C. Davison, Lt.-Col. A.R.G. Gordon, W. Grant, Maj. S.H. Hall-Thompson, J.J. McCarroll, H. Minford and E.S. Murphy.

'To inquire into the rentals now being charged for—
(a) Houses at present subject to the Rent Restriction Acts;
(b) Houses which were previously subject to the Rent Restriction Acts; but have become decontrolled by reason of their coming into possession of the owners;
and to report as to whether excessive rents are being charged . . . and to make recommendations . . . to prevent owners of such houses charging excessive rents, having due regard for the necessity of avoiding any steps which might tend to discourage the building of houses for the working classes, or placing any further burden on the Treasury . . . or on Local Authorities.'

The committee accepts that, for houses subject to the control of the Acts, the statutory rent laid down by legislation is reasonable. However, there are two types of case in which certain landlords of such dwellings are receiving an excessive sum. The first arises from the fact that the landlord may legitimately increase rent when his rates rise, but some landlords had failed to lower rents when the rates were reduced again. A suggestion for rectifying this is made. The second instance arises, on occasion, when landlords sell a house, through a hire-purchase agreement, rather than letting. There have been some very serious evasions of the Acts' provisions in some of these agreements, and it is recommended that legislation be introduced to check such evasion. In the case of the subletting of rooms in houses controlled by these Acts, it is suggested that provision should be made to ensure that rent charged to subtenants for rooms is a just proportion only of that paid by the tenant for the house as a whole.

Rents in decontrolled houses have risen extremely sharply because of the high demand for such dwellings, and steps are needed to check excessive rents being collected from the tenants.

It is urged that certain restrictions in operation prior to the Rent Restriction Act of 1925 be reimposed, with safeguards to avoid individual hardship. It is proposed that the Acts, with these amendments, should remain in force, the position being reconsidered in four to five years.

The committee is unanimous on most points, but there is an indication of two matters on which there was a division of opinion. There is a list of witnesses examined and a list of persons and institutions providing documentary evidence. In appendices are copies of hire-purchase agreements handed in; statistics of houses vacant in Belfast, 1914–1917 and 1921–1929; and details of corporation income and expenditure during 1931 with regard to houses erected under the 1910 Belfast Improvement Order. The bulk of the document is occupied by the minutes of evidence taken over a period of fifteen days.

Housing (in Northern Ireland)

Interim rep. of the Planning Advisory Bd. Cttee., 1944.
Cmd. 224, 53 pp.

Alderman S.B. Thompson (Ch.) and ten members—A.J. Allaway, Mrs. Amelia Bell, C. Caldwell, J.L. Clark, Miss E. Duffin, Alderman C.A. Hinds, T.H. MacDonald, J.H. Stevenson, Prof. W.J. Wilson, D. Winston. (In addition, an original member of the committee, J.E. Gamble, died in the very early period of deliberations, while two others, J. Dunlop and Miss D. Robertson, resigned during this time. A special technical sub-committee appointed by the committee included, in addition to Thompson, Stevenson and Winston, three others —H. Campbell, G. Hobart, and F. McKee.)

'To consider and report on the general housing problem . . . with particular reference to the clearance of slums and the provision of new housing in the post-war period.'

The technical sub-committee was asked:

'To consider and report on the problem of building the large number of houses which are urgently required . . . as quickly and economically as possible with special reference to:—

(i) the use of new materials and methods of construction;
(ii) standardization of planning structure and equipment;
(iii) permanency of structure;
(iv) insulation;
(v) water supply and sanitation.'

This, the first comprehensive picture of housing conditions in the province, was preceded by a housing survey which assessed houses with regard to structural conditions, overcrowding, lighting, heating, ventilation and water supply. The report indicates the results of this and goes on to discuss slum clearance, rural housing, rating systems, prefabrication, temporary housing, the acquisition of land, and the roles of housing associations and building societies. The provision of necessary minimum housing standards is discussed, and there are some comments on the density of housing, the provision of new estates, and the variety of housing that is necessary to cope with the numerous kinds of family units. It is revealed that, due to overcrowding and the need to replace unfit dwellings, approximately 100,000 new houses are required (apart from new needs arising while these are being constructed). Also some 230,000 houses need major or minor repairs. Legislation needs to be extended so that slum clearance can be carried out on a larger scale than at present and, where possible, occupants should be rehoused on the same site. Rural housing sites should be chosen and developed with due consideration for amenities, economy and facilities for community life. Detailed minimum standards are submitted for all new housing schemes, and machinery for the enforcement of these standards is recommended.

It is estimated that approximately 50,000 houses were built in Northern Ireland during the inter-war period, the largest number of subsidy houses constructed in any one year of this time being slightly in excess of 5,000 (average for the twenty-year span is 2,000 per annum). Suggestions to ensure the speedy and economic provision of houses are thus submitted; for the construction of the required 100,000 houses might, on past evidence alone, occupy almost two generations. Several proposals are made concerning the accumulation and local manufacture of materials and for planning an adequate labour force. It is deemed essential that rents should be within the means of those in lower income groups, and appropriate subsidies are urged. Because the present housing situation is grave, the example of Great Britain in providing temporary houses might profitably be followed. The committee cannot visualize new methods of construction or fresh ways of utilizing materials for permanent houses.

Appendices give notes on the number of houses required, unfit dwellings, assistance contributed by the government, and a list of those providing oral or written evidence. Numerous detailed statistical tables in the report and its appendices give information on houses needed; accommodation and overcrowding (with special tables dealing with overcrowding in Belfast and Londonderry); rural houses; state of water supply and sanitation; the productive capacity of and number of workers in the building industry; and the number of houses completed under the Housing Acts (with details of government financial aid afforded under these Acts).

Housing Costs Inquiry

Rep. of Tribunal, 1946 (reprinted 1948).
Cmd. 240, 19 pp.
Tribunal apptd., February 1946; rep. sgd. June 1946.

Sir William Robinson (Ch.) and two members — R.B. Donald and L.G.P. Freer.

'*For the purpose of inquiring into the cost of the provision by public authorities of houses for workers.*'

Prices are now very variable, and the building trades are in a state of transition. It seems, however, that tenders submitted in Northern Ireland might be excessively high when compared with those for similar houses in Great Britain. There has been a general rise in the cost of materials and labour. Inquiry shows the general level of tender prices in Northern Ireland to be not unreasonable, but that in one instance the problems presented by the site caused increased costs. Those responsible for house-building should proceed boldly, using the competitive tendering system; but the government should foster progress by use of the Civil Building Licensing Scheme, continue its efforts to apply effective supervision of the prices of materials and remain aware of the dangers of price-fixing 'rings'.

A statistical table compares tender prices in Northern Ireland and Great Britain.

Proposals for Dealing with Unfit Houses

[*A summary of proposals by local authorities under the Housing and Rent Restriction Law (Amendment) Act, 1956.*], *1959.*
Cmd. 398, 7 pp.

Details are given of the housing situation in various areas, and some 53,000 houses are revealed as unsuitable for human habitation, while another 41,000 are unfit but capable of repair. Londonderry has a much larger number of unfit houses than Belfast, but surveys in other areas reveal that rural districts usually have a larger proportion of unsuitable dwellings than do the urban areas. Statistical tables show the estimated 1958 population for each borough, urban district or rural district reporting; the total number of houses and the number of unfit ones; the estimated time needed to deal with all unfit houses; and remedial action planned up to the end of 1961.

Compensation of Compulsory Acquisition, etc., of Premises

Ministry of Health and Local Government, 1960.
Cmd. 422, 8 pp.

The existing law with regard to compensation is described. It is still in the process of being interpreted by the courts, but it is proposed to introduce legislation which will extend the provision for discretionary payments and authorize the payment of resettlement grants and 'good maintenance' payments to displaced tenants, which will be set off against any compensation which the courts may later award. Payments will also be authorized to owners of business premises and of owner-occupied houses purchased between 1944 and 1958. All occupiers of compulsorily acquired dwelling-houses will have a statutory right to be offered reasonable alternative accommodation.

2 BELFAST

Housing Scheme of the Belfast Corporation

Rep. of Inquiry held by R.D. Megaw (for the) Ministry of Home Affairs, 1926.
iv, 139 pp., charts. (A further 225 pages are occupied by the appendices.)

The extreme difficulty and complexity of the whole inquiry, initiated at the corporation's own request is explained in a preface. The report is partly concerned with serious allegations made as to the fulfilment of certain timber contracts, but it is also a more general investigation into the whole question of the corporation's administration of the Housing Acts over a five-year period. It appears that the allegations in the special inquiry unfortunately involve much more extensive matters than was originally believed, but the difficulty of obtaining accurate and reliable evidence is stressed.

The history of housing in Belfast since 1918 is traced. The charges that overpayments had been made to timber contractors and that the timber supplied was often seriously defective or worthless are asserted to be now fully proved. The report also comments upon factors contributing to these overpayments; the question of the choice and acquisition of building sites; contracts for house builders and for materials such as bricks, slates and sand; the organization of the corporation's Housing Department and its relation to the Treasurer's Department; labour conditions; the cost of housing; house allocation; and tenants' complaints.

As a much wider and very serious issue the responsibility and actions of the corporation and its Housing Committee are reviewed, and the matter of the suppression of documents in evidence (at first thought to be accidental) is commented upon, together with the role and attitude of officers holding major posts. The reporting inspector does not consider that this report, despite its length, is exhaustive. Much data was false, lacking or slow in forthcoming, perhaps because it was thought that publicity of abuses 'would be a greater evil than would be compensated for by the chances of reformed methods'.

Twenty-five appendices give the text of reports by firms and officials, analyses of accounts, comparison of tenders, appropriate statements, extracts from minutes, and correspondence. They also list the detailed proceedings of the meetings of the inquiry, give particulars of sites and cost of houses, and show the expenditure on housing by Belfast Corporation up to the end of 1925. Folding charts give statistics of the equivalent housing programme in six English cities.

Belfast Corporation Housing Allocations Inquiry

Ministry of Health and Local Government.
Rep. of Inspector, 1954.
38 pp.

Inspector apptd. October 1953; rep. sgd. February 1954.

T.A.B. McCall (Inspector).

'To hold an Inquiry in regard to whether there is any justification for allegations that payments, rewards or other considerations have been sought, offered, promised, made or received by or to any person or persons in connection with the allocation of housing accommodation provided by the Council of the County Borough of Belfast under the Housing Acts (Northern Ireland) 1890 to 1953, and, if so, in what circumstances the transactions took place and what persons were involved therein, and . . . to report.'

Allegations concerning improper methods in house allocation had been made by Councillor T.J. O'Sullivan. The resulting inquiry was held in public, and all witnesses who attended, whether on summons, voluntarily, or by invitation, gave their evidence on oath.

In view of the acute shortage in Belfast, a 'points' scheme (given in an appendix, together with the working rules in respect of the scheme) is used to determine the applicants' position on the waiting list. The scheme was adopted in 1946. By 1952–1953, points provided for loss of homes by enemy action or in respect of war service had ceased to be of any material significance, and the important factors were the degree of overcrowding and the presence of actual or suspected tuberculosis. The latter was the basis for allegations against doctors. Although there was evidence which

justified the making of the allegations, the inspector finds that no payment had been sought or received by Mr. W. Floyd, Dr. J.D.H. Mahony, Dr. H.F. Jackson, Dr. D.B. Emanuel and Mr. R. Young. He found that Miss Ann Copeland received, in all, £743 in connection with the allocation of housing; that Miss Sarah C. Madden received £512 on Miss Copeland's behalf and about £15 from Miss Copeland for her own benefit; that Mrs. Mary Valente (who denied that money was either offered or paid to Miss Copeland) paid a total of £65 indirectly to Miss Copeland and received £35 on Miss Copeland's behalf; and that Mrs. Meta Donnan sought a payment of £60 for her services in connection with the allocation of housing. Twenty-one cases are listed in an appendix in which it is admitted that money was paid directly or indirectly to Miss Copeland, and one in which it is admitted that money was offered to Miss Copeland. Appendices also list witnesses; give the judgement of the Right Honourable the Lord Chief Justice refusing the application by Dr. Jackson for a conditional order of prohibition to prevent Mr. McCall from proceeding with the hearing of the inquiry; summarize cases concerning Miss Copeland; and give copies of medical forms concerned with examinations of persons suspected of suffering from tuberculosis, who might thus be eligible for priority in rehousing.

XIII B TOWN AND COUNTRY PLANNING

1 General
2 Belfast and Environs

3 Other Areas

Note: Several important area studies are not parliamentary papers. Although some non–H.M.S.O. material is included here, it has been necessary to exclude technical reports prepared by teams of consultants and the reports of local government bodies, e.g., Belfast Corporation's reports on the Shankill and Whiterock areas, the Ballymena Devel-

opment Commission report on proposals for the new town centre.

Other area studies currently (1972) in hand include those for Newry, West Tyrone, and South-East Antrim.

On area planning in general, a useful publication for consultation is: *Seven Seminars: an Appraisal of Regional Plan-*

ning in Ireland, 1970, 121 pp. (Produced by Foras Forbartha, Dublin, and the Northern Ireland Ministry of Development, this is a report on a 1969 regional planning conference.)

1 GENERAL

Reconstruction and Planning

Ministry of Home Affairs. Preliminary rep. by W.R. Davidge, with a memorandum by the ministry, 1944.
11 pp.

This report was required to obtain expert technical advice from a consultant on certain particular questions: what area should be taken into account in preparing a town plan for Belfast, what should be the nature and scope of such a plan and what machinery should be set up to produce the plan? The consultant, therefore, is solely concerned with the procedure for the preparation of plans for a post-war programme to be carried out over a long term of years.

The consultant recommends a reconstruction plan for the city of Belfast and a large area around it, a plan for the city of Londonderry and the adjoining county, and plans for the improvement and development of the three inland counties. He also recommends that a planning advisory board be set up to make suggestions and advise on matters of principle arising during the preparation of the plan. There should be a planning commission of architects, engineers, surveyors, and planning officers, with a planning consultant appointed to act as a link between the advisory board and the technical planning commission.

The purposes of the plan will be to secure the fullest use of existing and potential resources; the improvement and development of transport, industry and agriculture, living conditions, water supply and sanitation; and the allocation of all land to its best use in the interests of the community.

The Ulster Countryside

Ministry of Health. Rep. by the Planning

Advisory Bd. on Amenities in Northern Ireland, 1946. Rep. sgd. August 1945. 44 pp., maps.

Committee on Amenities: D. Winston (Ch.) and seven members—D. Anderson, W.M. Capper, W. Duff, E. Estyn Evans, J. McGeagh, J. Seeds and F. Storey.

'To consider and report on means of safeguarding amenities throughout the Province with particular reference to:—
The provision of national parks and recreation grounds;
Advertisements and roadside structures;
The architectural control of buildings; and
The protection of access and legal rights of way.'

The need to preserve and improve amenities is stressed, as are the special dangers which the countryside faces in the immediate post-war years. There is a consideration and discussion of coastal preservation, roadside amenities, tree planting, architectural standards, ancient monuments and historic buildings, allotments, rights of way, smoke abatement, caravan siting, the landscaping of cemeteries and the advantages of crematoria, and the protection of special areas such as nature reserves or national parks. The responsibilities of local authorities are discussed and the need for overall control, through systematic planning, is agreed upon.

It is proposed that legislation be passed to ensure that public and private development aims at the conservation and improvement of existing amenities. Laws are also required on caravans and temporary structures, on advertisement control and to help improve road safety. More tree planting is urgently required, and a protected zone is envisaged for the coastline, in which the siting of buildings can be firmly controlled. There should be a continuous walking way around the whole of the coast. The appreciation of architecture needs to be promoted vigorously in the province, and a school of architecture at Queen's University would be an asset. The Planning Commission needs to be strengthened and reconstituted on a broader basis.

The various maps in the report are concerned with the protection of the coastal environment and with proposed national parks and similar inland reservations. Appendices consider nature reserves, field museums and suitable war memorials. A code for outdoor advertising is given, and extracts from the County Down by-laws regarding advertisements are quoted.

On this subject, see also Appendix: Select List of Annual Reports.

Provision of Recreational, Social and Physical Training Facilities

Interim rep. of the Planning Advisory [Bd.] Cttee., 1947.
Cmd. 246, 16 pp.

A.C. Williams (Ch.) and nine members—J. Blane, W.M. Capper, H. Casement, J. King Carson, W.I. Cunningham, W.H. Dawson, H.W. Neely, J.U. Stewart, Capt. Sir James Wilton.

This is the report of a subcommittee, four members of whom were members of the Planning Advisory Board appointed by the Ministry of Education. It is suggested that recreational activity should be aided by government grants but that these should be refused to voluntary organizations when requested for facilities that could be better provided by local authorities. In all towns there should be a minimum of five acres of public open space per thousand inhabitants, and blitzed sites in Belfast should be considered for conversion into children's playgrounds. Two and a half acres per five thousand inhabitants should at least be provided as children's playgrounds in the urban areas, and the needs of the countryside for physical training and recreational facilities must not be overlooked. Adequate provision of swimming baths, gymnasia and concert halls is urged, and authorities could consider closing certain streets to traffic so that children can play safely. No distinction need be made between the provision of facilities for different age groups.

The Ministry of Education ought to remain the central authority controlling facilities and grants, but the procedure for obtaining grants for different types of schools needs to be simplified. It is noted, in conclusion, that the proposals demand careful co-operation between local government and education and planning authorities. It is suggested, therefore, that the planning of new housing estates could include provision for the recreational and social needs of young people and adults in addition to the children's educational requirements.

Nature Conservation

Ministry of Home Affairs. Rep. of Cttee. 1962.
Cmd. 448, 24 pp.
Cttee. apptd. September 1960; rep. sgd. August 1962.

The Duke of Abercorn (Ch.) and eighteen members—A.G. Algeo, S. Anderson, J.V. Bateman, J.G. Calvert, A.E.P. Collins, H.J. Cromie, J. Cunningham, C.D. Deane, R. Eagleson, Prof. E.E. Evans, Prof. R.A.R. Gresson, A. Harkness, J. McK. Moon, R.E. Parker, H.T. Sheils, F.J. Silvester, N. Stephens, and L.J. Turtle. (J. McK. Moon died December 1960; J.E.C. Lewis-Crosby was appointed, April 1961.)

'To consider the protection of the natural fauna and flora and the physical features of scientific interest . . . and to make recommendations on measures for their conservation and control, including the protection of wild life.'

After some discussion of the historical background in Great Britain and in Northern Ireland, the case for developing a policy within the province is put. The functions and needs of a nature conservancy are considered, and these include the establishment and maintenance of nature reserves, staffing, and ways of promoting scientific research. An appendix shows a list of people and organizations which furnished evidence to the committee.

The numerous recommendations stress the urgency of a new approach and the irreversible effects of inaction. It is urged that a nature conservancy be set up and that national and local nature reserves be established. The national reserves should offer a balanced representation of Ulster flora and fauna. Cost of compensation to local authorities should be borne by government grant. The director and staff of the nature conservancy should be housed near to the Queen's University. The conservancy should have authority and means to promote research on matters such as land stability and erosion, soil fertility, peatland utilization and other topics of economic significance. The conservancy should publicize its work, and the local nature reserves should be within easy reach of population centres. The province should be divided into at least four areas for conservation purposes, each under the responsibility of a field officer.

The Administration of Town and Country Planning

[Ministry of Health and Local Government, Rep.] 1964.
Cmd. 465, 10 pp.

Under existing law there are thirty-seven local planning authorities. There is no overall plan, and planning decisions appear somewhat arbitrary and lacking in consistency. Surveys are needed, both regional surveys and more detailed town and village surveys. These should be the basis for a regional plan for the whole of Northern Ireland, and for area plans and town plans, which should all be subject to public debate. Professor Sir Robert Matthew, in his *Belfast Regional Survey and Plan* (Cmd. 451), drew attention to the advantages of a central planning authority which would be able to co-ordinate and guide development and would make more efficient use of the available professional staff. Public discussion and lengthy debate in the

House of Commons seem generally in favour of the idea, and the government proposes to establish a central planning authority, directly responsible to the minister of health and local government, which would work out policy and standards. The minister would be answerable to Parliament for all town and country planning. The local executive agents would be about ten local development committees, one for each of the six counties and two county boroughs, one for the New City area and one for the Belfast Harbour area. They would be mainly composed of elected councillors but with a few other local people nominated to represent important aspects of public life. There would also be a planning council of leading independent people to advise both on general trends and on individual cases of special importance, and there would be machinery for public hearing of eventual objections to plans and decisions.

The government invites discussion and informed comment on these proposals.

Area Development

Rep. of the Northern Ireland Economic Council, 1969.
49 pp.

Rt. Hon. B. Faulkner (Ch.) and seventeen members—A. Barr, W.J. Blease, G.E. Cameron, H.E. Campbell, A.H. Fetherston, W.D. Gilligan, Senator N. Kennedy, D.C. Lamont, W. McCormick, S. McGonagle, J. Morrow, J.T. O'Brien, Prof. J.R. Parkinson, Dr. D. Rebbeck, R.L. Schierbeek, W.L. Stephens, R. Thompson.

A high rate of unemployment in recent years in Northern Ireland has resulted from changes in industrial structure and an increase in population. Reductions in agricultural labour indicate that Northern Ireland's population will become increasingly urbanized. To cater for an increasing population, new industries will have to be attracted to Northern Ireland, and training schemes for all levels will be needed to match developments in industry.

Examining the Matthew/Wilson Reports and the published area plans, the council concludes that the fourteen centres recommended for Northern Ireland in the Matthew Report are too many and that a metropolitan area of Greater Belfast (including the towns of Carrickfergus, Bangor and Newtownards) and three centres, Craigavon, Antrim/Ballymena and Londonderry, could be developed to accommodate a large number of industries with other smaller centres having a more limited function. The council stresses that movement of population into the growth centres necessitates an urgent establishment of the administrative machinery to ensure growth on the scale and at the speed envisaged and also that services and amenities necessary in reception towns are provided in readiness for the increasing population. Smaller centres not potentially large enough to become growth centres are envisaged by the council as strong commercial, educational and cultural centres supported by a reasonable measure of industrial development. Movement of labour will need to be more positively encouraged and organized, and there is a need for an organization to tackle this problem. Rapid population growth in designated areas will necessitate an urgent development of primary, secondary and further education facilities. Plans for colleges of further education are outlined. University facilities for Northern Ireland are considered sufficient. The council feels that existing government training centres can be adequately developed to meet the changes of area development. The pattern of hospital services (see Cmd. 497, Hospital Plan, in Class XII) will support the suggested population development. Road development and expected expenditure involved are detailed in the report. Concentration will be on major regional routes and on urban systems. A radical administration reorganization is needed for water and sewerage, which would perhaps include the setting up of a central water authority. Economic development will be impeded if there are not sufficient houses provided by local housing authorities, and the council suggests that more sites be offered in key towns for private housing development. Improvement of cultural and social amenities in these areas must be kept up to date. Increasing demand for electricity supply, etc. can be met by forward planning on a regional basis. Port facilities ought to be investigated periodically to ensure that economic development is not impeded. Industrial land for the siting of new enterprises is already purchased by the Ministry of Commerce before immediate requirements, but further industrial sites will now be provided within new towns. The assistance given to industry under the Industries Development Act should not unduly influence industrial location.

Local government reorganization is urgently needed, as the present outdated system can impede economic progress and the development proposed; the Economic Council favours a small number of viable and effective local authorities. There is also thought to be a need for early introduction of comprehensive and up-to-date general planning legislation.

Appendices to the report include statistics showing the industrial structure of the working population, June 1966; tables and summaries of current estimates of population, housing and new manufacturing employment in key towns; and details of service industries and labour mobility.

Northern Ireland Development Programme 1970–1975

For details of this report see Class III p. 31-33.

2 BELFAST AND ENVIRONS

Planning Proposals for the Belfast Area

Rep. of Planning Com. Com. apptd. August 1942; rep. published 1945.

W.R. Davidge (Ch.) and eighteen members—J.W. Charlton, H.W. Craig, J. Crossland, R.B. Donald, R.D. Duncan, J. Getty, B.G.L. Glasgow, W. Grigor, A.S. Hamilton, E. McConnell, T.N. McLay, S.H.W. Middleton, Major J.H.A. Patton, T.F.O. Rippingham, E.D. Taylor, J.G. Wilkin, R.S. Wilshere, D. Winston.

'To prepare planning proposals for submission to the Ministry of Home Affairs and to make recommendations as to any legislative or administrative action necessary in connection therewith.'

Interim Report. *Sgd. September 1944. Cmd. 227, 18 pp., maps.*

Members of the commission are drawn from the county and county borough councils, Belfast Harbour Commissioners, Belfast Water Commissioners, and government departments of finance, home affairs, health and local government, agriculture, commerce, and public security.

The commission recommends a policy of gradual decentralization of Belfast, where, within the city boundary, population and industrial density are too high. Sites are suggested for building the many new and replacement houses which are needed. Industries at present in residential areas should be relocated. Certain towns are named as being suitable for further industrial development. Proposals are made for dealing with the traffic problem by such means as ring roads, and a new bridge to serve Sydenham bypass and a replacement for Queen's Bridge are suggested. A green belt, or agricultural zone, should be preserved around the city. Central Belfast has inadequate open space. A plan is proposed for the redevelopment of High Street by widening and planting trees, and for improving the river banks. There is a need for better car-parking facilities and bus termini; sites are suggested. Local authorities will need wide powers of acquisition and control, accompanied by strong financial aid from central government, and

appropriate legislation will have to be introduced.

Two maps illustrate the proposals made by the commission.

Planning Proposals for the Belfast Area

Rep. of Planning Com. Com. apptd. August 1942; rep. published 1952.

(Composition in June 1949–May 1951.) R.B. Donald (Ch.) and eighteen members—J.M. Aitken, J.C. Baird, J.W. Charlton, D.A. Davidson, R.D. Duncan, B.G.L. Glasgow, W. Grigor, A.S. Hamilton, R.H. McCullough, T.N. McLay, J. McRoberts, Maj. J.H.A. Patton, R.H.S. Patterson, T.F.O. Rippingham, Maj. H.K. Scott, J. Steel, R.T. Taggart, R.S. Wilshere. Consultant: W.R. Davidge.

'To prepare planning proposals for submission to the Ministry of Health and Local Government and to make recommendations as to any legislative or administrative action, necessary in connection therewith.'

And, in June 1949, *'To inform the Minister as to:—*
(a) the extent to which the recommendations contained in the Interim Report have been and are now being observed, and whether deviations, if any, are of a serious character; and
(b) the nature and extent of Belfast's "overspill" problem and the further steps, if any, which may be necessary to deal with it.'

Second Report. *Sgd. May 1951. Cmd. 302, 28 pp., maps.*

Members of the commission are drawn from the county and county borough councils, Belfast Harbour Commissioners, Belfast and District Water Commissioners and government departments of finance, commerce, health and local government, and agriculture. W.R. Davidge acted as consultant.

The commission concludes that the broad recommendations of the 1945 report do not require any considerable amendment, but is disturbed by the many departures from the original proposals, especially the contribution to suburban sprawl made by the proposed development in the Glengormley-Jordanstown and Finaghy-Suffolk areas.

The concentration of population and industry in Belfast is out of balance with that of the rest of the province, and an effort should be made to secure a more even distribution. This would only be achieved by a long-term policy of relocation of existing industry, supported by strong government encouragement. The commission advocates the building up of existing provincial towns and recommends provision of more adequate port facilities at Londonderry, Coleraine, Larne and Newry; the examination of the present system of freight charges; the offer of strong inducements by the government to secure dispersal, and close co-operation between central government, local authorities, housing, electric power and transport undertakings.

Certain areas on the outskirts of Belfast are indicated as suitable for housing development, but all practicable steps should be taken to preserve what remains of the green belt. The Belfast Corporation should press on with improved traffic routes in the city and should consider as a matter of urgency the cross-river traffic problem in the Queen's Bridge area.

Planning legislation is inadequate. The problem of compensation is a barrier to good planning, and the government should examine this matter with a view to introducing legislation which would enable the planning authorities to carry out their functions in such a manner as to cater for the best interests of the community.

Three maps show Belfast Corporation's planning proposals and road proposals and the Planning Commission's recommendations. Appendices list the members of the Belfast Area Subcommittee and bodies which submitted memoranda, and provide reports by W.R. Davidge, the Planning Commission Bridge Subcommittee and the Car Park Subcommittee.

Playing Fields in and about Belfast

Rep. of Youth Cttee., [1958].
Cmd. 381. 39 pp.
Cttee. apptd. October 1955; rep. sgd.
September 1957.

Wing-Com. J.S. Higginson (Ch.) and eleven members—L.A. Conlon, Rev. R.G. Craig, F. Jeffrey, Miss Mary Kerrigan, Rev. P. McCann, J.F. McClure, J. McGilton, Miss C.R. McKee. Rev. Canon H.A. McKegney, Miss Dorothy A. Meharg, D.G. Neill.

'To review the existing facilities for youth welfare, physical training and recreation, in the various localities . . . to direct public interest to the value of youth welfare . . . and to advise the Ministry.'

The Youth Committee, set up under the 1944 Youth Welfare Act, had been concerned about the poor provision with regard to sports fields and similar amenities. This report gives details of the number of pitches available for various sports and the number needed, of schemes proposed by local authorities and those existing through private provision, and of discussion with the authorities. Its chief recommendation is that, as a basis of a long-term policy, the ministry should increase the grant paid to local authorities from 50 percent to 65 percent of approved expenditure. It is also suggested that there should be facilities for authorities to recoup capital expenditure; that a capital sum of £250,000 should be set aside for urgent works; and that a consultative committee, with representatives from all the local authorities in the area, should be set up.

Appendices provide a statement by the National Playing Fields Association, a report on the condition of Belfast playing fields and a statement of schemes proposed, a statement of facilities available in nearby districts, and various appropriate statistical tables.

Belfast Regional Survey and Plan: Recommendations and Conclusions

Final Report. *Sgd. October 1962. Cmd. 451, 52 pp.*

Ministry of Health and Local Government. Rep. by Prof. Sir Robert H. Matthew. Apptd. October 1960. Reps. published 1961, 1963 (reprinted 1965).

'(a) to make a report on the Belfast region;
(b) to prepare an advisory outline plan for that region:
(i) in lesser detail so far as the City is concerned and concentrating largely on the population density, slum clearance and resultant problems of overspill;
(ii) taking account of the various plans adopted by the Belfast Corporation;
(iii) taking account of a plan recently prepared for Newtownabbey and adopted by the Urban District Council;
(c) to relate the survey and plan in the broadest terms to the geographical, economic and cultural pattern of Northern Ireland as a whole.'

Interim Report. *Sgd. January 1961. Published as a departmental report, Ministry of Health and Local Government. 19 pp., map.*

The interim report is necessary to enable development, especially housing, to continue while the regional plan is prepared. Sites approved for building are principally such as 'round-off and infill' existing development without encroaching on the high ground or lough-shore amenity areas around the city, or, except at Dunmurry, on good agricultural land. Six areas are recommended for public authority housing: Knocknagoney, Dundonald, Tullycarnet, Dunmurry, Doagh Road and Monkstown, and details and maps of the areas form an appendix to the report. Decisions about applications for private-enterprise house building present a problem in those cases where the site is not a 'rounding-off' of existing development; the government is requested to look into the matter of postponing such decisions.

The nature of the regional plan and survey is discussed, together with recent development, existing plans for town and country, and social and economic background. There has been much development with no co-ordination in planning. The quality of the environment is deteriorating. The ideal pattern is one of a capital city with all its facilities for government, industry and commerce, providing at the same time a good environment for living in all its aspects, and supporting and connecting with a widespread group of vigorous growing towns, themselves the centres on which agricultural life depends and to which the rural communities may look with confidence for services and recreation. In turn, the country would provide quiet and rest, but also stimulation for the townspeople, so that town and country together form an integrated whole. It is essential that population and employment be rapidly increased outside the Belfast urban area. Antrim, Ballymena, Bangor, Carrickfergus, Downpatrick, Larne, Lurgan, Newtownards and Portadown are suggested as centres for development, and Londonderry, Coleraine, Omagh, Dungannon, Enniskillen and Newry as key centres for industry. A new regional centre embracing Lurgan-Portadown is proposed, with an ultimate population of 100,000. The suggested population limit for Belfast would be made feasible by the increased attractiveness of these other centres.

A strict demarcation line should be made around Belfast between town and country. Housing in Belfast is discussed, and earlier reports and surveys are summarized. The limits of development now proposed include land for approximately 30,000–35,000 new buildings.

In the urban area, detailed surveys are required to cover: existing land use; densities of occupation; age and condition of buildings; buildings and other features requiring maintenance and preservation; the delimitation of areas of comprehensive redevelopment; location of areas for industrial expansion; location of open spaces; traffic requirements; areas requiring rehabilitation rather than reconstruction; landscaping, etc. An integrated planning authority for the urban area as a whole is urgently required. More study is needed to work out a comprehensive plan of communications that will meet both the broad needs of the region and the detailed requirements of the urban area.

On the fringe of the city certain areas are recommended for public purchase, including part of the Antrim Hills, as a regional park for general access by the townspeople. Wooded estates at present privately owned should be acquired for preservation as they come on the market. Steps should be taken to provide for protection, public access and rehabilitation where necessary, in the areas of eastern Lough Neagh, Shaw's Bridge, Strangford Lough and Belfast Lough. A development plan should make provision for camping, caravanning, picnics, carparking and the like, and any detailed survey should include a survey of all sites of scientific interest, of tree planting, and the condition of trees and rights of way.

It is important that the future regional planning organization should be concerned with the large number of miscellaneous matters relating to the maintenance of the countryside, from such basic improvements as removing smog from Belfast, to the rehabilitation of spoiled or neglected areas. A comprehensive cleaning-up process is needed—brushing up, making good, planting trees and landscaping. This means education, directly in the schools and indirectly by encouragement of local civic societies. The main recommendations of the 1946 *Interim Report of the Northern Ireland Planning Advisory Board on the Ulster Countryside* (see above) are strongly endorsed. The maintenance and enhancement of amenities is a responsibility of government at all levels. Improvement of tourist facilities should not be neglected, and the efforts of all interests should be co-ordinated.

Existing planning legislation is reviewed and suggestions made. A central planning authority is advised—the Ministry of Planning and Development Legislation should cover compensation grants to local authorities who acquire land for planning purposes and grants for preservation of areas and buildings of special interest, comprehensive development of town centres, areas in need of rehabilitation. Planning surveys should be carried out and development plans prepared for the whole province. The regional survey set up for the purposes of this report should be maintained and the survey be a continuing process.

Belfast Urban Area Plan

Ministry of Development. Belfast Urban Area Plan, 1969. Building Design Partnership in association with Nathaniel Lichfield and Associates, Derek Lovejoy and Associates and the late John Madge. May and September 1969. 2 vols.: Vol. I 163 pp., Vol. II 262 pp.; bibliography diagrs., illus., maps. Not published by H.M.S.O.

The period of this plan is nominally from 1966–1986, but in some aspects it looks ahead to the year 2,000. It is seen as capable of modification as it unfolds, but certain tasks are viewed as undoubted needs, and priority should be given to these. Between 1946 and 1966 capital expenditure in the Belfast urban area (at 1967 prices) was approximately £500 million. With or without a plan about twice this sum will be spent in the years 1966–1986. The plan is to 'guide' this inevitable expenditure according to sound social and economic priorities.

Volume I, the main report, provides a series of subject studies on such themes as land resources, population, industry employment, housing, shopping, education, recreation, landscape, social services, and public services. These are followed by full locality studies for each of the various regions within Belfast and nearby areas such as Lisburn, Dunmurry, Newtownbreda, Holywood, Dun donald, Newtownabbey and Andersonstown/Suffolk.

It is recommended that urgent acceleration of the development of growth centres and control of growth be provided. The establishment of a 'Housing Co-ordinating Agency' would encourage the planned movement of people to the growth centres, and house building should be encouraged in these centres; likewise an 'Industrial Agency', within the Ministry of Commerce, could co-ordinate industrial expansion. Suitable data for planning may be gained from an early consideration of the 1971 population census figures. Housing redevelopment needs a boost so that, by 1970, 1,500 dwellings per year will be cleared. Designated redevelopment areas should be completed by 1985. A population density standard is required. In the field of employment, ways in which the activities of the Northern Ireland Training Council could be extended are noted. A working party is needed to examine the supply of the educational system in relation to the changing needs of industry.

Office development could be concentrated in the proposed district centres, especially at Newtownbreda, Lisburn and Newtownabbey. The relocation of certain markets and the redevelopment of their present sites is urged. Eighty acres of land at Sydenham should be developed for light industrial and warehousing purposes, and Bog Meadows should soon be reclaimed and used for a new industrial estate. Car-parking standards in the City Centre require revision, and the elimination of through traffic there and in certain other areas is contemplated. Numerous other industrial recommendations relate to transport and to envisaged changes in the harbour and dock areas.

Major district leisure centres are proposed, and youth clubs should represent one per seven thousand population. The Lough and its shores should be developed for recreation, and the expansion of parks and the number of golf courses is discussed. The twelve district centres proposed must have excellent shopping facilities. Other shopping growth should be concentrated in areas where new housing is remote from the district centres.

Other proposals include a plan for integrated library development, compulsory purchase powers to aid the planned expansion of Queen's University, the enlargement of seriously substandard school sites, special housing facilities for the aged, retention of the Matthew Stop-line to conserve natural features, and the quickening of improvements to the sewage system including the long-term relocation of the main sewage works opposite the Newtownabbey plant. The report as a whole, with its numerous recommendations, represents a comprehensive, rational and ambitious plan for the growth and development of the Belfast area.

Volume II provides an appendix consisting of very specific information and technical analyses on ten of the subject studies. Appendices in volume I give the terms of reference, a list of complementary reports on planning for various areas in the Belfast region, a list of the planning objectives and of the planning team, a list of acknowledgements and a bibliography. A folding map is also provided as an appendix, and numerous relevant maps and plans are distributed throughout the text of the report.

3 OTHER AREAS

Ulster Lakeland

Ministry of Health and Local Government. A tourist plan for County Fermanagh, 1963.
88 pp., bibliography, map, photos.

This survey and plan was prepared by the planning staff of the Ministry of Health and Local Government at the request of the county council.

County Fermanagh's considerable potential as a tourist area is largely unexploited. The physical and social background, climate, population, industry, tourist facilities, and communications of the county are surveyed, and suggestions are made for developing tourist amenities and attractions in such a way that the peace and beauty of the area will remain unspoiled. Finally, the proposals are summarized in tabular form, so that for each location suitable for development or improvement, comments and suggestions are listed. These concern accommodation, catering, sports and recreational facilities, landscape, communications, and public services. Appendices list the persons, societies and departments from whom advice was sought, and the books and other publications consulted. There are twenty-six tables containing survey information, nine plans and diagrams, eleven plates and a map of the county.

New City (Craigavon)

Ministry of Health and Local Government. First rep. of the New City Design Group, 1964.
xvi, 126 pp. diagrs., maps, plates.

This preliminary statement of principles and objectives discusses the functions of the city, its area, and an outline of the plan and its implementation. Plates, diagrams and statistics indicate the present situation and the proposed layout of the new city, which aims at creating a new base for attracting industry to the province, the creation of a new centre which would contribute to the regeneration of the southern and western areas of Northern Ireland, and a residential zone which will relieve housing and traffic pressures on Belfast. The new community should house up to 100,000 persons by 1981, and such a city was described by Professor R. Matthew (in the Belfast Plan—see above) as the most important single new development suggested. The site proposed is midway between Lurgan and Portadown. Some twenty-five miles from Belfast and providing quick access to that city on the M1 motorway, it is on a natural line of development towards the west and south. Both Lurgan and Portadown were

'new towns' in the Ulster plantation period in the early seventeenth century, and their growth has continued to the present day. The manufacture of high quality linens and yarns is still a major source of employment in the area, but the industrial framework is being broadened. It is considered that the physical concept which best meets the objectives of the plan is that based on the principle of 'linear growth', thus giving the city a basic composition of town units (ultimately four with a population of up to 20,000 each), main centres, transportation network and a farm belt. The town units will each have about 5,000 dwellings. Up to 1,000 acres is allowed for industrial buildings, and three main sizes of site are proposed. The three major industrial regions should be Silverwood, which is to the north-west of Lurgan, Carn to the north-east of Portadown and the area between the boroughs on the southern edge of the city. Problems concerning education, landscaping and amenity provision are discussed. It is not considered that the new central area will adversely affect the commercial prosperity of the two boroughs.

A chapter on the implementation of the plan covers capital costs, financial returns and budgeting, with appropriate tables. Investment in the initial years will tend to be heaviest on preparatory works associated with the provision of engineering services and major roads. Diagrams in the report include an indication of communications, landscape and recreational facilities; the possible form of the city in the year 2000; the location of other new towns in the United Kingdom; and the age/sex structure in 1961 and 1981 for the city and for Northern Ireland as a whole.

[A second illustrated report (65 pp.) on Craigavon was published in 1967, but this was the work of the Development Commission for the city and is not a parliamentary publication. It presents more detailed plans of development to 1981 (particularly those scheduled to come into operation in the next few years) and offers a projection of further growth up to the end of the century.]

Antrim New Town

Ministry of Development. Outline plan, 1965.
52 pp., diagrs., map, photos.

Steering Cttee. apptd. September 1963; rep. sgd. July 1965. R. Moore (Ch.) and six members—G. Camblin, W.M. Cameron, J.H. Campbell, J.H. Lindsay, J. McDowell, G. Swann.

The plan was prepared by planning officers of the Ministry of Development, advised and guided by the steering committee. The population of Antrim town is about 3,000. The plan provides for a future population of at least 30,000, gradually achieved over fifteen years or more. British Enkalon Ltd. is the only large employer of labour, but it is hoped that many other industries may move into the expanding town, which is very favourably placed with regard to road, rail and air transport. The new motorway being constructed from Belfast to Ballymena, and ultimately to Londonderry and Coleraine, passes near Antrim. The new town should have two link roads to the motorway, connected by a system of secondary distributor roads. From the latter, minor roads will give access to houses and other buildings and to car-parks. Quite separate from the road system, a network of pedestrian ways is envisaged, such that journeys on foot will be pleasant and safe, and shopping centres kept free from motor traffic. A sketch plan shows the proposed redevelopment of the town centre, and a map of the whole area indicates sites for new housing estates, schools and industries. Suggestions are made for the development of existing scenic and recreational amenities, and for new play areas and sports facilities. Consideration must be given in new development to the maintenance of clean air, which is essential to the British Enkalon factory; to the water supply, which will be from Lough Neagh; to sewage disposal, for which a new disposal works will be required; and to electricity and telephones, for which expansion presents little difficulty.

No firm timetable can be laid down for implementation of the plan, but three stages are suggested for development of sewage, water and road works, and school buildings. The rate of provision of houses and playing fields will depend on the rate of industrial growth.

Tables in the appendix show the numbers or acreage of existing and proposed housing, industry, educational institutions, playing fields and the town centre.

Ballymena Area Plan

[Ministry of Development], 1966.
76 pp., bibliography, diagrs., map, photos.
Steering Cttee. apptd. May 1964; rep. sgd. October 1966.

J.D. Henry (Ch.) and eight members— G. Camblin, W.M. Cameron, R. Carson, W. Houston, A.N. Johnston, J.D. Loughridge, R. Moore, Maj. R.B. Morton.

The plan for Ballymena involves significantly different problems from that for Antrim, as Ballymena is already a vigorous and expanding township with a congested and tightly packed town centre. As with Antrim, it is planned to have a system of distributor roads linked to the adjacent M2 motorway (Belfast-Londonderry) and to minor access roads. Pedestrian routes and cycle tracks are recommended, forming a network quite separate from the road system.

There are many industrial firms in Ballymena which either provide for the needs of the farming community or are engaged in the processing of agricultural produce. Many existing industries are in the Harryville area, which is close to the town centre, but although this causes problems, it is accepted that these industries will remain. Areas for new industry are proposed at Broughshane Road, Toome Road, Galgorm Parks and Larne Road. New housing, of a variety of types, will be needed, and different areas are discussed. Housing development at Gracehill will need to be carefully designed to be in keeping with the character of this interesting village.

Redevelopment of the town centre will be difficult but essential. A ring road should allow traffic to circulate around this shopping and business centre and give access to car parks and service areas. In a new shopping and office sector, it is proposed to segregate pedestrians and vehicles, but it would be too difficult and costly to achieve this within the already developed town centre.

The accommodation of the present schools and other services is discussed. It is estimated that when the population reaches 60,000, seventeen new primary schools and five or six new secondary schools will be needed.

The area plan envisages a generous provision of open space throughout the urban area and recreational facilities of various kinds, including small intimate playing spaces for young children, equipped play parks for older children, and informal 'kick-about' areas, all within easy reach of the homes. A large park should occupy the area between the town centre and the motorway.

Expansion of the area's water supply is already in hand; the scheme includes two new reservoirs. Further trunk sewers will also be necessary, and there are plans for expansion of the existing Spencestown sewage works and additional new disposal works at the same site. No problem is foreseen in the necessary expansion of electricity, gas and telephone services.

It is undesirable that the countryside around the expanding town be marred by uncontrolled ribbon development. Plans for village communities at Ahoghill, Broughshane, Cullybacky, Kells and Connor are thus included in the area plan.

Finally, four stages are suggested for implementation of the plan; three of the stages should be complete before 1981.

Appendix I gives details of the population proposed for various housing areas, and the acreage occupied by or estimated for the town centre, industry, open space and schools. Appendix II is a report of Nathaniel Lichfield and Associates planning and economic consultants, entitled *Ballymena Town Centre: A Forecast for Shopping and Business Accommodation*. A short bibliography gives sources of published and unpublished data referred to. Appendix III lists public authorities and other bodies consulted.

Londonderry as a Location for New Industry

For details of this report see Class V p. 64.

Londonderry Area Plan

Ministry of Development. Londonderry Area Plan. James Munce Partnership, 1968. Rep. sgd. March 1968.
156 pp., diagrs., illus., maps, bibliography.
Not published by H.M.S.O.

Area Steering Cttee: A.W. Anderson (Ch.) and eight members—W. Beatty, R.C. Bond, J. Brown, J. Doherty, J.T. Lamberton, J. Mackey, J.H. Nicholl, J.J. Scott.

This report is, in part, a summary of nine detailed reports prepared for the steering committee by its consultants. Chapters deal with matters such as the nature of the region; population; employment prospects; shopping, housing, education, communications; and community services. There is also some discussion of landscaping, tourism, and residential growth patterns.

The basic objectives for the period to 1981 are to consolidate and revitalize the centre of Londonderry, to upgrade amenities to attract industrialists, to provide wisely sited residential development, to ensure adequate and well co-ordinated communications to accommodate the growth proposals, and to encourage tourism. In doing this, the inherent beauty of the region and the historic buildings in the city must be carefully conserved.

It is envisaged that, as more industrialization proceeds with the implementation of this plan over the next fifteen years and as population grows and is swelled by immigration from the west of the province, Londonderry will retain its rank as the second largest city. Population is expected to increase in this period by some 13,500 over the 1966 level. It is possible that a regional airport may eventually be provided as improved road communications and the expanded port stimulate industrial growth. Nearly 10,000 new houses will be built, with a large new residential area to the northwest of the city. The central shopping area of the city is to be restructured and supported by district centres in Waterside and at Ballyarnett-Shantallow. Planning includes the wise relocation of certain industries, improvement of traffic flow and the provision of a cultural-recreational centre. Towards the end of the plan period a second river crossing will be built. In education, the technical college will be expanded, and Magee College will, of course, form an important part of the New University. With regard to hospital services, it is envisaged that the Londonderry system will become one of the three area hospitals outside Belfast and that the city will have a very strong claim for the province's second medical school, if this is required. Details are also given of plans for the provision of sports facilities, the opening up of the riverside as a promenade and starting place for country walks, and the setting up of a tourist information office.

The phasing and cost of the plan are considered, and it is emphasized that it must be continually reviewed in the light of developments. It demands careful co-operation from all the local authorities involved. Appendices to the report list public authorities and other bodies consulted and provide a bibliography which includes a list of the technical reports prepared by the Munce Partnership. Maps, illustrations and diagrams throughout the report aim at showing land use, road proposals, population distribution, services, zoning plans, communications, and features envisaged to give the area the architectural character that is desired.

Coleraine-Portrush-Portstewart Area Plan

Ministry of Development. Rep. to the Steering Cttee., by R. Matthew, and Johnson-Marshall and Partners, in association with Percy Johnson-Marshall and Associates, 1968.
56 pp., illus., map, plans.

Steering Committee: J.W. Stewart (Ch.) and ten members—W. Millar Cameron, Lt. Col. D.J. Christie, J. Doherty, S.J. Henry, A. Kidd, W.R. Knox, R.G. Macauley, G.A. McIlrath, H.R. Neill, A.G. Thompson.

The study area is to be so planned as to accommodate a population of 74,000 people, with 60,000 of these in a new urban area which will eventually link the three towns to create a new scale of town (approximately equal in size to Stevenage, Hertfordshire—present population 60,500) which will 'attract and support a wider range of social, cultural and service facilities' and create a suitable environment for the expanding university. Coleraine, with a population of 13,578 in 1966, is the main centre in a total area of ninety square miles. 24,000 jobs could be created by 1981, and growth of urban population to that date should be approximately up to 46,000 people. Zones and community groups are planned within the region. Details are given of appropriate developments for recreation, tourism, housing and the countryside, and various alternative plans for the exact nature of the growth and development of the designated area are discussed.

Appendices give terms of reference; details on expansion of population and employment, with some statistics; and a discussion of transport patterns and public transport amenities.

Banbridge Area Plan

Banbridge Area Plan: a development strategy. Down County Planning Officer (H.J. Parson) in consultation with the Building Design Partnership, 1970.

32 pp., illus., plans.
Not published by H.M.S.O.

The first plan for the Banbridge area dates back to the latter part of the eighteenth century. The present report sets out 'to outline a general framework for development to the end of the century in an area of 145 square miles in West Down, comprising Banbridge and the surrounding countryside which is economically and socially related to the town as a source of employment, services, recreational and social facilities; [and] to keep the general public informed of the broad planning principles. . . .' A review is thus made of population, employment, housing, transport, landscape and recreation. A development strategy for the town centre is outlined.

Proposals include planned development to accommodate 32,000 people in the area by the year 2001, including 16,000 in the town of Banbridge; reservation of a large area of land within the town for the construction of 1,400 new houses by 1986; designation of two conservation areas and six development areas plus the construction of substantial additional retail floor space within Banbridge town centre; and the provision of landscaped car-parks. A new urban park for Banbridge is proposed, and there is to be a check on indiscriminate building within the area of the study. Buildings of historical or architectural merit are to be carefully conserved. The present redevelopment programme is to be completed by 1981. Banbridge is likely to change little in character, but it will depend more on Craigavon and less on Belfast.

Appendices give details of the new housing areas and programme and draw attention to a supplementary report which provides technical details in the form of work sheets and notes on population, employment, housing and traffic. Some statistics on these topics are provided within the present report.

Mourne

A study by technical officers of the

Ministry of Development, 1970.
viii, 85 pp., bibliography, maps, photos.

The area covered by the survey is bounded roughly by a line running from the head of Dundrum Bay to the north of Castlewellan Demesne, thence to Rathfriland and then turning south to the coast at Narrow Water, and it includes the main urban centres of Newcastle, Rostrevor, Warrenpoint, Kilkeel, Rathfriland and Castlewellan.

In the introduction, the report states the two main problems within the Mourne area as (a) the raising of living standards in an area mainly composed of small farms and (b) maintenance of the primary tourist attractions of unspoilt scenery and uncrowded conditions in the face of rapidly increasing use of the motor-car and outdoor recreational facilities.

Mourne is an area of rather sparse natural resources; lowland areas are predominantly agricultural, while the mountains provide sheep grazing, mineral working, forests, and extensive and valuable water catchment areas. The manufacturing industries are mainly in the holiday resorts of Newcastle and Warrenpoint. The road network, while possibly adequate for local needs, has not sufficient capacity for peak and seasonal traffic flows.

The major land uses in the area can be divided into agriculture, forestry, mineral working, manufacturing industry, service industry, public utilities, and residential and recreational. Three-quarters of the farm holdings in the area are less than thirty acres, and to amalgamate small farms would mean an increase in field size, and bigger farmhouses and structures (which are likely to be more obtrusive in the landscape than their predecessors). Entry into the Common Market might result in more land being released for forestry. All important commercial fishing is concentrated at Kilkeel. Mechanization has changed the scale and pace of stone working in the area, and today only nine quarries are in operation. The total employment in the area in the manufacturing industry is 1,500 persons, while in the service industry (hotel, catering and distributive trades), there are about 3,000 persons employed. About half of the occupied dwellings in the rural area are without piped water and indoor toilet facilities. The increasing demand for residential sites will, if not controlled, result in ribbons and pockets of suburban-type houses quite alien to the traditional landscape. The principal statutory undertakers whose operations affect the area are the Belfast City and District Water Commissioners, the Portadown and Banbridge Regional Waterworks Joint Board, the Electricity Board for Northern Ireland and the Post Office. The Mournes are a major recreational area in Northern Ireland, and facilities must be provided to benefit the greatest number of visitors and residents.

Proposals in the report cover landscape, roads, car-parking, access, signposting and the uninhabited landscape. Change is inevitable, but it is important that the rural landscape remain rural and not be sprinkled with outposts of suburbia. An increase in the afforestation programme could enhance the landscape and contribute to employment. Roads are a key feature in the development of the area. Minor improvements on existing roads, planning relief for traffic-congested towns, and considerable improvement on the main coast road are all essential. Increase in traffic necessitates a vast and urgent increase in car-parking capacity. Urban car-parks should be large and rural car-parks generally small with picnic facilities close at hand. Access to moorland, mountain and shore should be relatively unrestricted, but in the latter case the question of public rights of way is still relatively unexplored in Northern Ireland. Much more frequent and informative signposting is required. The wilderness area of the Mournes, i.e., that above 1,000 feet and especially that area inside the Belfast Water Commissioners' wall, must be maintained.

The report shows with maps and tables the population distribution and forecasts for the area and gives some suggestions for the improvement and long-term development of the urban settlements of Newcastle, Kilkeel, Warrenpoint, Castlewellan and Annsborough, Rathfriland, Rostrevor, Dundrum, Hilltown and Annalong.

The external appearance of the area is important. Litter must be kept to a minimum; rubbish tips are an essential and important public utility but are not visual assets, and so they must be screened and covered at frequent intervals. Derelict vehicles left by the roadside are another growing menace to the landscape, as are broken-down buildings, fences and gates; untidy quarries with rusting equipment; shabby and ill-maintained sheds and untidy spoil heaps. Public conveniences are a necessity with the increase of visitors, but they must be kept clean and tidy.

For the immediate future, implementation of development schemes is likely to be in the hands of the existing development authorities, between whom cooperation and co-ordination is essential.

The thirteen appendices take up about a third of the report and give details of the physical background of the area, communications, a pumped storage scheme, features of interest, small villages, caravan parks, camping, youth hostels and the souvenir industry. They further supplement the sections of the report on agriculture, car-parks and picnic sites, high car-parks, footpaths and recreation. The use of more than 100 tables and illustrations in the form of maps, photographs, diagrams and sketches gives a detailed guide to the contents of each section in the report. A bibliography and sources of information are found after the appendices.

North Down Area Plan

[*Rep. of a Steering Cttee.*], 1972.
168 pp., bibliography, diagrs., illus., maps.
Rep. sgd. November 1971.

Mrs. Georgina M. Stone (Ch.) and fourteen members — A.B.C. Baird, R.V.

Campbell, H.J. Cromie, J.S. Fowler, Captain D.J.R. Ker, J. McCormick, W. McCutcheon, H. McGimpsey, H.S. Porter, J. Scott, W. Spratt, R. Topping, F.C. Tughan, J. White. (Officers from the Ministry of Development and from the local councils also attended the steering committee meetings.)

An introduction sets out the historical background and reviews the present features of the area as a whole. Bangor and Newtownards are viewed as important growth centres. The former should have a population of 45,000 by 1981 and 60,000 by 1991; the latter experienced a slight population decline in the early 1960s but is expected to reach numbers of 23,000 in 1981 and 27,000 by 1991. The growth and expansion of other areas and the amenities of the villages of the Ards Peninsula demand consideration, and all measures taken must be compatible with the conservation of natural beauty. Areas adjoining Strangford Lough are in special need of protection from unsympathetic development.

Housing, employment, agriculture, transport, shopping facilities, recreation and landscape are viewed in a general context. Four separate chapters then consider the future planning of Bangor, Newtownards, Comber and Donaghadee under the headings—history, population, housing, employment, shopping, public utility services, community services, communications, recreation. The chapters on Bangor and Newtownards also have sections on the phasing of development and town centre planning. Another chapter considers plans for fourteen villages in the region—Ballygowan, Ballyhalbert, Ballywalter, Carrowdore, Cloughey, Crawfordsburn, Greyabbey, Groomsport, Helen's Bay, Kircubbin, Millisle, Moneyreagh, Portaferry and Portavogie.

Appendices indicate the survey work undertaken, shopping forecasts for the urban growth area, land use analysis, and details of buildings which are of architectural or historic importance and of archaeological sites. A bibliography is provided and acknowledgement made of the help given by various organizations in the preparation of this plan. The plan is liberally illustrated with maps, photographs of existing buildings and amenities, and diagrams showing envisaged projects, population structure, traffic flow in the main towns, and parking demand. Three detailed detachable maps concern recreational facilities, and specific proposals for Newtownards and Bangor.

XIV EDUCATION

1 GENERAL EDUCATIONAL POLICY

Educational Services

Ministry of Education. Reps. of Dept. Cttee. apptd. September 1921; reps. published [1922], [1923].

R.J. Lynn (Ch.) and thirty-one members —Rev. J. Bingham, J. Boyce, Rev. Canon J.E. Browne, Mrs. Dehra Chichester, Most Rev. C.F. D'Arcy, R.F. Dill, A. Duffin, J.G. Espie, Dr. H. Garrett, W. Grant, F.G. Harriman, Maj. G.A. Harris, W. Haslett, W.A. Houston, R.J. Johnstone, R.M. Jones, Prof. A. Larmor, J.B. McCutcheon, Miss A. Matier, A.S. Mayes, W.T. Miller, Prof. D.L. Savory, J. Sinclair, J. Smyth, Rev. W.H. Smyth, Maj. R. Stanley, Miss Elizabeth Steele,

J.H. Stirling, Rev. W.G. Strahan, Prof. R.A. Williams, A.N.B. Wyse. (Rt. Rev. C.T.P. Grierson apptd. November 1921 to take the place of the Most Rev. C.F. D'Arcy who resigned.)

'To inquire and report on the existing organization and administration of the Educational Services . . . and to make such recommendations as may be considered necessary for the proper coordination and effective carrying out of these services.'

Interim Report. *Sgd. June 1922. (Not signed by J.B. McCutcheon and J. Sinclair.)*
Cmd. 6, 104 pp.

Certain residual powers are to be transferred from other departments to the Ministry of Education, and an advisory council is to be set up to advise or make representations to the minister. County boroughs, urban districts and rural councils are to be the local units for administration and are to combine or subdivide their duties further as necessary, with ministry sanction. The ministry is to retain the power to prohibit unsuitable units. Three classes of primary school are distinguished, and suggestions are made for the allocation of state aid to them. There is to be separate religious instruction for children of all persuasions, and this should be part of the education given in preparatory and secondary schools, provided no system or rules are imposed. Compulsory school attendance is to be enforced with greater stringency. School buildings are to be provided through long-term loans rather than grant aid.

It is argued that the final selection of principals in important primary schools should be made by the ministry and that the ministry should maintain registers of teachers. Conditions of appointment and service for secondary school teachers are to be reshaped by the ministry. Recommendations for teachers' pensions are made. Among more specific suggestions, it is proposed that a rate be levied for technical education, that agric-

ulture should not be taught in schools, that workhouse schools should be closed, and that the ministry should limit its functions with regard to reformatory and industrial schools. A county scholarship is to be instituted; birth certificates are to be furnished in the case of each new school entrant; and meals provision for necessitous children is to be a shared responsibility of local authorities and the ministry. The financial implications of these recommendations, which constitute a comprehensive survey and critique of educational practice, are outlined. There are five, somewhat lengthy, reservations on various matters, signed by J.G. Espie and G.A. Harris; J. Boyce, F.G. Harriman and R.J. Johnstone; A.S. Mayes; A. Duffin; A. Larmor and J.G. Espie. Dr. Duffin's reservation presses, among other matters, for inter-denominational schools concentrating on secular education, although opportunity should be provided for religious instruction under the auspices of the churches. Appendices give statistics on the population and valuation of county boroughs and urban and rural districts; a classification of national schools existing in 1921; the number of teachers in April 1922; the number of intermediate and technical schools at this time; and details of state grants for technical instruction.

Final Report. *Sgd. June 1923. (R.J. Johnstone, J.B. McCutcheon and J. Sinclair did not sign.)*
Cmd. 15, 126 pp.

It is explained that, had time been taken to investigate every aspect of the educational problem, the report would have been delayed and urgently needed reforms postponed. It was thus decided to confine 'attention to those problems of educational administration which seemed most in need of reconsideration'. Five such areas are distinguished: teacher training, the co-ordination of the proposed educational system, the place of examinations, curricula, school inspection.

For the training of teachers, it is

proposed that the best student teachers intending to enter primary schools should be given an opportunity to obtain a degree at the end of their training. Continued study by primary school teachers is encouraged, but all such teachers should repay part of their training costs. All primary teachers should serve first as assistants. Teachers in secondary schools should have a degree and should usually pursue a post-graduate course in the history, method and practice of teaching. Recommendations are made for the qualifications needed by technical teachers, and it is regarded as beneficial that such teachers should work a two-year probationary period.

Among suggestions designed to achieve educational co-ordination, it is urged that the age for admission to an infants school be raised to four; that certain schools should be amalgamated for greater efficiency; that the teaching of domestic economy, horticulture and woodwork should be promoted; that, on an experimental basis, some new trades preparatory schools with an agricultural bias might be established; that there should be provision for intensive training in domestic science for older girls; and that research in technical schools should be assisted. There is insufficient demand to justify the establishment of central schools.

In the field of examinations, the existing technical school system is deemed to be satisfactory, although the establishment of a committee to investigate apprenticeship is recommended. There should be two primary-school public examinations with scholarships, one at age eleven or twelve for entrance to secondary school, the other at age thirteen or fourteen for a leaving certificate. Middle-grade secondary school examinations should be abolished, and two examinations (junior and senior), of a somewhat different character to the former ones, established. A detailed syllabus is laid down on the subject of school curricula. A wide range of themes, including temperance and kindness to animals, are suggested for pri-

mary school teaching. Recommendations on school inspection affect chiefly secondary and preparatory schools. No changes in the system of inspecting technical schools are envisaged.

The report has five signed reservations. The first, signed by A.S. Mayes, opposes a scholarship to secondary schools at the age of eleven years. W. Haslett and A. Larmor oppose some proposals relating to examinations and inspection. J. Smyth, J.G. Espie and J. Boyce signed a lengthy reservation concerning primary schools and the report's proposals for the inspection of such schools. A fourth reservation, putting the case for central schools, is signed by A.N.B. Wyse, J. Boyce, J.G. Espie and J. Smyth. The reservation signed by W.T. Miller and Mrs. Chichester supports central schools also, queries the teaching of the Irish language at state expense and urges the inculcation of loyalty to the state as a task for the primary school.

There are two substantial appendices, one being the report of a delegation visiting educational establishments in England and Scotland, the other being a memorandum by A.N.B. Wyse on teacher training in Britain. There are also some notes by R.M. Jones on schools visited in Birmingham and London and notes by Mr. Wyse on central schools in Britain and education for the mentally defective there. The statistical appendix to the report is concerned chiefly with tables indicating the number of teachers in certain areas of Northern Ireland in 1922 with an estimate of their efficiency. A list of the circuits and sections into which the country has been divided for the purpose of primary school inspection is given.

Educational Reconstruction

1944.
Cmd. 226, 43 pp.

The first part of this paper consists of a short survey of the development of educational services; the second part

EDUCATION 149

contains the government's proposals for their reconstruction. These proposals are concerned with age limits for compulsory school attendance; the provision of nursery schools where required; the provision of primary schools for children up to the age of eleven-plus, junior secondary schools for children from eleven-plus to fifteen, junior technical schools for boys from thirteen to sixteen. and senior secondary schools for which at least 80 percent of the pupils will have been selected by a qualifying test at eleven-plus; the size of classes; the provision of free books, etc.; university scholarships; compulsory religious instruction and collective acts of worship; building grants of 65 percent to voluntary primary and junior secondary schools under 'four-and-two' committees, and to voluntary senior secondary schools under certain conditions; part-time continued education and technical education; the provision of agricultural education in technical and junior secondary schools; adult education; physical training and youth welfare services; free medical and dental inspection and treatment; school meals and milk; the provision of special education for mentally and physically handicapped and maladjusted children; establishment of an advisory committee on conditions of service for teachers; finance; county education committees. Not all the proposals require new legislation.

An appendix on financial arrangements between the state and the education authorities lists the services and expenditure for which each is financially responsible, and a table shows estimated expenditure from public funds and estimated additional expenditure from such funds attributable to proposed developments.

[Quinquennial reports on educational reconstruction were later published, e.g., *Educational Reconstruction: The First Ten Years, 1959*, 24 pp.]

Special Educational Treatment

Rep. of Advisory Council for Education

1955.
Cmd. 331, 69 pp.
Council apptd. November 1951; rep. dated October 1954.

Dr. Eric Ashby (Ch.) and twenty members—T.C.C. Adam, D.H. Alexander, Rev. Br. T.A. Burke, Rev. J.H. Carson, E. Carvill, Rev. Mother Laurentia Corr, Rev. R.A. Deane, Mrs. Grace I.A. Faris, Dr. J.K. Forbes, A. Gibson, Dr. J.S. Hawnt, A. Hunter, Mrs. Sylvia G. Kastell, N. McNeilly, Mrs. V.F. Nelson, Rev. Dr. W.L. Northridge, F.P. Rose, W.H. Smyth, Maj. W. White, A.C. Williams.

'To consider the existing arrangements for the ascertainment of pupils requiring special educational treatment and for the provision of treatment for such pupils.'

The request for consideration of ascertainment and special educational treatment originated from the previous council.

An historical survey is followed by a summary of the principal current legislation and a discussion of the existing situation and facilities. Transfer of responsibility for the school health service from the local education to the health authorities has given rise to ambiguity and confusion which are not in the best interests of the child. The system found in England and Wales seems preferable and, accordingly, the council unanimously recommend that the school health service, together with responsibility for the ascertainment of handicapped children, should be integrated with the education service, by making the responsible medical officers joint appointments. The total cost of the service would be unchanged, but the new organization would greatly facilitate and improve the ascertainment of handicaps, would bring the medical officer and those in the educational service together as colleagues and so strengthen the influence of medical advice in the provision of special educational treatment, and it would remove certain administrative anomalies.

Every effort should be made to educate handicapped children in ordinary schools, with special facilities provided if necessary. In special schools, which should not be named as such, separate provision should be made for each type of handicap. Residential schools are not economical for fewer than twenty pupils, but surplus places might be welcomed by authorities in Great Britain. For academic education in special schools Northern Ireland should continue to rely on facilities available outside the country. Each local education authority alone should be regarded as requiring within the next decade an average of about two special schools in its area. Education committees should have discretion in notifying to the appropriate authority the withdrawal from school of educationally subnormal children at least, and the vocational guidance and facilities for further education of the handicapped should be improved. Each education committee should appoint a psychologist. Child guidance and speech therapy, which at present are health services, should become educational services.

Appendices include notes on administrative authorities; a list of those submitting evidence; copies of 'M1' and 'H.P.' forms certifying examination of handicapped children; and statistical tables giving the probable incidence of each handicap, a summary of the state of ascertainment and provision at 31 December 1952, some notable discrepancies in the records of health and education committees at 31 December 1952, and a list of special schools in operation on 31 December 1952.

Regularity of Some Scholarship Awards

For details of this report see Class I p. 18.

Educational Development

Ministry of Education rep., 1964.
Cmd. 470, 28 pp.

A foreword by the minister points out that there has been no major statement of government policy on education since the 1944 paper (Cmd. 226 above), which led to the 1947 Education Act. The present paper deals mainly with controversial issues and not with the whole educational scene.

The twenty-eight proposals of this paper include plans for the replacement of unsatisfactory primary school buildings and the reduction of the size of classes in large primary schools, statistics for primary teacher-pupil ratios being given. Reconstruction of the secondary school system—designed to eliminate selection at eleven-plus—will not be imposed by the government, but experiments towards that end should be encouraged. The title 'intermediate school' should be abandoned, and staffing differences between secondary and grammar schools reduced. The concentration of further education in a limited number of selected technical colleges is favoured. It is proposed to keep the age of transfer from primary to secondary school at eleven-plus, but it is urged that the qualifying examination be replaced, after 1965, by a different method of selection not involving formal attainment tests. The school-leaving age must be raised to sixteen, and this change should take place not later than 1970. Differences in holidays between schools should be eradicated. Experiments to meet the needs of less able children in a more adequate fashion are suggested.

Youth welfare is the subject of a separate paper (Cmd. 424 in Class XV), but it is stressed that a sports stadium at the Royal Ulster Agricultural Society grounds at Balmoral is required, if possible, and should be grant-aided. Financial details in an appendix show how grants are paid by the ministry to local authorities under existing legislation. Altogether, the Exchequer is meeting nearly 83 percent of the education expenditure, and there is no prospect of marked change in this position.

Public Education in Northern Ireland

Ministry of Education rep., 1964. 60 pp.

The Education Act (Northern Ireland) of 1947 provides the statutory framework of the education system as it exists in Northern Ireland today. This report begins with a historical outline of the education system up to that Act.

Public education in Northern Ireland (apart from university education) is administered centrally by the Ministry of Education and locally by eight education authorities, whose powers 'and duties are determined in the main by the 1947 Act and subsequent amending legislation.

There are two stages of public education: primary up to age eleven and secondary thereafter. The three types of secondary school are grammar, junior technical and secondary intermediate. Details of school attendance, transport, buildings, staffing, religious education, meals and milk, and health service are outlined briefly in the report.

Curricula, examinations and transfer from primary school to secondary school are examined in more detail. On the question of the Qualifying Examination, the report refers to the White Paper on educational development in Northern Ireland, 1964 (Cmd. 470), where it is proposed to discontinue this examination in 1965.

The opportunities for further education provided in Northern Ireland by the local education authorities are widespread. There are three central institutions — the Belfast Colleges of Technology, Art and Domestic Science—twenty-seven other technical institutions, and in addition, part-time classes are provided in more than fifty out-centres. Details are given of courses, subjects, day-release systems and Workers' Educational Association lectures and courses.

Teachers in Northern Ireland must possess qualifications prescribed by the ministry in its regulations. The three general training colleges in Northern Ireland, Stranmillis College, St. Mary's Training College and St. Joseph's Training College, are all within Belfast. A one-year course of professional training for graduates is provided also by the Department of Education of the Queen's University. There are also three institutions which undertake the training of specialist teachers of particular subjects: the Ulster College of Physical Education, the Belfast College of Domestic Science, and the Belfast College of Art.

Two chapters of the report are devoted to scholarships for the various types of education, and to finance—the cost of public education in Northern Ireland. The role of the Youth Service and Youth Employment Services are outlined in the report.

Appendices, with the use of tables, show the number of recognized schools, full-time teachers and pupils (1964); the number of technical centres, students and teachers (1964); and the cost of education services. Appendix III shows teachers' salary scales in operation on 1 August 1964, and publications concerning public education in Northern Ireland are listed in appendix V.

Local Education Authorities and Voluntary Schools

1967.
Cmd. 513, 10 pp.

The government proposes to introduce legislation to facilitate co-operation between local authorities and voluntary schools and to make certain financial changes. Voluntary primary, secondary (intermediate), special and nursery schools which accept local authority representation on their management committees (previously known as 'four-and-two' committees) would be known as 'maintained schools', and the local authority should become responsible for maintenance of their premises and for their equipment. Schools at present under such committees would have the option of reverting to purely voluntary management within a reasonable period, but thereafter the acceptance of maintained status would be irrevocable. New schools would be recognized only if 'maintained'. Voluntary grammar schools would have a similar option to accept representatives nominated by the minister on their governing body.

Building grants for maintained schools and for Group A voluntary grammar schools which have accepted representatives from the minister would be increased from the 65 percent received by schools with purely voluntary management to 80 percent. Similar grants would apply to local authority building expenditure. Certain other minor amendments are proposed.

2 TEACHERS

Salaries of Teachers

Twenty reps.:

Cmd. 48: 1925, 29 pp.
Cmd. 50: 1925, 20 pp.
Cmd. 230: 1946, 12 pp.
Cmd. 233: 1946, 11 pp.
Cmd. 243: 1947, 20 pp.
Cmd. 257: 1948, 9 pp.
Cmd. 290: 1951, 9 pp.
Cmd. 299: 1951, 4 pp.
Cmd. 321: 1954, 11 pp.
Cmd. 364: 1956, 20 pp.
Cmd. 365: 1957, 19 pp.
Cmd. 366: 1957, 16 pp.
Cmd. 403: 1959, 26 pp.
Cmd. 432: 1961, 24 pp.
Cmd. 442: 1962, 16 pp.
Cmd. 452: 1963, 11 pp.
Cmd. 489: 1965, 25 pp.
Cmd. 514: 1967, 15 pp.
Cmd. 529: 1969, 19 pp.
Cmd. 565: 1971, 16 pp.

The series of reports covering the reviews and recommendations made periodically and concerning various categories and grades of teacher begins (Cmd. 48, 50) by suggesting some salary reduction to reduce the cost to the state. This proposal is opposed in two minority reports to Cmd. 48 and in a signed protest by some committee members (in Cmd. 50). Cmd. 230 proposes that teachers with similar qualifications should have the same salaries whether they serve in primary or secondary

schools, while Cmd. 233 and 243 cover salaries for technical school teachers and conditions of teacher service, respectively. Papers 257, 290 and 299 urge parity with salary scales for teachers in Great Britain and propose appreciable allowance increases for the principals of smaller schools. In Cmd. 321, the principles laid down by the Black Committee (see 230, 233, 243, 257) are endorsed.

New scales to follow Burnham salaries in England and Wales are proposed in the 1956/57 reports (Cmd. 364–366), and a Burnham equivalent for technical schools is recommended. Cmd. 366 makes specific proposals on maternity leave, which should be without pay and for a minimum of eighteen weeks (a reservation suggests that a third of the salary could be paid for eleven of these weeks).

Further salary scale revisions for primary, secondary and special schools and Institute of Further Education teachers are proposed in Cmd. 403, 442 and 452. Cmd. 489 accepts most of the features of the 1965 Burnham scales, and Cmd. 514 and 529 do likewise for the 1967 and 1969 Burnham salaries. The 1971 Northern Ireland report also supports the Burnham proposals of the same year, but makes some separate recommendations relating to salary structure and some points of detail.

Appendices to these reports give the actual salary scales proposed for teaching staff. They sometimes provide also details of allowances, points scores, remuneration for part-time teaching, and scales relating to special posts.

The Recruitment and Training of Teachers

Rep. of Cttee., 1947.
Cmd. 254, 87 pp.
Cttee. apptd. May 1945; rep. sgd. July 1947.

Col. W.D. Gibbon (Ch.) and twenty members—T.C.C. Adam, Rev. Mother S.M. Ailbe, Prof. M.J. Boyd, Rev. G.A. Brady, Miss Mary Crawford, Prof. K.G. Emeleus, Mrs. Grace I.A. Faris, H. Garrett, R. Gingles, Major J.A. Glen,

Rev. Prof. R.L. Marshall, A. Martin, Miss E.F.K. McCormick, Rev. P.J. Mullally, Rev. W.H. Smyth, W.H. Smyth, J.U. Stewart, A.C. Williams, H.E. Winn, Maj. R. Workman. (The following resigned—R. Gingles, July 1945, Rev. Prof. R.L. Marshall, September 1945, A. Martin, May 1945, Rev. W.H. Smyth, June 1945, and they were replaced by H. O'Connor, May 1945, G.B. Leonard, July 1945, Prof. J. Haire, November 1945, Rev. Chancellor J. Quinn, January 1946, and W.B. Doak, March 1946.)

'To consider the recruitment and training of teachers for all types of schools recognized by the Ministry of Education, and to make recommendations.'

The report includes chapters on the existing educational system and the proposed new structure. It recommends that a university degree should not be insisted upon for teachers of 'general subjects' in primary and secondary schools, but that training courses should occupy at least three years. There is discussion of the content of courses and balance of subjects.

Courses provided for graduates should be of two types: to run concurrently with the degree course, or to follow it. Normally graduates wishing to teach in secondary schools should be trained in training colleges, and those for grammar schools in the university Department of Education.

The committee recommends the establishment of a physical education college, a college of music, a new training college for Roman Catholic men, and that the establishment of an institute of education be considered. Courses for specialist teachers should continue at the Belfast College of Art and at the Training College for Domestic Economy Teachers, which should find new premises, and provision should be made for specialist teachers of woodwork and metalwork. Training college and university students should be enabled to obtain Froebel qualifications. Technical school teachers should have suitable commer-cial or industrial experience in addition to professional qualifications. Only trained teachers should be appointed to posts in special schools.

No intending teacher should be debarred by lack of finance, and grants should be related to parental income. All students should have the advantage of residential training college life. Training college teachers should keep closely in touch with the schools, by secondment and the use of part-time serving teachers.

Short vacation courses should be organized for serving teachers, and one-year and refresher courses in religious education considered. A new system of bursaries would enable serving teachers to take advantage of these.

A reservation by Rev. Chancellor J. Quinn objects to the establishment of a training college for Roman Catholic men students when there has been no special provision for the training of Church of Ireland students.

Appendix I gives details of the schemes under which teachers trained as monitors or pupil teachers. Appendix II lists the bodies and individuals who gave evidence to the committee.

The Staffing of Technical Schools

Rep. of Cttee., 1956.
Cmd. 356, 23 pp.
Cttee. apptd. January 1954; rep. sgd. June 1956.

J.J. Graneek (Ch.) and eight members— D.H. Alexander, J.T. Esdale, G.H. Greep, Dr. W. Heron, K.A. MacCormac, J. McCoubrey, J. Malone, J. Scott, (T.F. Hall was appointed in addition in February 1954. Dr Heron resigned and was replaced by T. Cowan, November 1955.)

'To investigate the recruitment, educational qualifications and training of full-time teachers for institutions of further education; to consider whether the present requirements in regard to qualifications should be amended and whether improved arrangements should be made for training

these teachers; and to make recommendations.'

Difficulty has recently been experienced in appointing staff of the right calibre to technical colleges and schools. This is especially true in the case of science, maths, engineering and commerce. Deterrents such as travelling, broken working hours, excessive evening duties, and the difficulty of teaching heterogeneous classes are considered. Proposals are made for recruitment which are expected to be beneficial in the long term, and a revision of salary structure is urged, although the details of the latter would be beyond this committee's terms of reference. Observations are made on technical teachers' qualifications and training, on training courses and on the desirability of teachers in such colleges or schools having business or industrial experience. The latter is a desirable qualification, but most of the committee believe that to make it compulsory would be impractical and would further aggravate recruitment problems.

A schedule of qualifications for teachers of various subjects in further education establishments is set out, and it is proposed that the ministry should establish teacher training courses for commercial subjects. The suggestions for the content of such courses are indicated. Details are given separately of qualifications needed to teach metalwork, workshop practice and building trades subjects.

A reservation by J.T. Esdale and G.H. Greep insists upon industrial or commercial experience as a prerequisite for technical teaching; urges that travelling time of teachers in rural areas should be compensated by lowering their minimum teaching hours per week; and denies the need for full-time training courses aimed at commercial teachers, suggesting some alternatives.

Secondary School Organization

Conditions of Recognition

Supply of Teachers

Selection Procedure

Ministry of Education. Four reps. of Advisory Council for Education, 1964. Cmd. 471. 35 pp. Council apptd. May 1963.

Dr. M. Grant (Ch.) and thirty-six members—Miss M. McN. Anderson, Mrs. A.E. Biddle, D.W. Bleakley, Rev. Mother Laurentia Corr, J. Gallagher, Dr. J.F. Gillies, J.A. Glen, R.N. Greer, Mrs. M. Haughton, Dr. J.S. Hawnt, R.B. Hunter, A. Keith, Prof. H.M. Knox, Miss M. Leith, F.W. Logan, Miss Bessie H. Maconachie, D.V. McCall, R. McCormick, Senator J.A. McGlade, Very Rev. G.H. MacNamara, W.H. Mol, Rev. Br. J.M. Murphy, J.J. Napier, Rev. Dr. W.L. Northridge, Mrs. M.R. O'Hara, W.J. O'Riordan, Rt. Rev. Dr. W.A.A. Park, Dr. R.C. Pink, Col. M.C. Perceval-Price, Venerable G.A. Quin, Very Rev. Dr. P.C.J. Rogers, Prof. G. Seth, A.C. Stanley, Mrs. C. Stewart, A.J. Tulip, J.W. Walker, (J.J. Napier resigned February 1963, and Mrs. C. Stewart April 1964.)

Secondary School Organization. *Sgd. February 1964.* [*3 pp.*].

In view of the divergent opinions held by representative educationists, it would be unreasonable to insist on a uniform selective or non-selective secondary school system throughout the province. In areas of development and where conditions are favourable, the ministry should encourage provision of non-selective secondary schools, and any agreement among constituent elements of a selective system in a given area to end selection should be officially supported.

Conditions of Recognition of Teachers. *Sgd. February 1964.* [*10 pp.*].

The Fourth Advisory Council did not complete its study of the reference given it, December 1960:

'To examine the position in regard to the demand and supply of teachers for all kinds of grant-aided schools: to con-

sider measures to meet the prospective demand and the conditions under which teaching recognition is accorded: and to make recommendations.'

The study has been continued by the present council, which now reports on the latter part of the reference. A number of modifications of existing conditions are recommended, principally that after 1967 all teachers in primary and secondary schools should be required to take a course of training. Teachers in special schools should have special training, and this is also desirable for teachers of special classes in normal schools. The work of the University Department of Education and the teacher training colleges should be co-ordinated and modified in certain respects.

A supplement (sgd. June 1964) covers the training of teachers who have already received recognition, and especially the need for courses for teachers in institutions of further education.

The Supply and Demand for Teachers. *Sgd. May 1964.* [*8 pp.*].

(Terms of reference as for previous report.)

This report also is a continuation of the work of the Fourth Advisory Council. The council estimates that in 1970 about 1,900 more teachers will be required in primary and secondary school than may be expected to be available at the present rate of recruitment (450 primary and 1,500 secondary teachers). A working party should be set up to consider how the training facilities should be extended and how their extension can be phased to the school-building programme. Consideration should be given to the possibility of enabling students at training colleges to follow degree courses. Means of using the existing teacher strength more economically and more effectively should be carefully studied. A research project should be set up to investigate wastage. Consideration should be given to using suitable teachers of over sixty-five and to attracting into service mature persons from other occupations and married women who have formerly served as teachers.

Selection Procedure. *Sgd. June 1964.* [*6 pp.*].

The Qualifying Examination should be abolished after 1965, and in its place a system of selection based on teachers' scaled estimates and verbal reasoning scores substituted. A working party should be set up to decide whether a change in the age of transfer should be made to coincide with the raising of the school leaving age.

An appendix shows percentage of disagreements between classification of candidates based on official results and classification based on suitability scores or mean verbal reasoning quotients, divided into size of school and geographical position.

3 PUPILS AND THEIR SCHOOLS —SELECTION, CURRICULUM, EXAMINATIONS

The Programme of Instruction in Public Elementary Schools

Ministry of Education. Rep. of Dept. Cttee. of Inquiry, 1931.
Cmd. 136, 28 pp.
Cttee. apptd. March 1931; rep. sgd. November 1931.

J.H. Robb (Ch.) and thirteen members— J. Boyd, H. Garrett, J.R. Haslett, Miss Theresa Henderson, R.M. Jones, J.S. Mahon, A. Martin, Prof. W.B. Morton, W. Parr, R. Pears, Miss Dorothy Robertson, C. Webb, C. Wilson. (W. Parr died before the work of the committee was completed.)

'To report what changes, if any, are desirable . . . in order to secure the better education of the pupils, having regard to the general conditions of work in the schools, the time available for instruction, and the requirements of a sound modern education.'

The committee deal with the present standard of elementary education; the possibility that the programme is over-loaded; the inspection system in relation to the programme; the possibility of a standard programme; the special problems of the small school; senior schools; and subjects taught. A number of miscellaneous themes, such as book supply, homework and the teaching of additional subjects designed to encourage humane qualities, are also discussed. The committee advise and comment upon the syllabus for English, arithmetic, drawing, singing and other subjects taught. They consider small schools in rural areas, having only one or two teachers, as presenting the most pressing problem.

R.M. Jones adds a note on the value of the reading book in the teaching of English, and a reservation signed by C. Webb suggests that rigid enslavement to the present programme might well be to the detriment of elementary education. He favours more liberty for the teachers to plan the course of instruction and argues that children attending small schools are not likely to be any the weaker in essential subjects on this account. Appendices give a list of witnesses, a list of individuals and institutions supplying evidence and also a copy of a memorandum designed to help inspectors rate a teacher's ability and work.

The Scholarship System

Rep. of the Cttee., 1938.
Cmd. 192, 40 pp.
Cttee. apptd. January 1937; rep. sgd. March 1938.

J.H. Robb (Ch.) and twenty-one members—C.A. Abraham, J. Blane, W.H. Dawson, Mrs. Grace I.A. Faris, Very Rev. N. Farren, H. Garrett, P.F. Gillies, Prof. R.M. Henry, Lt.-Col. R.J. Howard, W.R. Johnston, Very Rev. Dean W.S. Kerr, H.A. Macaulay, R. MacDonald, Prof. R.K. McElderry, W.G. Pirie, R. Stanley, S.S. Steele, The Venerable Archdeacon J. Tierney, Prof. J.E. Todd, W. White, Capt. J.M. Wilton. (The report was not signed by W.G. Pirie and J.M. Wilton.)

'*To consider and report upon the working of the Scholarship System in Northern Ireland, and to make such recommendations as may seem desirable for its improvement.*'

Background historical detail on methods of awarding scholarships is given. The committee believes that scholarships of monetary worth should be granted only to students needing financial aid to continue their education, and sliding scales of parental income are suggested to assist education committees in making awards. For scholarships to secondary schools (involving a junior scholarship tenable for three years followed possibly by a two-year scholarship), English, English composition and arithmetic are proposed as the only subjects for the junior scholarship, and guidance is given as to the type of examination paper needed. It is proposed to extend the range of subjects on which the award of a senior scholarship depends. University scholarships should be granted only on the results of a special examination conducted by the university, awards to other university students being known as 'bursaries'. More attention should be given to the question of scholarships to junior technical and junior commercial schools, and the system of trade scholarships awarded by the ministry should be extended. No changes are recommended concerning special scholarships, or awards of scholarships to training colleges. Dr. Stanley is unable to agree with two of the recommendations relating to junior and senior scholarships at secondary schools. He claims that it is unwise to reduce the number of subjects for the junior scholarships to two and wants provision made for senior scholarships to be extended to a third year, in certain cases.

Senior Certificate Examination in Grammar Schools

Rep. of Cttee. Cttee. apptd. May 1948; both reps. published 1950.

Prof. J.K. Charlesworth (Ch.) and fourteen members—Rev. Br. T.A. Burke, J.S. Connolly, W.H. Crowe, Mrs. Grace I.A. Faris, Major J.A. Glen, Rev. Mother Alberta Grant, Mrs. Sylvia G. Kastell, Rev. J. McMullan, Mrs. E.A. MacQuillan, W.H. Mol, Prof. G. Waterhouse, Maj. W. White, A.C. Williams, H.E. Winn. (Professor Waterhouse resigned in January 1950.)

'To consider the present arrangements for the Senior Certificate Examination in grammar schools, and to make recommendations.'

First Report. *Sgd. December 1949. Cmd. 277, 32 pp.*

The examination should retain the name Senior Certificate Examination and should normally be taken at the age of seventeen-plus after six years in grammar school, but no lower age limit should be fixed. Passes (or compensation) should be required in a combination of six subjects which will indicate a balanced general education, and these passes must be gained in the same year. English language and literature should be compulsory, and English usage in other papers should be taken into account. Papers at 'ordinary' and 'advanced' levels should be set in most subjects, although the syllabuses for both should be the same. 'Pass' and 'credit' should be 40 percent and 60 percent for ordinary level, and 'pass' and 'distinction' should be 40 percent and 70 percent for advanced level. School assessments should be used as part of the examination in modern languages, music and the science subjects. No prizes from public funds should be awarded on the results of the examination, which should continue to be held in June and conducted by the ministry. Marks should be communicated to the candidates through the schools and later published.

Appendices contain statistical data, the committee's questionnaire and names of bodies and individuals who answered it or submitted evidence and of bodies who accept Senior Certificate as an entitlement to privilege or exemption.

Second Report. *Sgd. July 1950. Cmd. 282, 5 pp.*

A separate scholarship examination should be taken normally one year after the Senior Certificate Examination, which would be used as a means of awarding scholarships to students entering university, both state exhibitions and local education authority scholarships. Training scholarships to intending teachers should normally be awarded on the results of Senior Certificate. There should not be a fixed pass mark, nor a certificate indicating a pass in the examination as a whole, but marks should be supplied to the schools and candidates and published as is done for Senior Certificate. Three subjects should normally be taken, together with a qualifying paper in English to test the candidates' use of English and powers of expression.

Selection of Pupils: Secondary Schools

Rep. of Advisory Council for Education, 1952. Cmd. 301, 111 pp. Council apptd. April 1948.

Sir David Lindsay Keir (Ch.) and twenty members—T.C.C. Adam, D.H. Alexander, Rev. Br. T.A. Burke, Mrs. L. Irene M. Calvert, E. Carvill, Rev. R.A. Deane, Col. W.D. Gibbon, J.S. Hawnt, Mrs. Sylvia G. Kastell, the Rt. Hon. H.C. Midgley, Rev. P.J. Mullally, N. McNeilly, Mrs. V.F. Nelson, Prof. S.D. Nisbet, Rev. W.L. Northridge, Capt. the Hon. T.M. O'Neill, P.B. Webb, Maj. W. White, A.C. Williams, Rev. J.H. Withers. (Col. W.D. Gibbon, Sir David Lindsay Keir, the Rt. Hon. H.C. Midgley, Capt. the Hon. T.M. O'Neill and P.B. Webb all resigned during their term of office. The Rt. Hon. Lord Justice Black was appointed chairman, November 1949, and A. Hunter and P. Smiles as council members, June 1950.)

'To consider the problems involved in the selection of pupils for different types of

secondary schools and to report to the Ministry as to the most suitable methods of selecting pupils at about 11 years of age or later for education in

(a) secondary schools of the academic type (grammar schools)

(b) secondary schools of the non-academic type (intermediate schools including technical intermediate schools).'

Selection is based on performance in intelligence tests and attainment tests in the examination year, at present that year in which the child is below the age of 12 years 9 months. Two Moray House Intelligence Tests are given, with about a month's interval between. The attainment tests consist of two papers in English and one in Arithmetic. Marks are adjusted by adding an age allowance to the total marks of the younger children. Teachers' assessments are not used. Review procedures for 'misfits' were tried experimentally in Belfast and in County Londonderry in 1950.

The council considers it too early for any firm decisions to be made and indicates problems which require investigation, but it concludes tentatively that the existing machinery for selection at eleven-plus is already reasonably efficient; that a close watch will have to be maintained on the repercussions of the selection procedure on the life and work of the primary and preparatory schools; that many problems would disappear if all concerned had full knowledge of the facts and aims of the scheme, if there were sufficient secondary intermediate schools, and if there were a sound review procedure at thirteen-plus. There has been much research on the selection procedure, but more is still needed.

Nine detailed appendices give information about the 1950 Qualifying Examination; a calculation of the proportion of children who enter and the proportion who qualify; graphs illustrating numbers of children in the year group compared with numbers qualifying in 1950; details of the marking of English composition; comparison of results of intelligence tests in 1949 and 1950; two research reports

concerning follow-up of 1948 candidates; and teachers' assessments and reports from Belfast and from County Londonderry on the 1950 review.

Selection of Pupils: Secondary Schools

Second rep. of Advisory Council for Education, 1955.
Cmd. 335, 64 pp.
Council apptd. November 1951; rep. dated November 1954.

Dr. E. Ashby (Ch.) and twenty members —T.C.C. Adam, D.H. Alexander, Rev. Br. T.A. Burke, Rev. J.H. Carson, E. Carvill, Rev. Mother Laurentia Corr, Rev. R.A. Deane, Mrs. Grace I.A. Faris, Dr. J.K. Forbes, A. Gibson, Dr. J.S. Hawnt, A. Hunter, Mrs. Sylvia G. Kastell, N. McNeilly, Mrs. V.F. Nelson, Rev. Dr. W.L. Northridge, F.P. Rose, W.H. Smyth, Maj. W. White, A.C. Williams.

'To give further consideration to the reference [given the Council of April 1948] in the light of the previous Council's report and all other circumstances obtaining, [and]

'To consider . . . the age-limits within which the transfer of pupils to the different types of secondary schools should take place.'

The council reports briefly the introduction of a new procedure for 'borderline' and review cases. It concludes provisionally that the examination is on the whole a trustworthy method of selection for grammar schools. More investigations are essential if this is to be confirmed and if methods of selection are to be improved, and the council unanimously recommends that the ministry should see that these investigations continue. The problem of age of transfer cannot be solved until there is a uniform age of entry to primary school, and administrative decision must meanwhile be based on expediency.

Eight appendices give much statistical data: a summary of qualifying examination results, 1948–1954; a follow-up study of pupils who took the examination in 1948 and proceeded to grammar schools; sources of entry for the 1953 examination; the extent of 'Borderline Bands' in 1950–1954 and the effect of the new 'Borderline Procedure' in 1953 and 1954; an investigation into the differences between town and country; a summary of pupils reviewed at twelve-plus and thirteen-plus between 1950 and 1954; grammar school scholarships, enrolments, withdrawals and examination results; a comparison between Qualifying Examination papers in English and Arithmetic and standardized tests.

Selection of Pupils for Secondary School

Third rep. of Advisory Council for Education, 1960.
Cmd. 419, 74 pp.
Council apptd. November 1958; rep. dated July 1960.

Sir Eric Ashby (Ch.) and thirty-five members—the Rt. Hon. the Countess of Antrim, Mrs. A.E. Biddle, D.W. Bleakley, Dr. W.F. Bryson, Rev. Dr. J.H. Carson, Rev. Mother Laurentia Corr, W.H. Dawson, W.B. Doak, Dr. J.K. Forbes, J. Gallagher, Dr. J.F. Gillies, R. Gingles, J.A. Glen, P.J. Gormley, R.N. Greer, Mrs. J.W. Haughton, Dr. J.S. Hawnt, H. Holmes, A. Keith, Rev. Br. Stephen Kelly, D. Kennedy, Rev. R.E. Ker, Miss M. Leith, Prof. I.M.G. Llubera, F.W. Logan, Miss Bessie H. Maconachie, R. McCormick, the Very Rev. G.H. MacNamara, W.H. Mol, Dr. R.C. Pink, Col. M.C. Perceval-Price, Venerable G.A. Quin, C.B. Smith, A.C. Stanley, J.W. Walker. (The Rt. Hon. the Countess of Antrim, Sir Eric Ashby and Rev. Br. Stephen Kelly resigned, and Rev. Dr. J.H. Carson, W.H. Dawson and R. Gingles died during their term of office. Dr. M. Grant was appointed chairman, October 1959, and D. McCall, Rev. W.A.A. Park and Mrs. C. Stewart were appointed members in May, September and November 1959, respectively.)

'To review the arrangements for the selection of pupils for the different kinds of secondary schools . . .; to examine their suitability and general effect; to consider whether in the light of experience any changes are necessary and to report and recommend.'

A child may be entered for the Qualifying Examination in the year preceding the July in which he is aged between eleven and twelve years old. Two verbal reasoning tests, two English papers and an arithmetic paper are taken into consideration, with due adjustment of marks to compensate the younger candidates. The ministry fixes an 'absolute pass mark' and a lower 'not qualified' mark, while candidates in the 'border-zone' are dealt with by the education committee in whose area they reside. A review examination is conducted by the education committees, usually one year later.

The council recommends retention of a selective system of secondary school organization and a qualifying examination, but suggests that all pupils should take the verbal reasoning tests, so that suitable children may be advised to enter for the examination. A record card of attainments, attendance, medical history, character and temperament should be considered for all 'border-zone' candidates. Recruitment to junior technical schools should normally be at eleven-plus. Secondary intermediate schools should be permitted to organize courses leading to Junior Certificate, and successful candidates should then be permitted to transfer to grammar school or technical institution. The review procedure should be less formal and apply only to pupils in unreorganized primary schools and secondary schools without academic courses. Careful investigation is still required.

In reservations, D.W. Bleakley considers that there is insufficient evidence to warrant a firm recommendation supporting the present selective system and would also like to see the description 'intermediate school' replaced. Mrs. Haughton disagrees with retention of the examination, cites many arguments against it, and suggests an alternative organization of secondary education.

Nine appendices give statistical figures for the recent qualifying examinations and investigations connected with them.

Secondary School Examinations

[*Ministry of Education.*] *Rep. of Cttee., 1955.*
27 pp.
Cttee. apptd. April 1954; rep. sgd. March 1955.

Prof. A. Macbeath (Ch.) and fourteen members—T.C.C. Adam, L. Arndell, Miss M.W. Cunningham, Prof. T. Finnegan, Mrs. H.E. Freeman, P. Gilchrist, J.H. Grummitt, Dr. J.S. Hawnt, T. Holland, R.B. Hunter, Rev. P. Kerr, N. McNeilly, Rev. Mother M. Paul Martin, A.C. Williams.

'*To consider whether changes should be made in the present arrangements for the Grammar School Junior Certificate Examination; whether the Ministry should conduct an examination for pupils at about the age of 15 in other types of secondary school; and to make recommendations.*'

Grammar school pupils should not normally take an external examination between the Qualifying and Senior Certificate examinations, and the present Junior Certificate should therefore be discontinued. An optional examination, the Grammar School Preliminary Examination, should be instituted for a trial period and reviewed after five years. No external examination should be conducted for secondary intermediate schools, whose pupils should nevertheless be free to enter for any existing external examinations for which they seem to be qualified. It is considered that this arrangement would give greater freedom to the staff of these newly established schools to experiment with syllabuses and methods of teaching, and the position would be reconsidered in about ten years. Some minor modifications should be made in the Technical Day School Examinations, but they should be continued for five or six years and then reconsidered.

Bodies and individuals who gave evidence are listed, and statistics given, in the appendix, of candidates entering for the Junior Certificate Examination, Junior Technical Certificate Examination, Junior Commercial Certificate Examination, and Technical Day School Certificate Examination in 1953. Returns from seventy-six grammar schools tabulate the subsequent career of pupils who sat for Junior Certificate in 1952.

School Attendance

Rep. by Advisory Council for Education, 1956.
Cmd. 362, 43 pp.
Rep. sgd. October 1956.

Dr. E. Ashby (Ch.) and twenty-one members—E. Campbell, J.H. Carson, Miss Elizabeth B. Cathcart, Rev. Mother M. Laurentia Corr, E.P.M. Elliott, Mrs. Grace I.A. Faris, J.K. Forbes, Helen E. Freeman, A. Gibson, P. Gilchrist, R. Gingles, J.S. Hawnt, H.M. Knox, W.J. McClure, Mrs. V.F. Nelson, W.L. Northridge, F.P. Rose, A.J. Sheridan, M. Smith, W.H. Smyth, A.C. Williams.

'*To consider the extent to which the law relating to compulsory school attendance is observed and the suitability and effectiveness of existing arrangements for its enforcement.*'

Compulsory attendance is defined, and the state of such attendance and of absenteeism is outlined. Although truancy and shortcomings of the schools partly account for absenteeism, the chief reason is viewed as being parental laziness or a wish to keep children at home in order to put them to work. Difficulties in enforcing attendance arise from the slowness of the machinery for dealing with culprits, the abuse of the system of obtaining certificates from doctors and the failure of magistrates to impose adequate fines or to deal with cases consistently. It is stressed that attendance at most schools is good, but there are defects to be remedied, and the conditions under which attendance officers work demand improvement. It is proposed that the duties of these officers should be redefined and their title changed to that of 'education welfare officer'. Their numbers should be increased and their salaries reviewed, and the work should be undertaken exclusively by full-time staff. When these changes have been made, there will be no need for local authority attendance subcommittees. Other proposals concern leaving dates and the minimum leaving age, the promotion of close integration between the work of the education welfare officer and other welfare agencies, and the initiation of bylaws to control the part-time employment of children. Disciplinary action must follow more swiftly on offences through the more frequent visiting of schools by officers, and terms of responsibility for initiating prosecutions are outlined. Magistrates should be urged to impose larger fines, and it is proposed that medical certificates from general practitioners need no longer be demanded.

In appendices are given: the present statutory provisions dealing with school attendance and juvenile employment, details of the duties of the education welfare officers, a report on school attendance in Northern Ireland during the year 1954/1955, and a list of witnesses and of individuals and organizations providing evidence for the council. One appendix gives some attendance statistics, and these are supported by some tables in the body of the report which also give statistics on the number of school attendance officers compared with the school population, numbers prosecuted, and the range of fines imposed.

Primary Schools Programme

Rep. of Cttee. Ministry of Education, 1956.
8 pp.
Cttee. apptd. September 1952; rep. sgd. June 1955.

W.B. Doak (Ch.) and twelve members — E.K. Ashworth, R.J. Doolan, J. Duffin, S. Foster, R. Gingles, H. Hazlett,

R. Macdonald, B. McCartan, M.J. O'Neill, M. Smith, A.R. Taylor, A. Twyman.

'To consider the Ministry's Programme of Instruction for Primary Schools and to make recommendations.'

There has been no general curriculum revision since the 'Programme of Instruction for Public Elementary Schools, 1932'. The old programme was very rigidly followed, since it was widely regarded as a syllabus for the examination of pupils upon which efficiency ratings for teachers were assessed in those days. In putting forward a new 'Programme for Primary Schools', the committee have been advised by ten subject panels composed of committee members themselves and an additional forty teachers and twenty inspectors. The aim of the new programme is to foster a 'child-centred' approach, and, while retaining the traditional subject-divisions, the programme gives a broad picture of the standards a child should normally have attained at perhaps two or three appropriate stages in his school course, rather than a series of yearly syllabuses. The revised programme will demand of many teachers a new outlook and a change of values, and it therefore gives some guidance on points of teaching methods.

In view of the many unreorganized primary schools which have to cater for pupils for whom intermediate school accommodation is not yet available, courses were planned for these pupils also, and they are given in an appendix to the programme.

Appendices to the report list members of the subject panels, and bodies submitting evidence.

[The suggested primary school syllabus is considered at much greater length in *Programme for Primary Schools*, H.M.S.O. 1956, 222 pp.]

Examinations for Secondary Intermediate (including Technical Intermediate) Schools

Rep. of the Cttee., 1960.

Cmd. 413, 27 pp.
Cttee. apptd. May 1958; rep. sgd. April 1960.

Judge William Johnson (Ch.) and seventeen members—Capt. E.F. Anderton, E.D. Bunting, W.C.H. Eakin, Dr. J.K. Forbes, T. Holland, R.B. Hunter, A. Keith, R. MacDonald, R.B. Neilly, R. Newell, Col. M.C. Perceval-Price, Rt. Rev. Monsignor A.H. Ryan, A.C. Stanley, Col. C.E. Thompson, A.J. Tulip., W.J. Waring and D. Wright. (Captain Anderton and Mr. Bunting resigned in February and May 1959 respectively).

'To investigate the question of external examinations for pupils of secondary intermediate schools and to make recommendations.'

The intellectual ability of secondary school pupils and the existing examination system are discussed. The arguments for and against external examinations are noted. No new general external examination specifically aimed at secondary schools is thought to be needed. Suitable pupils can be entered for appropriate examinations if they wish to do so and have a chance of success. This, however, should not be at the expense of teaching facilities for the less gifted children. No pupil should take an external examination before completing four years on the secondary school course. Pupils from secondary schools should be eligible to take the Grammar School Junior Certificate Examination or to take individual subjects in it. Some of those who would not pass an examination demanding competence in a group of subjects may nevertheless achieve some success in individual papers, but they are expected to obtain at least 30 percent of the marks in English. The secondary school pupil may also, it is recommended, attempt (when appropriate) the Junior Technical and Junior Commercial certificates. If such children do not obtain the 'group subject' pass, they may again—depending upon performance in English—be awarded a certificate for the subject(s) in which they

are successful. No change is contemplated regarding the examination for the Technical Day School Certification.

The limited use of these examinations for the 'upper stream' in secondary schools, without this being detrimental to the majority of their pupils, is in broad agreement with the British White Paper *Secondary Education for All* (Cmnd. 604, 1959).

Appendices show educational and employers' organizations providing evidence to the committee, extracts from the regulations for the Grammar School Junior Certification and Technical Day School's examinations, and details of the special verbal reasoning test given in 1959 to secondary school pupils in the thirteen-fourteen age group.

Senior Certificate Examination

Three reps. of Cttee.

Dr. M. Grant (Ch.) and twenty-seven members—T.C.C. Adam, Prof. T.P. Allen (replaced, in November 1964, by Prof. T.M. Charlton), Prof. M.J. Boyd, Prof. J.C. Beckett, Reverend Mother Helena Collins, S.R. Dennison (resigned July 1961), J. Doherty, D.A. Dorman, Dr. B.C. Gee, A. Gibson, Dr. J.F. Gillies, Dr. H.J.G. Godin, R.B. Hunter, A. Keith, Prof. C. Kemball, Prof. H.M. Knox, Prof. F.J. Lelièvre, J.L. Lord, Miss Una McClafferty, Dr. R.C. Pink, Very Rev. Dr. P. Rogers, Miss N.M. Savage, J. Scott (replaced by J. Finney in November 1964), Very Rev. A.J. Sheridan, Dr. Dorothy Strangeways, A.J. Tulip, Miss F.C. Welch.

First Report. *July 1962, 25 pp.*

This report considers whether Northern Ireland should continue to operate its own secondary school external examination system at Senior Certificate level and if so what form the examination should take. The committee recommend that examination facilities controlled from within Northern Ireland should be continued and should comprise an examination leading to the award of a Northern Ireland General Certificate of

Education in individual subjects and also the award of a group certificate. Subject certificates should be available in 1963, and in the meantime the Senior Certificate should continue to be awarded. The new subject examinations should be open to all types of schools and to privately entered candidates over the age of sixteen and should be set at levels corresponding in standard with papers in examinations for the General Certificate of Education in England and Wales.

Second Report. *July 1963, 20 pp.*

This report deals principally with the requirements for the new group certificate, which, it is suggested, should operate with effect from 1965. The committee propose to adhere to the existing two-level structure for question papers and not to introduce 'Special' or 'S' papers at this stage. They are prepared to consider the introduction of additional subjects where there is reasonable demand and where they consider that there will be educational advantage in the introduction requested. Examinations should, as far as possible, be confined to the month of June. Grades should be used instead of marks to express examination results. The report shows the five groups of subjects for the new group certificate, to be known as the 'Northern Ireland Group Certificate', and recommends that the award of this certificate should not be conditional upon the completion of any defined course or attendance at any school.

Third Report. *July 1965, 26 pp.*

A review of the work done in the period covered by the previous reports is made. New work includes a scrutiny of the structure of subcommittees in anticipation of the appointment of a new Senior Certificate Examination committee. With regard to examinations, revised arrangements for holding oral and practical tests at advanced level are proposed, and alternatives should be offered, it is argued, to ordinary-level

modern-language candidates. 'A' Level domestic science and 'O' Level general science and Italian examinations should begin in 1967, and a test in the use of English (outside the G.C.E. structure) should be available from that date. Northern Ireland should participate in the Nuffield Foundation's science teaching project in chemistry. Supplementary winter examinations do not appear to be justified at present.

Appendices to the three reports include statistical information showing Senior Certificate Examination entries and candidates from secondary and technical schools taking G.C.E. subjects. A summary of results by grading and of cases where pupils taking Senior Certificate rather than G.C.E. were at a disadvantage is also given. Further appendices list those organizations and persons providing evidence and provide information on subcommittee structure and functions, and subject panel membership. Senior Certificate and G.C.E. results, 1961–1965, are given in a statistical appendix to the final report.

Secondary School Organization

Selection Procedure

The two reports concerned are published with two others concerning teacher recognition and the supply and demand for teachers. For details see p. 154 above in this class.

Curriculum of the Secondary (Intermediate) Schools

Ministry of Education. Rep. of the Wkg. Pty., 1967.
72 pp., bibliography.
Rep. sgd. April 1967.

A.J. Tulip (Ch.) (succeeded in December 1965 by R. MacDonald) and fifteen members—W.J. Dickson, J. Ferguson, Dr. B.C.Gee, R.A. Hamilton, E. Haslett, Miss S. Higgins, Sister M. Carmel Laverty, W.J. McClure, R. McKay, H.M.D. McWilliam, J.M. Malone, T. Moore, W.J. Patterson, W.J. Steele, Miss G. Woodrow. (W.J. Steele resigned in February 1966 and his place was taken the following month by V.J. McGeown.)

'To consider the curriculum of the secondary (intermediate) schools in the light of the Government's policy as set out in the White paper (Cmd. 470, 1964) on educational development in Northern Ireland.'

The working party stresses its concern with the personal development of pupils and the relationship between the schools and a changing society. A large part of the report is concerned with curriculum planning for a five-year course. Emphasis is given to subject distribution, the school as a community, links with further education, religious education and spiritual development. Factors affecting the curriculum, such as accommodation, facilities and size of classes, are emphasized. Examinations and assessment by school record, staff qualities and training, and extracurricular work are other topics considered.

It is proposed that secondary education planning should start with a professional concern for the students' development and that this should not be hindered by narrow specialization. There should be a five-year course with a common curriculum in years 1–3, but there is much room for experiment in the teaching of subjects (e.g. New Mathematics) and in internal organization. Years 4–5 should be more suited to careers and to the teaching of the character and structure of modern society. More teaching aids and careers guidance plus the expansion of further education seem necessary. Sex education should be a part of the curriculum. Adequate school records must be kept.

The number of public examinations should be reduced, although there need be no decrease in the number of candidates. There is a need for closer co-operation between primary and secondary school staffs and those of colleges of further education. Various proposals on teacher recruitment and training are made, and there is consideration of the role of educational study centres. The signatories have some difference of opinion on certain matters—such as whether pupils can profitably transfer to further education before the end of the year in which they reach school-leaving age—but the report represents the general body of their opinion and there are no stated reservations.

In appendices, there are provided: a list of those submitting evidence, an extensive reading list, and information and statistics resulting from the 1965 questionnaire sent to the province's secondary (intermediate) schools.

Certain Aspects of Educational and Vocational Guidance in Secondary Schools

Rep. of Wkg. Pty., 1968.
43 pp.
[*Not published by H.M.S.O.*] *Cttee. apptd. September 1966.*

G.B. Leonard (Ch.) and eight members —Mrs. K.M. Courtney, S.H. Dunlop, Miss K.M.V. Hall, Dr. J. McGilton, W.L. McIntyre, Miss E.D. Mitchell, J.M. O'Donoghue, M.G. Salters.

'To investigate the functions that careers teachers should undertake, the extent of the co-operation which would exist with the Youth Employment Service, whether careers teachers should have some form of training and what that training should be, the extent to which counsellors or counsellor/teachers should be employed in our schools and the amount of time which should be devoted to guidance work in the schools and its place in the curriculum.'

A questionnaire was devised and issued to all secondary schools in the province, in order to collect information on what is happening in schools at the present time in the general field of careers guidance.

Duties to be undertaken by careers teachers in schools vary from school to school, but consultation and co-operation with other members of staff form a continuous two-way process, which is essential if vocational guidance is to be really suited to the needs of the pupils and if pupils are to be brought to a true realization of their needs. There should be a specially equipped careers room in each school. Books on careers could be housed in the school library and career posters displayed around the school and in the careers room.

The careers teacher is the essential link between the youth employment officer and the pupils and parents; the youth employment officer is the career teacher's link with the vocational guidance, placement, and review of progress services operated by the Youth Employment Service Board. The youth employment officer has specialized knowledge about entry requirements for the professions, apprentice training schemes, job opportunities, and industrial conditions generally. Consultation and coordination with the local youth employment office should reduce the burden on the careers teacher and continue to widen the scope of the school's concept of guidance.

There must be a close liaison between counselling and vocational guidance work in the school, and to this end the committee feels that the careers teachers might be among the counsellors towards the latter part of the pupil's school life when vocational guidance is a more important factor in this work.

The committee recommends that a definite programme of training in guidance be made available. Part of the training should include at least the following—a broad view of psychology; the causes of educational retardation; principles of diagnosis and remedial methods; the social, cultural and biological detriments of normal and abnormal personality; the social significance of the school; the methods of school-organized curriculae environment for deprived children; the techniques of interpreting school policy to parents; the investigation of problems of attendance difficulties; the organization of in-school homework; and the easing of domestic relationships generally when there is a wide intelligence gap either way between children and parents. The committee feels that colleges of education and university departments of education should be able to devise comprehensive courses along these lines.

Appendices to the report show a copy of the questionnaire sent to schools, a summary of answers to the questionnaire on schools' careers work, and a plan for the proposed careers room for secondary schools.

Primary Education in Northern Ireland

Ministry of Education. Rep. of Advisory Council for Education, 1968.
120 pp., bibliography, photos.
Council apptd. February 1965; rep. sgd. July 1968.

Dr. M. Grant (Ch.) and twenty-two members—Miss M. McN. Anderson, Prof. M.J. Boyd, Rt. Rev. A.A. Buchanan, Miss Mary J. Duffy, W.C.H. Eakin, Col. J. Hughes, R.B. Hunter, Prof. F.J. Lelièvre, J.M. Malone, Miss E.H. Maxwell, D.V. McCall, Rev. Brother J.M. Murphy, Mrs. M.R. O'Hara, Very Rev. Dr. W.A.A. Park, Very Rev. Dr. P.C.J. Rogers, Sister M. Pacifica Rooney, S. Semple, Prof. G. Seth, Rev. P. Walsh, Dr. O.M. White, Dr. A.C. Williams, A.S. Worrall. (Dr. Grant resigned in August 1966, and Dr. N.A. Burges was appointed in September to succeed him as chairman. The following also resigned: Miss Anderson, Miss Maxwell in March 1967, and Professor Boyd in May 1967. Mrs. I.C.E. Jackson was appointed in April 1967, and the entire council, as it then stood, was reappointed for six months from February 1968).

'To advise the Ministry of Education upon such matters connected with educational theory and practice as they think fit, and upon any questions referred to them by the Ministry.'

In particular, in March 1967, 'to review the existing policies and practices in the field of primary education in Northern Ireland.'

Nursery education should be provided for all those who wish it, with priority in areas of overcrowding and bad housing, and provision should be made for suitable nursery accommodation in new housing development. The possibility of local education authorities making grants to approved playgroups should be investigated. The Ministry of Education, local education authorities and those responsible for the health and welfare services should re-examine the whole question of nursery education provision including provision for the mentally handicapped child.

The length of school day should be three hours in the first year of formal primary schooling, including the time devoted to religious instruction; four hours in the second year, divided into two sessions; and four and a quarter hours in the third year.

The formal primary school course should be six years following the fifth birthday, linked with the provision of nursery type education, and all children should have at least one year of nursery education, with more for the younger children of the age group. Meantime, present dates and conditions of entry to school should be maintained. Age of transfer and selection for secondary education should be jointly considered as a matter of urgency by either a new advisory council or a specialist working party.

The provision of up-to-date school buildings should proceed; a standing committee should be set up to provide information about design, standards and costs. Every school should have a telephone, and provision of television and radio receivers should not be dependent on the size of the school. The maximum number of pupils should be thirty in the upper classes, twenty-five in the lower, and fifteen in special classes, and in all schools there should be provision both for nursery and special educational treatment. More use should be made of techniques and devices to encourage individual learning, and the school's internal arrangement should be suffi-ciently flexible that both the highly intelligent and the 'slow learners' may proceed at a suitable pace. The enthusiasm of teachers can be fostered by closer liaison with the Schools Council in England and by the establishment of teacher centres.

Every school needs clerical assistance, but in small schools this could be undertaken by a new grade, 'general assistant', who would have some training and would also be able to assist in the classroom under a teacher's supervision. A more flexible approach to the employment of part-time teachers is advocated, and the use of peripatetic teachers for the handicapped should expand more where necessary. The problems of remedial education and the 'slow learner' require further investigation.

The present policy of closure and amalgamation of small rural primary schools should be continued, and efforts should be made to maintain contact with the parents in such cases. New rural schools should be made in no way inferior. Transport should be carefully planned and bus shelters provided at waiting points.

Homework set should have a useful educational purpose. There should be no homework for the first two years, fifteen minutes in the third, gradually increasing to an hour in the senior class, but none at week-ends and a reduced amount in the summer time. Punishment should never be given for inability to complete homework.

Co-operation between teachers and parents, school and home, should be improved, and preparation for such co-operation should form part of a teacher's professional training.

There is a reservation to the report, by W.C.H. Eakin, J. Hughes and D.V. McCall. They would prefer the period of primary education to be retained as seven years, so that if age of entry is to be five-plus, the age of transfer should be twelve-plus. The continuing adverse affects of selection could have been minimized by adoption of proposals (outlined in appendix I) for the abolition of statutory ages for compulsory education, and the substitution of a statutory minimum period of compulsory schooling. The proposals are linked with suggestions for flexibility in age of entry into, and promotion within, primary schools and in age of transfer to secondary education; they assume an extra year being added to compulsory schooling. Arguments are put forward in support of the proposals.

There is a bibliography of recent investigations and reports concerning primary schools. Appendices give the proposals discussed in the reservation, list the bodies and individuals who submitted evidence, give the text of a letter sent by the advisory council to all primary and preparatory schools, and show some examples of work done by primary school children.

Statistical tables throughout the report give figures for sizes of primary schools, numbers of pupils and teachers, management, building and reconstruction, cost per pupil, and also for costs, number of schools and numbers of pupils at nursery schools.

Northern Ireland General Certificate of Education

Rep. of Cttee., 1969.
41 pp.
Cttee. apptd. November 1965; rep. sgd. July 1969.

Dr. M. Grant (Ch. to August 1966); Dr. F.A. Vick (Ch. from October 1966) and twenty-eight members—T.C.C. Adam, Prof. M.J. Boyd, Prof. J.C. Beckett, Prof. J. Braidwood, Prof. T.M. Charlton, J. Doherty, D.A. Dorman, J. Finney, Dr. B.C. Gee, Dr. J.F. Gillies, Dr. H.J.G. Godin, Rev. Dr. J. Johnston, J. Kearns, A. Keith, Very Rev. Canon W. Larkin, Prof. F.J. Lelièvre, J. Malone, Prof. G. Owen, Dr. R.C. Pink, Very Rev. Dr. P. Rogers, W. Singer. *The following:* Rev. Mother M. Laurentia Corr, Miss M.W. Cunningham, Prof. N. Cuthbert, Prof. N.J. Gibson, Miss E.R. Gross, E. Howard, R. Macdonald, A.C. Stanley and A.K. Thomas joined the committee

at various dates, replacing Rev. Mother Helena Collins, J.L. Lord, Miss M. Leith, J.M. Malone, Prof. J.A. Parkinson, Miss N.M. Savage, A.J. Tulip.

'To direct the conduct of the General Certificate of Education examinations and to advise the Minister on matters relating to these. . . .'

The committee maintains that the standard of Northern Ireland G.C.E. examinations should be comparable to those of other examining boards and recommends that Northern Ireland join those other boards in undertaking further detailed investigations and in inter-board conferences.

If teachers from Northern Ireland served as assistant examiners and assistant moderators, this would increase teacher participation in the arrangements for the G.C.E. examinations. Communications between the committee and the schools should be strengthened by meetings with teachers, by annual reports on the examinations, and by arranging that teachers' views and/or suggestions for modifications of future syllabuses and examinations be conveyed to the committee and to the chief examiners.

Syllabuses and examining techniques should be kept under constant review, so that they will reflect the developments in teaching and examining which have been and are taking place in the various subjects.

Candidates following 'A' Level in any subject should be eligible for consideration for the award of a pass at 'O' Level in that subject. Practical tests for physics, chemistry and biology at 'A' Level should be supervised by teachers in their own schools, but tests for 'O' Level should be abolished. The introduction of new examination subjects should be kept under review, and the use of experiments in matters such as the multiple marking of English essays should be encouraged. Examinations in 'A' Level botany and zoology should be discontinued, as should the group certificate known as the Northern Ireland Senior Certificate.

The majority of the main decisions and recommendations of the committee, summarized at the end of the report, have already been implemented.

Appendices to the report show the functions of subcommittees and panels, and the membership of examination committees and subject panels. Tables show the number of candidates for G.C.E. examinations, 1966–1969, and also the results of the Senior Certificate and G.C.E. examinations, 1966–1969.

The Existing Selection Procedure for Secondary Education

Ministry of Education. Rep. of the Advisory Council for Education, 1971.
Cmd. 551, 32 pp.
Rep. sgd. October 1970.

N.A. Burges (Ch.) and fifteen members —Prof. D.J. Bradley, R.H. Brown, J.J. Campbell, Miss E. Conway, W.J. Dickson, J. Frost, Prof. J.A. Hendry, Prof. F.J. Lelièvre, Miss C. Macmahon, V.J. McGeown, Dr. J. McGilton, Mrs. M.R. O'Hara, E.G. Quigley, Dr. M.B. Sutherland, A.J. Tulip.

The council keeps strictly to its terms of reference, concentrating upon the *method* of selection rather than the *principle* of selection. After reviewing the existing selection procedure and possible modifications considering possible criticism of the procedure method, and noting the present 'review' procedure and the age of transfer from primary to secondary schools, it is decided that the present method—if supported by recommendations in this report—is the best available. Although the principle of selection is outside the scope of this report, some concern about it is expressed and the move away from selection elsewhere in the United Kingdom is noted. An appropriate study by the council is under way.

It is proposed, in the present report, that all eligible pupils should be entered for verbal reasoning tests; that boys' and girls' verbal reasoning test scores should be standardized separately; that

a new 'border-zone' scheme be devised which would help to standardize borderline-case treatment in all educational areas; and that the percentage of entrants qualifying automatically should be increased and the size of the 'borderzones' appropriately decreased. Principals of schools provide an order of suitability as a separate and independent means of assessment, and an explanation of the importance of this could be added to the ministry's circular of instructions. Investigation of both close correlation and lack of correlation between the principal's order of suitability and the results of verbal reasoning tests should be made. Under-age entrants should be treated as special cases by the local education authority, and pupils who, through illness or other reasons, miss two terms or more of a seven-year primary school course should have another year there.

Appendices give a list of bodies and individuals providing memoranda of evidence plus a suitable extract from a 1964 report by the council. Statistical tables in the report concern entrants, grades, 'border-zone' cases, and scholarships awarded in recent years (1966–70) in the various educational areas.

4 EDUCATION FOR PARTICULAR SUBJECTS OR VOCATIONS
Bible Instruction

Correspondence between the Ministry of Education and the Armagh Regional Educational Committee on the subject of Bible instruction in transferred schools, 1928.
Cmd. 84, 14 pp.

Four letters written during the months of March and April 1928 are included together with copies of relevant extracts from reports of an Armagh subcommittee.

The initial letter is from A.N.B. Wyse as secretary to the ministry, and it points out that the Lurgan Clerical Union has drawn attention to the fact that the Armagh authority has not inserted in the transfer deeds of schools the clause relating to simple Bible instruction which was arranged for in the 1925 Education Act. W. Dawson, secretary of the Armagh committee, replies with an extract from a report signed by H.B. Armstrong the chairman of the education authority's Transfers and Building Subcommittee. This extract argues that there is no one relevant clause on Bible instruction and that the Armagh committee's policy is involving some such instruction and is in no way materially different from that of other local education committees.

The next letter from the ministry states the clause in question and asserts that it, or a very similar clause, has been accepted by every other education committee which has entered into agreements for transfer. The Armagh committee is again exhorted to adopt the clause. The final letter includes a document signed by J.S. Carrick, the new Transfers and Buildings Subcommittee chairman. This reiterates that the necessary Bible instruction is taking place, alleges that the clause has not previously been submitted to the committee, that no such clause has been made generally applicable in transfer deeds in other areas, and that the only real fear of those complaining is that future Armagh education committees may not continue the present policy. No complaints have been received about the religious instruction, and it is argued that education authorities should have full power to prescribe the Bible instruction programme in their schools.

Rural Education

Rep. of Advisory Council for Education, 1952.
Cmd. 300, 48 pp.
Council apptd. April 1948.

Original council was Sir David Lindsay Keir (Ch.) and twenty members—T.C.C. Adam, D.H. Alexander, Rev. Br. T.A. Burke, Mrs. L. Irene M. Calvert, E. Carvill, Rev. R.A. Deane, Col. W.D. Gibbon, J.S. Hawnt, Mrs. Sylvia G. Kastell, Rt. Hon. H.C. Midgley, Rev. P.J. Mullally, N. McNeilly, Mrs. V.F.

Nelson, Prof. S.D. Nisbet, Rev. W.L. Northridge, Capt. the Hon. T.M. O'Neill, P.B. Webb, Maj. W. White, A.C. Williams, Rev. J.H. Withers. (Col. W.D. Gibbon, Sir David Lindsay Keir, the Rt. Hon. H.C. Midgley, Capt. the Hon. T.M. O'Neill, and P.B. Webb all resigned during their term of office. The Rt. Hon. Lord Justice Black was appointed chairman, November 1949, and A. Hunter and P. Smiles as members of the council, June 1950.)

'To examine the problem of rural education . . . , to enquire into the educational facilities available to country dwellers and to make recommendations to the Ministry as to the improvements which should be made in the various forms of such educational services, taking into account
(a) the part the new intermediate schools should play in the improvement of rural education and amenities,
(b) the extent to which schemes of further education should have relation to the distinctive needs of the countryman, and
(c) the extent to which courses in rural science, rural technology and agricultural science should be provided.'

Immediate attention is needed to bring rural school buildings up to a reasonable standard, especially of hygiene, and all should have adequate space for a playground and school garden. Suitable teachers must be attracted to work in rural areas and encouraged to remain there by having as good financial prospects as teachers in towns.

More variety is desirable in the primary schools' curriculum, and the value of physical education and music is emphasized. Teaching should be related to a country environment.

In both intermediate and grammar schools, there should be special provision for remedying shortcomings in the use of languages and for social training. General science, including biology, should have a special place. A variety of special courses should be provided in the later years at intermediate school, and there should be better facilities for domestic science. Both types of school require a relatively liberal staffing ratio so that children need not go to larger towns to have a wide choice of courses. The council does not agree with the Agricultural Enquiry Committee's recommendations for junior agricultural courses at technical intermediate schools.

Technical schools should cater for voluntary full-time preparatory vocational courses, and for part-time courses for those who wish to remedy a deficiency in their early education or to develop a special skill. Part-time courses for women in domestic and cultural subjects are advocated. The technical school should normally be the cultural and recreational centre for the community, failing which, the centre should be the intermediate school. An experimental village college, of the Cambridgeshire type, might be tried. The public library service should be reorganized and linked with the institutions of further education.

The appendix lists those bodies which gave evidence, and the publications which were consulted.

Technical Education for the Textile Industry

Rep. of Cttee. 1955.
Cmd. 329, 15 pp.
Cttee. apptd. December 1952; rep. sgd. October 1954.

Lt.Col. J.R. H. Greeves (Ch.) and seven members—M.F. Gordon, Dr. W. Heron, F. Hughes, Sir J. Graham Larmor, K.A. MacCormac, A.C. Menzies, H. Ruben. (Additional members appointed March 1953—A. Black, W.J.K. Hamilton, R.C. Jefferson, F.J.W. Shannon.)

'To investigate the needs and problems connected with technical education for the textile industry . . . and to make recommendations.'

The textile industry is the largest single manufacturing industry in Northern Ireland. Linen still predominates, although employment in the woollen and cotton industries has increased and there have been important developments in manmade fibres.

Classes for education in textiles are held in a few centres, but mainly in the Belfast College of Technology. The value of suitable training for recruits to the industry is stressed. Representatives of the trade would like to see a more practical approach in the classes provided, but the committee found apparent apathy, especially with regard to the trade scholarship courses, and some blame for the present state of education for textiles must be borne by the trade itself. The committee recommend the provision of courses for all types of workers, an increase in day and half-day release arrangements, and concentration of the majority of senior and advanced classes in the College of Technology. The staffing, premises and equipment of the college are discussed. The committee also advocate the establishment of an advisory committee which would disseminate information about courses available, encourage the writing of textbooks, secure financial support for suitable students, and foster co-operation between the schools and the industry.

5 HIGHER EDUCATION

Possible Development of Magee University College

Rep. of Cttee., 1950.
Cmd. 275, 49 pp.
Cttee. apptd. January 1949; rep. sgd. November 1949.

Sir Frederick Ogilvie (Ch.) and eight members—Sir James G. Acheson, G.C. Duggan, Maj. H.B. McCance, Lady (Louise P.) McDermott, Prof. P.S. Noble, Capt. the Hon. T.M. O'Neill, A.C. Williams, S.H. Wood. (S.H. Wood resigned March 1949 and was replaced by J.W. Parker. Sir Frederick Ogilvie resigned, April 1949, and Sir James Acheson became chairman.)

'To consider the possible development of Magee University College, Londonderry, in relation to the provision of University

education in Northern Ireland; and to make recommendations.'

An historical introduction describes events leading to the opening in 1865 of Magee Presbyterian College. Its original function was to provide a complete training for candidates for the Presbyterian ministry, and to this end it was divided into an arts and a theological department. The development of Magee College in relation to the universities and university colleges of Ireland is traced, and the gradual relaxation of control by the General Assembly of the Presbyterian Church in Ireland is indicated. The college suffered many handicaps, was never able to grant degrees, and with the exception of one fellowship, received no government assistance until 1938, when an annual grant of £2,500 was provided for the Arts Department. The college still consists of only two departments. Students may prepare for a degree of Trinity College, Dublin, spending part of their time in each institution, and intending Presbyterian ministers may take the first year of their three year divinity course at Magee University College.

Early in 1948, the government set up a committee of three members—Col. W.D. Gibbon (Ch.), Dr. H. Garrett and Lt.-Col. A.R.G. Gordon—to investigate the possibilities of the development of Magee and of the increased contribution which it could make in the future to university education in Northern Ireland. The report of this committee and a statement of the college's views on the report form an appendix to the present report. Colonel Gibbon's committee recommends the setting up of an experienced committee to consider in detail how the college can be fully developed as a university college catering for the arts. Theology should be transferred to the Assembly's College, Belfast; consideration should be given to forming a link with the Queen's University in addition to the link with Trinity College, Dublin; and the government should give financial assist-ance to develop the college. A minority report by Dr. Garrett stresses the need for changes in the college's governing body. The college, in their statement, welcome the proposed committee and agree with many of the report's recommendations. They consider that retention of theology and some development of a science department would create a better balanced college, and that the finances of the Theology Department could be kept separate from the rest of the college, as already is done.

Sir Frederick Ogilvie's committee concludes that the increase in university students in the next decade will not be sufficient to warrant the development by government grants of a true university college in Londonderry, and that science and social science departments should not be established. The college should become truly undenominational by closing the Theology Department and changing the nature of the governing body. A full range of arts courses should be provided, up to degree standard, with separate classes for honours. The college should be linked either to the Queen's University and Trinity College or to the latter alone, and it should be known as 'The University College of Londonderry'. A superannuation scheme should be introduced, and staff should retire at sixty-five. Annual grants should be assured from relevant local authorities. Discontinuance of government aid should be considered if the student body has not risen to at least 200 within seven years.

Other appendices give statistical information about the students at Magee College, and comparisons with other university colleges; the main provisions in the schemes governing the trusts of Magee College; and lists of bodies and individuals who submitted evidence to the committee.

Adult Education

Ministry of Education. Rep. of Cttee., 1964.
Cmd. 473, 55 pp.

Cttee. apptd. March 1963; rep. sgd. July 1964.

Sir Charles R. Morris (Ch.) and five members—Mrs. Helen I.A. Dales, Major J.A. Glen, J. McCoubrey, A.J. McGonigal, G. Pepper.

'To consider the basis on which Adult Education . . . could most usefully be organized, developed and financed in the future; and to make recommendations.'

Adult education, within the context of this report, is deemed to deal with liberal education linked with university extramural departments and bodies such as the Workers Educational Association. Indeed the appointment of the committee followed a joint request from the vice-chancellor of the Queen's University and the chairman of the regional W.E.A. There is a review of the present position as revealed in the work of Queen's, Magee University College, local authorities and the W.E.A., comparison being made with equivalent courses in the rest of Britain. It is thought that the university's joint committee for adult education should no longer be the sole recipient of Ministry of Education grants, as there is much need for work at a level below that which the university could generally undertake.

Details of proposals for new arrangements are set out, and discussions and recommendations consider both university and non-university level classes; grants and finance; co-ordination and control; and the question of establishing a centre for residential courses. It is recommended that provision of adult education classes should be at two levels in future, one to be organized by the Extramural Studies Department of the university, and the non-university-level work to be administered by the local district of the W.E.A. The bodies should establish a consultative committee, and there must be opportunity for voluntary bodies or a second university to participate in adult education provision. Other proposals concern the future financing of the respective levels of courses, the need for aid for the W.E.A. in appointing full-time organizing staff, and the value of a committee which could advise the ministry on adult education and on the grants to be paid.

A list of bodies and individuals providing written or oral evidence is given in an appendix, and another appendix provides relevant extracts from a report on adult education in England and Wales. Other appendices offer statistics of enrolments in W.E.A. and other classes, 1946–1963, and financial details of adult education courses recently provided at the Queen's University plus the likely financial requirements for the fuller participation of the W.E.A. There are also programmes indicating the range of adult courses offered recently by the Belfast branch of W.E.A. and by the university.

Higher Education

Rep. of Cttee., 1965.
Cmd. 475, xiv, 317 pp., 2 maps. Cttee. apptd. November 1963; rep. sgd. November 1964.

Sir John Lockwood (Ch.) and seven members—Maj. J.A. Glen, R.B. Henderson, Sir Willis Jackson, W.H. Mol, Miss A.R. Murray, Dr. D. Rebbeck, Sir Peter Venables.

'To review the facilities for university and higher technical education, . . . having regard to the report of the Robbins committee, and to make recommendations.'

The report first examines the general background, gives an account of existing facilities for higher education, and summarizes the development plans of the institutions concerned. The committee then examine and advise upon the university situation and teacher training, and discuss the remaining aspects of higher technical education and other relevant matters. An attempt is made to cost the proposals.

By 1980 there should be provision of 12,000–13,000 full-time university places,

3,000 places for intending non-graduate teachers and at least 4,000 full-time places in other higher-education courses.

The Queen's University should revise undergraduate courses to reduce overlap with school work and allow able students to embark on honours courses immediately upon admission. There should be greater provision for post-graduate courses. Consideration should be given to the foundation of a government research establishment associated with the university and directed towards research for industrial development. Interchange of university level students within the United Kingdom should be encouraged, and about 10 percent of university students should be from overseas. The Queen's University should not exceed 7,000 students by 1980, 6,000 of which should be undergraduate; the balance of the various faculties is indicated. All degree work in applied science and technology should be the responsibility of the Queen's University; the Joint Authority for Higher Technical Studies should be abolished, and a recent similar arrangement for degree studies in architecture abandoned. An adequate area in Belfast should be designated as a university precinct, and legislation introduced to permit powers of compulsory acquisition.

There should be a second university, with an enrolment by 1980 of between 5,000 and 6,000 full-time students directed mainly towards biological and related pure and applied sciences, environmental and social sciences, the humanities, and teacher education. The second university should have one or more research institutes associated with it, possibly government sponsored but at least government supported. Initially, it should not include a medical or a veterinary school but should establish a school of agriculture, after which the existing arrangement between the Ministry of Agriculture and the Queen's University should be terminated. The committee found it impossible to deal satisfactorily with the academic problems of a new university outside the context of its general location, and were informed through their assessors on behalf of the government, that they were free to recommend a location if they so desired. The Coleraine area is proposed, where a suitable site should be presented by the sponsoring local authorities, an endowment fund established, and academic planning board set up without delay. Priority should be given to the provision of facilities for teacher education and agriculture, and the first students admitted in October 1968.

Government grants to Magee University should be progressively reduced, the staff permitted to transfer to the new university or, if senior, to retire, and the buildings should later be used for non-university courses of varying types and duration.

An education centre should be established within the framework of the new university, preferably by 1966 or 1967, providing B.A. or B.Sc. degree courses (not B. Ed.) and diploma courses for non-degree students, and with a variety of other functions including provision of religious education courses, and training facilities for teachers in the agricultural colleges. In view of the developments in teacher education, the nature and duration of the probationary period for teachers should be reconsidered.

The Queen's University should enter partnership with the Ministry of Education and the Belfast training colleges to assume responsibility for producing teachers for all types of schools. The governing bodies of the training colleges, renamed 'Colleges of Education', should include university and staff representation, and their courses should be revised. Training facilities should be available for 'in-service' training of technical teachers, in addition to the existing full-time arrangement with colleges in England and Wales, and also for training part-time technical teachers and newly appointed and other interested university teachers.

There should be a regional college of technology in Belfast, with an associated group of area or local colleges from which students completing appropriate courses could transfer to the regional college. There should be an increase in sandwich and block-release courses, and Queen's University should reconsider the Ordinary and Higher National Diplomas and Certificates as qualifications for admission or for credit in degree courses. The Regional College of Technology together with the Belfast Colleges of Domestic Science and Art and the proposed colleges of commerce, catering, music and drama should form a combined 'Ulster College' under a single board of governors and financed by direct government grants. An adequate precinct should be designated. Meantime, there should be no change in the management or organization of the Ulster College of Physical Education.

The government should consider setting up a body to secure co-operation within higher education and to absorb the functions of existing bodies such as the Council of Queen's University and Schools and the committee which directs the examination for the Northern Ireland General Certificate of Education. Both universities should join or form an association with the Universities Central Council for Admissions.

Miscellaneous recommendations include the supply of adequate reading rooms for students, pending improved residential facilities; abolition of employment conditions for student grants; more facilities for part-time degree study; extension of extramural activities; exploration of the potentialities of television; establishment of a school of communications at the Queen's University. The Queen's University and the Ulster College should have adequate facilities for musical and theatrical productions. There should be a substantial development of public library services. More entrants to medical auxiliary occupations should be trained in Northern Ireland. Loughry Agricultural College should engage in applied research and in other higher-degree work in association with the second university.

Higher education should be periodic-ally reviewed.

All major local authorities should make significant annual grants to the universities and the Ulster College.

In addition to lists of sources of evidence and institutions visited by the committee, there are seven appendices. These give extracts from the Robbins Report; a summary of the history, organization, regulations and future plans of the Queen's University; details concerning higher education—the Joint Authority for Higher Technological Studies, courses available, trade scholarships, proposed expansion of the work of Belfast College of Technology, and arrangements with regard to architectural education; the history and regulations of Magee University College and of the training colleges; miscellaneous information on the development of television in this and other parts of the world; a table showing professional and technical staff engaged in the health and hospital services, together with their educational requirements and further training; a description of the Northern Ireland Council for Educational Research and the charter of the Council for National Academic Awards. The seventh appendix consists of a hundred statistical tables concerning such things as numbers of students in different sectors of higher education; the qualifications and performance of university students; considerations of geographical distribution, age, social class, etc.; and central government expenditure on different institutions.

Higher Education

Government statement on the report of the committee appointed by the Minister of Finance, 1965.
Cmd. 480, 3 pp.

The Government accepts the Lockwood Committee's recommendations on future development at the Queen's University, principally expansion of its work in science and technology; on the training of teachers and the concept of an education centre within the new university;

on the need for an increase in facilities for non-university higher education, and the establishment of an Ulster College. While agreeing with the recommendation that a new university should be sited in the Coleraine area, the government does not accept that Magee University College will have to discontinue and will investigate further.

6 LIBRARIES, MUSEUMS

LIBRARIES

Libraries

Rep. of the Dept. Cttee., 1929.
Cmd. 101, 45 pp.
Cttee. apptd. June 1928; rep. sgd. July 1929.

R.L. Praeger (Ch.) and eight members— H.B. Armstrong, D.A. Chart, J.D. Goldsbrough, Col. R.J. Howard, Very Rev. R.G.S. King, Prof. G.G. Smith, Maj. G. Thomson, and Maj. R. Workman.

'To inquire into the library provision . . . and its adequacy, particularly for the securing and preservation of works of the higher branches of learning and historical research; to consider the means of extending and improving library facilities, whether by the establishment of a State Library, co-ordination of existing public and other libraries, or otherwise; and to make recommendations.'

Present library provision in Northern Ireland is viewed as inadequate, especially for those engaged in research. Public library provision is scanty and uneven, and there is no guarantee that other libraries can satisfy needs which the public service does not meet. It is proposed that a state library, known as the Ulster Library, be established as the centre of a co-operative system and to procure works required for serious study. The existence of such a library might encourage some owners of private collections to donate material. Although such a library could not be complete, it could achieve a vital role in co-ordin-

ation and house many important works relating to the interests and problems of the province. To promote economy in book purchase, a central catalogue of books held by various libraries could be compiled and maintained in the Ulster Library.

While the report is chiefly concerned with the establishment of this state library and means of encouraging rational co-operation, information is also given on the public libraries of Belfast and Londonderry and of the six counties. The county is viewed as the viable and logical unit for the development of a public library service. Other proposals concern methods for encouraging library use, ways of developing the parliamentary libraries and libraries in schools, and the importance of fostering relations with library services in Great Britain and the Free State. Appendices state districts in which no public library service yet exists, give descriptive notes on the resources and facilities of the chief non-public libraries, and provide statistics on public library income, expenditure, stock and operations.

The Parliamentary Library

Special and final reps. of Jt. Sel Cttee., together with proc., mins. of ev. and app., 1948.
H.C. 778, 44 pp.
Cttee. apptd. May 1947; rep. o.p. February 1948.

Prof. R. Corkey (Ch.) and five members —Maj. J.C. Boyle, Mrs. Irene Calvert, C. Healy, Mrs. Dinah McNabb, Capt. T.M. O'Neill.

'To examine the present [Parliamentary] Library facilities and make recommendations for their improvement.'

The special report merely indicates that the committee believe the terms of reference to be too narrow and that they should be identical with those of the equivalent Westminster committee appointed in 1945. The committee resumed its sittings after being assured that the terms were wide enough to cover staff questions.

In the final report, it is argued that the library should be able to provide detailed factual data for members, offer good reference facilities, house a relatively comprehensive collection of Northern Ireland material, and co-ordinate its own services with those of various departmental libraries. There are therefore a number of constructive proposals, a principal one being that a library advisory committee be established. It is also recommended that the range of material provided be greatly extended; that plans for the exchange of books be developed; that catalogues, staffing, lighting and heating all warrant improvement. An annual sum of £500 should be voted in estimates for book purchase, and, in addition, a capital sum should be made available to overcome existing deficiencies. The library should be available to the civil service as well as to M.P.s.

Most of the report is occupied by the evidence of the three witnesses heard—the parliamentary librarian, the librarian of the Queen's University, and an engineer whose advice on lighting was sought—and the committee proceedings. Appendices provide a memorandum on the work the library staff should perform, as envisaged by the librarian, and a brief statement on the ways of improving lighting and heating.

The Public Library Service

Rep. of Cttee., 1966.

Cmd. 494, 63 pp.
Cttee. apptd. September 1964; rep. sgd. December 1965.

Dr. J.S. Hawnt (Ch.) and twelve members—Prof. M.J. Boyd, J.J. Campbell, I.A. Crawley, W.H. Fenning, Mrs. May A.F.E. Haughton, P. Havard-Williams, H.J. Heaney, W.S. Henderson, Mrs. R.I. Lillie, A. McGonigal, J. Malone, L.J. Mitchell.

'To consider the Public Library Service ... and to make recommendations for its development, having regard to the relationship of public libraries to other libraries.'

The historical development of the public library services of Northern Ireland is described. The main principles of the Roberts Report (*The Structure of the Public Library Service in England and Wales, 1959,* Cmnd. 660) and of the Working Party (*Standards of Public Library Service in England and Wales, 1962*) are found to be relevant to the service in Northern Ireland. Only the eight county and county borough authorities serve populations of over 40,000 (the minimum viable unit, according to the working party), while all authorities are substantially below the standards recommended by the working party in terms of book and staff provision. A radical reorganization of the service is necessary. It should be based on viable units of population: urban library authorities should be required to relinquish their library powers to the appropriate county authority, and certain authorities should be encouraged to amalgamate. Present financial arrangements, depending entirely on local rates, are unable to meet the demands of a modern library service. The Ministry of Education should provide and administer grant-aid. A grant formula is suggested, designed to encourage the less developed authorities to reach an acceptable standard of service within a reasonable period. Recommendations are made as to suitable library buildings. The service should be able to attract qualified staff; standards in staff and salary should not fall below those in Great Britain.

The Ministry of Education should supervise the public library service and should promote legislation to ensure its development and the attainment and maintenance of prescribed standards. A library adviser should be appointed to the ministry, and a statutory advisory council set up. A provincial library should be established which would provide many central services, and it should be based on the book stock and services of the Belfast Central Library.

Recommendations cover standards of library services, schools library service and library co-operation. The Linenhall Library and Armagh Public Library should be assisted from public funds.

A reservation to the report, signed by six members (I.A. Crawley, Mrs. Haughton, P. Havard-Williams, W.S. Henderson, Mrs. Lillie and A. McGonigal), disagrees with the proposal to separate the present Belfast Central Library from the Belfast Public Libraries in order to form a provincial library. The Belfast Public Libraries should be retained under one control, administered by the corporation, with an adequate government grant and contributions from other library authorities in recognition of its services to the rest of the province.

There are nine appendices, which summarize the Roberts Report; the Report of the Working Party on Standards; the Public Libraries and Museums Act, 1964; public library legislation in Northern Ireland; and staffing and salary scales. Bodies which submitted evidence are listed, and details are given of questionnaires sent to all public, private, special and academic libraries in Northern Ireland, and also analyses of returns covering such things as expenditure, book stock, staff, reader and branch numbers. Statistical tables show library authorities' expenditure and receipts, 1964–1965; the scheme for distributed expenditure designed to encourage the less developed authorities; and results of a survey to examine the effect of improved library facilities on demand.

MUSEUMS

Ulster Folk Museum

Rep. of Folk Museum Cttee., 1954.
Cmd. 326, 11 pp.
Cttee. apptd. March 1954; rep. sgd. August 1954.

Sir Roland Nugent (Ch.) and seven members—Mrs. Florence E. Breakie, G.N. Cox, Maj. H.M. Donaldson, Prof.

E.E. Evans, R.J.R. Harcourt, K. Leacock, C.R.M. Wood. (K. Leacock did not sign the report.)

'(a) To examine and make recommendations on the proposal to establish an Ulster Folk Museum in Belfast illustrative of Ulster life, culture, arts and crafts of the past;
(b) to enquire into the desirability of the establishment and maintenance of such a Museum on a national basis;
(c) to enquire into the prospective capital costs of the proposal and the costs of administration and maintenance, and to make recommendations.'

The benefits of preserving, in Ulster, items which illustrate its life and culture are indicated. The report recommends that an authority representative of Belfast Corporation, local authorities, the Queen's University of Belfast, and the government should be constituted to establish a folk museum on a national basis. It is suggested that the folk museum be set up in Belfast; that the area of the Folk Park in the grounds of Belfast Castle should be enclosed and that exhibits should be completed with a view to opening the museum in two to three years; that the daily control of the museum should rest with a curator-in-charge, appointed by the governing body in consultation with the Belfast City Council; and that the government should make a reasonably substantial contribution towards the capital costs of establishing the museum. The government should consider the possibility of empowering the museum authority to borrow from government funds, and an annual grant should be made towards the current expenditure of the museum. The Ministry of Education should consider grants made by local education authorities towards the costs of the museum as expenditure qualifying for a grant under the Education Act (N.I.), 1947. The Northern Ireland Tourist Board should make an annual grant to the museum to acknowledge its appeal to tourists.

Two appendices give the plan for the

proposed museum site (this appendix is not included with the report) and details of the proposed mobile exhibition.

Museums in Northern Ireland

Ministry of Finance. Rep. of Standing Commission on Museums and Galleries, 1965.
Cmd. 488, 13 pp.

The Rt. Hon. the Earl of Rosse (Ch.)

Terms of reference given December 1964:

'To advise on any questions which they considered relevant to the most effective development of the Ulster Museum as a national institution. In particular . . .
(a) what should be the level of purchase grants made available by the Government of Northern Ireland;
(b) what steps might be taken to promote co-operation both between the Ulster Museum and national institutions in Great Britain and also between the Ulster Museum, the Ulster Folk Museum and other museums in Northern Ireland;
(c) what should be done to stimulate increased interest and support by industrialists and the public at large;
(d) what should be the relative status of the Director for the purpose of salary compared with similar officials in Great Britain, both at the present stage of development of the museum and when the proposed extension is completed.'

The commission visited the Ulster Museum, the Transport Museum, the Ulster Folk Museum, and the County Museum and Regimental Museum at Armagh.

It is favourably impressed by the progress made in the planned extension for the Ulster Museum and by the high standard of work at all the museums. If the Ulster Museum is to continue its promising development, the pay and conditions of staff must be comparable with similar United Kingdom institutions. The director's salary should be on the scale of the smaller national museums in the U.K.

The present purchase grant of £17,500 is comparable with £18,000 for the Royal Scottish Museum and £20,000 for the National Museum of Wales. In its present stage of transition from a local to a national institution, the museum may need a larger grant to enable it to build up its collections to the necessary level; this could be either an increase in grant over a critical period, a special allocation for a special purpose, or sympathetic government consideration over the next five or ten years of any requests for special grants to permit acquisition of outstanding material. All museums now must have some degree of specialization. Collection of Irish art, furniture, glass and ceramics would seem essential, but in Irish archaeology the major treasures are already in Dublin, and a comparative collection of European archaeology could become the concern of Belfast. For the present, the world of art can best be presented to the Belfast public by means of temporary exhibitions, and there might be a policy of restraint in acquisition of paintings and sculpture other than Irish and modern.

The director of the Ulster Museum is already a member of the Directors' Conference. All professional staff should have occasional opportunities of meeting their colleagues in Great Britain, the Republic of Ireland and abroad.

Plans for removal of the Transport Museum to a site at Craigavad are approved; there would then be a strong case for its absorption by the Folk Museum and its financing in the same way as the latter. The consequent share in government responsibility would mean that co-operation between the two and the Ulster Museum could be encouraged. Provincial museums, such as the Armagh County Museums, might be aided by government grant for building and development where there is genuine need and the local authority is contributing to the full extent of its powers. Increased support for the Ulster Museum other than from public funds might be stimulated by formation of an association of friends of the museums. Sunday opening, even for a few hours, is most important.

A school museum service, to circulate museum objects to the schools, is of especial value in a region much of which is far from any museum, and the Ulster Museum should study the organization in Wales and other places with a view to setting up a similar organization.

XV SOCIAL PROBLEMS

1 **General**
2 **Charities, Clubs**
3 **Care of Children**

4 **Juveniles**
5 **Gambling, Drinking**
6 **Problems of War**

1 GENERAL

World Poverty

First rep. from the All-Party Cttee., 1969.
8 pp.
Cttee. apptd. February 1967; rep. sgd.
December 1968.

Capt. W.J. Long (Ch.) and eight members—R.A. Ardill, J.J. Brennan, H. Diamond, Miss B.H. Maconachie, Miss S.M. Murnaghan, E.G. Richardson, F.V. Simpson, J.D. Taylor.

'To examine and report on Northern Ireland's responsibilities in world poverty relief and to make suggestions relating to schemes which might be initiated with a view to the most effective use of the efforts being made and to maintain contact with the Ministry of Overseas Development at Westminster.'

Reasons for providing aid to developing nations and the work of appropriate voluntary organizations in the province are outlined. Gifts of seed potatoes and dried milk have been arranged, and a donation of £1,000 has been received from the Tughan Trust, through the interest of F.C. Tughan, for use in appropriate projects. The community is becoming more aware of world poverty, and there is now a Northern Ireland equivalent of the Voluntary Committee on Overseas Aid and Development. Support received by NIVCOAD from organizations and the Ministry of Overseas Development is encouraging. There are close links between NIVCOAD and the present committee.

A Record of Constructive Change

For details of this report see Class XVI p. 221.

2 CHARITIES, CLUBS

Charitable Loan Societies

First rep. of the Ministry of Finance as successors . . . to the Loan Fund Board, [1925].
Cmd. 36, 12 pp.

The period covered by the report extends from 1 January 1922 to 31 December 1924, but until 9 May 1923 certain difficulties prevented transfer of the relevant papers and funds from the Department of Agriculture and Technical Instruction in Ireland, previously responsible for the functions of the Loan Fund Board. Particulars of this money are given in Table I of the appendix. With the spread of ordinary banking facilities, the number of charitable loan societies has decreased. On 1 January 1922 there were seven in Northern Ireland. A summary of their transactions for 1922, 1923 and 1924 are given in Tables II-IV. During the period, two of the societies, Drumquin and Londonderry, decided to dissolve, and the winding up is nearly completed. Owing to certain defects and irregularities, the ministry decided to dissolve the Irvinestown society; a receiver has been appointed and the society's assets are being realized.

A bill is to come before Parliament which would enable the ministry to use undistributed surpluses of dissolved societies and similar sums, for loans to farmers in times of distress, and to allow better control and superintendence over the societies. Table V of the appendix gives an account of the moneys received and paid by the ministry as successors to the Loan Fund Board.

Administration of Charitable Donations and Requests, 1922–1924

Ministry of Finance, Rep., 1925.
Cmd. 52, 11 pp.

The ministry is successor in Northern Ireland to the Commissioners of Charitable Donations and Bequests for Ireland. A charities advisory committee was appointed in June 1922, composed as follows: 'The Chairman shall be or shall have been a Judge of the Supreme Court of Northern Ireland or a County Court Judge. Not less than two members shall be ministers of religion of different denominations, and not less than three members shall be persons professing the Roman Catholic faith. Not less than two members, in addition to the Chairman, shall be persons having legal qualifications.' The committee are to advise on the administration of the law relating to charities; the construction of wills and documents; dealings with charitable property; acceptance of funds applicable for charitable purposes; framing and amendment of schemes governing the administration of charities and educational endowments; matters of policy, religion, ecclesiastical practice and finance. The first committee consisted of the late Rt. Hon. Sir Denis S. Henry (Ch.) and eleven members—J.M. Barbour, Rt. Hon. Mr. Justice Brown, Sir William F. Coates, Sir Robert N. Anderson, Very Rev. T.G.G. Collins, F. Kerr, Rev. W.J. Lowe, Sir Frederick Moneypenny, Mrs Julia McMordie, Sir William Whitla, J. McSparran.

A summary is given of funds transferred to and the amount held by the ministry. Further details appear in schedule I of the report. A portion of the Queen's Jubilee Fund of the Royal Irish Constabulary was paid to the ministry for administration of the scheme in Northern Ireland. The ministry also appeared in the case concerning the Seaton Association Fund which benefits wives and children of soldiers serving or having served in Ireland, and was successful in preventing alteration to the scheme. Proceedings have been instituted to secure transfer of certain funds held in Dublin. It is the policy to dispose of Free State securities where possible, as the exemption from Free State income tax is only temporary. A detailed list of funds (other than funds transferred by order of the Joint Exchequer Board) lodged with the ministry during the period is found in schedule II.

Charity

Rep. of Cttee., 1959.
Cmd. 396, 48 pp.
Cttee. apptd. September 1956; rep. sgd. January 1959.

Prof. F.H. Newark (Ch.) and fifteen members—C.J. Bateman, J.M. Benn, T. Brown, R.A. Corscadden, Dr. V.T.H. Delany, Most Rev. Dr. N. Farren, Mrs. J.W. M.A.F.E. Haughton, J.G. Lennon, R.L.E. Lowry, F.C. MacNeice, H.A. McVeigh, C.A. Nicholson, Sir Lucius O'Brien, H.M. Thompson, Capt. R. Watts. (H.A. McVeigh resigned, October 1956, and K.R. Shimeld was appointed, September 1957.)

'To consider and report on the law (except as regards taxation) relating to charitable trusts in Northern Ireland including their application cy-pres with particular regard to
(a) the powers and duties of the Ministry of Finance as successor to the Commissioners of Charitable Donations and Bequests in Ireland;
(b) the report of the Committee on the Law and Practice relating to Charitable Trusts in England and Wales (Cmnd. 8710) and the White Paper entitled "Government Policy on Charitable Trusts in England and Wales" (Cmnd. 9538),

and any legislation which may be passed to implement the White Paper; and
(c) the reports of the Inter-departmental Committee of 24th July, 1954, and 25th April, 1955, on Schemes made under the Educational Endowments (Ireland) Act, 1885.'

Interim Report. *Sgd. May 1958. Appendix A of report.*

Legislation should provide for the establishment of a combined trust fund by any body of trustees where proper administration is assured, and the establishment of an independent investment trust in which the trustees of the smaller charitable trusts may invest.

Final Report.

The charity laws of England and Wales and of Ireland have a common origin and are broadly the same, and, for reasons given in the report, it is prudent not to disturb this uniformity. Yet there are important minor differences, especially in the field of administration. It is recommended that a board of ten commissioners, constituted on the model of the Irish Charity Commissioners, should be established to take over the functions performed by the Ministry of Finance in relation to charity matters, and most of the committee's recommendations relate to the powers and functions of this proposed charity authority.

Appendices list the bodies and individuals who gave evidence, give figures for charitable donations and bequests notified to the Ministry of Finance, 1952–1957, give details from statutes and legislation referred to in the report, and list the proposals for dealing with the provisions of the Charitable Donations and Bequests (Ireland) Acts, 1844, 1867 and 1871.

Registered Clubs

Ministry of Home Affairs. Rep. of Cttee., 1960.
Cmd. 410, 24 pp.

Cttee. apptd. January 1959; rep. sgd. December 1959.

Rt. Hon. Sir Anthony B. Babington (Ch.) and fourteen members—Air Marshall Sir George R. Beamish, A.S. Boyd, Miss A.A. Campbell, J.J. Campbell, W. Craig, T.A. Crowley, W.E. Dornan, Mrs. Margaret Drennan, A.V. Froggatt, F.L. Hopkins, J. Jackson, F. Jeffrey, R.R.J. Miller, W.J. Morgan (Vice-Chairman).

'To consider the operation and enforcement of the law . . . relating to registered clubs and recommend whether and in what respects amendment of the law is necessary and desirable in the public interest.'

Registered clubs generally are well administered and properly supervised. The law governing registration and conduct of registered clubs is set forth, and recommendations of the committee are concerned with stricter requirements for applications for registration and renewals; opening hours and exemptions for residential clubs, nightworkers' clubs and special occasions; keeping of books and submission of accounts; control of visitors; and irregularities which should be statutory offences. Appendices list witnesses to the committee and give figures relating to numbers of clubs, numbers of members, amount spent in purchase of intoxicating liquor, inspection of clubs by police, and particulars of objections by police to registrations and renewals of registration.

3 CARE OF CHILDREN

Children in Care

Rep. by the Northern Ireland Child Welfare Council, 1956.
35 pp.
Prepared by two study groups.

Adoption and Boarding Out Study Group

J.P. Murphy (Ch.) and seven members—
H.I. Brown, Miss F. Harrison, T. Lynch,
Miss M. McAleese, Mrs. J.I. Suttie, Rev.

W.G.M. Thomson, Brigadier Jessie Thorniley.

Home Study Group

D.G. Neill (Ch.) and nine members— J. Bebbington, E. Geary, R. Getgood, Mrs. D.C. Harrison, J. Keating, Br. S. Kelly, Miss M. McAleese, Mrs. M.I. Simpson, Mrs. J.I. Suttie. (R. Getgood resigned and E. Geary died before the completion of the investigation).

'To investigate the various aspects of child care and welfare in Northern Ireland and to make suggestions on the basis of their investigations.'

Part I, dealing with adoption and boarding out, covers the difficulties and problems of adoption, fostering and illegitimate children. Ideally the best age for a child to be adopted is before two years old, as it gives a stronger sense of stability and security within the family group. General difficulties arise such as cost of fees, failure of the public to realize the needs of the abandoned child, doubts by prospective adopters, necessary guarantees by landlords and housing authorities that the child will be permitted to live on the premises. In addition to the foregoing general hindrances to adoption, there are often special difficulties in particular cases. Mental, physical and psychological defects in children can be serious drawbacks to adoption, as can also be the difficulty of obtaining parental consent and the fact that many children in care cannot be regarded as wholly abandoned. The greatest care should be taken in the selection of suitable adopters with regard to their physical and mental health, age and character. The child in care has a right to a home of his own as much like other children's as possible. Legal adoption is admittedly the best way of providing this, but where it is not possible, boarding out is considered to be the most satisfactory alternative. The illegitimate child presents a special problem; failure to arrange for a satisfactory adoption or boarding out at an early age often leads to his passing through a series of systems and institutions, each catering for the failure of the previous ones, until he is mentally unfitted for normal life. The report goes on to outline the several problems of illegitimacy and the reasons for the wish of the parents to rid themselves of the unwanted child; much more care should be taken to provide accommodation for mother and child and where this is not possible to arrange for adoption at an early age.

For the child who is denied the privilege of growing up in his natural family or substitute family (i.e. by adoption or fostering), a voluntary home is needed to give affection, understanding, and security. There has been an experiment in establishing family group homes where a husband and wife are given the responsibility for a number of children besides their own child or children. Although this system is successful and satisfactory, it is not always possible, and larger homes are necessary to cater for much larger groups of children. Part II of the report outlines both cases and gives recommendations and standards necessary to the successful working of a large home, giving consideration to the importance of maintaining the individuality of each child and providing a life as near as possible to that of the child in its natural home as regards pocket money, holidays, outings, etc.

The special need of advice and guidance in the important years following a child's leaving a welfare authority voluntary home—referred to in part III of the report as after-care—is discussed, and recommendations are made by the council under such aspects as education, leisure-time activities, vocational guidance and training, co-operation with the employer, emigration and Forces apprenticeship schemes, residential hostels and lodgings.

The council, in part IV, puts forward general recommendations on children's services, the voluntary organizations and the needed co-operation with welfare authorities and stresses the need for financial assistance to voluntary homes both for day-to-day expenses and the added expense of boarding-out allowances for those children who would benefit more from living in a family group.

Appendix A gives a table showing the numbers of children in care at 31 December 1955. Appendices B and C show the present legal conditions of adoption and the agreement a foster parent has to sign on acceptance of a child to his or her home. Standards of sanitary accommodation for nurseries and homes for children over five years of age are shown in appendix D, and lastly, in appendix E is listed the information which should be available in case records.

Child Guidance and Speech Therapy

[*Ministry of Health and Local Government.*] *Rep. of Advisory Cttee., 1958. 27 pp.*
Cttee. apptd. September 1956; rep. sgd. July 1958.
F.F. Main (Ch.) and eight members—F.M.B. Allen, J.M. Benn, W.F. Bryson, N. Dugdale, J.S. Hawnt, J. McG. Jackson, W.G. Swann, Rosemary J. Webb.

'To consider how the Child Guidance and Speech Therapy Services in Northern Ireland may best be developed, and to make recommendations.'

The need for a second full-time clinic in Belfast for the child-guidance service is stressed, with part-time clinics to be set up in other parts of the province as soon as circumstances permit. All clinics should be open to all children under and above the compulsory school age. Until clinics are established at convenient centres, it is suggested that a visiting psychological service could serve the rural areas. On staffing for a child-guidance clinic, it is recommended that each should have as a working team a psychiatrist, doctor, psychiatric social worker and psychologist, with the former the leader of the team. General social workers and health visitors would be acceptable in the absence of enough psychiatric social workers. If possible, a speech therapist should be associated with each clinic.

Health and education authorities should be more closely associated with the work of the clinic, including staff exchanges. The existing clinic should remain a responsibility of the Northern Ireland Hospitals Authority and serve as a point of referral for the province. There should be a close functional relationship between the hospital, school health and psychological services. Additional clinics should be supplied by the Hospitals Authority, which in most cases might also employ the psychiatric social workers and make their services available to the health authority. Otherwise the psychiatric social worker or substitute should be employed jointly by the health authority and the Hospitals Authority. The local education authority should supply the psychologist.

To combat the shortage of psychiatric social workers, educational psychologists and psychiatrists, the Hospitals Authority should give urgent consideration to the arrangements for providing specialist training in child psychiatry. Modifications are needed in the conditions governing the award of grants to teachers who propose to take a B. Ed. specializing in psychology. Consideration should be given to the establishment of a mental-health course for training psychiatric social workers. In-service training both for psychologists and health visitors who are to be employed on child-guidance work should be provided by secondment to clinics, supported if possible by a theoretical course.

In conclusion, the report recommends that the development of the child-guidance service be supervised by a consultant psychiatrist and that people or bodies interested in the work of the child-guidance clinics should be able to make full use of the facilities available. The need for boarding schools or hostels for maladjusted children and the need for psychiatric in-patient beds should be carefully considered.

Speech therapists should be principally employed by the Northern Ireland Hospitals Authority, but their services should be made available to local authorities. Work should give opportunities for professional and specialist consultation. While the shortage of speech therapists lasts, only the severe cases reaching hospitals and clinics should be dealt with by the speech therapist and then only after filtering by a medical examination.

The shortage of speech therapists necessitates a training school for speech therapists in Belfast, efforts to stimulate recruitment, and financial assistance from the Hospitals Authority to those trainees who undertake to give two years' service after training. Short courses for teachers on the correction of minor speech defects are advisable.

Appendix A gives details of all sources of evidence in the report and is followed, in appendix B, by recommended accommodation for a child guidance clinic.

Operation of Social Services in Relation to Child Welfare

Rep. by the Northern Ireland Child Welfare Council, 1959.
11, 45 pp.
Prepared by a study group.

Lady E.H.R. Ashby (Ch.) and ten members—H.I. Brown, J. Dixon, Mrs. Grace I.A. Faris, Miss W.E. Hadden, Mrs. S.T. Harrison, J. Keating, Miss M. McAleese, J.A. McGlade, D.G. Neill, Rev. W.G.M. Thomson.

'To report on the operation of social services in relation to child welfare.'

Every year many children are taken into care by welfare authorities and voluntary organizations for one reason or another. This survey was undertaken to classify those reasons and to·assess their importance numerically. The report outlines some of the circumstances in which children are taken into care, such as illegitimacy, neglect or abandonment by parent(s), illness of parent(s), orphaned children, death or desertion of parent, family homeless, unsuitable foster homes, parent or guardian in prison, etc.

Part II of the report consists of a series of particular studies, covering the reasons

why children came into the care of the eight welfare authorities and the six largest voluntary homes, the distribution of children in homes according to age groups, the time which welfare authorities devote to child care, and the extent to which contact with parents and relatives is maintained during the period in care. The fifth and sixth studies in part II concern the persons or agencies who place children in care (optional contacts) and the place of birth of the children in the care of the voluntary and statutory bodies.

Following the report the committee lists in part III all conclusions and recommendations arising from their findings.

The report concludes with sixteen appendices showing statistical tables for the following: (1) reasons why children come into care; (2) percentage distribution of children committed to the care of welfare authorities by Fit Persons Orders of the courts, according to the reasons why they were brought before the court; (3) number of children in care of welfare authorities and voluntary homes, classified according to status at birth and age group; (4) total and illegitimate birth rate for the six counties, the two county boroughs, and Northern Ireland as a whole, for 1953–1956; (5) comparison of children in care of welfare authorities in 1952 and 1957 with the number boarded-out and placed in voluntary homes; (6) distribution of children in the care of the welfare authorities according to the reasons why they came into care; (7) distribution of children in care of the six largest voluntary homes according to the reasons why they came into care; (8a) and (8b) distribution according to age groups of children in care of the eight welfare authorities and five of the largest voluntary homes; (9a) number of children in care per 1,000 of the estimated population of Northern Ireland on 30 June 1957, by age groups; (9b) distribution of children in the care of welfare authorities according to the number of years they have spent in care;

(10) distribution of the time which welfare authorities devoted to child care according to the age of the children; (11) distribution of time which welfare authorities devoted to child care according to the reasons why children came into care; (12) contact with parents or relatives related to welfare and voluntary care, and to legitimacy; (13) comparison between the eight welfare authorities and the six largest voluntary homes in relation to the maintenance of contact with relatives; (14) original contact in placing the children in care in each of the eight welfare authorities and the six largest voluntary homes and in all the voluntary homes; (15) place of birth of children in the care of welfare authorities and voluntary homes. Appendix 16 gives an example of the information required for the central register of children in care of welfare authorities or voluntary organizations.

Adoption of Children

Rep. by the Northern Ireland Child Welfare Council, 1963.
51 pp.
Rep. sgd. October 1962. Rep. prepared by appropriate subcommittee.

D.G. Neill (Ch.) and three members—
H.I. Brown, F. Crilly, Rev. W.G.M. Thompson.

'*To examine critically the law and procedure in Northern Ireland in relation to the adoption of children, to contrast this with the present position in Great Britain, and to make such recommendations as the Council think fit.*'

Legal adoption was introduced in Northern Ireland by the Adoption of Children Act (Northern Ireland), 1929. The report outlines the existing adoption law in Northern Ireland and makes comparison with adoption legislation in Great Britain. Certain aspects of the operation of the Adoption of Children Act (Northern Ireland), 1950, in the quinquennium from 1 January 1955 to 31 December 1959 and for the years 1960 and 1961 are given in the report, with

accompanying tables showing statistics for application for adoption orders, 1955–1959; reasons for refusal and withdrawal; age and sex of infants (who were the subjects of applications); prospective adopters and their age groups; the religious affiliation of the children and the applicants; and lastly the person or organization placing the children for adoption. For comparison, the report supplies summaries of some of the statistics for the years 1960 and 1961.

The committee stresses the importance of a regular review of the work of the adoption societies to ensure that the necessary requirements are being fulfilled, with perhaps a closer link established between some of the voluntary homes for children and adoption societies, so that children in the former who are suitable for adoption will not be overlooked. A lower age limit for adopters must be retained, but no rigid recommendation is made with regard to an upper age limit. The committee considers that there is no strict need to maintain a difference of twenty-one years between the elder applicant and the child. A mother should, if she wishes, express the religious persuasion in which her child is to be brought up. An adoption order should not be made unless the child has been continuously in the care and protection of the applicants for at least three consecutive months immediately before the date of the hearing. Consent of the mother to place her child for adoption should be witnessed by a commissioner for oaths. The committee does not think that anything can be gained by concealing information about the child's parentage.

A uniform rule needs to be established as to whether or not the child concerned should be required to attend the court hearing. A general right of appeal from the decision of a court to grant or refuse an adoption order should be created by statute. Welfare authorities should provide necessary information to the court, such as specific information on the child and his parent, and particulars of the prospective adopters.

There should be available to the court a full medical report on the health of the child and of the proposed adopters.

The fact that amendments to the Adoption Act, 1958, are absent from the Northern Ireland adoption legislation should be examined to ensure that the situation in Northern Ireland is similar to that of Great Britain. All documents necessary for the child should, upon adoption, be changed regarding name. The necessity of telling the child that he has been adopted should be impressed upon the adopters.

An example of the petition for adoption is shown in an appendix.

Role of Voluntary Homes in the Child Care Service

Ministry of Home Affairs. Rep. by the Northern Ireland Child Welfare Council, 1966.
36 pp.
Rep. sgd. June 1966. Prepared by a subcommittee.

D.G. Neill (Ch.) and five members— L.R. Andrews, H.I. Brown, Miss Kathleen B. Forrest, J.H. Parkes, S. Pennington.

'To consider and report upon the rule, in the child care service, of the organizations providing voluntary homes . . . and the principles adopted by such organizations in the caring for children and young persons.'

The council makes recommendations under six sections, admissions to children's homes, children in homes and their relation to the community, staffing, the role of voluntary homes, finance and co-operation between voluntary child-care organizations. On admission to children's homes, the council considers it is vital that the decision to admit a child should be taken by someone who, as well as knowing the circumstances, is fully qualified to assess the relative merits of various solutions, especially if the admission is to be a long-term or perhaps permanent arrangement. The relationship between homes and the

rest of the community should be kept on as normal a basis as possible. Every effort should be made to preserve a child's relationship with his parents where this can be the basis of significant development, and where the ultimate object will be the re-establishment of the family if there is any possibility of its functioning normally. Teaching and child care are two different occupations which are concerned with two entirely separate parts of children's lives, and the responsibility for these two functions should not be vested in one person. Opportunity to mix naturally with children from other backgrounds should always be given if possible, so that children can develop contacts and relationships with a natural environment. Voluntary homes should be encouraged to arrange boarding out for all the children who would benefit from this arrangement. For a child who ceases to be in the care of the voluntary organization because of age limit, there should be someone appointed, either from a voluntary source, home, or welfare authority, to look after the child's needs for advice and friendship in the community in which he lives.

The most important aspect of the environment of a children's home is the staff. Insufficient staff is a problem in the voluntary home, resulting in unreasonable demands on existing staff and lack of sufficient individual attention to children. Single-sex institutions present the deprived child with no compensating home influence; therefore there should be staff of both sexes employed. Qualified field staff and trained staff for homes are essential, and every effort should be made to obtain the services of such staff or to give existing staff opportunity for training with full salary. Day-release courses are at present organized by the Belfast Education Authority for staff in voluntary homes in and around Belfast. Similar courses should be arranged for the benefit of staff in homes in provincial areas. Staff cannot be expected to give of their best unless their own needs are considered, and they are given adequate standards of comfort and privacy.

While one essential role of the voluntary home is to give freedom of choice to parents or guardians in placing their children away from home, voluntary homes should work in closer co-operation with welfare authorities to ensure that the child's best interests are catered for and that the case-work service and trained staff which welfare authorities provide are used. The committee feels that the lack of confidence shown by some voluntary bodies in welfare authorities is, in general, unjustified, but some welfare authorities might make a more positive effort to ensure that there are sufficient Roman Catholic staff at all levels of seniority in their children's homes to make sure that the religious upbringing of Roman Catholic children in their care will be safeguarded. Voluntary homes should review the rigid segregation of age groups and sexes and should examine the part they can play in making available a wider variety of types of care, experimenting with new and more adventurous methods, and catering rather more for children with special handicaps and problems.

In voluntary homes as a whole, there is no consistent uniform method of calculating costs, and this needs rectification. Many homes could make more use of the financial loans and grants from the government and welfare authorities to improve standards of care.

The Northern Ireland Council of Social Service should be invited to form a Northern Ireland association of voluntary child-care organizations and if possible arrange for its application to the national body to benefit from the discussion of common problems that corresponding committees receive in Great Britain.

Four tables at the end of the report give statistics on appropriate aspects of child care.

4 JUVENILES

Reformatory and Industrial Schools

For details of this report see Class XVI p. 195.

The Protection and Welfare of the Young and the Treatment of Young Offenders

Rep. of Cttee., 1938.
Cmd. 187, xii, 240 pp.
Cttee. apptd. December 1935; rep. sgd. October 1937.

Sir Robert J. Lynn (Ch.) and ten members—Rev. D.D. Boyle, R. Crawford, Prof. Sir Robert J. Johnstone, Miss Anastasia McCready, A.P. Magill, P.J. O'Donoghue, Mrs. Dehra Parker, Capt. J.R. Perceval-Maxwell, F. Thompson, W.H. Welply, (P.J. O'Donoghue died before completion of the report.)

'To inquire into the existing provisions of the law . . . for the protection and welfare of the young and the treatment of young offenders, and to report what changes, if any, are desirable.'

The inquiry is restricted to persons under twenty-one, although the report does not accept this age limitation when considering the treatment of young prisoners and of borstal inmates. The committee discusses and makes detailed recommendations for many areas of social welfare, although the historical introduction that is usual in such comprehensive reports is omitted.

Recent changes in the appropriate laws of England and Wales are considered first of all. There is then an account of the extent and nature of present-day juvenile delinquency in Northern Ireland and the varied factors which may affect it—betting and gaming, cinemas, dance halls and street trading are considered in this context in addition to unemployment and inadequate housing. Recommendations are made to curb social evils contributing to juvenile crime. For example, it is proposed that the law should prohibit street trading by those under the age of seventeen, that dance halls should be more closely supervised, and that general recreational facilities should be improved. A central child-guidance clinic might be established by the Queen's University with the aid of a government grant. It would have a full-time social worker on its staff and the assistance of a psychologist.

The juvenile court, its working and the nature and extent of its jurisdiction are then considered, together with the question of the remand of the young before and during the court hearing. Suggestions are made for changes in the membership and procedure of this court; it should be constituted, in future, only of persons with suitable qualifications. With regard to the question of remand in general, it is thought that a remand home for boys should be created. Under the heading 'methods of treatment', the committee examines closely the probation service and the system of approved schools. Probation should involve a considerable degree of discipline and should be clearly distinguished from dismissal or binding-over. 'Welfare officer' is thought to be a more satisfactory title than 'probation officer'. The number of such officers, their conditions of service and the cost of the probation system are dealt with in specific recommendations. In the realm of probation, it is urged that many of the recommendations made recently by a special committee* appointed by the Westminster government be adopted in Northern Ireland. With regard to approved schools, the old distinction between reformatory and industrial schools could profitably be abolished.

The committee next comes to the matter of young persons in need of care and protection and prevention of exposure to cruelty or to physical or moral danger. Various amendments are suggested to existing legislation in this area, and it is urged that boards of guardians should pay a reasonable sum in respect of each child that needs to be boarded out. Advertisements to take young children for nursing should be prohibited unless they clearly identify the would-be nurse. The ordinary courts

should be empowered to refer children and young persons involved in cases of cruelty or neglect to the juvenile courts for treatment.

The treatment of offenders over the age of seventeen warrants a separate section in the report. Such persons should continue to be tried under the usual criminal jurisdiction of the ordinary courts. Bail may be granted where possible, but the fines imposed on such youths should continue to be the same as for adults. The minimum age limit for capital punishment should be raised to eighteen at least, but the minimum age for committal to borstal should remain at sixteen, with the length of sentence three years in all cases. The power to commit inmates of approved schools to borstals should be retained, and it may be necessary to consider the transfer of exceptionally difficult cases to institutions in England. There should be some training in mechanical trades and in clerical work at the borstal institution. It is also urged that if an incorrigible inmate needs to be transferred from borstal to prison, the prison sentence should be much less than the residual time scheduled to be spent at the borstal institution.

There are nine appendices to the report occupying some fifty pages. These include a list of those giving oral or written evidence and a list of institutions visited; details of juvenile welfare and the probation service in Scotland; memoranda on remand homes; an outline of the information sought by confidential reports used by lady visitors at H.M. Prison, Wormwood Scrubs; and specimen reports submitted by probation officers to juvenile courts. Many of the appendices are statistical in character, and there are some statistical tables in the report itself. Among Northern Ireland statistics provided are a return of persons under twenty-one charged with indictable and non-indictable offences during 1935; details of the use of certified schools as places of detention in the years 1931–1935; details of those on probation in 1935; admissions to

* *Report of the Departmental Committee on the Social Services in Courts of Summary Jurisdiction,* 1936. Cmd. 5122.

reformatories and industrial schools in 1922 and in 1927–1936; admissions to borstals during these years; the scale of Treasury grants to reformatory and industrial schools; prosecutions against children and young persons in each county during 1936; and details of children at nurse, boarded out or in the workhouse during the week ending 27 February 1937. One or two of the tables contrast Belfast statistics with those for the rest of the province.

The Instruction of Unemployed Juveniles

For details of this report see Class X p. 102.

Youth Welfare

Report of Cttee., 1944.
Cmd. 220, 54 pp.
Cttee. apptd. February 1942; rep. sgd.
December 1942.

H.M. Thompson (Ch.) and fifteen members—E.M. Brown, J.J. Campbell, S. Gihon, Mrs. M.J.I. Gilmore, J.H. Grummitt, Dr. J.S. Hawnt, F.J. Holland, Miss Mary Kerrigan, H. King, Miss Anastasia McCready, Miss Mary A. McNeill, Miss Janie G. Magill, Mrs. Dehra Parker, Dr. Elizabeth M. Robb, W.H. Smyth. (H. King resigned before completion of the report.)

'To consider the problems affecting youth welfare . . . and make recommendations as to their solution.'

War-time conditions of restricted recreational facilities and relaxed parental supervision have accentuated problems of youth welfare. The committee's recommendations are of two kinds: those which should be implemented immediately, and those which are desirable but cannot be implemented during the war.

The general needs of youth are discussed, and parental responsibility is stressed. Housing and environment are important to family life, and the interests of youth should be represented on the Planning Advisory Board of the Ministry of Home Affairs. Other recommendations are designed to encourage the provision of more physical training and recreational facilities, playgrounds with trained youth leaders, youth centres with facilities for organizations, clubs and non-technical educational classes, and more nursery schools. School-leaving age should be raised to sixteen; there should be part-time education up to eighteen and, in certain cases, opportunities for full-time education after entering employment. Civics should be taught to older pupils, and more attention should be given to home-making and the domestic arts, appreciation of beauty, responsibility and service to others. Class sizes in public elementary schools should be reduced, and school attendance laws revised and enforced. Other recommendations deal with advice to and welfare of young people in employment and the responsibility of employers. Institutions are needed for young mental defectives and other young people requiring special provision. Cinema films, fun fairs, dance halls and suggestive literature should be more strictly controlled, and street trading by young people largely prohibited. The law protecting adolescent girls should be strengthened, and more women police appointed.

There are two reservations: H.M. Thompson's is concerned with school-leaving age and with the expense involved in certain of the recommendations, and F.J. Holland also raises matters concerned with school-leaving age and continued education. A list of witnesses is provided in an appendix.

The Protection and Welfare of the Young and the Treatment of the Young Offender

[Rep.], 1948 (reprinted 1959).
Cmd. 264, 43 pp.

The existing position is surveyed, and proposals made for future legislation. The government considers it essential that all aspects of legislation affecting the care and protection of the young and the treatment of the young offender be dealt with by one government department, the Ministry of Home Affairs.

Welfare authorities in relation to their responsibilities for children will come under the control of the ministry; voluntary organizations operating homes for children will be required to comply with certain conditions; managers of institutions for delinquent children and young persons will be subject to measures of control; new conditions governing the adoption of children and the care of illegitimate children will be laid down; juvenile courts will be established on a new basis and the probation system extended; after-care schemes for all children and young persons coming directly within the scope of the new legislation will be instituted. An advisory committee, the Child Welfare Council, will deal with all matters relating to children coming within the scope of the government's proposals.

Appendix I gives statistics for children under the care of welfare authorities, 1939–1946. Appendix II reports on 179 cases of juvenile delinquency, giving home conditions and background of each child.

Juvenile Delinquency

Interim rep. of the Northern Ireland Child Welfare Council, 1954.
27 pp.
Sub-Appropriate Study Group apptd. March 1953.

J.M.B. Donaldson (Ch.) and six members—S.R. Bell, Mrs. D.C. Harrison, J.A. McGlade, Miss M.A. McNeill, W.H. Smyth, Mrs. J.I. Suttie.

The report, following the introduction of the rise of juvenile delinquency in Northern Ireland, outlines the causes of juvenile delinquency, the influence of the parents, the children's activities, and the effect of the community on the child. The causes of juvenile delinquency have been studied in many countries and from many angles, but there is no simple cause responsible for the problem as a whole. Many factors are involved, such as lack of religious training and parental control, incompetent parents, broken homes, mothers at work, poverty, overcrowding, irregular attendance at school, intelligence, lack of play space, cinemas, comics, sensational journalism, and employment. The report studies each of these factors in turn and makes recommendations.

On the influence the parent has on children and the subsequent delinquency which can arise from irresponsibility and incompetence, the council recommend and suggests that solutions to the various problems could be training of parents, rehousing, community centres to increase satisfaction and richness of life for the rural population to help check the drift from the country to the towns. They stress the need for security and development of responsibility in the parent.

Playgrounds, adventure playgrounds and youth welfare organizations are thought by the council to be invaluable for children's activities where open spaces for children's play are restricted. Special attention should be given to the influence of cinemas, comics and children's libraries on children. Excessive visits to the cinema are harmful; the spread in this country of the type of comic which glorifies and stimulates violence or sexual appetite and encourages racial prejudice should be stopped, and children should be encouraged to use the library and find suitable and good literature. Irregular attendance at school must be investigated more promptly, and suitable employment found for the young school leaver. Many first offences by a juvenile are committed more or less by chance; therefore a child should be caught and properly dealt with to discourage subsequent offences. Finally, churches, schools and the home should provide adequate training to the young for the duties and responsibilities of citizenship.

A statement of the number of children and young persons found guilty of indictable and certain non-indictable offences, by counties and county boroughs, and of percentage increases for the years 1938, 1946, 1952 and 1953 is shown in appendix A. Appendix B lists a summary of recommendations in the report and is followed in appendix C by a list of people who contributed to the evidence of the report.

Operation of Juvenile Courts

Rep. by the Northern Ireland Child Welfare Council, 1960.
24 pp.

Prepared by Study Group: F. Crilly (Ch.) and ten members—L.R. Andrews, C.E.B. Brett, Mrs. E.M. Glendinning, Mrs. S.T. Harrison, Br. S. Kelly, J.P. Murphy, Miss M.A. McNeill, D.G. Neill, Mrs. M.I. Simpson, R.J. Young.

'To consider the operation of the juvenile courts, with particular reference to the maintenance of the principle that these courts shall have regard to the welfare of the child or young person.'

The evidence of the report divides into five sections covering constitution of the juvenile court, procedure, amalgamation of juvenile courts, age of criminal responsibility and a miscellaneous section which covers such areas as questioning of juveniles by the police, appeals, police cautions, records, etc. The report shows many ways in which the juvenile court needs to change, to act properly for the welfare of the child. The council finds it undesirable that a resident magistrate in a juvenile court is removable only by death, voluntary retirement, or by joint address to the governor by both Houses of Parliament. Magistrates, on their appointment to the juvenile court, should be given adequate training to assist them in their work. Lay members of the juvenile courts are unfortunately dominated and overawed by their legal professional colleagues.

Legal phraseology should be kept to a minimum in favour of a simple language suitable to the child's age and understanding. The juvenile court should not be regarded as a minor version of the adult court.

The large number of very small juvenile courts, sometimes held in very un-suitable conditions, has led the council to a consideration of an amalgamation of juvenile courts. The council recommends that the age of criminal responsibility should be raised to twelve years and that children under that age who are brought to court should be dealt with as being in need of care or control. It is unfortunate that records are kept of all convictions against juveniles and that these can be held against them in later life.

In the miscellaneous section, many important aspects of the juvenile's home circumstances, his welfare in police questioning, in court, and after care are considered, and recommendations made by the council on each subject The council considers that, due to an under-staffed probation service, difficulties arise when female probationers have to be supervised by male probation officers.

Reservations on advice and legal aid were made by Mrs. G.I.A. Faris, Mrs. Sylva T. Harrison and Miss M.A. McNeill, and these follow the main report. Appendix A shows an example of a notice to a child or young person committed to a training school. The suggested distribution of juvenile courts is set out in appendix B.

Development of the Youth Service

Ministry of Education, 1961.
Cmd. 424, 27 pp.

The paper first gives an outline of the youth service as it is today, followed by the ministry's proposals designed to foster further development. Local authorities could take a more active part by making premises available for youth organizations and providing instructors. The Housing Trust and local authorities should be encouraged to provide playing fields and play space in new housing areas. Grants should be given to assist provision of premises for youth organizations, and grants for full-time youth leaders should be increased. The youth committee which advises the minister should represent wider interests. Specialist youth clubs should be encouraged as well as those with a balanced programme.

Appendix I summarizes present legislation, and appendix II details grants made to voluntary youth organizations during the year ending 31 March 1960.

5 GAMBLING, DRINKING

GAMBLING

Betting Laws

Rep. of Cttee., 1947.
Cmd. 251, 119 pp.
Cttee. apptd. June 1944; rep. sgd. April 1947.

Capt. Sir James Wilton (Ch.) and sixteen members—Mrs. Lilian D. Anderson, N. Booth, A. Dalzell, H.G. Fleet, Rev. T.J. Gray, Maj. S.G. Haughton, A.F. Heggarty, F.J. Holland, W.E.G. Johnston, Very Rev. W.M. Kennedy, D. McKee, Dr. D. McSparran, W.J. Price, G.E. Robinson, Rt. Rev. Monsignor A.H. Ryan, Rev. J.N. Spence. (Rt. Rev. Monsignor A.H. Ryan resigned and was replaced by Rev. D. Gogarty, October 1944. Very Rev. W.M. Kennedy died, July 1945, and was replaced by Rev. J.S. Cameron, August 1945. H.G. Fleet resigned, August 1945. Sir James Wilton died, February 1946, and Maj. S.G. Haughton became the new chairman, March 1946. Rev. J.S. Cameron resigned and was replaced by Rev. J.H. Carson, April 1946.)

'To inquire into the existing law and the practice thereunder relating to lotteries, betting, gambling and cognate matters, and to report what changes, if any, are desirable and practicable.'

The report opens with an historical survey and a statement of the law, followed by a description of the existing position. It appears that certain customs have evolved with regard to enforcement of the law. The law and position in Great Britain and in Éire are also examined.

The majority report recommends that small private lotteries should be exempt-

ed from the law, which should be clarified and consolidated in a new act prohibiting large public lotteries. Off-the-course cash betting should be legalized, the bookmakers licensed and their premises approved. Football betting should be allowed to continue as a postal system, and the Ready Money Football Betting Act, 1920, should be repealed. Gaming machines and gaming houses should be prohibited, and fun-fair machines and games should be subject to police decision. The gaming laws need to be consolidated in a new act. A betting tax is suggested.

Four of the nine members signing the majority report were in favour of a licensing system for on-the-course bookmakers, and two were not in favour of a betting tax.

The minority report, signed by six members, would prefer to prohibit all lotteries. Cash betting offices should be suppressed, and a new act consolidate and clarify the laws. Ready-money football betting should not be legalized. Greyhound track licences should be annually renewable and in the hands of the local authority. A betting tax should not be imposed.

The question of totalizator betting was considered separately. Ten members considered that totalizator betting should not be legalized, whereas five recommended that it should be, under licence and with restricted hours.

Appendices list the witnesses to the committee, summarize replies to the questionnaire circulated to chief constables in Great Britain, and give statistical details of prosecutions under the Betting Laws (N.I.), examples of football coupons, a greyhound track licence, and figures of yearly attendance at the four greyhound tracks.

Betting and Lotteries

[Rep.], 1956.
Cmd. 349, 8 pp.

The best approach to the problem of betting and gambling lies in control rather than suppression. It is suggested that licences should be introduced for bookmakers and their premises; suggested licence fees are £25 and £250 respectively. The county court would refuse licences to unsuitable persons or premises, and also whenever there were already an adequate number of licensed premises in the district. Only licensed bookmakers would be allowed to operate on racecourses and at point-to-point meetings. Rules for conduct of licensed premises are proposed and would be enforced by any authorized member of the Ministry of Finance or any member of the Royal Ulster Constabulary.

It is suggested that legislation should be introduced to restrict fixed-odds football betting to licensed bookmakers (who must be Northern Ireland residents) and to reduce the 30 percent rate of duty to 10 percent.

Legislation similar to the Betting and Lotteries Act of 1934 should be introduced, so that small lotteries would be legalized subject to certain conditions—limited prize value, no private gain, no advertisement, etc.

Permission has been sought to instal totalizators at the Maze and Downpatrick racecourses. If this be allowed, then the 30 percent excise duty to which bets would be liable under Section 56 of the Miscellaneous Transferred Excise Duties Act (N.I.), 1953, should be reduced or removed, and totalizators should also be permitted at dog racecourses.

DRINKING

Intoxicating Liquor Act (N.I.), 1923

Rep. of Claims Tribunal. Reps. published [*1925*], [*1926*].

Under this Act compensation is payable to those who have lost their licence to sell intoxicating liquor by reason of the Act's provision that such trade may not be carried on in conjunction with any other trade, or because of the Act's provision for the abolition of licences where there are too many in a district. Claims for compensation go before a claims tribunal.

To meet the compensation awards and the expenses, the tribunal has two sources of revenue.

(a) an annual licence (compensation) levy;

(b) borrowings from the Consolidated Fund.

Compensation may be for depreciation in the value of premises, loss of profits, value of fixtures and fittings.

Interim Reports, together with a prefatory note by the Ministry of Finance. *Sgd. May 1925 and August 1925. Cmd. 45, 30 pp.*

(a) Report of the Claims Tribunal as constituted to deal with claims in the Borough of Belfast.

His Honour Judge H.M. Thompson (Ch.), J. Roche, A. Miscampbell, J. Brown, W.D. Scott. (W.D. Scott was replaced by R.J. Walsh, J. Brown by R.N. Kennedy. J. Roche died when the sittings were practically completed.)

(b) Report of the Claims Tribunal in regard to claims received from persons in the area outside Belfast. The constitution of the tribunal varies from district to district. The nominees of the minister of finance and the minister of home affairs, R.J. Walsh, J. Roche and A. Miscampbell, are common to all. (J. Roche died and was replaced by P.J. O'Donoghue.) These common members approved the report.

These reports cover all the activities of the tribunal to 31 August 1925 and include statistics of the amounts claimed, the number of claims, and the amounts awarded. The finances of the scheme will require reconsideration by Parliament.

Final Report. *Sgd. September 1926. Cmd. 67, 8 pp.*

This report covers the period up to 30 June 1926, when the tribunal ceased to function and responsibility passed to the Ministry of Finance. The report contains statistics of the total amounts claimed and awarded and the total number of claims and awards, under the headings of Spirit Grocers' Licences, 'On' Licences and Wine Licences; and of the expenses of the tribunal including the interest on Treasury advances. A separate table sets out the apportionment of the amounts of awards and expenses as between each of the six county areas and the Borough of Belfast. The financing of the scheme was set on a firmer basis by the Intoxicating Liquor (Finance) Act, 1925.

Intoxicating Liquor Law

Review of the operation of the Intoxicating Liquor Acts in Northern Ireland, 1955 (reprinted 1958).
Cmd. 346, 8 pp.

While the current legislation (principally the Intoxicating Liquor Acts of 1923 and 1927) has done much to check drunkenness and subject licensed premises to police supervision, it is commonly agreed that revision of certain aspects is desirable. At present, trading hours may be longer in the larger urban areas than in smaller urban and rural areas; it is suggested that opening hours throughout the province should be from 11.00 A.M. to 2.30 P.M. and from 5.30 P.M. to 10.00 P.M., which would, without hardship, reduce the total trading hours. The general law prohibiting opening on Christmas Day and Sundays should remain unchanged.

A resident in a hotel should be permitted to purchase and consume liquor up to one hour after closing time, and on Sundays he should be permitted to purchase drinks for his guests to drink with a meal. Diners in hotels or restaurants should be permitted to consume drink purchased before closing time up to one hour after closing time, and on Christmas Day, during ordinary licensing hours. Permits for special dinners or entertainments should cover sale of liquor as well as consumption. A public bar cannot at present be provided in a new hotel, and the 'dispense bar' which is permitted has no advantage and facilitates adulteration of drink. Special wine licences for certain catering establishments might be granted and could be valid between 12.00 noon and 2.00 P.M.

Stricter control of registered clubs is desirable. They should be restricted to the same total daily hours as licensed premises, with midnight closing. Short hours, e.g., 12.30 P.M. to 2.00 P.M. and 5.30 P.M. to 10.00 P.M., should be stipulated for Sundays. Right of entry to clubs should be given to head constables and sergeants of police.

Applications for occasional licences, which enable an existing licensee to sell drink at a place other than his licensed premises, should be heard by resident magistrates at petty sessions, and at least twenty-four hours' notice should be given to the district inspector of police.

Provision should be made for granting new licences to airports; some elasticity of licensing hours might be needed in future. 'Public transport' refreshment rooms should be, in law, in the same position as railway refreshment rooms, or alternatively, it should be legal to transfer a licence from any railway station to the nearest omnibus station serving the substitutionary road services.

Where licensed premises are involved in slum clearance, there should be provision for transfer of the licence to a new building, or if there is substantial transfer of population, to the new area.

Granting of licences to new areas of population and old towns which have expanded should be left to the discretion of the licensing court.

6 PROBLEMS OF WAR

Air Raid Precautions

Rep. of Advisory Cttee., (1937).
Cmd. 178, 20 pp.
Cttee. apptd. August 1936; rep. sgd December 1936.

Lieut.-Col. A.R.G. Gordon (Ch.) and fifteen members—W.Y. Chamberlain R.B. Donald, A.S. Hamilton, J. Mackintosh, A.W. Mann, Capt. J. McIntyre, Commander R.P. Pim, Lt.-Col. J. Sargent, Maj. P.E. Shepherd, J. Smith,

J.D. Smith, D. Thompson, M.J. Watkins, C.F. Wheeler, F.H. Whysall. (Capt. C.H. Ensor, S. Gray, W.R. Knox, Maj. M. Speir, and C.S. Thomson were added to the committee in Autumn 1936.)

'To advise and assist the Government in the consideration and preparation of schemes for protecting the civil population and for the maintenance of essential services . . . in the event of attacks from the air in time of war.'

Suggests the appointment of an air raid precautions officer, with a branch in the Ministry of Home Affairs to deal with air raid safety measures by keeping in touch with the latest developments in such precautions within Great Britain, by keeping essential services and local government informed of such precautions and by supervising the preparation of local authorities' schemes. A draft scheme is included; this sets out recommendations for air raid warnings, lighting restrictions and medical services. It also comments on the need for air raid wardens, decontamination squads, and the enlistment of an auxiliary fire brigade.

Coal Rationing

For details of this report see Class VI p. 71.

Northern Ireland in the Second World War

Rep. by John Blake, 1956.
569 pp., maps, photos.

Professor Blake reviews the establishment and history of the state, its population and resources, and its constitutional position in time of war. He then describes preparations for war and gives an account of the development of the war effort. The latter, which comprises the bulk of this volume, discusses events overseas and the war at sea, in addition to the setting up of United States forces bases in Northern Ireland, and the roles of the agricultural, shipbuilding and linen industries. Defence and internal security measures are also described, as are the air raids and the A.R.P. services. The record of the military units associated with Northern Ireland is considered at some length.

Maps show civil defence boundaries in Northern Ireland and details of the war campaign in various European countries. Appendices provide details of numbers unemployed in Northern Ireland in the war years, by sex and for each of the principal industries; a list of ships built by Harland & Wolff; the number of agricultural workers; acreage, production and yield per acre of principal crops; details of agricultural machinery; and numbers of labour transferees.

XVI LEGAL ADMINISTRATION, POLICE, THE LAW

1 **Miscellaneous Matters involving the Law**
2 **Legal Aid**
3 **Law relating to the Family**
4 **Law of Property; Buildings and Land**
5 **Police**
6 **Civil Unrest**

1 MISCELLANEOUS MATTERS INVOLVING THE LAW

Reformatory and Industrial Schools

Rep. of Dept. Cttee., [1923].
Cmd. 14, 65 pp.
Cttee. apptd. January 1923; rep. sgd. May 1923.

T. Moles (Ch.) and ten members— D.A. Chart, Col. W.R. Dawson, W.A. Houston, A. Miscampbell, S. M'Guffin, Col. J. Morwood, Rev. J. Murphy, J.D. Williamson, Mrs. Barbara Carey and Miss Florence F. Clark.

'To inquire into the number and character of committals to Reformatory and Industrial Schools . . . ; into the care of boys and girls after leaving the Schools; into the financial position of the Schools, including the cost of maintenance; into the pro-

portion that should be borne by the Exchequer and Local Authorities, respectively, of the cost of the Schools; into the extent to which a proper contribution is obtained from parents; and into the question of the provision of a Borstal Institution for youthful offenders committed in Northern Ireland.'

Much detail is given on the early history of such schools, in addition to the consideration of their cost and administration. It is considered that juvenile courts should be held in separate buildings, that children sent on remand to reformatories should be kept apart from those already committed, that 'Training School' is a better title than 'Reformatory', and that magistrates should thoroughly investigate each case brought before them. Parental contributions should be enforced, and the government and the local authorities should, between them, pay a weekly capitation grant to certified auxiliary homes. If suitable buildings at reasonable cost can be obtained, there should be established a borstal institution, but only for boys. Other recommendations include a statement that much of the responsibility for these schools should be transferred from the Ministry of Home Affairs to the Ministry of Education.

A reservation to the findings of the report, signed by D.A. Chart, concerns after-care and the cost of the schools. Appendices include statistics on local authorities' contribution to industrial schools on 31 December 1922; the scale of existing Treasury grants to the schools; and the number of children committed in the years 1920, 1921 and 1922, with particulars of cases, details of deaths in the schools from 1911 to 1920, and other items of statistical information. There is also a list of regulations for the certified industrial schools and a copy of the questionnaire addressed to Northern Ireland magistrates, together with their replies.

[On this subject, see also Appendix: Select List of Annual Reports.]

The Jury System

Rep. of Dept. Cttee., [1924].
Cmd. 25, 71 pp.
Cttee. apptd. May 1923; rep. sgd. February 1924.

The Hon. Lord Justice J. Andrews (Ch.) and sixteen members—His Hon. Judge A.H. Bates, S. Bradley, M.J. Burke, D.A. Chart, S.D. Cheyne, E. Cowdy, S.G. Crymble, J.C. Culbert, J.Hill Dickson, J.F. Gordon, H.C. Kelly, Sir F. Henry Miller, J. MacBride, T.E. McConnell, S. Watt, J. Williamson.

'To inquire into . . . the qualifications required for Jurors, common and special; the procedure for the annual revision of the Jurors Lists and the remuneration to the persons concerned; the statutory exemptions for cause granted by the Court; the preparation of the panel by the Sheriff; the travelling and other expenses of Jurors; and any other matters relevant.'

The work of grand, common (petit), and special juries is considered and much information given on their historical development in Ireland. Among the chief recommendations, it is thought that grand juries should be abolished at quarter sessions and recorder's courts but retained at assizes in the counties. In the opinion of the committee, persons with incomes of over £250 who are not rated as householders or landed proprietors should serve as petit jurors, and those with larger incomes as special jurors. Many other recommendations are made relating to legislative and administrative changes involving one or another of the three types of jury, especially the petit and special juries.

It is proposed too that remuneration for officers preparing jurors lists and books should be a fixed sum, and that certain categories of people should be removed from the list of those exempted from jury service. The payment of petit jurors should be given statutory sanction, and the number of jurors in criminal cases should remain at twelve. Other proposals relate chiefly to right of challenge, trial by judge only, matters in court and court accommodation, the Oaths Acts, the coroner's jury, and the printing of jurors lists and of other necessary cards and documents. To reduce the inconvenience of jury service, it is suggested that the presiding judge be empowered to subdivide the jury panel into sections and thus excuse certain jurors at specified and appropriate times.

There are reservations made by certain members of the committee. That opposing the abolition of grand juries at quarter sessions and recorder's courts is signed by S. Watt; the suggestion that civil servants could act as jurors is opposed by D.A. Chart, S.G. Crymble, J. Hill Dickson, Sir Henry Miller and S. Watt; a proposal that a relaxation of the duty placed on women to serve as jurors should be made is criticized by D.A. Chart, S. Watt and J. Williamson on the grounds that this should not be considered separately from the issue of women's right to the franchise.

An appendix to the report gives a list of witnesses examined.

Explosives Act, 1875

First Rep. [for 1924] of the Government Inspectors of Explosives for Northern Ireland, [1925].
Cmd. 38, 7 pp.

H.M. inspectors of explosives were appointed government inspectors of explosives for Northern Ireland in April 1924. The Explosives Act (N.I.), 1924, was passed in May 1924 and amends the Explosives Act, 1875. No explosives are manufactured in Northern Ireland, and the report deals only with the keeping and conveyancing of explosives, and accidents in connection with this. The regulations as to licence to keep explosives are summarized. At the end of 1924 there were four magazines licensed, those at Carrickfergus and Silent Valley Water Works being in use, and those at Upper Ballysillan, County Antrim, and Gobnascale, County Londonderry not

in use. Five stores licensed by local authorities are in use, and one now disused. Four hundred and seven premises are registered with local authorities, all but seven being for the keeping of fireworks only. In general, storage of explosives was satisfactory; some gelatine dynamite in Carrickfergus magazine was found to be in a dangerous condition. There were two accidents in connection with the use of explosives for blasting. One of these was due to improper heating of frozen gelignite. A brief description is given of the proper procedure for thawing nitroglycerine explosives.

The inspectors conclude by pointing out that the normal conditions for the storage of explosives have not yet been completely restored in Northern Ireland. They propose to make one or more annual visits.

[This was the only annual report published. Later information on this subject appears in the annual reports of the Ministry of Home Affairs.]

The Law relating to Personation at Elections

For details of this report see Class I p. 1.

Ulster Transport Authority versus Tyrone County Council and Others

Transport Tribunal for Northern Ireland, 1965.
34 pp., map.

This matter began with a notice given on 4 March 1964 by the Ulster Transport Authority to terminate wholly the railway transport services between Portadown Junction and Londonderry, via Omagh, and between Dungannon and Coalisland and Warrenpoint to Goraghwood, and to withdraw general freight train services from the remaining sections of the authority's railway system. The authority took this step towards eliminating its railway losses in an endeavour to save the transport undertaking from final bankruptcy.

The tribunal considered the matter at a hearing which lasted seven days and at which oral and documentary evidence for and against the application was received, and on 30 October 1964 it made an order authorizing the authority to terminate those services in the application.

On 18 November 1964 Tyrone County Council, objecting to the authority's application, appealed to the Supreme Court to reverse the tribunal's order. Lord Justice McVeigh heard the appeal and determined that the tribunal had the right to defer the application until such times as the roads are able to take safely any increase in the weight of traffic. The tribunal, at a second hearing on behalf of the authority and other parties, made an order refusing to defer the coming into operation of the said order dated 30 October 1964.

Again Tyrone County Council appealed, seeking an order reversing the tribunal's order of 16 January and an order to postpone the closure of the railway for three to five years. They also argued that the tribunal had at the second hearing exhibited bias and shown itself incapable of objectively reviewing its own decision. Mr. Justice Lowry, on 22 February 1965, came to the conclusion that the tribunal, having satisfied itself with regard to the adequacy of the proposed road services (and the financial case being a strong one on any basis), was certain to reach a decision in favour of an immediate order. The appeal failed.

Enforcement of Judgements, Orders and Decrees of the Courts

Ministry of Home Affairs. Rep. of the Jt. Wkg. Pty., 1965.
123 pp.

A.E. Anderson (Ch.) and six members— G.J. Cairns, G. Courtney, J. Kernohan, J.A.L. McLean, J.J. Napier, R.S. Neilson.

'To consider the administration and adequacy of the existing methods of enforcing judgements, orders and decrees of the courts in Northern Ireland; to consider the setting up of a unified system for the enforcement of judgements, orders and decrees of all courts in Northern Ireland whether by seizure, instalment orders or otherwise; to consider what changes should be effected, by legislation or otherwise, to improve, modernise and unify the present system and its administration; and to make recommendations.'

A description of the present legislation relating to writs of execution and the work of under-sheriffs and bailiffs is provided. The present system of enforcement execution by seizure of the judgement debtor's goods and chattels is outlined, and a new system considered.

The report's fifty-seven principal recommendations include proposals that writs of execution be abolished and an office for the enforcement of judgements established, with a register kept there of all judgements lodged. The period within which a judgement may be enforced should be limited. When an application for enforcement has been made, an officer should have power to take possession of a debtor's goods, to list them, and to interview the debtor as to his means. Various methods of enforcement, which should be within the power of the office, are outlined. Costs of enforcement should be recoverable from the judgement debtor. Insurance policies should be among goods capable of seizure. An officer should be allowed to enter a debtor's premises by force, if necessary, to remove goods. If the office certifies that judgement cannot be enforced because there are no assets, then the debtor is to be deemed bankrupt. The office should have power to restrain a company from paying director's fees or dividends to a debtor in appropriate circumstances. A new procedure on an application for committal is also recommended.

Appendices provide a list of organizations and persons giving evidence or submitting memoranda; statistics relating to writs, bankruptcies, cost of execution of judgements, the remuneration of bailiffs, and the execution of county court and petty session decrees; specimen forms including those for use under an order of seizure; and appropriate definitions. They also show the proposed system of registration of judgements, present practice and suggested changes on entering judgement in the Queen's Bench Division, and the procedure relating to charging and restraining orders.

Law Reform

[*First*] *rep. of Director of Law Reform, 1967.*
Cmd. 507, 11 pp.
A.G. Donaldson apptd. June 1965.

This paper summarizes the administrative machinery for law reform, the first plans, and the work which has been done. In selecting branches of the law for consideration, regard has been had to the work done by bodies such as the Lord Chancellor's Law Reform Committee, the Home Secretary's Criminal Law Revision Committee, and the work of the Law Commission and the Scottish Law Commission.

It is proposed to initiate a long-term survey of land law; it is useful that reports are pending on law relating to registration of title and on long leases. Studies are also being made in criminal procedure—the system of taking depositions, certain aspects of the law of contract, and the law of tort.

Bills are in preparation to abolish the distinction between felonies and misdemeanours; to permit payment of compensation to persons who suffer substantial personal injury as the result of a criminal offence; to permit the award of costs to successful defendants in criminal cases; to provide a uniform system for the enforcement of judgements as recommended in the 1965 Report of the Joint Working Party; to consolidate the law relating to building societies, superannuation, registration of clubs and plant health; and to amend and consolidate the law on insurance companies. As a first step towards the production of a statutory public health code, it is proposed to start with a bill amending the law relating to infectious diseases and port sanitary authorities.

The following Northern Ireland Consolidation Acts were the responsibility of the Law Reform Office—Factories, 1965, National Insurance, 1966, Health Service Contributions, 1966, Family Allowances, 1966, National Insurance (Industrial Injuries), 1966, Hire Purchase, 1966, Statute Law Revision (Consequential Repeals) Act (N.I.), 1966.

Reprints, as amended, have been produced of the Drainage Act (N.I.), 1947, and the County Courts Act (N.I.), 1959.

Second rep. of Director of Law Reform, 1970.
Cmd. 543, 23 pp.

Completion of certain aspects in the law reform programme has led to acts having been passed on the following subjects—amendment of registration of deeds, theft, compensation for criminal injuries to persons, costs in criminal cases, increase of fines, abolition of obsolete offences, committal procedure, criminal evidence, innocent misrepresentation, abolition of torts of maintenance and champerty, age of majority, family provision, and enforcement of judgements.

The major part of the report covers the main branches of the law on which the Law Reform Office continues to work, i.e., land law, criminal law and procedure, the law of contract and the law of tort, while the heading of family law has been added. Consolidation of the statute law continues to be a part of the Law Reform Office's work—selecting subjects for consolidation, the drafting of the necessary bills, and assisting in making the statute law accessible. A list is given of those Northern Ireland Consolidation Acts dealing with subjects mentioned in the first report, namely, Superannuation, 1967, Registration of Clubs, 1967, Plant Health, 1967, Building Societies, 1967. In addition, the following Consolidation Acts are the result of the work of the Law Reform Office—Development Loans (Agriculture and Fisheries), 1968, Firearms,

1969, Fire Services, 1969, Public Health, 1967, Insurance Companies, 1968, and Industrial and Provident Societies, 1969.

The report also provides a short account of the other work of the office. It ends with a summary of work completed and in progress and lists the main subjects for future work as land law reform; proceedings against estates; interest on damages; personal injuries litigation; financial provision in matrimonial proceedings; restitution of conjugal rights; actions for damages for adultery, enticement, etc.; and breach of promise of marriage.

Law on Performances by Children

Ministry of Home Affairs, 1971.
31 pp.

This guide to the Children (Performances) Regulations of 1971 and related provisions under the Children and Young Persons Act of 1968 is intended to assist parents, local education authorities and employers. It sets out details of the legislation and deals with restrictions and conditions on the granting of licences, broadcast and recorded performances, and other performances—including those for which a licence is not required. Limitations on performances, hours of work and rest, circumstances in which school absence may be authorized, and penalties and offences under the Act are among the topics covered. Information is provided on applying for a licence, the form of licence, records to be kept by licence holders, and the number of hours per day allowable in law for children of various ages who take part in broadcast and recorded performances.

2 LEGAL AID

Legal Aid and Advice

Ministry of Home Affairs. Rep. of Cttee.,
1960.
Cmd. 417, 104 pp.
Cttee. apptd. August 1958; rep. sgd.
June 1960.

Gen. Sir James S. Steele (Ch.) and twelve members—J.L. Baxter, T.A. Blair, J.J. Campbell, L.I.G. Fox, J.M. Gray, Mrs. Audrey M. Irwin, R.L.E. Lowry, J.J. Napier, S. Napier, W.F. Patton, J.M. Shearer, Mrs. Eileen B. Wallace.

'To consider and report whether it is desirable to enact legislation providing for a scheme of legal aid and advice in Northern Ireland; if the committee consider that such legislation should be introduced, then to advise as to the form and nature of the provisions to be made.'

The report deals separately with criminal and civil proceedings.

Part I outlines the background to the problem.

Part II summarizes the results of the inquiries, and the recommendations made with regard to criminal proceedings. No fundamental alteration in the system by which legal aid is provided in criminal cases is necessary. The Ministry of Home Affairs should investigate the question of giving the superior courts power to award costs to an acquitted defendant proceeded against by indictment.

Parts III and VI deal with civil proceedings. It is desirable that legislation be enacted to provide for a scheme of legal aid and legal advice. Recommendations cover the circumstances when legal aid should properly be given, the facilities and conditions for legal advice, the conduct and administrative machinery of the schemes, and the appointment of an advisory committee to the minister for home affairs on questions concerning the operation and effect of the scheme.

T.A. Blair, J.M. Shearer and J.L. Baxter, in a signed reservation, state that an adequate case has not been made out for the introduction of a general scheme of legal aid in the Supreme Court. They do not agree with the suggested procedure for approving applications for legal aid in the county courts, which could cause delay and be liable to abuse.

R.L.E. Lowry makes a separate report, being in disagreement with the majority. Introduction of a legal aid scheme is not justified, has not been proven necessary, and would have a number of disadvantages which are enumerated. Mr. Lowry recommends certain steps to ease the burden of litigation.

A memorandum by W.F. Patton sets out those parts of the majority report with which he is in agreement. He would like to see a system of legal advice established but not of legal aid, and he makes recommendations about the payment of costs in appeals, and the need for review of the system of costs taxation. A memorandum from the Bar Council of Northern Ireland on the best form of legal aid for Northern Ireland, if a scheme were introduced, forms an appendix to Mr. Patton's memorandum.

Appendices list witnesses and give statistical details on numbers and types of cases and on remission of court fees. They also outline the acts governing legal aid schemes and give some account of the poor person's procedure rules. There is also a memorandum, presented by the Incorporated Law Society, on a legal aid scheme for Northern Ireland.

Legal Aid Scheme

Reps. of the Incorporated Law Society of Northern Ireland, and the comments and recommendations made by the Advisory Cttee. [appointed under the 1965 Legal Aid and Advice Act].

Advisory Committee: D.J. Little (Ch.) and seven members—A.E. Anderson, H.G. Bass, B.G. Finnegan, C.M. Mullan, F. Newark, G.B. Newe, G.R. Purcell.

1965–66 Report. *O.p. November 1968. H.C. 1892, 37 pp.*

Under the 1965 Act, a Legal Aid Committee was set up with T.Q. King (and later R.W. Porter) as chairman. This report indicates the regulations made under the Act and gives details of the legal aid scheme, together with its operation and finance and relevant statistics.

The advisory committee believe that the Law Society has devised an appropriate method for the administration of their duties, but the scheme has been in operation for such a short time that no useful conclusions can yet be drawn. No recommendations are, in fact, made.

1966–67 Report. *O.p. November 1968. H.C. 1893, 31 pp.*

The Law Society reports that the number of persons seeking legal aid is showing a uniform pattern which, it is believed, is indicative for the future. Four hundred and fifty cases were concluded in the period under report. Appendices include statistics of these and also of numbers of applications received, civil aid certificates issued, case results, and an account of receipts and payments of the Legal Aid Fund.

The advisory committee are satisfied that the scheme is working well, in that no unnecessary delay is incurred between the time of an individual's application for legal aid and the granting or refusal of a certificate to that person, but they are not fully convinced that delay has been adequately restricted during the passage of cases through the courts. The Law Society's attention is drawn to the fact that there is an undue time-lag between the service of a notice of appeal and the determination of the application for legal aid. Machinery should be devised to cope with this problem, and the Legal Aid Committee must ensure that an assisted person's legal advisers do not cause delay. The section of the Act relating to legal advice should become operative as soon as possible. The public do not, at present, appear to be making full use of the legal aid service, and the centralization of the administration in Belfast may have been off-putting to prospective applicants from outside the city.

The advisory committee agrees with recommendations of the Law Society concerning appeals to the Legal Aid Committee and the removal of limitations on certificates.

3 LAW RELATING TO THE FAMILY

Law of Intestate Succession

Rep. of Cttee., 1952.
Cmd. 308, 20 pp.
Cttee. apptd. November 1951; rep. sgd. June 1952.

His Hon. Judge W. Johnson (Ch.) and ten members—P.M. Bass, T. Brown, Mrs. Irene Calvert, H.J. Curlis, E.M. Doris, A.H. Elliott, M.W. Gibson, Lt.-Col. T.F. Glass, H.A. McVeigh, Prof. F.H. Newark.

'To inquire into the law in regard to intestate succession to real and personal property in Northern Ireland and to recommend what alterations are necessary or desirable.'

The report describes the background to the subject and the existing law of intestate succession, which has altered little for 250 years. Memoranda were received from a number of bodies and officials, who are listed, and representations were also made by private individuals.

The scheme of distribution of the estate recommended by the committee is illustrated in tabular form. The division of property into 'real' and 'personal' would be abolished; the same rules would apply to all property. The value of real estate would be its market value at the date of the intestate's death. The rights of a widow would be increased, and it is considered that there should be no distinction between the rights of widow and widower. The law of primogeniture, and all distinction between sexes and whole-blood and half-blood relationships would disappear. Representation by issue would apply to every line of succession. Within a class, e.g., brothers and sisters or uncles and aunts, all members would take equally. Shares of members would be contingent on their attaining twenty-one years of age or marrying thereunder. A county court would be enabled to authorize expenditure of the capital of an infant's share where it is desirable for maintenance, education or benefit of the infant. Next of kin would be limited to grand-uncles and grand-aunts and their issue. Special cases, where provision should be made for certain classes of dependants and other persons for whom the estate might reasonably have been expected to make provision, should be dealt with by the High Court or county court. Failing next of kin or special provisions, the estate would be declared bona vacantia and would go to the crown.

A reservation by A.H. Elliott states general agreement with the report with the exception of the recommendations affecting bona vacantia. He considers bona vacantia to be outside the terms of reference of the committee and outside the powers of the Parliament of Northern Ireland, and he finds the recommended court procedure too elaborate, duplicating certain investigations, and possibly disadvantageous to persons having moral claims on the estate.

Family Provision

Rep. of Cttee., 1955.
Cmd. 330, 19 pp.
Cttee. apptd. September 1953; rep. sgd. October 1954.

His Hon. Judge W. Johnson (Ch.) and eleven members—T. Brown, Mrs. Irene Calvert, H.J. Curlis, M.W. Gibson, R.R. Hastings, H.A. McVeigh, Prof. F.H. Newark, W.B. Rankin, Mrs. Eileen B. Wallace, Mrs. Hilda F. Wilson, J.O. Wylie.

'To consider . . . whether it is desirable to empower the courts to order that provision shall be made out of the estate of a testator for the maintenance of his dependants, and, if so, the extent to which such provision should be made; and to make . . . recommendations.'

A testator in Northern Ireland has complete freedom at present, with the exception of a restriction relating to gifts of land for charitable uses, which are void unless the will is executed at least three months before the testator's death. An historical survey traces the evolution of this freedom, and the situation in Scotland, England and the British Commonwealth is examined. In England, the Inheritance (Family Provisions) Act, 1938, amended by the Intestates' Estates Act, 1952, allows for provision by the courts for maintenance of dependants, and the main provisions of the Act are summarized.

Letters were received by the committee from individuals; certain bodies (listed) submitted their views; and oral evidence was also heard. The evidence is summarized, and this is followed by brief statements of the main arguments for and against introduction of family-provision legislation. The committee find the arguments fairly evenly balanced, but they favour the introduction of legislation. They oppose the principle of giving dependants interests of a fixed amount and consider that courts should be enabled to vary the will in favour of dependants for whose maintenance the testator has failed to make reasonable provision. This would have the advantage that the case law and interpretation of the English Act would be applicable in Northern Ireland. Some amendments to the English Act are suggested—designed to alleviate potential hardship or to clarify parts of the Act. The existing restriction on charitable gifts of land should be abolished.

In a minority report, H.J. Curlis, F.H. Newark, and J.O. Wylie disagree with the conclusion that legislation should be introduced arguing that, in the light of evidence received, it would be superfluous.

4 LAW OF PROPERTY; BUILDINGS AND LAND

Law of Landlord and Tenant in the Case of Non-Agricultural Holdings

Rep. of the Dep. Cttee., 1929.
Cmd. 96.
Cttee. apptd. January 1928; rep. sgd. January 1929.

R.D. Megaw (Ch.) and six members— T.J. Campbell, J.C. Davison, T.J. Elliott, T.S. McAllister, J.H. Monroe, J.H. Robb.

Majority Report. *39 pp.*

The committee realizes that the principal matter for attention is the position existing on the expiration of leases and the termination of tenancies. Grievances have arisen, especially in Portrush and Bushmills, over legislation whereby a leaseholder must, on the expiration of the lease, pass over to the landlord any building erected by the leaseholder during his tenancy. However, the report also reviews previous inquiries and discusses the variety of relevant existing legislation, especially the 1906 Town Tenants Act. It is proposed that this Act is more suitable as a basis for legislation than the Landlord and Tenant Act (England and Wales) of 1927. Any new legislation should be self-contained, as at present there are too many references to various Acts. Other recommendations concern compensation for tenants who have carried out improvements, the suggestion that a new lease for a term not exceeding fourteen years should be granted in cases where a monetary sum would not compensate a tenant for loss of goodwill, extension of the powers of those who are tenants for life, compensation for unreasonable disturbance, and the continuation of the county court as the tribunal for the purposes of the Act.

A summary is given of the points of difference between the two reports, as seen by the majority.

Minority Report. (signed by T.J. Campbell and T.S. McAllister).
24 pp.

This agrees with most of the proposals in the majority report but considers some additional matters, such as the Ulster Custom (fair rent, fixity of tenure, and free sale) for agricultural tenants and its possible extension to the case of urban tenants, the question of the law relating to repair of property, and the acquisition of ownership by occupying tenants. Specific points of difference relate to some matters concerning compensation for improvements, disturbance compensation, the constitution of the tribunal having jurisdiction over the recovery of possession of small premises, and the compulsory renewal of leaseholds. In the latter case, for example, the minority favour a succession of renewals, if need be, while the majority do not.

Business Tenancies

Special and final reports of Jt. Sel. Cttee., together with proc., min. of ev. and app. H.C. 1359, 126 pp.
Cttee. apptd. November and December 1958; rep. o.p. October 1959.

H.V. Kirk (Ch.) and nine members— R. Armstrong, J. Fisher, I.G. Hawthorne, J.S. Johnston, A. McConnell, J.A. McGlade, R.H. O'Connor, W. Oliver, F.V. Simpson.

'To compare the present position of occupying tenants of premises . . . used for business, trade, or professional purposes, with that of similar tenants in other parts of the British Isles and to advise—
(1) Whether the first-mentioned tenants should be given a right to renewal of their tenancies and, if so, the terms (particularly as to rent and duration) on which any such renewal should be granted;
(2) whether further provision should be made for giving to those tenants a right of compensation for improvements and goodwill on the termination of their tenancies; and
(3) what machinery should be provided to . . . effect any recommendations.'

The special report, presented to Parliament in January 1959, merely indicates that the committee was unable to complete its work and suggests that a similar committee be appointed during the next parliamentary session to continue the inquiry. This was agreed upon, and the final report, produced by the same body of people in the new parliamentary session, considers particularly

the questions of compensation for loss of business and the condition on which a lease should be renewable. In the one case, the question of what should be taken into consideration when awarding compensation merited especial attention, while the rights of the sitting tenant warranted primary regard in the other.

It is concluded that legislation dealing with business tenancies should be made permanent, subject to certain conditions. These include recommendations to the effect that a court should be given power to grant a longer lease than the five years allowed at present; that the possibility of setting up an impartial tribunal to deal with future cases be considered; that the term of four years limitation of possession prior to the 1952 Act be removed; and that in the case of mixed tenancies (where the tenant is not actually resident), either landlord or tenant should be able to apply to the courts to place a fair rent on the business portion of the tenancy. It should be compulsory for landlords to serve a second notice on tenants who do not wish to surrender their right to the property, and in any case where the tenant is dispossessed, he should be given compensation paid on a rateable value principle. If a landlord wishes to reconstruct a property for reletting, the existing tenant should have the option of a new lease at a rental equivalent to the market value of the redeveloped property. Property owned by the Ulster Transport Authority or Belfast Harbour Commissioners is to be excluded from any permanent legislation in the sphere of industrial and commercial tenancies.

The witnesses contributing to the minutes of evidence are listed, and they include representatives from Belfast Chamber of Trade, Belfast Harbour Commissioners, the Chartered Auctioneers and Estate Agents Institute, the National Union of Small Shopkeepers, the Royal Institution of Chartered Surveyors, and the Ulster Transport Authority. There is provided, in tabular form in an appendix, a comparative statement on the main legal provisions on industrial tenancies in various parts of Britain and Éire. A further appendix gives some regional statistics on the numbers of premises covered by the existing temporary Act and on the number of cases in which recourse has been made to the courts under the Act's provisions.

Compensation on Compulsory Acquisition ... of Premises

For details of this report see Class XIII A p. 129.

Long Leases

Ministry of Home Affairs. Rep. of Cttee., 1967.
Cmd. 509, 19 pp. Bibliog.
Cttee. apptd. June 1964; rep. sgd. March 1967.

Judge R.H. Conaghan (Ch.) and eleven members—J.L. Baxter, H.A. Brown, T. Brown, W.M. Cameron, E.M. Doris, The Hon. J.C. MacDermott, H.A. Frazer, W.S. Hill, J. McMullan, R.W. Porter, D.M. Stevenson.

'(a) To consider and report on the law ... relating to leases of land on which permanent buildings, whether business or residential, have been erected by the lessee or his predecessors in title and also on the law relating to other long leases.
'(b) To make recommendations to the Minister of Home Affairs on all aspects of such leases and in particular on what steps should be taken for the avoidance or alleviation of any hardship which may arise on the expiration of such leases.'

Long leases can be divided into 'short' long leases of 50–99 years, and 'full' long leases of more than 99 years. Many nineteenth-century building leases were for 99 years. At the expiration of the lease any building on the land passes to the landlord. There is no statutory provision for leasehold enfranchisement —i.e., the compulsory purchase by the leaseholder of the fee simple of his holding, together with any intermediate leasehold interests. There is no great evidence of a present general social

problem in the acute form of eviction of lessees on the expiry of long leases. Such a grave social problem will emerge as more long leases fall in, and as lessors may increasingly be tempted to take advantage of lessees lacking the protection and security of tenure available in other jurisdictions.

It is recommended that a 'short' long lease should be perpetually renewable for the same period as the original term and at a modern ground rent. There should be provision in the renewal for review of the ground rent at intervals. Where a landlord successfully opposes a tenant's application for renewal, he shall pay compensation for the structure and the loss of right to renew. Similar conditions should apply to 'full' long leases. The committee does not feel justified in recommending right of enfranchisement in the absence of either demand or hardship. Tenants should be able to apply to the county courts when it is desired to modify restrictive covenants. The position of subtenants should not be overlooked. Consideration of leases for blocks of flats should be deferred; harbour authorities should be excluded from any proposed legislation; and in such cases as hospital accommodation and land used for sport, rights to renew leases should be given over and above those conferred by the Business Tenancies Act (N.I.), 1964. Disputed cases should be judged in the county courts.

A minority report by the Honourable J.C. MacDermott and R.W. Porter advocates a right of enfranchisement for all lessees holding leases for terms of over fifty years, and it would prefer jurisdiction in the case of disputes to be given to the Lands Tribunal.

A minority report by H.A. Frazer cites many points of disagreement with the majority report. He would like the provisions of the Business Tenancies Act (N.I.), 1964, to be extended to dwelling houses, and disputes to be referred to the Lands Tribunal.

A reservation by T. Brown dissents from the recommendations that reviews of ground rent should be possible during the term of a lease, and that land used for sport should have special treatment. The Lands Tribunal is the proper forum for disputes.

Bodies from whom the committee received evidence are listed in an appendix, but not names of individuals, in order to avoid a breach of confidence. There is a bibliography of background material, relating to all parts of the British Isles.

Registration of Title to Land

Rep. of Cttee., 1967.
Cmd. 512, 94 pp.
Cttee. apptd. August 1958; rep. sgd. June 1967.

The Hon. Mr. Justice R. Lowry (Ch.) and fifteen members—D.W. Bleakley, Sir Percival Brown, Prof. V. Delany, I. Hawthorne, W.E. Henry, J.P. Higgins, C.K. Holden, T.Q. King, S. Lomas, Dr. P.F. McGill, G. McSpadden, P. Maxwell, L. Moody, H.J. Perkes, W.B. Rankin. (L. Moody resigned in December 1958 and was replaced by D.B. Murray. I. Hawthorne resigned in August 1960 and was replaced by W.S. Hinds, who later resigned and in February 1963 was replaced by J.W. Kennedy. Sir Percival Brown died in October 1962, and H.A. Frazer was appointed. Prof. V. Delany died in January 1964.)

'To examine the law and practice relating to the Registration of Title to land . . . and to consider—
(a) what changes are desirable;
(b) in particular whether any and, if so, what action should be taken to encourage the registration of the ownership of land . . . ; and
(c) what other steps might be taken to facilitate the transfer of ownership of land.'

In Northern Ireland, as in England and Wales and the Republic of Ireland, there are two separate and distinct conveyancing systems for transferring land, houses and other buildings from one person to another—

(a) the private deeds system, which operates under little or no governmental control and in Northern Ireland deals mainly with property in towns; and

(b) the public registry system, which operates under the direct control of a government office called 'The Land Registry' and in Northern Ireland deals mainly with property in country areas.

The public registry system is more efficient, quicker, and costs buyer or seller less in legal fees. Compulsory registration should be extended gradually to the whole of Northern Ireland, provided that the existing system is modified in the twenty-four ways suggested in the report, that such features of the English system as are necessary for efficiency and speed are introduced, that additional Land Registry staff are recruited and trained, and the ordnance survey maps for an area are up to date and large scale before extension of the compulsory system to that area.

A detailed survey of the substantive land law should be carried out under the director of law reform. Certain principles and law amendments are recommended. Local authorities should do all they can to give quick answers to pre-contract inquiries. The three registries — Land, Statutory Charges and Deeds—should preferably be located in the same suite of offices.

Organizations and individuals who gave evidence are listed in an appendix. Other appendices give statistics for dealings in the Land Registry and the Registry of Deeds, 1955–1965; Land Registry expenses and receipts for Northern Ireland and for England and Wales; tables of costs for unregistered and for registered conveyancing; and comparisons of solicitor's costs and registration fees on sales of unregistered and registered land.

Building Regulations

Rep. of the Cttee., 1970.
Cmd. 540, 26 pp.
Cttee. apptd. December 1967; rep. sgd. October 1969.

R.W.B. McConnell (Ch.) and ten members—J. Cairncross, R.N. Collins, I.G. Doran, M.N. Hayes, G.R. Hyde, W.P. McIlmoyle, H.R. McIlveen, R. Maginnis, R. Montgomery, P. Shea.

'To examine the existing law . . . in the light of recent changes in Scotland, England and Wales and to advise upon the changes which might be necessary to secure a control of building standards which would operate as uniformly as possible and be flexible enough to take account of the development of new techniques and materials.'

It is proposed that the present control of building under local acts and local authority by-laws should be replaced by a new act similar to the Building (Scotland) Act, 1959. Regulations must be uniform throughout Northern Ireland and should be enforced by local authorities—preferably by a few large authorities. Exemptions should be laid down in the regulations rather than in the Act, and the regulations must be kept under review by an advisory commitee. Any time limit on the life of a building proposed by the regulations must be enforced.

Some other recommendations on specific points are made, and attention is drawn, in an appendix, to matters which require further study in relation to the industry in Northern Ireland. The appendices also indicate matters which come under the scope of regulations in England, Wales and Scotland, and recent proposals for alterations in the England and Wales building regulations.

Survey of the Land Law of Northern Ireland

Rep. to the Director of Law Reform by a Wkg. Pty. of the Faculty of Law, the Queen's University, Belfast, 1971.
425 pp.
Wkg. Pty. apptd. November 1967; rep. completed March 1970.

L.A. Sheridan (Ch.) and three members —B.W. Harvey, E. Tenenbaum, J.C.W. Wylie.

'To survey the substantive land law . . . and to make proposals for its reform in pursuance of recommendations in the Report of the Committee on the Registration of Title to Land (Cmd. 512, 1967) paragraph 140.'

It is pointed out that the 1967 report (mentioned in the terms of reference) criticized the present law relating to strict settlements; regarded English property legislation as having sound principles which would be valid for Northern Ireland; and suggested reforms relating to settled land, co-ownership, and the length of title a purchaser may require of the vendor on an open contract.

The present survey excludes the statutory regulation of agricultural and business tenancies. Rent restriction, planning law, and taxation are also viewed as being outside its terms of reference. It deals at very great length, however, with many aspects of the law of property, including legal estates and tenure; settlements; co-ownership; contracts and conveyances; fees and commissions; periodic rents; mortgages; powers of attorney; landlord and tenant; perpetuities; wills; husband and wife; easements, profits, and covenants; equitable interests; and voidable dispositions. Principles kept in mind by the working party (but alas sometimes in conflict with each other) include the need to simplify titles and conveyancing, the removal of doubt as to existing law and of injustices, easy accessibility of the law, the value of assimilating land law with that governing other types of property, and the utility of standardization of the law with that in England. One hundred and fifty-seven specific recommendations are made.

Appendices indicate those organizations which were consulted or which provided evidence to the working party, and give suggested drafts of bills for property and periodic rents in Northern Ireland. Tables of relevant statutes and cases are provided, and the report is indexed.

5 POLICE

Police Reorganization

Reps. of Dept. Cttee. of Inquiry. Cttee. apptd. January 1922; reps. published 1922, [1925].

L. Campbell (Ch.) and fourteen members—Sir Robert N. Anderson, Sir Wiliam F. Coates, J. Cooper, W. Coote, J. Cunningham, Sir Joseph Davison, J. Hill Dickson, G.C. Duggan, W. Grant, J. Roche, J.V. Stevenson, P.J. Tiernan, S. Watt, Lt.-Col. C.G. Wickham.

'To report on . . . (a) the alterations in the existing organization, which would be necessary in establishing a Police Force . . . ; (b) recruitment and conditions of service . . . ; (c) the extent to which the new Force should be composed of existing members of the Royal Irish Constabulary and of existing members of the Special Constabulary; (d) the strength of the new force and what provision should be made by way of a temporary Force, and (e) the cost involved.'

Interim Report. *Sgd. March 1922.*
Cmd. 1, 15 pp.

Proposals include the idea that there should be a single force for the whole of the province, rather than administration on a local basis as in Great Britain; that the total force should not exceed 3,000; and that certain benefits should be offered to members of the Royal Irish Constabulary and the Special Constabulary who join the new force. The pay of such men should be the same as the remuneration previously received, but new recruits should receive a lower rate of pay than that now recommended. There need be no increase in the number of policewomen. The new force should recruit one-third of its men from suitable Catholics in the R.I.C., and if any portion of this fraction is not available from that source, it should be made up by new Catholic recruits. The remainder of the force is to be Protestant, drawn mainly from the R.I.C. and Special Constabulary.

Details of the situation with regard to pay, allowances and pensions for the R.I.C. men in 1920 are given in appendices. There are nine signed reservations involving, in all, no less than ten members of the committee. Most of these reservations concern pay, pensions and transfer benefits for R.I.C. men. However, J. Cooper, J. Hill Dickson and G.C. Duggan believe that there should be an increase in the present extremely small number of policewomen, and G.C. Duggan and J. Roche query the wisdom of dividing the force on sectarian lines, while P.J. Tiernan believes that it is inequitable to reserve only one-third of the places for Catholics.

Final Report. *Sgd. June 1924.*
Cmd. 34, 6 pp.

Of the three matters on which the committee intended to report, it has been decided that both the question of modification of the R.I.C. Code to adjust it to the needs of the new Royal Ulster Constabulary and the question of increasing the number of policewomen should be dealt with departmentally. The third issue concerned possible reduction of pay. In Great Britain it has recently been decided by an appropriate committee that there should be no immediate change. The Northern Ireland Government should consider the suitability of applying the same decision, remembering that their force is supported by central government rather than by the rates and that the cost of the force and the responsibilities of its members are greater in Northern Ireland than in Britain.

A reservation, signed by W. Coote, urges a modified scale of pay for entrants to the force after the enlistment of three thousand men.

Report of Findings of a Police Inquiry

Rep. of W.F. Patton, 1966.
Cmd. 498, 91 pp.
W.F. Patton apptd. March 1965.

'To examine upon oath into the truth of certain allegations contained in speeches made by Mr. H. Diamond, M.P., in the House of Commons [on the 25th day of February 1965, and on the 2nd day of March 1965] against the conduct of certain members of the Royal Ulster Constabulary.'

Mr. McGonigal, Q.C., and Mr. Nicholson were instructed by Mr. B.M. McCloskey representing the tribunal, and in due course sixty-eight complaints involving eighteen members of the R.U.C. were formulated. These were divided into ten blocks, or series, of cases which arose out of the same set of facts. An eleventh series covered two matters mentioned by Mr. Diamond and not dealt with in the ten series. The inquiry was held in public, the first sitting being on 1 September 1965.

Five persons were cited by Mr. Diamond as having cause for complaint against the police: Alexander Donnelly, Josephine Andrews and her mother, Charles Robin McBrien and his wife. The McBrien and Andrews cases are linked to some degree by the fact that Miss Andrews was a witness at trials of Mr. McBrien.

Alexander Donnelly died of a gunshot wound in Brown Square Police Station on 4 December 1958. Mr. Diamond cast doubt upon the verdict of suicide and quoted an allegation against a detective head constable. In fact, the verdict of the coroner's court had been that 'Deceased died from a bullet wound self inflicted and there being no evidence to show the state of his mind or whether it was accidental'. Mr. Patton concludes that the wound was accidental and that there was no breach of the current regulations as to care and custody of firearms, although there had been negligence in leaving Mr. Donnelly alone. The detective head constable named was not in the police station at the time of the incident, and the allegations are 'a gross slander'.

C.R. McBrien was said to have been wrongfully and oppressively detained and interrogated, and assaulted by the police at Ballymoney in September 1959, the incident already having been the subject of an inquiry shortly afterwards. The interrogation did take place and was prolonged on account of Mr. McBrien's reluctance to tell the truth about his movements on the night when a crime had been committed. He consented to be taken to Ballymoney and could have requested to be taken home at any time. There is no truth in the allegations of physical assault by the police. The detective sergeant who was said to have taken the most active part in attacking him was at that time physically incapable of such an attack.

Mr. McBrien admitted stories to be false in which he said he had been offered bribes to withdraw allegations against the police and that he had been attacked and stabbed by a detective constable. Nothing in the police files supports the allegation that the police conspired to persecute him. On every occasion on which he was arrested, there were reasonable grounds for arresting him. There is no foundation for allegations that he was 'framed'.

Miss Andrews, it was alleged, was arrested, kept all day without a break, refused permission to see her mother or a solicitor, and browbeaten into making a statement. There was no credible evidence that the police exceeded their powers or exercised their powers in an unreasonable manner. Miss Andrews came to the Ladas Drive Police Station for the express purpose of giving what information she could in regard to a robbery, but, having arrived at the station, she changed her mind and refused to speak. Allegations that on other occasions Miss Andrews was beaten by the police and that a detective head constable had threatened her and attempted to intimidate her into giving certain evidence are found to be quite untrue. On yet another occasion, a persistent interrogation of Miss Andrews following stab wounds is found to be justified, and also the detention of her damaged clothing, and the allegation of a bribe offered subsequent to this incident is untrue.

Mrs. Andrews and Mrs. McBrien retracted statements that members of the police had interviewed them and attempted to tamper with their evidence.

An appendix to the report names the police officers concerned and the subject of complaint. Extracts are given from transcripts of C.R. McBrien's three trials. A third appendix lists 'points for discussion' concerning treatment of persons being interrogated by the police.

Police in Northern Ireland

Rep. of Advisory Cttee., 1969.
Cmd. 535, 50 pp.
Cttee. apptd. August 1969; rep. sgd. October 1969.

Baron J. Hunt (Ch.) and two members — Sir James Robertson and Robert Mark.

'To examine the recruitment, organization, structure and composition of the Royal Ulster Constabulary and the Ulster Special Constabulary and their respective functions and to recommend as necessary what changes are required to provide for efficient enforcement of law and order. . . .'

Production of the report was a matter of urgency, and it was not possible for the committee to make as detailed an examination as it would have wished. Inquiries were informal and confidential. To have invited submissions from all sources would have delayed completion without adding to the technical information on which many of the recommendations are based. The committee is convinced that nothing less than the full implementation of their proposals, within the shortest time possible, can suffice to lay a sound foundation for the good order and security of the province.

The history of both forces is briefly surveyed, together with their organization. The principal recommendations aim to increase the efficiency of the Royal Ulster Constabulary, to improve its relations with the public, and to bring it into full partnership with the police forces in Great Britain. In future it should not undertake duties of a military nature, and firearms should not normally be carried. Responsibility for the force should lie in a police authority representative of different groups in the community, and a police advisory board should be established for consultation between minister, police authority and all ranks of the force. The Central Representative Body should be reorganized. The name of the force should remain, but the uniform should be changed to blue, and exchanges of personnel with other forces should be encouraged. The effective strength of the force should be increased and a volunteer reserve police force set up. The practice of reserving a specific proportion of vacancies in the force for Roman Catholics should be discontinued, but vigorous efforts made to increase the number of Roman Catholic entrants. The procedure for dealing with complaints against the police should be changed, and the chief officer of police made vicariously liable for wrongful acts committed by members of the force. The Scottish system of independent public prosecutors should be adopted, so that the police should no longer be responsible for deciding who shall be prosecuted nor acting as prosecutor. Other recommendations concern improved organization for the force and possible measures for enhancing public relations.

All threats to the security of Northern Ireland from armed incursions and attacks are a proper military responsibility and should rest with the government at Westminster. There is great merit in the continuing presence of a local force, with local knowledge, capable of being at instant readiness, and a locally recruited part-time force, under the control of the G.O.C., Northern Ireland, should be raised as soon as possible for such duties as may be laid upon it. This force, together with the police volunteer reserve, should replace the Ulster Special Constabulary.

Appendices give details of numbers and deployment of the R.U.C., numbers of offences and proceedings taken, 1965–1968, the strength of the U.S.C. and their rates of remuneration.

Royal Ulster Constabulary Reserve

Ministry of Home Affairs, 1969. Cmd. 536, 4 pp.

The government's decisions on the Royal Ulster Constabulary Reserve, one of two forces to replace the Ulster Special Constabulary, as recommended by the Advisory Committee on Police in Northern Ireland, are that members of the new force will assist and be supervised and trained by regular members of the Royal Ulster Constabulary and will wear uniforms distinguished from the latter by a metal shoulder badge. They will not be issued with firearms. Members will be citizens of the United Kingdom, aged between twenty-one and fifty-seven, subject to security vetting and medical and educational tests, and will take an Oath of Allegiance. A bounty of fifteen pounds per year will be paid to special constables who attend twenty-four two-hour training parades, or equivalent, per year, and patrols in excess of this obligation will be paid at nine shillings per hour. Higher ranks will receive appropriate rates. Initial establishment will be 1,500; recruiting will commence on 1 January 1970; and the Reserve will become operational on 1 April 1970.

Public Prosecutions

Rep. of the Wkg. Pty., 1971. Cmd. 554, 70 pp., charts. Wkg. Pty. apptd. February 1970; rep. sgd, December 1970.

J.C. MacDermott (Ch.) and eight members—B.J. Campbell, J. Faulkner, J.A. Gilliland, D.A. Haggan, A.W. Jack, S.T. Killen, P. Maxwell and W.G. Robinson. (D.A. Haggan left the working party in September, upon taking up an appointment outside the province).

'To carry out further study upon the recommendations contained in paragraph 142 of the Report of the Advisory Committee on Police (Cmd. 535) that the Scottish system of independent public prosecutions should be adopted in respect of the initiation and presentation of summary prosecutions in Northern Ireland, and to devise and make recommendations thereon.'

The paragraph mentioned draws attention to the fact that prosecutions in the lower courts are at present undertaken by police officers. The impartiality of the police could be questioned if they both decide who shall be prosecuted and act as prosecutor. A mistaken impression of the relationship between the courts and the police could also arise.

The working party examined the existing system and found that approximately 98 per cent of the cases involved in magistrates' courts concerned the police in the role of prosecutor. It is urged that this practice should cease, with the crown case being presented by members of the legal profession, and that 'police work' and 'court work' should be separated, except in the case of minor offences. It is stressed that the Royal Ulster Constabulary have, in the working party's unanimous view, carried out this dual role with competence and integrity, but they should not be expected to continue to act as prosecutors. A new system is needed, but that adopted in Scotland would be impractical in the province. It is thus recommended that an independent Department of Public Prosecutions be set up as soon as possible and a director appointed. The department would be solely responsible for prosecuting and for the handling of prosecutions in all the courts. Appointment of the director and of prosecutors should be made by an independent body such as the Civil Service Commission. There is some discussion in the report on the availability of lawyers of sufficient calibre to form a group of prosecutors, of the relationship between prosecutors and existing crown solicitors, and of the problem of distinguishing between major and minor cases.

Much of the report is taken up by the appendices, which set out in detail the existing machinery for prosecutions in Northern Ireland and the Scottish position with regard to the role of the public prosecutor and the institution of criminal proceedings. Statistics are provided of summary offences in Northern Ireland in 1968—cases where persons were prosecuted in a police officer's name. Further appendices give the dates of magistrates' courts sittings in the province and provide extracts on the police as prosecutor, from British government papers and a relevant journal article.

A reservation to this report, by W.G. Robinson, suggests that the recruitment of suitable prosecutors will be difficult. If the report's proposals are implemented, he contends that help may be needed from the Incorporated Law Society for the recruitment and training of the right kind of men.

6 CIVIL UNREST

Disturbances in Northern Ireland

Rep. of Com., 1969.
Cmd. 532, 123 pp., 5 maps.
Com. apptd. March 1969; rep. sgd. August 1969.

The Hon. Lord Cameron (Ch.) and two members—Prof. Sir John Biggart, J.J. Campbell.

'To hold an inquiry into and to report upon the course of events leading to, and the immediate causes and nature of the violence and civil disturbance in Northern Ireland on and since 5th October 1968; and to assess the composition, conduct and aims of those bodies involved in the current agitation and in any incidents arising out of it. . . .'

The commission was given the usual powers of royal commissions. These do not include any power to insist upon the attendance of witnesses or to place any witness on oath. The opening session, in April 1969, was held in public, but

thereafter the sittings were in private, so that witnesses might speak with full freedom and the inquiry might not be used as a propaganda platform. The attorney general undertook that no statement made to the commission would be used as the basis of a prosecution, or in evidence in any criminal proceedings.

A general introduction and a summary of the government's legal powers to maintain order are followed by a description and analysis of each of the occasions of civil disturbance. The causes of the disorders are discussed and the actions of government and police examined. The organizations involved are described, and the report ends with a summary of conclusions.

The events fall into three phases. The first began when Mr. Austin Currie, Nationalist M.P. at Stormont, occupied a house at Caledon on 20 June 1968 as a protest against housing policy in the area. This led directly to a march from Coalisland to Dungannon on 24 August 1968, organized by the Northern Ireland Civil Rights Association. During the same period, there had been recurring 'sit-ins' and squatting in Londonderry, also designed as a protest against local housing policy.

The next phase began when a proposed Civil Rights march on 5 October in Londonderry was directed by a ministerial order from its planned route, and there was a consequent clash between the police and marchers seeking to evade the ban. This march was mainly organized by local groups in Londonderry, but it was under the nominal auspices of the Northern Ireland Civil Rights Association. During the next two months, there was constant protest marching in Londonderry, and counter-demonstrations were held. On 13 November, the minister (Mr. W. Craig) banned all processions within the walls of Londonderry for one month. This ban was ineffective. On 22 November, the government announced a number of reform proposals, including the establishment of a development commission for Londonderry to supersede the corporation.

However, the government was not then prepared to introduce universal adult suffrage in local elections. On 30 November, a Civil Rights march in Armagh, which had been sanctioned by the authorities, was unable to follow its planned route because of a counter-demonstration by Dr. Paisley and Major Bunting and their supporters, who had occupied the town centre. The police feared they could not keep the peace if the march proceeded. During the whole of this second phase, it is fair to say that non-Unionist opinion was critical of the Northern Ireland Government and on the whole sympathetic to the Civil Rights movement.

During December the third phase began. Mr. Craig, the minister of home affairs, who has regarded the Civil Rights movement as a front for Republican activity, was dismissed from office. This tended to moderate the attitude of the government. On the other hand, divisions began to appear in the Civil Rights movement when an organization called the People's Democracy proposed to organize a march from Belfast to Londonderry. This received the nominal support of the Civil Rights Association but was undertaken contrary to the wishes and advice of the Derry Citizens Action Committee. The march took place between 1 and 4 January 1969 and was accompanied throughout by violence and counter-demonstrations. Its arrival at Londonderry was the signal for sectarian violence, rioting, and allegations by Catholics of police misconduct and partiality. The latter have been the subject of a special investigation by County Inspector H. Baillie of the Royal Ulster Constabulary, the full text of which was placed before the commission. On 11 January, there was a People's Democracy march in Newry. This developed into a riot. At a later stage serious rioting broke out in Londonderry on 19/20 April, following the prohibition by ministerial order of a proposed North Derry Civil Rights Association march from Burntollet to Londonderry in face of the risk of serious violence.

Since the setting up of the Government of Northern Ireland, there has not developed any united parliamentary opposition supporting the existing constitution and presenting a possible alternative governing party. This situation leads to complacency in the party in power and a loss of sense of responsibility in the opposition. There has been a widespread sense of political and social grievance for long unadmitted and therefore unredressed by successive governments. The root cause of the disturbances are basically housing and employment and arise partly from a tradition that Protestant and Catholic representatives in local government ought primarily to look after 'their own' people in the matter of jobs and housing. In Londonderry County Borough, Armagh Urban District, Omagh Urban District, Dungannon Urban and Rural Districts and in County Fermanagh, the electoral boundaries have been producing unfair results, weighted against non-Unionists, and in all these Unionist-controlled councils, appointments have benefited Protestants. Council housing policy has often been distorted in order that the political balance will not be disturbed. Restriction of local government franchise to ratepayers and their spouses, while it affected all sections of the population, was felt to operate mainly against poorer elements and in particular against Catholics. The reality of these grievances is supported by the recent government moves on local franchise, administrative boundaries, housing allocation, and machinery for dealing with grievances against local authorities. A table gives population, housing, and local government representation figures in certain areas from which complaints were received.

There was also agitation against the continued existence of the Civil Authorities (Special Powers) Act (N.I.), 1922, among the various organizations supporting or professing to support the cause of civil rights.

The Ulster Special Constabulary (''B' Specials') were considered by the Catholics to be partisan and sectarian. The use made of the 'B' Specials in the disorders was marginal and certainly not in the maintenance of law and order, as only a few were mobilized for service with the R.U.C. There were, however, a number of complaints that among 'loyalist' groups in clashes with Civil Rights demonstrators were known members of the 'B' Specials.

On the Unionist side, the fears and apprehensions have solid and substantial basis in both past and present—the absence of full recognition of the Northern Ireland constitutional position by the Republic; the ambiguous attitude of the Roman Catholic hierarchy in Northern Ireland; the opposition to the constitution and hostility to Great Britain among a proportion of Catholics; the continuing I.R.A. attacks; the steady decline of Protestant population in the South; the influence of Roman Catholic doctrines there on government in such matters as censorship and birth control; and the fear that a higher birth rate among Catholics will produce a Catholic majority which would lead to widespread Catholic discrimination against Protestants and a general lowering of living standards, as well as jeopardizing Northern Ireland's place in the United Kingdom.

The separate educational facilities of the Catholics are said to perpetuate sectarian feelings and antagonism.

Membership of the Unionist party is in theory not limited by faith or creed, but theory and practice have not kept pace, and few Catholics seek membership on this account, as well as because of the link between the party and the Orange Order.

The partial prohibition of the Civil Rights march in Londonderry on 5 October had the effect of increasing the number of those taking part. The police handling of the demonstration was ill co-ordinated and inept. There was widespread use of unnecessary and ill-controlled force in the dispersal of the demonstrators, only a minority of whom acted in a disorderly and violent manner.

The wide publicity given by press, radio and television to particular episodes inflamed and exacerbated feelings of resentment against the police which had been already aroused by their enforcement of the ministerial ban.

There were insufficient police available to enforce the second ban on processions taking place within the walls of Londonderry, or to give adequate protection and control in Dungannon on 23 November and 4 December 1968, in Armagh on 30 November 1968, at Burntollet Bridge and in Londonderry on 4/5 January 1969 and 19/20 April 1969. Apart from a few isolated incidents of indiscipline in Armagh on 30 November, the conduct of the police and the handling of the situation by the officers in charge deserve commendation. Instances of police indiscipline and violence towards persons unassociated with rioting on 4/5 January in Londonderry provoked serious hostility to the police and an increasing disbelief in their impartiality towards non-Unionists.

The Northern Ireland Civil Rights Association was founded in February 1967. There was early infiltration both centrally and locally by subversive left-wing and revolutionary elements which were prepared to use the movement to provoke and foment disorder and violence. The course of events in Londonderry on 5 October 1968 was due partly to the association not planning and controlling the march, to inadequate stewarding and communications, and to the fact that some of the marchers were prepared to accept or to provoke violence. The first chairman of the movement was Miss Betty Sinclair, who was succeeded by Mr. Frank Gogarty.

The People's Democracy group has no accepted constitution and no recorded membership. It grew from the protest meetings at the Queen's University following 5 October 1968 and at first had very wide support at the university, representing many political opinions. It was decided that the group should be open to everyone. Moderate support diminished. The decision not to undertake the Belfast/Londonderry march, made at a largely attended meeting during the university term, was reversed during the recess when only about forty persons were present. People's Democracy provided a means by which politically extreme and militant elements could and did invite and incite civil disorder. The leaders of the movement include Eamonn McCann, Michael Farrell, Cyril Toman and Bernadette Devlin. They propagate ideas which are far more politically extreme than the objects for which the Civil Rights Association has campaigned and represent a threat to the stability and existence of the Northern Ireland Constitution. However, they reject a sectarian basis for their political actions.

Derry Citizens Action Committee was formed at a meeting on 9 October 1968, with five of the committee representing the five organizations responsible for the 5 October march, and ten other members. Its influence throughout has been honestly exercised towards non-violent protests, and there is no sign of any concealed or subversive purpose. There is no formal constitution, but accounts are audited and in regular form. Mr. John Hume from the beginning has taken the lead and shown himself both responsible and capable.

There is evidence that members of the Irish Republican Army are active in the Civil Rights Association, but there is no sign that they are in any sense dominant or in a position to control or direct policy. As stewards they have been noticably efficient, and there is no evidence that they incited to riot or took part in acts of violence. At the same time, closer attention should be given to the extent to which their policies and objectives are directed to the same ends politically and socially as the extreme left-wing elements of the People's Democracy. No evidence was found that other Republican organizations played an active part in the disorders.

The Ulster Constitution Defence Committee has a membership of twelve and is a self-perpetuating body with Dr.

Paisley as chairman. It is the governing body of the Ulster Protestant Volunteers, commanded by Major Bunting. It has not been possible to obtain clear evidence of any association with the Ulster Volunteer Force, a proscribed organization. The use of force was contemplated both in Armagh on 30 November and in Londonderry on 4 January, as evidenced by weapons seen. The holding of a meeting in the Guildhall, Londonderry, on 3 January was an act of the greatest irresponsibility. Dr. Paisley and Major Bunting and these organizations with which they are concerned must bear a heavy share of direct responsibility for the disorders in Armagh and at Burntollet Bridge and also for inflaming passions and engineering opposition to lawful, and what would in all probability otherwise have been peaceful, demonstrations.

In the disorders which occurred in Londonderry and Newry, the local hooligan element played a significant part which must not be underestimated. It was prominent in the later phases of the events of 5 October and almost wholly responsible for the rioting on 3 January and the night of 4/5 January. It took advantage of the situation in Newry on 11 January and the Londonderry riots of 19/20 April.

The commission suggests setting up an independent tribunal to investigate complaints concerning the police, and a change in the method of appointment of senior local government officials.

Appendices list the persons and bodies providing evidence to the commission, and those who refused or ignored a request to provide evidence (Rev. J. Brown, Major R. Bunting, W. Craig, D. Hutchinson, Rev. I.R.K. Paisley); the constitutional position of Northern Ireland and the organization and powers of the police are described, and the terms of the ministers' prohibitions on marches are given. A full list of events relevant to the inquiry is given, and five maps show Northern Ireland as a whole, and street plans of Londonderry, Armagh, Newry and Dungannon. The constitution and rules of the Ulster Constitution Defence Committee and Ulster Protestant Volunteers are set out, as are the constitution and rules of the Northern Ireland Civil Rights Association, a list of Civil Rights committees and associated bodies, and a manifesto of the People's Democracy, February 1969.

A Commentary by Government of Northern Ireland to accompany the Cameron Report, incorporating an account of progress and a programme of action.

1969. Cmd. 534, 17 pp.

In this paper the government of Northern Ireland summarizes the measures it has already taken to meet legitimate demands and indicates some further lines of action. Command 532, the Cameron Report, is commended for public study. Attention is drawn to the rapid economic and social progress in the province prior to 1968, especially to the provision of large numbers of houses in post-war years, of which provision in Londonderry stands well above the average. The government emphasizes the strenuous, consistent and sustained efforts made over many years to improve conditions in Northern Ireland and refers to the many inquiries, studies and development plans commissioned in recent years.

The violence and civil disturbance which the Cameron Commission was asked to examine started on 5 October 1968. On 22 November 1968, the government announced a series of reforms:

(1) Allocation of houses: the government undertook to ensure that all housing authorities placed need in the forefront in the allocation of houses, and that future housing allocations would be carried out on the basis of a readily understood and published scheme.

(2) Investigations of citizens' grievances: the government agreed to consider the need for effective machinery to investigate grievances in an objective way, and in the area of central government activity, to introduce legislation to appoint a parliamentary commissioner for administration.

(3) Implementation of the Londonderry Area Plan: the government announced that it would take all possible steps to ensure that prompt and effective action would be taken to implement a plan, designed to transform the economic and social life of the city, and to assist this objective by the appointment of a strong, well-qualified and objective development commission.

(4) Reform of local government including the franchise: the government indicated its firm intention to complete a comprehensive reform and modernization of local government structure within a period of three years—that is, by the end of 1971—to review the franchise in the context of the organization, financing and structure of the new local government bodies; and to abolish the company vote in local government.

(5) Special Powers: the government announced that after discussions it had agreed with the United Kingdom Government that—(i) as soon as the Northern Ireland Government considered this could be done without undue hazard, such of the Special Powers as are in conflict with international obligations would, as in the past, be withdrawn from current use; but (ii) in the event of the Northern Ireland Government considering it essential to reactivate such powers, the United Kingdom Government would enter the necessary derogation.

Progress has been made in implementing these reforms. Forms of guidance and a model scheme for allocating houses have been prepared, and adopted by the Housing Trust and the majority of local authorities. Only a few have yet to submit their schemes. A parliamentary commission for administration was appointed and at work by 1 July 1969. In addition, legislation is to be introduced in autumn 1969 to appoint a commission to deal with citizens' grievances against local and public authorities and to set up a community relations board. The Londonderry Development Commission, established in February 1969, took over on 3 April 1969, the municipal functions of the Londonderry County Borough and Londonderry Rural District Councils. The prime task of the commission will continue to be the rapid implementation of the Londonderry Area Plan, which was prepared by the James Munce Partnership and was generally welcomed by the community in Londonderry when it was published early in 1968, well before any troubles began. Housing has been given top priority, and a crash building programme has been instituted. Excellent progress has already been made in implementing the jobs target in the Area Plan: in the past three years negotiations with twelve new firms and expansion of others will provide many new jobs. In 1968, one-third of the total jobs negotiated for the whole province were for Londonderry. Almost one million square feet of factory space has been or is being provided, and a government training centre at Maydown is fully operational.

Discussions on reshaping local government, begun in March 1966, have resulted in a White Paper (Cmd. 517) in February 1968, and a second (Cmd. 530) in July 1969, ahead of schedule. The government undertakes to have a new local government system in operation by 1971, to abolish the company vote in local government, to postpone the local government elections ordinarily due in 1970 until 1971, to introduce in time for these elections universal adult franchise, and to appoint an independent statutory commission to determine the new electoral divisions. Discussions are proceeding on the making of senior appointments in local government, the new integrated structure for the health and welfare services, and the structure of the education and public library services.

In existing circumstances, the Northern Ireland Government has felt unable to withdraw any of the provisions of the Special Powers legislation, an attitude endorsed by the United Kingdom prime minister.

Following a meeting at 10 Downing Street on 19 August 1969, a declaration was issued by the United Kingdom government and the Northern Ireland government reaffirming the position of Northern Ireland in the United Kingdom; the ultimate responsibility of the United Kingdom government for maintenance of law and order, in accordance with which troops have been provided on a temporary basis; the intention of the Northern Ireland government to take into account at all times the views of the United Kingdom government regarding the status of citizens; the approval of the United Kingdom government for the proposed reforms; and the belief of both governments that every citizen is entitled to freedom from discrimination. The full text is given.

An advisory board was set up on 26 August 1969 under Baron Hunt to examine the Royal Ulster Constabulary and the Ulster Special Constabulary. On 27 August 1969, a tribunal was set up under Mr. Justice Scarman to inquire into the civil disturbances between April and August 1969.

The Northern Ireland Government pays tribute to the achievements of Mr. Callaghan, the British home secretary, and Lord Stonham on their visit in August 1969. The text is given of a communique issued on 29 August reporting on Mr. Callaghan's visit and the progress and principles of reform. Joint working parties of officials of the two governments were recommended to report on housing allocation, avoidance of discrimination in public employment, and promotion of good community relations. These have been set up. Arrangements are in hand for the proposed visit by officials of the Ministry of Technology, the Board of Trade and the Department of Economic Affairs to assess economic and industrial prospects in the light of recent events. A committee has been set up for the promotion of good community relations, and a minister for community relations will be designated.

An explanation is given of the Baillie Report mentioned in the Cameron Report. It is an internal report within the

Royal Ulster Constabulary and was available in full to the Cameron Commission. Arising from it, displinary charges were preferred against sixteen members of the force. Criminal proceedings against two policemen were not directed because of the general amnesty embracing the times in question.

Violence and Civil Disturbances in 1969

Rep. of Tribunal of Inquiry, 1972. Cmd. 566, Volume 1: 249 pp.; Volume II: 60 pp., maps, tables. Tribunal apptd. August 1969; rep. sgd. February 1972.

The Hon. Mr. Justice Scarman (Ch.) and two members—G.K.G. Lavery and W. Marshall.

'for inquiring into a definite matter of urgent public importance: that is to say, the acts of violence and civil disturbance which occurred . . . and resulted in loss of life, personal injury or damage to property.'

The tribunal of three members inquired into the violence of July and August affecting Belfast, Londonderry and Armagh, but other acts of civil disturbance during March–August 1969 were investigated by the chairman alone. Certain disturbances, such as those in Lurgan, were excluded from the terms of reference, but the tribunal nevertheless sat (though not continuously) from September 1969 to June 1971. It had the power to enforce the attendance of witnesses, to examine them under oath and to compel the production of documents. The total cost of preparing its report exceeded £460,000.

Volume I of the report opens with a general survey of the course of events, consideration of the origin and nature of the disturbances, and an examination of the role and actions of both the police and the Ulster Special Constabulary. There is then a chronological description and extensive assessment of individual disturbances—attacks on public utilities and post offices during the spring; the mid-summer disturbances; the Londonderry riots of August; and the spread of

rioting to Belfast, Dungannon, Coalisland, Newry and Dungiven. The features of the Belfast riots of 14–16 August are fully examined. Separate chapters deal with civil disturbance in Armagh and Crossmaglen, while other chapters consider the constitutional implications of army involvement and official discussions over deployment of troops, and the far reaching social costs—deaths, damage, injuries, displacement of persons, and intimidation. Many individual incidents involving particular streets or locations are described and considered in very great detail. It is indicated at the beginning of the prefatory general survey that the terms 'Catholic' and 'Protestant' are used merely as sociological labels for the clear and concise identification of Northern Ireland's two distinct communities. The second volume of the report consists entirely of the appendices and appropriate maps. The tribunal stresses that it has only made findings and conclusions in those cases where it is sure that the truth has been brought to light.

The relevant events prior to 1969 are outlined in the initial general survey. It is accepted that the attacks on electricity and water installations from 30 March to 25 April 1969 were the work of Protestant extremists who wished to bring about the downfall of Captain O'Neill's government: the attacks on the post offices, however, were probably the work of the Irish Republican Army (I.R.A.). There was a very short period of relative calm after Major Chichester-Clark became prime minister and announced an amnesty for offences. In May, however, there was some civil disturbance in the Ardoyne district of Belfast, and in June there was trouble in the predominantly Catholic town of Dungiven in association with Orange Lodge events there. The large Orange march of 12 July was followed by disturbances, by way of response, in Belfast, Dungiven and most especially Londonderry. In that city, the Citizens' Action Committee was superseded by a more militant Derry Citizens' Defence Association, which undertook the 'protection' of the Bogside. In Belfast, the Protestant group, the Shankill Defence Association, encouraged the movement of families and the decline of the 'mixing of religions' in streets within the working-class area in and near the Ardoyne. In early August, there was Protestant rioting on the Shankill Road of a severity which paralleled that of Catholics in Londonderry during the previous month. There were also riots by Catholics in August within Dungannon and Coalisland.

On 12 August, the traditional (Protestant) Apprentice Boys' Parade took place in Londonderry. It was decided not to impose a ban, as detailed arrangements had been made for the route and for appropriate stewarding. The parade was controlled and orderly, but was stoned by some young hooligans whose action released the pent-up tension of the (Catholic) Bogside. 'From this small beginning developed not only three days of disturbance in Londonderry, but the many disturbances elsewhere, including in particular the very serious disorders in Belfast'. The night of 14 August was the one of the worst Belfast violence. There was intense and prolonged rioting, and the police, believing that they faced an armed uprising, employed guns. They shot four Catholics dead, and one Protestant was killed by a shot from a Catholic rioter. Death and destruction continued on the fifteenth, with Catholics burning factories and Protestants destroying public houses and the homes of Catholics. Two people (one of each religion) died that day from civilian shooting. The rioting in Londonderry had also been prolonged and extremely intense and the army entered the city on the evening of 14 August. They entered Belfast on the fifteenth but remained in the Falls Road area: after the events in the Ardoyne and Crumlin Road on the fifteenth, the troops went there also on the following day. The worst of the disturbances died away, but some barricades remained in streets, and defence committees were set up. The spread of the severe rioting to Belfast and elsewhere, following the parade in Londonderry, owed much to measures taken to reduce police pressure on rioters in the Bogside through causing further disturbance which prevented the sending of police reinforcements to Londonderry. The Northern Ireland Civil Rights Association was involved in such measures.

The tribunal rejects the idea that there was a plot to initiate an armed insurrection or to overthrow the government, but notwithstanding the absence of any such planning, it is clear that the young hooligans who started the violence in most cases were manipulated and encouraged by those seeking to discredit that government. 'The public impact of the activities of this element was tremendously enhanced by the coverage given by the mass media of communication.'

A few violent acts were planned by extremists from either end of the political spectrum, but the main sequence of rioting sprang from a complex political, social and economic situation. There was an I.R.A. influence at work in Londonderry, Belfast and Newry, but the riots were not planned or started by that organization; nor did the Civil Rights Association plan rioting, although this organization did help to spread the August violence and bears a 'heavy, albeit indirect, responsibility'. There is no evidence that an Ulster Volunteer Force, as a Protestant army comparable to the structure of the I.R.A., exists. Protestant participation in the disorders was often—although certainly not always—violent reaction to disturbances begun by the Catholics. In some riots, there were no Protestant civilians involved, and it was simply a battle between a Catholic crowd and police. Against this it could be said that the Orange Order persisted with parades which were bound to initiate jeering and disruption from elements in both communities. These two communities showed 'the same fears, the same sort of self-help (e.g. vigilante patrols and defence committees), the same distrust of lawful authority. Catholics and Protestants were haunted by the same ghosts and retreated in fear to their respective ghettos while attributing to each other the responsibility and the blame.' One side saw the police as a tool of the Protestants: the other thought police leaders were often lenient with 'rebels'. There were, on both sides of the divide, leaders who had the habit of inflaming rather than controlling mob passions. Mr John McKeague and Rev. Paisley probably incited rather than calmed Protestant fears and militancy: Miss Devlin encouraged continued violence among the Bogsiders after the disturbances of mid-August had begun, and Mr. E. McAteer's speech at Celtic Park on 10 August must have greatly increased Catholic tension and aggression in Londonderry prior to the Apprentice Boys' Parade.

The majority of policemen in the Royal Ulster Constabulary consistently did their difficult work well, although certain mistakes were made, and there were occasions when some individual officers reacted wrongly. The police acted against either or both communities as was necessary, but the character of the rioting meant that they were often facing Catholic crowds, and for numerous reasons the hostility and resentment of many Catholics against the Royal Ulster Constabulary grew stronger. Six occasions are mentioned when, it is argued, the police were certainly at fault: it is stressed, however, that they were doing what was usually an excellent and always non-partisan job, often handicapped by casualties, severe fatigue and shortage of numbers. The occasions in August when mistakes are judged to have been made arose from a wrong impression that the police were facing an armed insurrection devised by the I.R.A. The role of the Ulster Special Constabulary was more difficult and contentious. The use of these men was a success on at least one occasion in an exclusively Protestant area in Belfast, but on another occasion they enraged Catholics without managing to restrain militant Protestants. When used for riot control outside of Belfast, they showed lack of discipline at times—especially in their use of firearms.

The section of the report on the constitutional issues raised by the calling in of the army makes it clear that it was long realized that the British government would be reluctant to allow its troops to be used by another government which might be viewed as one expressing a particular religious outlook. A report from the *Financial Times* for 6 August, to this effect, is quoted. It is clear that the Ulster Special Constabulary was generally viewed as a force which should be used before the army could possibly be called in; it is plain that the Northern Ireland government realized this and knew also that to request military aid from Westminster would raise constitutional implications.

A final chapter in volume I tries to assess the social costs of the rioting and other violence, with the aid of appropriate tables. Ten civilians died in the disturbances under review, and over 500 were injured. Three hundred and sixty-six policemen, ten firemen and two special constables were also hurt. Large numbers were also in need of first aid or treatment for the effects of the CS gas. The gas was used against hostile crowds, but such was the complex problem of the disturbances that many other people were inevitably affected by it. Another table shows the compensation made for damage to buildings and vehicles—costs (somewhat conservatively assessed) exceeded £2 million, with numerous claims still outstanding. There was very extensive damage to licensed premises, which in most cases within Ulster are owned by Catholics. The most insidious result of the strife is, however, seen in the displacement of persons and intimidation. Statistics of the former and of the latter (as far as it was reported to the police) are given. In Belfast, where migration due to real or alleged intimidation was most severe, Catholics suffered especially from displacement of their households (5·3 percent of all Catholic households were displaced, but only 0·4 percent of Protestant households).

The second volume, containing the appendices, opens with details of the procedure, organization and administration of the tribunal. A descriptive list of exhibits follows: these exhibits include reports, photographs, maps, forensic science documents, broadcast extracts and other sources of evidence. The text of some documents from the exhibits is quoted in the report. Information quoted in full in this way includes the speeches and statements of the prime minister (Major Chichester-Clark) on 14, 15 and 17 August; press releases by Cardinal Conway on the fourteenth and seventeenth and a statement dated 23 August; a statement by the Irish Republic's Taoiseach, Mr. Lynch, dated 13 August; a copy of an I.R.A. political and military plan; and a report of 18 August from the Royal Ulster Constabulary to the Ministry of Home Affairs.

An alphabetical list of witnesses is given, and statistics show, for each region, the number of lay witnesses, clergy, police and others who gave evidence. Details of legal representation at the tribunal are provided and a 'timetable' or chronology of events from January to June 1969 is shown. Thirteen maps, many of them detailed, aid reference to localities concerned in the disturbances. These maps cover Northern Ireland in general, Londonderry, Central Londonderry, Dungiven, Armagh, the Shambles area in Armagh, Coalisland, Dungannon, Newry, the main riot areas of Belfast, the Belfast police districts, displacement of Belfast families, and high velocity bullet damage to the Divis Flats.

A Record of Constructive Change

(Rep.). 1971. Cmd. 558, 14 pp.

Legislation and administrative change, in relation to the joint statement of policy made by the Westminster and Stormont governments in 1969 (known as the Downing Street Declaration), is set out. A series of specific aims which were made in communiques following that declaration are listed, together with action taken. Commitments include matters concerning the police; the place of the Special Powers Act; the replacement of the Ulster Special Constabulary; the appointment of a commissioner for complaints; fair electoral representation for minorities; equality in public employment; an anti-discrimination clause in government contracts; a review of other forms of discrimination; and the reorganization of local government (in relation to the latter see Cmd. 546 in Class 1). In addition, a ministry of community relations and a community relations commission (the latter independent of the government) have been set up, a points system for housing has been devised and legislation passed to combat incitement to hatred and the circulation of wild rumour. The text of the Downing Street Declaration appears as an appendix.

Apart from action related to the declaration and subsequent communiques, three functional committees—covering social, environmental and industrial services, respectively—with salaried chairmen, have recently been proposed. The Opposition was invited to provide at least two of the chairmen; it is stressed that this offer of participation, made before the Social, Democratic and Labour Party withdrew from Parliament, is still open.

Economic and social progress are also briefly discussed, and the 1970–75 Development Plan (see Class III) commented upon. Public investment, in relation to the aims of that plan, has been satisfactory, but civil unrest has somewhat hampered private investment and the quest for full employment.

Political Settlement

For details of this report see Class I p. 4.

APPENDIX I
WESTMINSTER REPORTS CONCERNING NORTHERN IRELAND

Apart from the fact that certain activities —national finance, inventions, and post office services—have always come within the scope of Westminster's publications rather than those of Stormont, there have been a few reports on Northern Ireland issued by the British government during the fifty-year span. These include Justice C.L. Sheil's committee reporting on the *Supreme Court in Northern Ireland,* issued in 1957 as Cmd. 227, and the *Conviction and Sentence at Belfast, 30th November, 1954 of T.J. Mitchell,* on a charge of an attack on and within a military barracks in Omagh. This was issued in the 1955/1956 sessional papers as H.C. 32.

The most significant of such reports, (apart from two major Westminster 'declarations') from the point of view of enduring interest, may well be two arising out of the civil commotion and violence of the last few years of the period under review. These are the Compton Report concerning allegations of brutality to men taken into custody during 1971, and the Widgery Report of the rioting and deaths in Londonderry in January 1972. These four reports are catalogued and summarized below.

Northern Ireland.

Text of a communiqué issued following discussions between the Secretary of State for the Home Department and the Northern Ireland Government in Belfast on 9 and 10 October 1969, 1969.
Cmnd. 4178, 8 pp.

It is agreed that the Royal Ulster Constabulary should be unarmed, provided that the security situation permits this. A new security force is required and the Ulster Special Constabulary should remain until this force is available. Sir Arthur Young has been recommended as the new R.U.C. Inspector-General.

Economic assistance and industrial progress are reviewed. A minister of community relations has been appointed and a bill introduced to establish a commissioner for complaints. An anti-discrimination clause is to be introduced into government contracts, but the civil service in Northern Ireland has a good record with regard to impartiality in employment. Despite the efforts of local authorities, a central housing authority is now proposed as an essential step towards the solution of housing problems.

Mr. James Callaghan and the other ministers present agreed that the measures taken constitute a comprehensive programme for the achievement of concord and prosperity.

Allegations Against the Security Forces of Physical Brutality

Home Office. Rep. of the Inquiry, 1971. Cmnd. 4823, 73 pp.
Cttee. apptd. August 1971; rep. sgd. November 1971.

Sir Edmund Compton (Ch.) and two members—Edgar S. Fay and Dr. Ronald Gibson.

'To investigate allegations by those arrested on the 9 August under the Civil Authorities (Special Powers) Act (Northern Ireland) 1922 of physical brutality while in the custody of the security forces prior to either their subsequent release, the preferring of a criminal charge or their being lodged in a place specified in a detention order.'

On 9 August, 342 men were arrested and a total of 980 had been detained by noon on 10 November. When the inquiry began, 105 of the original number had been released and the remainder were in HM Prison, Belfast, or detained on the depot ship, *Maidstone,* following their arrest and initial movement to one of three regional holding centres—Ballykinler, Magilligan, and Girdwood Park.

The Northern Ireland Civil Rights Association rejected this inquiry into complaints because it was undertaken in private (to minimize risk to the safety of members of the forces) and because of its constitution. All but one of the complainants thus refused to come forward, but it was possible to investigate the allegations of some forty men by utilizing press reports and material supplied by newspapers. The cases investigated cover all aspects of the operation on 9 August, but the inquiry could not be truly comprehensive—the non-appearance of those making allegations frequently made it difficult to form judgements, especially where the evidence conflicted.

The nature of the evidence available and the problem of defining 'brutality' are considered. A review is then made of the arrest and holding operation and the pattern of complaints. The latter concern methods of depth interrogation, about which the allegations of eleven men reached the committee. They also involve alleged incidents concerning an obstacle course, a helicopter, and late release (all at Girdwood Park) and the imposition of special exercises at the Ballykinler centre.

Interrogation in depth may involve wall-standing, hooding, bread-and-water diet and subjection to continuous noise. Government policy in relation to such interrogation is outlined, and it is pointed out that torture and degrading treatment are prohibited. Daily visits by a medical officer are a safeguard. Strict discipline and a sense of isolation for the suspect may help to increase the flow of information regarding terrorist operations. Such information is essential to capture murderers, arms, and explosives and to save innocent lives. Isolation was also considered necessary in view of likely I.R.A. vengeance against informers. The complaints regarding interrogation procedures are considered individually: several cannot be sustained in the light of medical and other evidence. In other cases, physical ill-treatment took place, but not brutality if the latter is defined

as 'a savage form of cruelty . . . coupled with indifference to, or pleasure in, the victim's pain'.

The other groups of allegations and the evidence concerning them are also considered in detail. Investigation of the 'helicopter incident' involved six complainants. This was, in fact, a deception manoeuvre to suggest that detainees were being transferred to another location. A measure of ill-treatment took place here, and some unintended hardship occurred in relation to the 'obstacle course' at the same centre, about which a group of twelve complaints was considered. As far as late releases are concerned, it is pointed out that although the hour was late and some detainees thought departure at that time involved hazard, the men concerned were not forced to leave there and then, and some actually remained at Girdwood for some further hours by their own choice. The special exercises at Ballykinler caused some unintentional hardship, but no deliberate ill-treatment took place. In all, in addition to the 'five groups of allegations', twenty individual complaints are also examined. There are three individual complainants who are deemed to have suffered ill-treatment or accidental injury. One of these was the solitary man who appeared before the committee. In some cases, internal evidence of inaccuracy of complaints, the use of medical data, photographs, or visits to inspect the topography or accommodation of a centre led to the above conclusions or to the view that a complaint could not be upheld. Some charges remain unproven simply because 'it would offend against the principles of justice if we were to reach conclusions which assumed that the credibility of witnesses we have examined was superior to the credibility of those we have not seen'. A list of all those whose complaints were examined appears as an appendix.

Attention is drawn to lack of consideration of medical arrangements in the planning and administration of the arrest operation. It is unfortunate that, at

Girdwood Park, individuals were not medically examined at arrival. Many of the complaints relate to this centre, and there are not parallel systematic medical records to those that exist for Magilligan and Ballykinler. Medical officers carried out unexpected duties well, but the authorities showed a lack of awareness of the medical hazards involved in such an operation of arrest and detention.

An introduction to the report by the home secretary, Mr. Maudling, comments upon the recent events in Northern Ireland that led to the introduction of internment, the work of the I.R.A., the difficult task of the security forces in the internment operation, and the complaints which are considered in detail in the report. He stresses that no evidence has been found of physical brutality, brain-washing or torture. 'The Government reject any suggestion that the methods currently authorized for interrogation contain any element of cruelty or brutality. The report . . . confirms this view. But it also brings out the difficulty of implementing the rules in detail in circumstances in which rigorous and intensive interrogation is vitally and urgently necessary.'

Deaths in Londonderry

Rep. of the Tribunal apptd. to inquire into the events on Sunday, 30 January 1972, which led to loss of life in connection with the procession in Londonderry on that day, by the Rt. Hon. Lord Widgery. 1971–1972, H.L. 101, H.C. 220, 45 pp. map.
O.p. by both the House of Lords and House of Commons 18 April 1972.

Parades had been prohibited in Northern Ireland since 9 August 1971, but the Civil Rights Association (NICRA) organized a march for 30 January in order to protest against the internment policy. After some improvement in the law situation in the Bogside and Creggan areas of Londonderry since 1969, the situation had worsened from mid-summer 1971, and the terrorists had gained effective control of these areas. The army

thought that the march through the city should proceed only up to a certain point and then be blocked, as a hooligan element—backed up by gunmen—would take control. There was, in fact, considerable violence, and British soldiers opened fire, shooting thirteen civilians dead and injuring a like number.

Lord Widgery's introduction covers the appointment of the tribunal and the reason for its location at Coleraine, the terms of reference, the representation of relatives' interests, and the sources of evidence. The latter include statements taken from individual citizens by NICRA, the evidence of soldiers, photographs taken by professional photographers, and evidence given by some of the wounded. A hundred and fourteen witnesses were called, but many more statements were taken and considered. The remainder of the report then examines the narrative of events and the question of responsibility, and offers conclusions. It is stressed that it is a fact finding exercise to reconstruct, if possible, events objectively and in sequence—to provide a reliable basis for those who wish to form judgements. Evidence was sometimes conflicting, but conclusions were 'not reached by counting heads or by selecting one particular witness as truthful in preference to another'. They were 'gradually built up over many days of listening to evidence and watching the demeanour of witnesses under cross-examination'.

The narrative explains that the marchers were mainly orderly and good-tempered, but some insisted on a confrontation with the army at the latter's William Street barrier, despite the efforts of their stewards to persuade them to take the Rossville Street route. A crowd spat and shouted at the soldiers, hurling stones and other objects. An army plan to use the First Battalion Parachute Regiment to arrest hooligans and rioters was enforced. This operation can be both praised and criticized: an attitude of mere containment would certainly have reduced later incidents, but the grave threat to future order posed by a hard core of rioters made arrests an understandable security objective. Unfortunately the rioters and marchers were never really separated. Shooting began shortly before 4 o'clock, and it is considered that at least one sniper opened the firing from the Rossville Flats area. The action in the Rossville Flats' courtyard and in Rossville Street is then described with extracts from the evidence of appropriate witnesses. Initial firing from the Rossville Flats area was not heavy, but both army and civilian evidence suggests that many in that area were armed.

The question of responsibility gives rise to two further questions. Were any of the deceased, who are considered individually, carrying firearms or bombs? Were the soldiers justified in firing? Soldiers gave evidence with confidence and without contradicting themselves or each other. In considering their own firing, the problems of split-second decisions, the difficulty of clear identification and definition of firearms in the hands of rioters, and certain allegations of brutality in the making of arrests are mentioned.

It is concluded that there would have been no deaths if NICRA had not pressed on with this illegal march and brought about its virtually inevitable clash. There was no general breakdown in discipline, and the stated intent of the army to use the Parachute Regiment for an arrest operation but *not* for any other militant purpose, such as to give the Bogside residents rough treatment, is considered absolutely true. 'There is no reason to suppose that the soldiers would have opened fire if they had not been fired on first'. None of the deceased or wounded is proved to have been shot when handling a gun or bomb, and some are completely acquitted of such action; evidence leads to a strong suspicion that others had used guns or bombs earlier and that yet others had been closely supporting gunmen or bomb throwers. Nail bombs were found in the pockets of one of the dead. The army may well have under-estimated the hazard to

civilians brought about by the arrest operation. Without this operation, a 'low-key' attitude might have been maintained and deaths avoided.

The standing orders contained in the 'Yellow Card' are, in Lord Widgery's view, satisfactory, but temperament and training affect decisions which must be taken very quickly. Several soldiers showed great responsibility, but in Glenfada Park the firing 'bordered on the reckless'. Soldiers engaging gunmen near to peaceful civilians are set an impossible task, and it is not remarkable that some innocent persons were hit. Individual soldiers ought not to have to decide whether or not to open fire in this type of confused situation.

Appendices to the report list the thirteen men who died and the twelve men and the woman who were wounded. They indicate the names of civilians, priests, reporters, soldiers (identified by letters of the alphabet), police and medical experts giving evidence. A folding map of the relevant area of Londonderry, including the position of army barricades to halt the march, is provided.

The Future of Northern Ireland.

A paper for discussion (presented by the Secretary of State for Northern Ireland),* 1972.
VI, 98 pp.

The foreword by the secretary of state, Mr. William Whitelaw, explains that the object is to set out and try to reconcile the views and aspirations of the Northern Ireland people: 'to find a system of government which will enjoy the support and the respect of the overwhelming majority . . . there has to be a lengthy process of consultation.' The paper tries to provide a sound basis for wide-ranging further discussions.

Part I *Historical background*: A review

* This paper is, strictly speaking, outside the chronological scope of the volume since it appeared after the prorogation of the Stormont parliament. It is fitting to end with it, however, since in a very real sense it represents a summary of past and present political views and attitudes and endeavours to point the way ahead.

of events and attitudes—from the time of the partition of Ireland to the present violence and civil unrest—is provided. This explains succinctly and clearly how deep-rooted divisions have arisen. Northern Ireland has had legislation which differs on certain 'sensitive' matters from that for the rest of the United Kingdom, but has also been subjected to recurring bouts of violence from extreme republicans. Whatever distinctive features have existed with regard to the franchise, the continuous power of the Unionist Party has been based on a just mandate from the electorate and substantial advances have been made in numerous fields during the last half century. Several Catholic protests have nevertheless been legitimate, although others have been due to imaginary bias or to 'non-participation' by some of those belonging to this northern 'minority'.

Part II *Proposals and possibilities*: The proposals of the Unionists, the Social, Democratic and Labour Party (SDLP), Alliance, the Northern Ireland Labour Party, the Liberals, and the New Ulster Movement are outlined and considered. No proposals had been received from the Nationalist Party or the Republican Labour Party, but the chief wishes of these parties are clearly known. The Democratic Unionist Party favours the complete integration of Northern Ireland with the rest of the U.K., but its proposals were not received in time for inclusion. All these viewpoints have been considered, as have the views of some 2,500 individual citizens, who responded to an invitation to write to Mr. Whitelaw. The theoretical possibilities and alternatives are carefully considered. A bill of rights, for instance, seems to be widely favoured. If introduced, certain problems must be overcome to ensure that it is practical and not merely an empty declaration. Complete integration of Northern Ireland with the U.K. would have many problems including the relationship of local to central government, the reversal of tradition and legislative difficulties it implies, and the antagonism it

would arouse in the Republic of Ireland. The majority of the parties oppose it. Various alternative institutions for a Northern Ireland parliament or assembly and its powers, representation and finance are discussed and considered.

Part III *Towards a settlement*: Here some basic facts about finance and security for the province are set out. Any form of political solution or change implying independence for Northern Ireland would be unrealistic in terms of economics, security and political stability. The United Kingdom interests and links are then briefly considered along with the position of the province within Ireland as a whole. The latter statement about the 'Irish dimension' discusses the wishes and fears of the minority, the need for co-operation between North and South and the importance of seeing unification as a goal which could be obtained but only *if* the bulk of the people in the North so wish. The United Kingdom interest is to see the province secure, at peace, and making progress; the U.K. has obligations to Northern Ireland's majority and minority communities and they have obligations to it.

Part IV *The way forward*: The present system of 'direct rule' government is essentially temporary and further discussion on numerous points outlined in the paper must proceed in order to arrive at a general and pragmatic consensus. Eight conditions, which must be satisfied by any new scheme of government, are stressed. They include a consideration of the 'Irish dimension' along with the perpetuation of the British link provided the latter is what the majority wish; recognition of the sovereignty of the U.K. parliament and due division of powers between the national and regional authorities; an insistence that new institutions be simple and businesslike, based on a suitable consensus, as befits a regional assembly, and capable of winning the confidence and participation of all the community members. Westminster must, at least for the present, retain control of security and have an involvement in its future control. It is emphasized that 'there is no definite answer to questions as difficult and long-standing as these . . . the ultimate truth is that the people . . .need each other and that to squander their great talents in bitter conflict is to diminish the prospects of them all.'

Nine annexes are provided. These concern a review of some main provisions in the 1920 Government of Ireland Act; some developments in North-South relations; change and reform 1968–1972; and the detailed statements of the Unionist Party, the SDLP, and the Liberal Party. The latter statement includes an appendix on proportional representation and proposed constituencies. There is also a statement drawn up by the New Ulster Movement, concerning a fresh constitution for the province. There is much agreement between several of the parties concerning a declaration of rights, the repeal of the Special Powers Act and the need for North-South co-operation, but the Unionists differ from Alliance and Labour in seeking a regional parliament rather than an assembly and wishing it to have a positive role with regard to security. The SDLP statement stresses the 'Irish dimension' and urges Britain positively to encourage eventual unity of North and South, by consent.

APPENDIX II

SELECT LIST OF ANNUAL AND OTHER RECURRING REPORTS

Agricultural statistics	1925–1930	Cmd. series
Agriculture, Ministry of	1922–	Originally dept. reps. Later published in Cmd. series.
Births, marriages and deaths (Registrar General)	1922–	H.C. series.
Capital grants to industry	1955–	H.C. series.
Charities	1965–	H.C. series.
Commissioner for Complaints	1970–	H.C. series.
Companies	1922–	Dept. reps. (Min. of Comm.), later in H.C. series.
Development, Ministry of	1965–	Cmd. series.
Economic report	1964–	Dept. reps. (Cabinet).
Education, Ministry of	1922– (not issued in war years)	Cmd. series, but published as H.C. Papers for a time.
Factories	1949–	Cmd. series.
Family expenditure survey	1967, 1968/69	The only surveys of this kind restricted to Northern Ireland.
Finance, Ministry of	1927–29	One rep. only, Cmd. 117.
Fisheries, Sea and Inland	1926–	Dept. reps. (Min. of Comm.), later in Cmd. series and H.C. series.
Friendly societies, registrar of	1947–	Cmd. series, later dept. reps.
Health and local government services (originally called local government services)	1922–	Cmd. series.
Home Office services	1927–	Cmd. series.
Kitchen and refreshment rooms (parliamentary)	Irregular	H.C. series. See p. 19.
Labour	1922–1924	Two reps. only. First is dept. rep., second is Cmd. 41.
Local authority financial returns (originally called local taxation)	1921/22–	1st rep. H.C. Paper, remainder in Cmd. series.
Lunatics	1924–1927	Five reps. only. Continued from 1928 in Home Office services reps.
Maternal deaths	1956–1967 (irregular)	Dept. reps.
National Assistance Board (originally Unemployment Assistance Board)	1934–1965 (not issued in war years)	H.C. series.
Nature Reserves Committee	1968–	H.C. series.
Prisons	1923–1927	Five reps. only. Continued from 1928 in Home Office services reps.
Public records	1924–	Cmd. series.

228

Reformatory and industrial schools	1921/22	Dept. rep. (Home Affairs). One rep. only issued, then continued in Home Office services reps.
Tourist Board	1948/49–	Originally Cmd., then in H.C. series.
Ulster Countryside Committee	1966–	H.C. series.
Youth Employment Service Board	1963–	Dept. reps.

INDEX OF CHAIRMEN AND AUTHORS

This list includes, in addition to chairmen of commissions and committees, other personal or corporate names closely associated with reports—such as the names of consultants, assessors, or investigators. Military designations have been omitted as, in many instances, they change over a span of time. The index is a finding device, but it does not necessarily identify persons, as there may be a change of name or a change of an individual's practice in signature.

INDEX OF TITLES

To help this index to serve as a quick locating device for individual reports, the first word of each title has been indexed. Entries under key-words other than the first are designed to display subject associations not shown by the classification or to assist when a title is imperfectly remembered. Titles of annual reports and Westminster papers have been omitted.